Organizational Cognition and Learning:

Building Systems for the Learning Organization

Luca Iandoli
University of Napoli Federico II, Italy

Giuseppe Zollo
University of Napoli Federico II, Italy

 Information Science Publishing

Hershey • New York

Acquisition Editor:	Kristin Klinger
Senior Managing Editor:	Jennifer Neidig
Managing Editor:	Sara Reed
Assistant Managing Editor:	Sharon Berger
Development Editor:	Kristin Roth
Copy Editor:	Katie Smalley
Typesetter:	Jamie Snavely
Cover Design:	Lisa Tosheff
Printed at:	Yurchak Printing Inc.

Published in the United States of America by
Information Science Publishing (an imprint of IGI Global)
701 E. Chocolate Avenue
Hershey PA 17033
Tel: 717-533-8845
Fax: 717-533-8661
E-mail: cust@igi-pub.com
Web site: http://www.igi-pub.com

and in the United Kingdom by
Information Science Publishing (an imprint of IGI Global)
3 Henrietta Street
Covent Garden
London WC2E 8LU
Tel: 44 20 7240 0856
Fax: 44 20 7379 3313
Web site: http://www.eurospan.co.uk

Library of Congress Cataloging-in-Publication Data

Iandoli, Luca, 1972-
  Organizational cognition and learning : building systems for the learning organization / Luca Iandoli and Giuseppe Zollo, authors.
       p. cm.
  Summary: "This book presents a theory of learning based on a model of organizational memory, explaining organizational processes and dynamics through which organizational memory is built and updated. It provides a methodology and tools to elicit and map organizational memory contents, examples of applications, implications for practice, and a research agenda for the development of systems for learning organizations"--Provided by publisher.
  Includes bibliographical references and index.
  ISBN 978-1-59904-313-5 (hardcover) -- ISBN 978-1-59904-315-9 (ebook)
  1. Organizational learning. 2. Corporate culture. I. Zollo, Giuseppe. II. Title.
  HD58.82.L32 2007
  658.3'124--dc22
                              2006039750

British Cataloguing in Publication Data
A Cataloguing in Publication record for this book is available from the British Library.

All work contributed to this book is new, previously-unpublished material. The views expressed in this book are those of the authors, but not necessarily of the publisher.

Organizational Cognition and Learning:
Building Systems for the Learning Organization

Table of Contents

Section I:
Organizational Learning

Chapter III
Organizational Action: Persistence and Change

Chapter IV
Collective Memory

Chapter V
The Paradox of Learning

Section II:
The Emergence of Organizational Learning

Chapter VI
The Construction of Shared World

Chapter VII
Constructing Explanations

Foreword

by Giancarlo Michellone
President of the Area Science Park of Trieste (Italy)
Former President of the FIAT Research Center

During the 1980s the prevalent approach to strategic thinking was based on the consideration that the competitive advantage was mainly based on the characteristics of the industry. Consequently, the aim of strategists was to devote considerable resources to the analysis of competitors, markets, and customers. In the 1990s, the environmental conditions changed dramatically, as the globalization of markets and technologies, together with a new wave of technological innovations, raised the ambiguity and the uncertainty of the external environment.

The result has been that firms started to consider human resources internal competencies and learning capabilities as a stable and reliable source of value and competitive advantage. The new strategic approach is based on the learning organization loop, a circle of competence building and leveraging, which creates and exercises strategic options and opportunities of value creation. Nevertheless, after about two decades of debate on the new role of learning within organizations, many methodological and practical issues have been left unresolved, mainly because of the difficulty of the companies in abandoning the mechanical way they organize their own resources and capabilities.

This cultural resistance represents the first obstacle for the effective management of a learning organization. The second obstacle, obviously related to the first, is the lack of new management systems suited to the characteristics of the learning organization.

While at the cultural level the dominant rhetoric view, which assumes intangible assets, knowledge, human resources, and continuous learning as the key competitive resources, is widely recognized and accepted, in everyday practice, managers still behave as if nothing has happened. Management is still considered something that has to do with power and control. But creativity, problem solving, motivation, and all the other ingredients for individual learning cannot be analysed, controlled, measured, evaluated, at least in the traditional sense, by the old managerial apparatus that is still influenced by a mechanistic view of organizations.

This book provides readers with original and effective ideas both at the cultural and systems level. The authors investigate thoroughly what a learning organization is, and provide an original theory for organizational learning and competencies building. Then they go forth and build methodological tools that are not only coherent with a new way to look at the organization but that can be applied in practice, as they did on several occasions within different research projects about knowledge, learning and competencies management in collaboration with the FIAT Research Centre and other international industrial partners in the last 10 years (Cannavacciuolo et al., 1996; Cannavacciuolo et al., 1999; Zollo & Michellone, 2000).

I share with the authors some fundamental assumptions that actually shape our common view of the organization and that are described in detail in this book.

First, knowledge creation cannot be controlled by the organization, neither internally nor externally. The capability of an organization to access knowledge from external sources is always limited. What is clear and accessible to anybody has of course little strategic value, while valuable knowledge is often hidden in details and weak signals. Thus, the problem is not to have access to something that is "out there" but to have the capability to interpret creatively what is often close at hand, to observe the world from different perspectives, to exploit internal variety and solicit individual initiative.

Second, in order to cope with an ambiguous and increasingly uncertain environment, organizations must learn to look within them for the answers that traditionally they search for outside. In the last 15 to 20 years, organizations have turned themselves inside out looking for resources and capabilities able to generate value. All major managerial revolutions that have happened in the last 20 years such as business process reengineering, total quality management, cost management and more recently knowledge management can be considered as attempts in this direction. Through these attempts, in many cases organizations have ended up with discovering that value is the result of the projection of their competencies on the external world and that strategy is not about managing a battle against external enemies but is rather like making a painting of the world real.

These managerial revolutions were accompanied and partly inspired at the end of the 1980s by a theoretical revolution in the strategic management literature, that is the birth of the resource-based theory. The resource-based theory (RBT) questioned that the sources of competitive advantage lied in the structure of industrial sectors and posited that strategic management was mainly about acquiring and internally developing rare, inimitable, and value creating resources (Amit & Shoemaker, 1993; Prahalad & Hamel, 1990).

Whereas with quality management and business process reengineering (BPR) the old attitude of managers toward control and power has worked effectively, with the new challenges of knowledge and learning management the old "Taylor world" has come to a crisis. So, after more than a decade of the Knowledge revolution, there are still many uncertainties and perplexities about what it means to manage learning and competencies strategically.

What does it mean to look inside your own organization for value creating resources and capabilities? From the theoretical point of view that Iandoli and Zollo develop in the first two parts of the book and especially with their MEP model (Memory, Experience, Plan, Chapter IX), the picture is quite clear. Value is created by learning and competencies development through a cycle like the one depicted in Figure 1.

The value creation cycle is based on two main processes:

1. The competencies building process through which the learning organizations creates new strategic options, that is the opportunities to generate future cash-flow.

2. The competencies leveraging process through which the learning organization implements and exploits some of the available options and generates cash-flow.

In order to work properly, this cycle requires an essential condition: *the organization must be able to generate always more options than those it is able to exploit. Redundancy and continuous learning are the ways through which this result can be achieved.*

Without this internal variety and capability to solicit, identify and (only) finally exploit new possibilities of actions, it is impossible to grow and prosper in an unpredictable world.

Figure 1. The value competencies cycle (Adapted from Sanchez & Thomas, 1996)

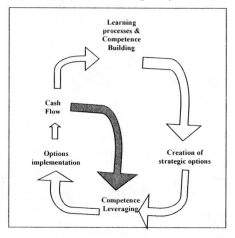

All the difficulties in the implementation of this cycle lie in the developments of new methods to construct new competencies and to identify the available options. If I were to sum up in one sentence what this book tries to do is: *to provide a theory and a method* to construct new competencies and identify available options. The authors provide methods to investigate learning from the discourses through which organizational members construct everyday knowledge and experience. Through an original blend of qualitative and linguistic methods and advanced computational techniques such as fuzzy logic, the tacit knowledge contained in those discourses can be mapped and elaborated into verbal models that can help organizations to analyse, store and reuse their knowledge.

Managers that want to go down to the everyday battlefield from the celestial Empyrean heaven of Figure 1 have to accept some radical changes in their work:

1. Learning and competencies can not be identified, controlled and developed with a top down approach, since they are generated from the bottom by individuals who actively interpret events, construct new theories, develop new resources. Top managers have rather the task of acknowledging the new emerging competencies, integrating them into an organic vision, reinforcing the capability of the organization to generate new options, *whatever they will be*.

2. It is not possible to encapsulate competencies and learning within strict and unambiguous definitions, procedures and practices, nor to understand a-priori which is the level of detail in the description and development of learning processes. *Learning stops when the learner decides so, competencies are such when someone recognizes me as competent*. Learning and competencies building are collective processes based on mutual agreement and reciprocal adaptation. No manager can fully establish their start and their end, the "how," the "when," and the "what" of learning.

3. *Any description is provisional*. Competencies and learning are generated and modified continuously on the base of new experience and stimuli. The tomorrow competency speaks often with a weak and low voice today, a voice that managers must be able to listen to in the middle of a roaring storm.

These changes can be possible if managers have the courage to renounce a mechanistic view of the organization and are able to tolerate ambiguity, redundancy, uncertainty, to manage delegation, to uncover talents, to build trust, to solicit participation and involvement of their collaborators. They are required to construct open environment where, while pursuing collective objectives, individuals are free to grow, to express their diversity, subjectivity and initiative.

Competence building and competence leveraging help to transform routine workers into what Iandoli and Zollo call *cognitive workers, that is a new worker endowed with three fundamental capabilities: the capability to evaluate and make decisions, the capability to learn, the capability to persuade.*

To manage learning, organizations must be able to promote the development of these three capabilities both within the traditional know-how domain of the organization and in the exploration of new territories.

References

Amit, R., & Schoemaker, P.J.K. (1993). Strategic assets and organizational rent. *Strategic Management Journal, 14*(1), 33-46.

Cannavacciuolo, A., Capaldo, G., Michellone, G.C., & Zollo, G. (1996, November 10-13). *Understanding and managing organizational paradox with fuzzy logic.* III Congreso SIGEF, Buenos Aires.

Cannavacciuolo, A., Iandoli, L., & Zollo, G. (1999). The performance requirements analysis with fuzzy logic. *Fuzzy Economic Review, 4*(1), 35-69.

Prahalad, C.K., & Hamel, G. (1990). The core competence of the corporation. *Harvard Business Review, 68*(3), 79-93.

Sanchez, R., Heene, A., & Thomas, H. (Eds.). (1996). *Dynamics of competence-based competition. Theory and practice in the new strategic management.* London: Elsevier.

Zollo, G., & Michellone, G.C. (2000). Competencies management in knowledge-based firms. *International Journal of Technology Management, 20*, 134-158.

Preface

The Crisis of the Fordist Paradigm and the Emergence of Cognitive Work

In 1885, Frederick W. Taylor presented a paper to the *Society of Mechanical Engineers* in which s/he proposed a method for analyzing the timing and movements of work. In 1913, Henry Ford and his partners perfected an assembly line in the Highland Park factory adopting Taylor's principles. In Taylor's framework and Ford's factory, the timing and movements of work were determined by an objective technical system rather than an arbitrary factory hierarchy. In the spring of 1914, the technological and organizational model now known as the Fordist paradigm was a reality.

Perhaps the most relevant aspect of the Fordist factory is that the work is organized, evaluated and regulated on the basis of *standards* that prescribe both the results and the timing of the work, as well as the ways it is carried out. The process of defining standards proceeds from the formal planning of the work, it is further developed through the definition of procedures and is sustained by an intense activity of measuring each operation.

Once the standards have been constructed, human needs can also be taken into account, but always with the awareness that every mediation means moving further away from the ideal, causing a weakening of "rational" action. *The recurrent problem in managing the work in a Fordist factory is how to impose the "rationality" of the standards and how to defuse the threats to order arising from the individual's subjectivity and initiatives.* Historically, this problem was resolved in different ways within the diverse ideologies and power relationships operating outside and inside the factory, but always with respect to the Fordist paradigm, that sees in the standard a point of reference which cannot be renounced.

Even the toughest paradigms are not eternal. Around the middle of the 1960s, the Fordist paradigm began to wear thin due to a series of social, economic, technical and cultural reasons. Surely one of the most relevant changes came in the technological center of gravity of the companies, following the spread of automation, information and communication technologies. One of the main innovations introduced by the technologies is linked to the availability of infrastructures for multimedia communication, which is thorough and global at the same time, opening up possibilities for opportunities and types of business that were not feasible in the past.

By removing individuals from the simple execution of manual tasks and routines, which was more and more the prerogative of "intelligent" machines, the new communicative infrastructure profoundly transformed work and its organization, anchoring work activities to knowledge sharing and transformation, instead of to the standardization and division of labor. The new processes of transformation are now based more and more on the widespread cognitive capacity of the subjects called to integrate modules of specialist knowledge. Knowledge that, as Rullani (2002, p. 34) affirms, in post-Fordism produces value "because it generates sense and therefore opens new horizons for possible production, giving meaning to objects, behaviors, situations that were previously without value."

In new organizations, the worker, independently from the role that s/he occupies and the function that s/he has, becomes a *cognitive worker*[1], called to *gather and interpret data and information, to understand the world in which s/he operates, to make sense of her/his own actions, to explain and infer her/his own evaluations and her/his own decisions, and to construct, with other individuals, common courses of action.* The cognitive worker does not only work on the explicit knowledge contained in documents and tables, but also on personal experiences, discourses, relationships, evidence, and emotions. The task that s/he is asked to carry out is to make sense of the events that fall into her/his own area of responsibility, directing and widening the range of opportunities for her/his own organization.

Cognitive work is work invested with reflexivity (Cillario, 1990): The worker generates events, observes them, reflects upon them, and possibly modifies the ways of generating future events. The cognitive worker is perpetually involved in redesigning her/his own actions, and s/he develops a continuous activity of construction and reconstruction of sense, partly tacit and partly explicit, in messages that s/he exchanges with her/his interlocutors. The activities carried out by the cognitive worker are defined in the proposals by Choo (1998) for the *knowing organization*:

1. The activity of *sense-making,* necessary for reducing the ambiguity and equivocation of events

2. The activity of *decision making*, necessary for making choices and allocating resources

3. The activity of *knowledge creation*, necessary for enriching the organization with new frames of reference to be used in the future

The cognitive worker[2] contributes to the processes of creating values through activities that allow him/her to direct her/his actions, overcoming obstacles coming from paralyzing dilemmas in the form of paradoxes (Cameron & Whetten, 1983). The paradoxes are presented as intrinsic contradictions between elements that cannot be traced to a coherent unicum in the area of an existing conceptual system. The objective of the cognitive worker is to resolve the paradoxes by questioning the dominant point of view, the routine, the beliefs and the values system that is taken for granted. Only by overcoming the dominant rationality and creating a new system of reference can the paradoxes that block the action be resolved.

For cognitive work, what has been written by Pinchot and Pinchot is quite true: "*The nature of knowledge work, which requires gathering information, imagination, experimentation, the discovery, and the integration of new knowledge in a wider array of systems has as a consequence that the bosses cannot control the knowledge workers as if they were ditch diggers or workers on an assembly line. If knowledge workers do not know how to do their work, they can learn what to do before their bosses. Knowledge work has a strong component of self-management and group work, and is blocked by the long-distance control of a boss. [...] When a team of doctors administer a life-saving therapy, the members of the group must apply hundreds of instruments, medicines, and procedures to a variety of patients, each of which is unique, and they learn continuously, also because knowledge and technogies are improved continuously. This is true both for technicians and doctors. A society of knowledge workers will be completely different than what it was before*" (Pinchot & Pinchot, 1993, p. 47).

The centrality of the cognitive aspects in the creation of values radically modifies the rules of the organizational game. Most of the work done by cognitive workers consists in the emission and reception of messages through rituals of interaction with the social and organizational network. *Meanings, decisions, and shared knowledge are constructed with these messages.*

Organizational charts, procedures, planning and control systems, informative systems are not very effective in defining and organizing *a priori* the activities of the cognitive worker. The first and most stringent conflict is the asynchronism between the time needed for cognitive work, which is the time for creativity, research, innovation, and the time, methods and standards imposed by the productive machine.

Although most managers are aware of this challenge, in practice there is a strident contrast between the rhetorical exaltation of the centrality of knowledge, creativity and the managerial apparauts still strongly inspired by the Tayloristic approach.

Managing Knowledge: From Individual Sense-Making to Organizational Learning

Most managers illude themselves that knowledge resources and the creative and learning processes can be governed with the old logic of observation, measurement, and control. The failure of this approach, arising from the crisis of the Taylorist model, has caused many organizational and management researchers to look for new forms of organizations and to study some possible alternatives in the governance of learning and knowledge management.

Some scholars have analyzed the concept of organizational cognition. Lant and Shapira (2001) classify approaches to organizational cognition within a dichotomy between the hard, objective, and quantitative information processing approach (March & Simon, 1958) and the soft, subjective, and qualitative sense-making approaches (Daft & Weick, 1984). In particular, following the latter, fruitful research efforts have been directed toward the representation of organizational cognition and information flow in groups and organizations, such as cognitive mapping (Eden & Ackermann, 1992; Huff, 1990), and qualitative methodologies such as ethnography and discourse analysis (Heracleous & Barrett, 2001).

Despite the development of many methodological approaches, there is scarce integration between qualitative approaches, mainly oriented to consulting applications, and quantitative approaches, usually developed at the academic level for research purposes.

Second, on the theoretical side the different perspectives developed in literature and managerial practice have focused on different aspects and have used different level of analysis and background without providing a holistic theory of organizational learning and knowledge creation.

Third, there is a lack of literature addressing the issue of organizational learning from the practitioners' perspectives, and providing feasible methodologies and tools for organizational learning management able to merge the in depth level of analysis usually achieved by qualitative inquiry and the rigor and analytic power of quantitative modeling techniques.

In order to try to fill this gap, this book is based on a multidisciplinary approach to organizational cognition and learning and, in a broader sense, to knowledge management. Such an approach can be positioned at the intersection between sociology, cognitive psychology and "hard sciences" such as computer science and advanced computation. It proposes in integration of qualitative methodologies (discourse analysis and mapping) and quantitative methodologies (fuzzy logic and soft computing) to model cognitive processes starting from the analysis of discourses through which people *make sense* of their own and others actions in organizations.

In the sense-making perspective (Weick, 1979), understanding is a matter of choice. Choice is only the final act of an ongoing process in which individuals make sense of the uncertain external environment drawing on previous knowledge accumulated through action in terms of past experience and interaction with other people.

In the sense-making perspective, individuals create knowledge in a three stage process made up of enactment, selection, retention. In the enactment stage, individuals, on the basis of their preexisting knowledge, select clues and signals belonging to the ongoing and uninterrupted data flow from the environment. Through enactment, people try to reduce ambiguity of incoming information. In the selection stage, people draw from their memory models of actions (e.g., recipes, scripts, theories, etc.) constructed through experience and learning that proved to be useful in the past. In the retention phase successful models of action are stored for possible future reuse.

Being influenced by and strictly interrelated with action, *cognition is necessarily situated*, and, as such, influenced by the particular organizational context in which it develops (Blackler, 2002). Actually this means that enactment, selection and retention may be strongly conditioned by the presence of shared values, traditions, procedures, socially accepted behaviors, rules, culture, etc.

By adopting a sense-making perspective to investigate organizational learning and knowledge creation with respect to a specific context of action, one needs to analyze how individual cognition takes place concretely in organizations in terms, for instance, of how people frame problems, which values and beliefs influence or draw their actions, how existing models of action influence current and future choices, how people make and justify their choices and perform their action through the use of organizational artifacts. This understanding is essential for managing change in organizations, in order to grasp resistance and obstacles to change as well as to bring to the surface tacit knowledge, local learning, and emerging competencies.

According to this approach, a new event is interpreted when an individual is able to link it to an existing previous body of individual and collective knowledge. Natural language is the most immediate tool to express such knowledge, because it allows individuals to represent nuances, ambiguities, uncertainties, and conflicts usually neglected by formal methods in order to achieve coherence, simplicity and certainty. *Furthermore discourses can be used to communicate and share knowledge by convincing other organizational members through reasonable arguments. In order to convince other people one needs to share with others, at least to a certain extent, a common body of knowledge and a same language.*

It is possible to have an idea of the complex contextual knowledge used by an individual when s/he explains the motivations of his/her judgment to other people. Actually, through an explanatory discourse, people introduce hypotheses on the base of their own background knowledge to explain some evidence by relating new facts to known ones. More precisely with explanatory discourse we mean any spoken or written discourse through which an individual try to make explicit the reasons justifying a choice.

Starting from this theoretical background the main ideas proposed in this book are summarized as follows:

1. Individual knowledge is incorporated into mental schemata and organizational procedure. Patterns of action, scripts, models of behavior, facts, shared values, and stereotypes resulting from an ongoing sense-making activity are stored in both individual and collective/organizational memory.

2. Organizational as well as individual memory are socially constructed thanks to an ongoing activity of individual interpretation and collective interaction (Berger & Luckmann, 1966; Nicolini & Meznar, 1995).

3. Ambiguity related to input coming from the surrounding environment is resolved through explanation (Schanck, 1986; Thagard, 1994). Through explanatory discourses, people relate new facts to known ones by introducing or implicitly assuming hypotheses to explain (enacted) "evidence" on the base of their own background knowledge.

4. Natural language is the most direct tool to express such knowledge, because it allows the representation of nuances, ambiguities, uncertainties and paradoxical assertions (Quinn & Cameron, 1983).

5. By combining qualitative and quantitative methodologies we can define a methodological approach to build management systems for the learning organization by representing individual and collective knowledge through "verbal models."

6. Verbal models can be used to elaborate knowledge for different aims, e.g., for simulation of organizational members reasoning and decision processes, for decision making support, to perform organizational analysis, to map and store useful and reusable knowledge, to support knowledge exchange and creation, to help groups in the problem setting phase.

How the Book is Organized

Learning and creativity are the fundamental dimensions of cognitive work. The objective of this volume is not to analyze cognitive work at the individual level, but to see how it unfolds in organizations. This means investigating the processes of learning and creating new knowledge at the collective level.

The learning organization is the organizational paradigm for the exercise and development of cognitive work and is the primary object being studied in this text. A learning organization is not only an organization that favors and provides incentives for learning and creativity among its own members, but in some way supports it, amplifies it, appropriates it and makes it available to the other members of the organization and its stakeholders.

Consequently, organizations wanting to transform themselves into *learning organizations* need to understand, model, and in some way, govern collective learning and manage cognitive work. They also need new and concrete ways and tools for analyzing and managing organizational processes. In order to provide some possible answer to these needs, this text deals with the following questions:

1. What are the building blocks of organizational learning?
2. How does the organization build learning by itself?
3. Which methods and systems can facilitate learning?
4. How should a learning organization be governed?

The text is divided into four parts followed by two appendixes:

a. In the first section (Chapters I-V), the principle object of study, organizational learning, and its main components (organizational change and collective memory) are defined;

b. In the second section (Chapters VI-IX), the processes through which organizational learning is developed are taken into consideration, in particular the role that language and discourses have in generating, making explicit and utilizing organizational knowledge.

c. In the third section (Chapters X-XV), the concept of verbal model is introduced, and is used to identify, codify and model the organizational knowledge contained in discourses. Moreover, we demonstrate how verbal models can be used to build systems and tools for managing knowledge and supporting decisions. Finally we present a case study aimed at illustrating a practical application of the proposed methodological approach.

d. In the fourth section (Chapters XVI-XVIII), the managerial implications for governing cognitive work more effectively are highlighted, and a research agenda for the development of methodologies within the paradigm of the learning organization is outlined.

e. In the appendixes we provide two further examples related to the application of some of the methodological tools proposed in this book (fuzzy verbal models, agent-based simulation).

Section I: Organizational Learning

The first section of the volume (Chapters I-V) aims at answering the question "What is organizational learning?"

In Chapter I we show how digital technologies have contributed to the need of managing a critical new resource: knowledge. After giving a brief history of the birth and evolution of knowledge management (KM), we will show how the paradigm of the learning organization is able to answer to some of the main criticism moved to the modern approaches to KM.

Our analysis of organizational learning assume as starting point that organizations emerge when there is a need to impose an "artificial" order on the spontaneous and chaotic flow of social action. This order guarantees the regularity and rhythm of collective actions and such regularity is generally recognized from the outside. Each of us identifies an organization based on the objectives that it pursues and on what it really "does" or "produces" *regularly*. The same regularity, together with the output that the organization produces, is one of the most evident products of organized collective action (Chapter III).

The regularity of collective action is usually achieved through standardization, controlling behaviors, and sacrificing subjectivity in the pursuit of collective aims "at a higher level." In order to guarantee this regularity, organizations develop the tools and shared values through which they condition, more or less openly, the behavior of individuals. Conditioning is therefore, instrumental and psychological at the same time. Rules, procedures, division of labor, formal systems, but also missions, and slogans, are practical examples of how organizations attempt to assure *their own persistence*.

In their pursuit of regularity and the rational use of resources, organizations are often compared (and sometimes confused) with machines (Morgan, 1997). However, in addition to being the result of an organizational and efficiency-oriented rationality, organizational action is the product of the social game and individual intiative within a group (Crozier & Friedberg, 1977). It is the result of two essential cycles: The cycle of persistence, that is manifested through the attempt to reduce the entropy of social action within recognizable and stable forms, and the cycle of change, through which the individuals create space for action in order to attain individual advantages within the limits imposed by the dominant rationality (Chapter IV). Every organizational action is developed within this continuous tension between persistence and change.

The regularity of functioning in an organization is always potentially up for discussion. This is usually pursed is three ways: (1) *at the political level*, through the management of power and of the social game, (2) *at the technical level*, through the maintenance of the formal apparatus (control and technology systems), (3) *at the cultural level,* through the construction of shared values. If organizations are systems that impose and maintain order to guarantee continuity and an identity that is recognizable to collective action, then they are systems that are *intrinsically predisposed to avoid change*, because every deviation from the constituted order is seen as a dysfunction, disturbance, or anomaly. *Collective learning, then, is always manifested as an anomaly and only as an attempt of questioning the status quo, within and through the social game and individual initiative.*

There is no change if there is no memory. Change, in fact, is not a blind leap into the future but the regeneration of memory beginning with the possiblity of action that memory itself allows. In Chapter IV, the concept of collective memory is analyzed and a model is proposed. Organizational memory is seen as a system of shared values and artifacts that guide the action. Artifacts are products of human thought that at the same time guide ad condition action. In the organization the artifacts are usually explicit rules and tools necessary for the coordination of collective action. The following examples represent typical organizational artifacts: utensils, projects, marketing plans, reports, manuals, procedures, signals, regulations, labels, glossaries, images, equipment, software programs, missions, declarations, Web sites, uniforms and clothing, training material, contracts, sales orders, etc.

In Chapter V the relationship between organizational change and memory is analyzed. It is this relationship that in this text is considered organizational learning. In particular, the intrinsically paradoxical nature of collective learning is highlighted. Learning occurs when an organization is capable of modifying its memory, and therefore its value system and artifacts. Memory is not so much the goal of learning as much as it is its starting point.

The content of organizational memory can be distinguished by the amount of *sharing* among its members, the degree of *prescriptiveness* in directing action, the degree of *specificity* with respect to specific courses of action. When these contents are widely shared, prescriptive and specific, then the organization exercises a high level of control on organizational actions, with the unpleasant consequence that the higher the control exerted on the actions, the less likely it is that an individual can create variety.

In reality, organizational memory is characterized by a graduality of sharing, of prescriptiveness, and specificity that is inevitably translated into *ambiguity*. It is this graduality that allows the cognitive worker to express variety; and it is the ambiguity that allows the organization to modify its own memory and to transform itself, into a learning organization.

On the other hand, an excessively weak and ambiguous collective memory can turn out to be too fragile to generate and sustain change inasmuch as it does not in itself contain sufficient history and cohesion.

The paradox of learning is the paradox of experience: Memory is a prison and a space to explore, a restriction and an opportunity, an obstacle and a resource for change, all at once. The future is, more often than not, the projection of the image that we have of our past.

Section II: The Emergence of Organizational Learning

The second section of the volume (Chapters VI-IX) is dedicated to answering the following questions: How does the learning organization learn and through what processes? How much and in what way is it possible to model and govern the processes of learning in an organization?

If learning is the offspring of memory, then it can be stated that learning only takes place *within a tradition* (Polanyi, 1967). Whether learning is a continuation or a break with the past of a group, it can be verified only from within a social world that shares values, rules, systems, tools, and knowledge. This social world is the shared representation that is constructed and settled over time from within a group that has a history and that is what sociologists call constructed reality (Berger & Luckmann, 1966). Collective memory is therefore the result of a process of social construction (Chapter VI).

In organizations, social reality is constructed less spontaneously and more quickly than in an unstructured group, through the identification of a set of shared meanings and language that facilitates the coordination of collective actions and the persistence of the organization. The process of learning in organizations is above all learning about how the organization "works." Individuals are constantly engaged in the construction of a sense to give to their own actions and those of others within the social reality of an organization.

To make the world more predictable, individual cognition does not hesitate to use the interpretive schemes and proconstituted models; learning in a social reality is above all learning these schemes, that is the way things should be "seen' (Chapter VII). Once these schemes have been learned, it is enough to put each event in its place within a well-known world (Nisbett & Ross, 1980). Paradoxically, learning by schema becomes a formidable obstacle to deeper learning, that is to say at the second level, relative to the capacity to question the schema or to create new ones (Argyris & Schön, 1978).

Whether at the first or the second level, collective learning is tied to a problem of consensus: I cannot learn without a language, a tradition, a set of explanations of events and situations, and if I want to transfer the results of my learning to the group, I have to use the rules and the language of the group—either that or I have to modify them so that I can be understood.

How can this world of shared, often implicit and fleeting meaning be identified? A central role in the process of construction of sense and consensus is played by language and by discourses (Daft & Wintington, 1979). Individuals communicate their realities through discourses and they share it and attempt to explain it to themselves and their interlocutors. Explanatory discourses represent a very direct way to use the constructs of collective memory. It is through explanatory discourses that organizational members offer and ask for reasons. It is through discourse that events, behaviors and choices acquire meaning and are legitimized (Chapter VIII).

The explanations provided by members of an organization describe the "theories" that guide the action. At the first level, they can be analyzed to understand how to organization works, how their members interpret the events, which schema they use and how these schema are made.

At a more sophisticated level, explanations are not the simple activation of schema, but the creative construction of hypotheses, conjectures and mechanisms that better explain the existing schema, or ambiguous and unusual events.

Through *confermative* explanations, organizational memory is activated and consolidated, while through *creative* explanations, the organizational knowledge present in its memory is declined and regenerated in order to be adapted to new contexts of action. The vagueness and blurriness of memory play a decisive role in the effectiveness of the adaptation from old to new situations. Only through language is it possible to realize the complex process of transfer and generalization of knowledge from past experiences to new experiences. As a matter of fact, the ambiguity of verbal language allows evaluations and explanations to be maintained even though they are not necessarily coherent with each other (Chapter VIII). The logic of explanatory discourses is not the rational pursuit of truth, but the production of consensus. It is the logic of conviction, of rhetoric, of communication. The rationality of social action is not to demonstrate the truth, but the convince and build sense and consensus.

On the basis of the theoretical elements described in the first and second part of the book, in Chapter IX a model of organizational learning is presented: The MEP model (memory, experience, plan). It represents the starting point for the construction of the methodologies and tools proposed in the third part of the volume.

In the MEP model, the logic of learning and of cognitive work is realized with regard to three fundamental coordinates: The coordinate of accumulated knowledge that is consolidated through learning (memory), the coordinate of the intentions and anticipatory vision (the plan), the coordinate of interaction and comparison with the world (experience). The logic of learning is a logic of action. An action is self-made through a continuous comparison between the schema of sense contained in memory, the flow of raw data coming from the outside world and the intended plan.

According to the rational approach of the theory of decision, the action is a final product of the sequential process that originates from deliberate intentions and requires the elaboration of objective data.

In Figure 1, the rational character of the action is shown instead through its cyclical development between the coordinates of memory, planning and experience, and its continuous returns and revisions: the schema of sense contained in the memory influence the way in which the reality is tested, the result of the perceptions force the schema to be modified, and the intentions guide the activation of the schemes and the search for information, but it can be modified and adapted to the available data and unconfirmed expectations.

Through action, the logic of explanation begins to take shape: The cognitive worker constructs hypotheses, conjectures, inferences, suspicions, images, representations through a continuous comparison between memory, intention and concrete experience. Finally, s/he is able to build convincing explanations in the attempt to transfer or simply communicate the results of one's own learning to the community.

The action of the cognitive worker requires a balanced mix of the use of memory, experience and planning ability. Upsetting the balance of the action toward just one of the dimensions creates pathologies that are then transmitted into the organizational networks.

The action that is carried out above all along the lines of memory is typical of a *self-referential organization*, which reinterprets the world exclusively in the light

Figure 1. The coordinates of action

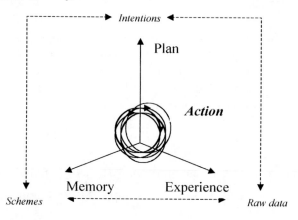

Rational action is developed within three temporal coordinates. The first coordinate specifies the action as determined by "intentionally disposed needs" (Bonfantini, 1987). It is the coordinate of intentions, objectives, desire, goals, planning, willingness, and the imagined future being sought. The second coordinate specifies the action in terms of experience, means and resources that are offered for the action, the opportunities to be taken advantage of, and problems to resolve. It is the *present* that is continuously regenerated during the course of the action as a set of events to interpret and to put back together in the flow of action. The third coordinate specifies the action in terms of the accumulated knowledge of the actor, as a possible result within the framework of the rules, the values and the knowledge that the actor has at his disposition. It is the *past* that allows the actor to acquire awareness of the action.

of the past; the action is cemented into its memory. The weight of the past blocks the capacity to construct the future. Bureaucracies are typical examples of self-referential organizations.

The action that is carried out mostly along the planning axis is typical of *utopic organizations*, with their elevated capacity for planning that is not founded upon history and its capacity to deal with the outside world. This is what often happens in small, innovative companies that often are not able to survive their own birth or disappear when the creative impulse of the founder-entrepreneur is exhausted.

The action that is usually carried out along the axis of experience is typical of *empirical organizations*, which rely upon experience, empiricism and contingency. Small companies are often examples of empirical organizationas, centered around the figure of the entrepreneur and her/his action, inspired by the myth of artisanship that is often organizational craftsmanship, and because of structural, cultural or contextual limitations, have a hard time developing a proactive type of action and a vision relating to the project.

Section III: Methods and Tools for the Learning Organization

Which methodological tools can be used for analyzing the organizational learning process and to build systems for the management of knowledge and the support for decisions in the learning organization? In the third part of the volume, a methodological approach is presented for the identification, mapping and modeling of explanatory discourses for the construction of tools:

- In support of organizational analysis
- For modeling and management of the knowledge contained in discourses
- For the development of tools for the support of decisions

In Chapter X, the methodology is described at the overall level and suggestions are made for the identification of explanatory discourses. In this phase, the methodological approach is qualitative, but structured. A protocol is illustrated for the identification of discourses through interviews and examples from research in the field.

In Chapter XI, the problem of codifying discourses is explored. The codification comes through "mapping" the contents of the discourse, typically classified in terms of concepts and relationships between concepts. A mapping technique is presented in detail and reference is made to a larger portfolio of methodologies that allow for the creation of cognitive maps, meaning representations of belief systems in the light of which individual or groups interpret a situation or a problem.

The discourse mapping approach derives in part from the field of cognitive psychology and operations management and in part from the typical approaches of the so-called knowledge engineering, which is the branch of computer science specializing in building systems for managing information and knowledge in support of decisions. Among the latter, those most closely resembling the approach presented in this volume are the so-called expert systems, computer systems that, by modeling the knowledge of an expert in a certain field of application (domain), reproduces the reasoning of a human expert in the resolution of localized problems such as in the elaboration of a diagnosis beginning with the symptoms and experimental measurements.

In Chapter XII and XIII, through the introduction of the concepts of verbal models and linguistic variables (Wenstøp, 1975b; Zadeh, 1973), some basic elements are provided for modeling discourses and linguistic variables by using some mathematical techniques, fuzzy logic in particular.

A verbal model is a mathematic representation of the variables (concepts) contained in a discourse and of the relationships between these variables. A linguistic variable is a variable that assumes linguistic values for example, the variable "performance" can assume the values of disappointing, poor, satisfactory, above average, excellent, and so on.

A verbal model can be implemented through the use of appropriate algorithms on a computer: The model accepts both quantitative data and qualitative evaluations as input, in the form of verbal judgments, and fuzzy algorithms allow for the rigorous and reproducible simulation of the effects of the reasoning contained in the discourses. This way, the logic of explanation can be seen in action.

In Chapter XIV, some examples of verbal models are developed in reference to applications in the organizational and managerial fields. Verbal models can contribute to the construction of a wide knowledge base and an analysis of the results of the simulations can be used for various purposes, which can be classified into two main typologies:

a.   **Analysis and description:** The representations can be used to analyze and describe the cognitive schemes through which members of an organization classify or interpret a problem: How can a collaborator be evalutated? What is a good supplier? How should I act in a given work situation? How can I resolve that type of problem? These analyses can be used for training purposes, to plan some improvements, or to understand the causes of resistance to change, etc.

b.   **Decision support and synthesis:** The models can be used for resolving complex prolems and for building systems to support decisions. The approach is similar to the one used for creating expert systems. The hypothesis is that organizational memory contains the answers to a new problem. Or one supposes that the members of a work group can use these representations as a support for reflecting upon a problem, comparing alternative points of view, arriving at more elaborate representations following the aphorism proposed by Weick (1979): How can I say what I think until I see what I say? The models are, in effect, visual representations of mini-theories.

Finally, in Chapter XV, we illustrate the application of the proposed methodological approach to a real world case study. In the case study we use causal maps to elicit and represent the grey knowledge used by software developer's involved in a project of development of a new software.

Section IV: Implications and Perspectives

In the fourth section (Chapters XVI, XVII, and XVIII), the managerial implications for the effective management of cognitive work are underlined and a research agenda is proposed for the development of methodologies regarding the learning organization paradigm.

In Chapter XVI, some criticalities and methodological implications for organizational analysts who intend to adopt the approach and the tools proposed in this book are discussed. Our approach assumes discourses as data. And yet, this is problematic data, with quite different characteristics from those of the quantitative data of traditional empirical research.

The fundamental difference between the numerical data and qualitative verbal data lies in the fact that while objective meaning can be associated to the first, sense can be made of the second only after a process of subjective intepretation of the data. For example, to say that "Today, the outside temperature is 30°C" is not the same as saying "It's hot today."

In particular, in this chapter, the question of the reliability of data is discussed, and an answer is given to questions like: How can we be relatively sure that the content of the discourses are interpreted correctly by the analysts? When is an intepretation acceptable? Is more than one intepretation admissible? Is it possible to identify and evaluate errors of interpretation?

Chapter XVII is dedicated to managerial implications. We highlight that one crucial aspect of the processes found in a learning organization is not so much in its capacity for achieving certain results, but in the process itself. The results of learning are difficult to predict and even more difficult to plan. The process of learning is destructured and uncontrollable. It can go in unexpected directions and give unhoped for results. Serendipity, or the luck of finding something new and interesting while intending to search for something else, is a recognized characteristic of the learning process (Merton & Barber, 2004). Individuals must be given a certain degree of freedom and room to maneuver. All of this requires a new cultural and managerial attitude with respect to time and space management, as well as work relationships. Times, places, and relationships marked by creativity and innovation, before production, hierarchy and efficiency.

Some suggestions are proposed in this chapter for managers who intend to supervise learning and cognitive work in this perpective.

Chapter XVIII is dedicated to identifying possible future research perspectives and development for the methodological approach presented in this text. The methodological argument is taken up again from a wider perspective in order to propose a truly innovative approach. For each of the salient moments of the proposed approach, that is, the identification, mapping and modeling of discourses, the available or potential alternative methodologies are mentioned briefly and possible developments are outlined.

The two final appendixes are aimed at providing the readers with further detailed examples of application of the methodological approach proposed in our book. The first example presents the step-by-step construction of a verbal model to represent and evaluate the voice of the customer in new product development, the second appendix describes an agent based model to simulate collective learning processes in competencies development.

How to Read This Book

Given the objectives of this work, the text was conceived as a sequence of short Chapters that attempt to give complete descriptions of the specific concepts within them. Nevertheless, there are some alternative ways to read this book, for people who are less interested in the methodological aspects or would like to read about them later.

For these readers, we advise reading all of the chapters in the first two parts, the first chapter of the third section (Chapter X) and to skip directly to the final chapters (Chapters XV, XVI, XVII, XVIII). For readers who are interested in the methodological aspects, but less interested in the quantative aspects, we suggest following the same procedure with the addition of Chapter XI.

Reading Chapters XII, XIII, and XIV does not require special mathematical knowledge. We have preferred to give the minumum amount of detail and mathematic formalism, saving it for the appendix or other readings, perhaps to the detriment of the rigor of the presentation, but with the advantage of a higher degree of legibility of chapters even by an audience that does not have a background in quantitative studies. Nevertheless, the methodological approach presented in Chapter X can be applied as a first step, without necessarily moving on to a "hard" modeling of discourse, limiting it to the phases of identification and mapping.

The text can be used with a specialized course of business organization at the graduate level, for masters and for PhD courses, training courses for organizational analysts, personnel managers, and personnel trainers. Most chapters have been designed so that the material can be covered easily and completely in a single two hour lesson.

The text can also be used as a "secondary" source for in-depth study and reflection. Many summary boxes and detailed descriptions of the illustrations have been provided for this reason. Some boxes are extra information for "detailed study," and contain brief reviews of specific topics and essential bibliographical references. Other boxes contain examples, metaphors, digressions and suggestions, often taken from narrative literature or the figurative arts, whose function is to give readers interpretative keys and explanations of some concepts in nontraditional and, we hope, more meaningful and interesting ways. The citations at the beginning of every chapter have also been chosen in order to represent as closely as possible the content and what is to us the deeper sense of the chapter.

To avoid interrupting the flow of the chapter we have limited the footnotes and end notes to those that are strictly indispensable. At times the notes contain information that would have been more appropriately shown in boxes, but we decided to limit the use of this tool to avoid overusing it. Instead we have highlighted or illustrated just those concepts that we believe are most important to the objectives of the text.

For Whom This Work was Written and What You will not Find in it

The text was written for everyone who believes that the future of organizations lies in learning and those who would like to know how to build and manage a learning organization. To those readers we offer a theory of organizational learning in which the central concepts are those of memory, experience and planning. A methodological approach is presented along with some tools that can be used to analyze explanatory discourse, which are the starting point of every attempt at organizational learning.

An example of an information box: Organizations as cognitive systems

The origins of the cognitive approach to the sudy of organizations goes back to the contributions made by March and Simon (1958) in which organizations are essentially considered as systems for the elaboration of information (*information processing*). Organizations allow us for the partial obviation of the limits of the rationality of individuals, inasmuch as they are able to process a larger quantity of information collectively. It was from these approaches that the metaphor of the organization as a computer or a brain was born (Morgan, 1997).

A second line of thought that put the cognitive process at the center of the analysis comes from the analysis of the decision-making process in March (1988), Mintzberg et al. (1976), and Quinn (1988). Unlike the *information processing* approach, the experts of organizational *decision-making* place the emphasis on the chaotic, destructured, political, and apperently irrational character of the decision-making process. In particular, March analyzes the role of ambiguity as an intrinsic characteristic of organizational decision-making processes (March, 1988).

A third line of study is tied to organizational *sense-making*. Followers of this approach (Weick, 1979; Daft & Weick, 1978; Choo, 1998) consider organizations as intepretative systems that elaborate and create meanings instead of as complex processors of information from the objective, or at least non-problematic meaning. In the sense-making approach, the interpretation is not antecedent to the action but is the result of the action and the interactions in organizations; moreover, organizational processes are conditioned by the presence of preexisting intepretative schema created by individuals through the accumulation of experience and the construction of collective beliefs. The sense-making approach had remarkable methodological effects in the field of *cognitive mapping* (Huff, 1990; Eden & Ackermann, 1992); the methodologies of mapping aim at identifyig and representing the interpretative schema that guide the actions of members of an organization.

Lant and Shapira (2001), editor of a volume that contains many contributions on the recent developments of *organizational cognition*, highlight a growing contrast in the literature between the supporters of *information processing* and *organizational sense-making*. The works contained in the volume nevertheless show that organizational cognition can gain remarkable advantages from the integration rather than the contrast of these two approaches.

The emerging paradigm of *social cognition* (Conte, 2002) promotes the integration between the cognitive and sociological approaches, and recent advances in the field of artificial intelligence in virtue of the recognition of the reciprocal influence between individual cognition and social interaction. The chosen methodological tool for the analysis of this complex problem is *simulation based on agents* through the creation of virtual organizational scenarios implemented through algorithms in which various typologies of independent agents interact with their peers and with their surroundings causing the emergence of aggregate phenomena and mass tendencies that can be explained starting from individual behaviors and ways of interaction.

Quite little attention is paid to the pyschological aspects tied to individual learning. Instead, proper consideration is given to the political and relational aspect of learning. The use and application of methodological tools presented in this volume assume that the learning organization has adequate conditions (psychological, relational and political) to carry them out.

The text is aimed at people studying organizations, consultants, managers and anyone who is interested in actually building a learning organization. In the entire universe of books and articles on the theme of "learning organizations" the present text has a very specific, and in some ways original place among them.

Specific, because it casts its attention on a specific tool of organizational learning, which is explanatory discourse. It firmly sustains that explanatory discourse triggers organizational learning, summarizing in a rational construct of memory, experience and planning.

Original, because it provides a bridge between the theory and the practice of organizational learning by proposing an innovative methodological approach. This connection allows us to lay down the base for the construction of new organizational systems that can envelop and circulate knowledge and "soft" information usually ignored by traditional systems.

References

Argyris, C., & Schon, D.A. (1978). *Organizational learning. A theory of action perspective.* Reading, MA: Addison-Wesley.

Berger, P.L., & Luckmann, T. (1966). *The social construction of reality: A treatise in the sociology of knowledge.* New York: Doubleday.

Bifo Berardi, F. (2003). Che significa oggi autonomia? www.republicart.net

Blackler, F. (2002). Knowledge, knowledge work and organizations. In C. W. Choo & N. Bontis (Eds.), *The strategic management of intellectual capital and organizational knowledge.* Oxford: Oxford University Press.

Bonfantini, M.A. (1987). *La semiosi e l'abduzione.* Bompiani, Milano.

Choo, C.W. (1998). *The knowing organization.* Oxford: Oxford University Press.

Cameron, K.S., & Whetten, D.A. (1983). *Organizational effectiveness.* New York: Academic Press.

Cillario, L. (1990). Il capitalismo cognitivo. Sapere, sfruttamento e accumulazione dopo la rivoluzione informatica. In A.A.V.V. (Ed.), *Trasformazione e persistenza (Saggi sulla storicità del capitalismo).* Milano: F. Angeli.

Conte, R. (2002). Scienze dociali e scienza cognitiva. *Sistemi intelligenti, XV*(1), 7-31.

Crozier, M., & Fiedberg, E. (1977). *L'acteur et le système.* Paris: Editions du Seuil.

Daft, R.L., & Wintington, J.C. (1979). Language and organizations. *Academy of Management Review, 4*, 179-191.

Daft, R.L., & Weick, K. (1984). Toward a model of organization as interpretation systems. *Academy of Management Review, 9*(2), 284-295.

Eden, C., & Ackermann, F. (1992). The analysis of causal map. *International Journal of Management Studies, 29*(3), 310-324.

Heracleous, L., & Barrett, M. (2001). Organizational change as discourse: Communicative actions and deep structures in the context of information technology implementation. *Academy of Management Journal, 44*(4), 755-778.

Huff, A.S. (Ed.). (1990). *Mapping strategic thought.* Chirchester: Wiley

Lant. K.T., & Shapira, Z. (Eds.). (2001). *Organizational cognition: Computation and interpretation.* Mawah, NJ: Lawrence Erlbaum Associate.

March, J.G. (1988). *Decision and organization.* Oxford: Blackwell.

March, J.G., & Simon, H. (1958). *Organizations.* New York: John Wiley & Sons.

Merton, R.K., & Barber, L. (2004). *The travels and adventures of serendipity: A study in sociological semantics and the sociology of science.* Princeton,NJ: Princeton University Press.

Mintzberg, H., Raisinghani, D., & Theoret, A. (1976). The structure of unstructured decision processes. *Administrative Science Quarterly, 25*, 465-499.

Morgan, G. (1997). *Images of organizations* (2nd ed.). Thousands Oaks,CA: Sage.

Nicolini, D., & Meznar, M.B. (1995). The social construction of organizational learning. *Human Relations, 48*(7), 727-746.

Nisbett & Ross (1980). *Human inference: Strategies and shortcomings of social judgment.* Englewood Cliffs, NJ: Prentice-Hall.

Pinchot, G., & Pinchot, E. (1993). The rise and fall of bureaucracy. In G. Pinchot & E. Pinchot (Eds.), *The end of bureaucracy and the rise of intelligent organizations.* Berret-Koehler Publishers. (Reprinted in Myers, P.S. (ed. by), *Knowledge Management and Organizational Design*, Butterworth-Heinemann, Boston, 1966, pp. 39-53).

Polanyi, M. (1967). *The tacit dimension.* New York: Doubleday.

Quinn, R.E., & Cameron, K.S. (1983). Organizational life cycles and shifting criteria and effectiveness. *Management Science, 9*, 33-51.

Reich, R. (1991). *The work of nations: Preparing ourselves to the 21st century capitalism.* London: Simon and Schuster.

Rullani, E. (2002). Produzione di conoscenza e valore nel postfordismo (an interview by A. Corsani). In Y. Moulier Boutang (Ed.), *L'età del capitalismo cognitivo. Innovazione, proprietà e cooperazione delle moltitudini* (pp. 23-35). Verona: Ombre Corte.

Schank, R.C. (1986), *Explanation patterns: Understanding mechanically and creatively.* Hillsdale, NJ: Lawrence Erlbaum.

Thagard, P. (1992). *Conceptual revolution.* Princeton,NJ: Princeton University Press.

Weick, K.E. (1979). *The social psychology of organization* (2nd ed.). Reading, MA: Addison Wesley.

Wenstøp, F. (1975b). Deductive verbal model of organizations. *International Journal of Man Machine Studies, 8,* 301-357.

Zadeh, L. (1973). Outline of a new approach to the analysis of complex systems and decision processes. *IEEE Transactions on Systems, Man and Cybernetics, 3*(1).

Endnotes

[1] The term "cognitive work" has been used in Italy within the Marxist contrast between work and capital (Bifo, 2003). The use of the expression in our treatment is instead to be considered without political connotations, even though some political fallout may originate from our conceptualization. This debate naturally goes beyond the limits and the objectives of this volume.

[2] The term "knowledge worker" is often use to mean cognitive worker (Blackler, 2002; Reich, 1991). This concept recall the definition proposed by the National Labor Relation Board negli USA (1996), the professional is "a worker that executes intellectual job activities, with high discretionality, that produces non standard outputs, and that possesses specialistic knowlegde acquired through superior training or the exercise of the professional activity." As Cillario observes (1990), nevertheless we should not mistake cognitive work with intellectual work. What distinguishes cognitive work from noncognitive is in the end traceable to the capacity for observation, reflection on one's own work, and autoomous reorganization.

Acknowledgment

To Teresa, for sharing with me her life, and also ideas, conversations and work in the writing of this book.

To my parents, Ida and Vincenzo, for their love and support.

Luca Iandoli

To Rosalba, for giving me the love, the space and the time to toy with my ideas.

Giuseppe Zollo

The theory, methods, and examples contained in this book have been developed and/or used in various field studies by the authors in several different companies. Such field studies have given us many precious occasions to confront the principle question that companies and organizations in the real world must face in terms of knowledge and learning in organizations. Throughout these experiences we were lucky enough to have the support of some managers and professionals who made the learning organization their paradigm of reference and faced the daily challenges at work.

A special thanks goes to Giancarlo Michellone, former president of the FIAT Research Center and to the managers of CRF who were involved in our research activities, Alessandro Cannavacciuolo in particular.

We would also like to thank Francesco Ruggiero, personnel director of the Automobile Club of Italy (ACI) and the work group at ACI coordinated by the Director of Organizational Development, Simonetta Petruccini (Valeria Cipollone, Rossella Forti, Luigi Mingrone, Nicoletta Troiani). Finally, we would like to thank Valerio Teta and Mario Capaccio for the study developed together at GEPIN Engineering.

We would like to thank all of the colleagues at the Department of Business and Managerial Engineering at the University of Naples, Federico II who discussed and exchanged ideas with us about the arguments in this book, and particularly Guido Capaldo and Cristina Ponsiglione, who shared some of the experiences illustrated here. We also need to thank the students who worked with us and helped us to explore various themes and aspects found in this book more in depth in their degree theses and doctoral dissertations (Francesca Borrelli, Lorella Cannavacciuolo, Vincenzo D'Angelo, Laura De Maio, Francesca Di Lucchio, Pierluigi Rippa, Giusy Iacoviello).

We gratefully acknowledge the support of the staff of the COINOR (Center for Communication and Organizational Innovation) at the University of Naples Federico II, and in particular Sara Cavaliere and Maria Grazia Mergenni in the editing and graphic layout of the text.

Special thanks also go to all the staff at IGI Global, whose contributions throughout the whole process from its inception of the initial idea to final publication have been invaluable. In particular, to Lynley Lapp, Meg Stocking, and Lynn Day, who continuously prodded via e-mail for keeping the project on schedule.

Deep appreciation and gratitude is due to Dianna Pickens who helped with the translation of this text. Her professional manner and punctuality, as well as her enthusiasm and encouragement, were fundamental in finishing this work.

Of course we have many scientific debts to the many scholars and thinkers quoted in this book. In a few cases, we were lucky enough to have met some of them in person and to have their advice and ideas that we used fully in writing this text. A warm thanks to our friends Barry Shore and his wonderful wife, Carol, and to many colleagues at the Whittemore Business School of the University of New Hampshire, in particular to A.R. Venkatachalam and Carole Barnette.

Thanks goes to Maya Evans who encouraged us to continue with this project.

Many of the results and ideas described in this volume have been presented at various international meetings and in scientific journals. On these occasions, some precious advice and influence has been useful in the development of the research. We thank, in particular: Jaime Gil Aluja (U. of Barcellona), Colin Eden (University of Strathclyde), James Hayton (Utah State University), Gerry Hills (University of Illinois at Chicago), Anne Huff (Advanced Institute of Management Research at the London Business School), Nigel Gilbert (University of Surrey), V. K. Narayanan (Drexel University) and Deb Armstrong (University of Arkansas), Prashant Palvia (University of Carolina at Greensboro), Kurt Richardson (Institute for the Study of Coherence and Emergence at Mansfield USA), Lorraine Uhlaner (Erasmus University Rotterdam) as well as the many friends and colleagues from whom we received during these last years valuable feedback at the Global Information technology Management Conferences, the Italian association for Management Engineering (AiIG), the International Society for Fuzzy Sets and Management (SIGEF).

A special thanks goes to Lotfi Zadeh and Piero Bonissone for their conversations, hints, and suggestions during their visiting at the University of Naples Federico II.

Section I

Organizational Learning

Chapter I

Managing Knowledge in the Cognitive Organization

We have wheels in our knees, funnels as ears and discs impressed in our brains. Pliers as hands, pivot in our elbows and shoulders; muscles & nerves are tiny and intertwined chains; pulleys and transmission shafts driven by two interconnected engines, the heart and the brain.

~ Fortunato Depero, W la macchina e lo stile d'acciao

Abstract

Digital technologies have played an important role in the diffusion of knowledge management (KM). The distinction between hardware and software, between platform and logical layer has revolutionized the concept of the machine. Machines become intelligent, while knowledge becomes an independent virtual object. An analogous revolution has occurred in organizations: the metaphor of the organi-

zation as a machine is replaced by that of the organization as a computer. In this type of organization there is a need to manage a critical new resource: knowledge. Organizations are different from machines and computers in one fundamental way: They are able to generate new knowledge through learning. After giving a brief history of the birth and evolution of KM, in this chapter, we will show how the main criticism of modern approaches to KM are due to the inadequacy of the metaphor of the computer. Finally, we show that in order to overcome such limits, KM needs to be framed within an organizational learning theory and the metaphor of computer organizations substituted with the paradigm of the learning organization.

The Digital Revolution and the Cognitive Machine

In 1996, the governor of the Federal Reserve, Alan Greenspan, declared that a radical change had come about in the American and world economy: the progressive loss of volume. In particular, he observed that:

Accordingly, while the weight of current economic output is probably only modestly higher than it was a half century ago, value added, adjusted for price change, is well over threefold.[1]

This paradox questions a basic rule of economic exchange. This rule says that the value of wealth produced in a market correlates to the mass of products which are produced and exchanged.

Dematerialization is a phenomenon that concerns not only the final products, but also the processes of production, and is due to a series of technological innovations, which have played a major role in miniaturizing electronic circuits and information technology (IT) in general.

Underlying all of the relevant innovations produced by the advent of new technologies is probably the intuition of Claude Shannon. In the 1930s, as a doctoral student at MIT in Boston, he understood that an electronic circuit could be used to implement the capacity to do logical operations, such as those used in the logic of propositions, onto a device.[2]

In many ways, everything that is considered IT, and in particular all types of software, can be traced back to this invention. Circuits that are no different than those invented by Shannon are now the fundamental components of the architecture of all the electronic processors and all the existing machines that process digital information.

The consequences of Shannon's invention and the implementation of the first logical circuits through the introduction of transistors were noteworthy, and not only on a purely technological level. *Shannon's circuits revolutionized the concept of the machine*, from various points of view.

The functional logic of any Shannon circuit can be described first "in words," that is, by describing the rules "if ... then ... " to be codified in the circuit, then in a more synthetic way through algebraic expressions according to Boole's algebraic formalisms. Given the equations, the physical realization of the circuit is reduced to an assembly of standard components. More generally, we can say that the functioning of the machine can, for the first time, be described through formal language (Boolean equations). Although it is rigid and formalized, this language can describe operations carried out by the processes of human reasoning.

Secondly, with the introduction of circuits and programmable logic, the description of its functioning is incorporated into the machine as if it had been transferred from outside. Thanks to this operation, the machine has been given a form of "intelligence," which is also extractable from it.

At nearly the same time, the pioneering studies of Turing (1937, 1950) and Von Neumann and Morgenstern (1946) deepened and expanded upon this intuition. In those same years, the cybernetics (Wiener, 1948) thought of machines as examples of more general models formulated in system theories, able to react appropriately to stimulation coming from the external environment by following their own internal logic. That is how machines have become sophisticated systems which are able to process information and react to external stimulation by using high-level descriptions of their own functioning. Their "reprogramming" through human intervention would not necessarily require rethinking their physical structure.

Products have also been subjected to this transformation. An "intelligent" product is not only a material object but also a combination of a physical support, which is getting smaller and smaller, and a certain amount of "knowledge" that is virtually something else inside the object. However, this "knowledge" can also be separated from it, transferred to another similar object, and modified without changing the container in any way.

The possibility of giving machines knowledge introduces two more very important ideas:

1. It is possible to add or expand the functions of a machine without changing its basic configuration, while reducing its space and weight thanks to the miniaturization of its components.

2. It is possible to develop general purpose machines that are not specifically dedicated to the execution of well-defined tasks, but able to contain in the same

device several personalized functions, according to the needs of the specific application.

In the end, machines become physical platforms for knowledge, describable through formal language formal language with a syntax and semantics similar to human language. Moreover, this knowledge can be transmitted, modified, shared by several machines, just as if it were a physical object. However, it is undeniable that we are talking about a special kind of object which does not wear out and seems to have many characteristics that make it similar to a description, as approximate, simplistic and crude as it may be, of human knowledge.

Programming a machine means "injecting" an object with the capacity to carry out a certain number of functions described in software language. Software is the way we not only describe and impose behavior on a machine, but also the way we create the conditions for a new form of interaction between the man and the machine. *The act of giving intelligence to machines makes them more similar to ourselves. Just as we need machines to be intelligent so that we can delegate some tasks, machines need to interact with our intelligence to complete their plans of action.* This new type of relationship between human beings and intelligent machine is much more flexible and ambiguous than that of a traditional machine because, in the first case, the interaction assumes a different, and more profound, meaning.

One example of the type of interaction that takes place might be when the graphic interface is represented through metaphoric language (the desktop). The machine offers its computational intelligence, and we complete that intelligence with our ability to generate metaphors. Although the metaphor of the desktop influences the way we interact with it, it is purely incidental and allows us to create a large set of possible interpretations and uses (file, document, archive, trash, etc.).

The idea that knowledge can be an object, though a strange one, comes from this suggestion: Machines are transformed into "thinking" machines, which are the combination of a physical platform and a certain amount of knowledge.

Even organizations have been unable to remain indifferent to a revolution such as this.

At the beginning of the twentieth century, the application of the scientific method to work organizations by Frederick Taylor and the mechanization of production changed the face of industry, transforming factories into giant mechanisms (Morgan, 1997). The metaphor of the machine was immediately successful, so it became an organizational model that was adopted in many different sectors. Still today, we tend to think of organizations as machines.

Similarly, the digital revolution has imposed new organizational paradigms based on the dualism between hardware and software, material resources and the intangible capital made up of people and knowledge: the computer metaphor (Simon, 1981).

Taylor's machine had to work, at least in theory, like a giant clock in which every mechanism had to do its part. There was no separation between the system and the man, and the system and the machine.[3] We can call it a clockwork organization. In Simon's machine, which we can call a cognitive organization, this "harmony" has been lost forever.

The Digital Revolution and the Cognitive Organization

In the computer metaphor, organizations can be thought of as the integration between hardware (the technical system) and software (the social system),[4] but the added value is mostly created by the software part, i.e. through human and intangible resources. However, organizations are different in that they can create new knowledge through the individual and collective learning process.

If the management of knowledge and learning become critical processes, even traditional organizational models are no longer valid.

In the clockwork organization, the contribution of individuals is primarily by carrying out standard tasks or giving "portions of attention" to monitor repetitive events.

Instead, the cognitive organization can be thought of as an intelligent machine, as a combination of a hardware platform of technology, structures, machines, property, and a "software" or "wetware"[5] component, which is essentially the people, processes, and mechanisms which coordinate collective action.

In the passage from the clockwork organization to a cognitive organization, immaterial resources are given more and more importance with respect to hardware. In the most extreme cases, organizational forms become almost virtual, and their material resources are considered secondary.

In new organizations, individuals do not carry out tasks or dedicate their attention passively; both of these actions are mostly given to intelligent machines governed through a formal symbolic language. Instead, individuals are asked to manage unexpected situations, to transform themselves into knowledge workers (Blackler, 2002), and to go from manipulation of nonambiguous objects and information to manipulation of problematic symbols and information (*Symbolic workers*, Reich, 1991). They become cognitive workers and their main task is to make evaluations and decisions instead of carry out standard tasks.

The roles that have been most involved in these changes are those in middle management and the front-office. In many cases they have been changed from controllers/executors to *professionals,* characterized by "*nonroutinary and intellectual job activity, discretionary power, nonstandard outputs, specialized knowledge acquired through high education and/or training on the job*" (National Labor Relation Board, USA, 1996).

The increasing weight of immaterial resources in the creation of values and the growing emergence of professionals has changed how technical systems and human systems in organizations are seen to interact. While in a clockwork organization the technology forces individuals to follow its rhythms and transforms them into a part of the machine itself, in a cognitive organization, this aspect becomes more and more problematic, and the relationship between the person and the machine is primarily based on the concept of interaction instead of subordination.

Moreover, interaction with the machine is no longer just manual and prescriptive, but conceptual and creative, and the individual is not only asked to control the machine, but to discover more efficient ways to use it. Just as cognitive machines interpret human language in some way, the knowledge worker must also interpret the language and the capacity of the machine creatively and effectively. Finally, the interaction between man and machine is above all symbolic and metaphorical in nature.

In the clockwork organization, the interface between the human system and the technical system is guaranteed by a strong, prescriptive rationality, perceived as being outside the system and sometimes incomprehensible to most of its members. The coordinating mechanisms based on the rules, the procedures, the hierarchy, as well as the subordination of human action to that of the machine, prevent individuals from bringing their own rationality into play, and essentially ask them to conform to an objective, top-down rationality that is unquestionable, because any questioning of it would put the entire system itself at risk.

But a clockwork organization, like any other machine, can only work effectively and safely in a stable environment. The complexity, instability and ambiguity of technological scenarios and the competitive environment have made this organizational paradigm inadequate. In these contexts, the prescriptivity has been transformed into rigidity, intended as the incapacity to react quickly and effectively to changes.

A profound change was therefore made necessary: Along with the *strong* and *centralized* rationality, more and more often we find a *weak* and *distributed* rationality that is locally generated by the system itself through continuous and adaptive learning processes. The rationality of the interface in the new organizational paradigm:

- Is *weak*, in that it is adaptive: The continuous interaction with a problematic and changing environment forces individuals to question it constantly and to react flexibly to its demands.
- Is *subjective*, in that it depends on the experience, ability and degree of autonomy of each individual.

- Is *distributed* in the organization because it is locally generated through individual creativity and interaction between individuals within learning networks for sharing knowledge.

- Is *transactional* since it develops at the interface between the human system and the technological and organizational system.

Cognitive organizations have to confront problems that clockwork organizations do not have to face.

In the first place, they have to reach a delicate balance between the need for centralized control and local learning, that is to say between a strong, centralized rationality and a weak, subjective, and local rationality. In the second place, they must adopt policies which favor the growth and development of the capacity for learning. In the third place, they must be able to take advantage of the results of individual learning, which we will define in Chapters III and IV of this book as organizational learning.

The accumulation and development of knowledge, therefore, becomes a strategic factor in the development and growth of cognitive organizations and creates a double challenge for them: (a) to create an appropriate environment which is able to attract and generate relevant knowledge through individual and collective learning processes, and (b) to use this knowledge regardless of the individuals who possess it in order to modify, transfer, manipulate, or share it; in other words, to "manage" it, possibly in the same way the codified object knowledge is managed: By transforming knowledge into a code to be "injected" into machines.

The Emergence of Knowledge Management

The concept of knowledge as an object, and the hardware/software dualism has strongly influenced the first attempts of managers to provide effective answers to the problems raised by the knowledge-based competition. The attempts is at the heart of a new managerial discipline known as *knowledge management (KM)*.

KM is the process of creating, capturing, and using knowledge to enhance organizational performance. It refers to a range of practices and techniques used by organizations to identify, represent, and distribute knowledge, know-how, expertise, intellectual capital, and other forms of knowledge for leverage, reuse and transfer of knowledge and learning across the organization. KM is most frequently associated with two types of activities. One is to document and appropriate individual's knowledge and then disseminate such knowledge through such venues as a company wide databases. The second one includes activities that facilitate knowledge exchanges using such tools as groupware, e-mail, and the Internet.

We must also recognize that, if the first software technicians and engineers had not tried to reduce knowledge to an object, thanks to the possibilities offered by electronic, computer and web technologies, KM would never have been invented—at least not in the form it has taken today.

In the following paragraphs, we will go over the essential phases in the evolution of KM.[6] We will also demonstrate that one of the main weaknesses of current approaches to KM is in their relative lack of integration with organizational learning management.

KM: A Movement with Two Beginnings

According to Karl Sveiby (1997) the expression "managing knowledge" appears for the first time in a context of artificial intelligence at the end of the 1980s. In 1988, an article entitled *Managing the Knowledge Assets into the 21st Century* was published by Debra Amidon, a researcher at Purdue University.

The first researchers in the field of KM were interested in the possibility of using information technology to support the process of individual learning.

Again in the artificial intelligence (AI) community, Karl Wiig (1993) was one of the first scholars to recognize the limits of a primarily technological approach and to define KM in terms of *creation, learning, sharing (transferring), and using or leveraging knowledge as a set of social and dynamic processes that needed to be managed.*[7]

Almost at the same time in Japan, Ikujiro Nonaka and his research group conducted a series of studies on the management of the process of innovation within large Japanese companies. These studies, together with the total quality management movement and the concept of continuous improvement (kaizen), reevaluate the overall role that human resources play at all levels in organizations discovering what was not yet obvious (and is still not obvious in many contexts) in organizational practice: the centrality of the individual in the knowledge creation process and the consequent need to recognize the person's necessary level of competence and autonomy. In 1995, Nonaka and Takeuchi published the results of their research in *The Knowledge Creating Company*, a text that would revolutionize KM, emphasizing the concept of tacit knowledge and the social processes that allow for the creation and transfer of knowledge in organizations.

Most of the contributions in the vast literature on KM can be reduced to one of these two approaches or attempts to integrate the two perspectives.[8] A summary for a possible classification of the various contributions available in the literature can be found in Table 1 (Sveiby, 1997).

Table 1. Fields of KM research

Focus on Level	Information technology Knowledge = object	People Knowledge = process
Organizational level	Reengineering	Theoreticians of business organization
Individual level	AI- specialists E-specialists	Psychologists Cognitive scientists

This matrix identifies four possible areas on the basis of two variables: Level of analysis (organizational or individual) and connotation of knowledge (knowledge-as-an-object vs. knowledge-as-a-process).

Knowledge as an Object

It is undoubtedly true that the promoters of the knowledge = object approach from the engineering/informatics culture, tend to consider knowledge management as the sophisticated management of information that takes more advantage of the potential of the tools offered by technology. It is equally easy to show that the promoters of the knowledge=object approach are not unaware of the organizational role of knowledge creation, transferal and sharing; on the contrary, they often warn against the indiscriminate use of the new technologies in this field (Schreiber et al., 1999). However, they do not go any deeper into the question and they focus on studying the methodologies of representation and codification of knowledge and the technologies that can support these processes, and above all on the tasks that a KM system must implement: *identify, organize, file, find, share and transmit knowledge* (Satyadas et al., 2001).

In each of these tasks, knowledge is undoubtedly considered as an object to identify, manipulate and transfer; in other words, it has all of the characteristics of a piece of software code: Knowledge that is explicitly describable in formal terms, and is transferable to any means of support (electronic device, paper, human, etc.), within an acceptable cost and time.

The attitude is to concentrate on making software platforms and management tools that allow us to carry out more or less sophisticated operations, taking for granted, or at least for untreatable through analytical means, all of the soft processes that Nonaka and Takeuchi (1995) consider as fundamental for the creation of knowledge and which are traceable to the human variable and to the processes of social interaction in organizations.

One of the definitions of KM that best shows the IT-based approach is the following (Satyadas et al., 2001) *"KM is a discipline that provides strategy, process, and technology to share and leverage information and expertise that will increase our level of understanding to more effectively solve problems and make decisions"* (p. 429).

In the same way, the definition of knowledge in the knowledge = object approach is *actionable information,* meaning the information that is necessary to act or that can more efficiently guide action. This definition is based on an important assumption: The individual is the one who is given the task of identifying the information/action combination, and the process that leads to the creation of new knowledge is a black box that the knowledge engineer is not interested in.[9] His/her job is substantially limited to creating technological systems that are able to support the sophisticated and widespread management of complex information. The emphasis is on the characteristics of the platform that best allows for the management and in part, the interface between the platform and the individual.

The following is a list, which is certainly not complete, of the KM applications which this line of research has mainly concentrated on:

1. **Content management:** Creation, archiving, distribution, aggregation, filtration, retrieval, building taxonomies

2. **Portals:** Single-sign-on, user interface, personalization, search and navigation

3. **Collaboration:** Chat rooms, e-meetings, virtual agents, virtual workspaces, e-mail (Smith, 2000)

4. **Learning:** Just-in-time learning, self-teaching, collaborative learning, face-to-face learning

5. **Business intelligence:** Data warehouse, analytical treatment of information, decision support systems

6. **Business integration:** Processes, application integration, data aggregation

The IT-based approach to KM has been very successful and, in particular since the 1990s, it has produced a strong proliferation of tools that have been widespread commercially, above all in some sectors such as business integration, e-learning and customer relationship management.

The main advantages of this approach is in the creation of management tools and applicative tools that have often contributed to improving the efficiency of the very process of creation and elaboration of new knowledge. The impact of the application of KM systems in business has been noteworthy above all in terms of the improving productivity and lowering costs rather than in increasing the ability to create innovation (Martin et al., 1996).

The reasons why businesses have implemented KM systems are varied. Sveiby (1997), after collecting the experiences relative to about 40 cases in business, clas-

Table 2. Initiatives for knowledge management (Adapted from Sveiby, 1997)

External structure initiatives	Internal structure initiatives	Competencies initiatives
Acquire knowledge from clients	Build a knowledge-sharing culture	Career management based on KM
Offer additional knowledge to clients	Create new revenue from existing knowledge	Create microenvironment for transferring knowledge
	Capture individual knowledge, store it, spread it and reuse it	Support the learning through ICT
	Measure the process of knowledge creation and intangible assets	Learn from pilot project simulations
Benetton, General Electric, National Bicycle, Netscape, Ritz Carlton, Agro-corp, Frito-Lay, Dow Chemical, Skandia, Steelcase	3M, Analog Devices, Boeing, Buckman Labs, Chaparral Steel, Ford Motor Co., Hewlett-Packard, Oticon, WM-data, McKinsey, Bain & Co., Chevron. British Petroleum, PLS-consult, Skandia AFS, Telia, Celemi	Buckman Labs, IBM, Pfizer, WM-data, Hewlett-Packard, Honda, PLS-consult, Xerox, National Technological University, Matsushita, IKEA

sified the KM initiatives with respect to three different types of initiatives: External structure initiatives, internal structure initiatives, and initiatives for the management of competencies (Table 2).

Knowledge as a Process and the Limits of the IT-Based Approach

Those who sustain this approach tend to give a central role to individuals and the interaction processes that happen between them in organizations when creating and elaborating knowledge. Usually, the background of the people belonging to this area is in the social sciences. Consequently, the emphasis is not on the instruments that implement the KM systems, but on the psychological, social and organizational factors that influence the process of creation of new knowledge in organizations.

Within this group of researchers, we can find two different attitudes toward technology: One that is fundamentally skeptical, which stamps the IT-based approach as reductive and ineffective; the other a "compromise" approach, which, instead, recognizes its merits and follows its development carefully, but in the end, gives priority to studying the human factor. Nonaka and Takeuchi (1995) belong to the first group, while the European school derived from the Swedish one led by Sveiby makes up the second.

Nonaka and Takeuchi start from the basic idea that the revolution of knowledge-based competition requires a complete revision of the role of the individual in an organization. They recognize, along with Drucker (1993), that *"The central activities in the creation of wealth are not the allocation of capital in productive employment, nor work [...] Value is created today by productivity and innovation, which are both applications of work knowledge."*

Nevertheless, they affirm that their position on KM is quite different from the Western approach. Why did the Japanese choose a different line? They respond to this question by affirming that limiting oneself to methodically managing information and measuring intangible capital does not influence the capacity of the business to create innovation.

Nonaka's position reaffirms the concept that a large part of business knowledge has nothing to do with data, but is based on a sort of informal operative knowledge that he, repeating a concept expressed by Polanyi (1958, 1966), defines as *tacit knowledge,* which is impossible to codify in otherwise sophisticated management systems. The presuppositions of the Japanese school can be expressed as follows:

- Knowledge can not be reduced to a set of data or information that can be stored in a computer, but it also involves emotions, cultural values, and intuition.

- Businesses should not limit themselves to managing knowledge but have to give priority to processes that spark creation.

- Every member of an organization must be involved in the creation of business knowledge.

- Middle management plays a critical role for managing knowledge and, in a cognitive organization, constitutes the transmission belt from bottom to top and vice versa, while in the machine organization constitutes the transmission belt of control.

Nonaka and his team refuse the dualism typical of Western culture between the knower and the known object, body and mind, action and reflection. Instead, they consider action as the starting point for individual learning. They do not accept the metaphor of the thinking machine and the hardware/software dualism. In the Japanese approach, hardware is considered irrelevant and the reduction of knowledge to software, meaning explicit and encodable knowledge, is considered misleading.

According to Nonaka, knowledge is created in the tight network of social relations that run through an organization and the revelation of knowledge is an important moment, but one that is secondary to the process of creation itself. That is why they prefer the expression "knowledge creation" to "knowledge management," and they underline that the concept of creativity competes with the concept of control which dominates organizational theory and Western culture.

The fundamental processes of creation of knowledge are those of *socialization*, through which individuals share the results of individual learning, and those of *internalization* through which the individual adopts and processes the shared knowledge. Only when knowledge is sufficiently socialized and internalized it can be made explicit through *externalization* and recombined with existing explicit knowledge (*recombination*). These four processes make up a cycle that can produce new knowledge in the end, both at the individual and at the organizational level.

For supporters of the people-based approach, knowledge cannot be made perfectly explicit and spread unevenly in an organization (Boisot, 2002). *KM makes no sense because an organization cannot manage knowledge; what an organization can do is to create the favorable conditions in which creative expression and socialization of knowledge can take place.*

The problem areas identified by these studies are quite varied and comprise themes such as the generation of tacit knowledge, the study of decisional processes in organizations, the creation and sharing of knowledge in organizations, and studies on the people-machine interface.

In Table 3 we report the main differences between the approaches that we have presented with respect to the three variables: The definition of knowledge, the definition of KM and the purposes of KM.

Table 3. Review of the differences among the various approaches to KM

		Definition of Knowledge	Definition of KM	Purpose of KM
IT-based		Actionable information	Process of creating, capturing, and using knowledge to enhance organizational performance problems understanding and effective decision making	Archiving, capturing, organizing, distributing, codifying knowledge Making it available and reusable at the right moment, for the right person, in the right place
People-based	**IT skeptics**	Knowledge as know-how, creativity intuition, importance of cultural values and social conditioning, distributed unevenly, tacit-explicit opposition	None	Favoring processes that spark the creation of new knowledge; involvement, participation, autonomy, individual and organizational development
	IT Confident		The art of creating value out of intangible assets by using technology a instruments of support.	Solicit, stimulate and motivate people to improve, evaluate and share their own knowledge

Filling the Gap Between Knowledge and Learning

In the *knowing organization* model, Choo (1998) summarizes the many important contributions in the literature on so-called *organizational cognition* (see box in the preface of this book), in particular in reference to Weick's theory of *sense-making* (1979), in organizational decision-making and in the line of research on knowledge creation processes and information in organizations (Nonaka & Takeuchi, 1995).

In Choo's model (Figure 1) the entire process of creation and elaboration of knowledge in organizations has a cyclical form in which three fundamental sub-processes alternate: the sense-making process, knowledge creation process and the decision-making process. The three phases have an almost sequential relationship, but there is also intense feedback in each of the three phases.

In the *sense-making* phase, individuals are primarily concerned with what Karl Weick calls sense-making. According to Weick, individuals are not passive receivers of environmental stimuli, but they actively select (*enact*) the stimuli they receive through the continuous flow of experience. From this flow, some stimuli are actively selected while others are ignored (*bracketing*). Typically, the selection activity is guided by preexisting mental models with specific expectations.

Figure 1. Choo's knowing cycle (Adapted from Choo, 1998)

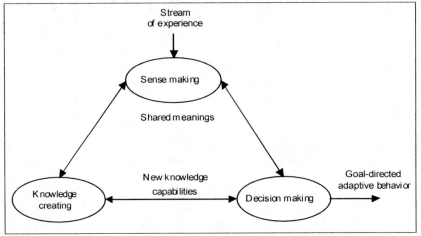

Note: In Choo's model, the process of knowledge creation in organizations is carried out according to a cycle articulated in three fundamental processes: the sense-making process, which aims at the reduction of ambiguity and the construction of shared meaning, the knowledge-creation process, in which new knowledge and capabilities are generated, and the decision-making process, which is goal directed. The cycle is fed by intense feedback activities between each phase and describes adaptive behavior.

The process of interpretation is aimed at the resolution of ambiguity. The creation of sense is ex-post and the action, in particular social interaction, is the fundamental mechanism through which individuals construct knowledge. The sense-making phase is important because it can signal a knowledge gap that is sufficient to spark the next phase of *knowledge creation*.

In the *knowledge creation* phase, preexisting mental models can be changed or new representations and rules can be created. Finally, in the *decision-making* phase, a particular pattern of action is selected.

In order to carry out a classification of the domains of research in KM, we hypothesize that the passage between two opposing poles of *knowledge-object* and *knowledge-process* as a continuum, and we place the three moments of the knowing organization cycle along the perpendicular axis: sense-making, knowledge creation, decision-making, as illustrated in Figure 2.

Finally, we add the areas of research which are part of KM. The horizontal axis represents the *degree of difficulty of knowledge representation and codification*, which is assumed to grow as the knowledge-object becomes the knowledge-process; the vertical axis represents the *degree of ambiguity of the knowledge being analyzed*, which grows with the passage from the decision-making phase to the sense-making phase.

In this type of representation, the lower left corner shows the application of IT technologies to KM, while the upper right corner (the knowing organization area) belongs to the social science approaches. When looking at Figure 2, four possible areas of research emerge, of which two are more traditional, one is defined as a *gap area*, and one is on the technological edge:

Figure 2. A classification of the research areas in KM

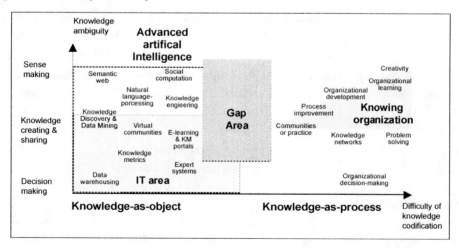

- Two preexisting **traditional areas** mentioned many times in this chapter on the IT-based approach and the people-based approach.

- The **technological edge area**, which correspond to the most advanced areas of artificial intelligence, whose objective is to develop tools for modeling complex cognitive and perceptive processes.

- The **gap area** which corresponds to an area that is scarcely covered and should be the integration between the two dominant approaches. We can define this are as an area of interface management between the individual and the machine, or more generally between the human system and the technological system of organizations.

In an exhaustive review of the literature on KM, Rubenstein-Montano et al. (2001) identify the most evident limitations to the current approaches to KM as the following:

- Most of the approaches proposed in the literature are excessively prescriptive and task-oriented.

- The integration between KM and organizational learning is fairly lacking.

- There is a severe lack of a theory or a unifying and solid conceptual system that more clearly defines the theoretical assumptions of KM.

- The interpretations of basic concepts (knowledge, information, learning, etc.) and tasks that KM should contribute are extremely different and sometimes contradictory, just as the weight that some of these fundamental concepts have in different approaches.

Looking closely, these criticisms mostly concern the IT-based approaches to KM. In practice, the excessive rigidity and the objective difficulty in integrating such systems effectively with social and complex organizational processes is questioned.

In our view, the limitations that arise from the inadequacy of the metaphor of the computer hinges on the exasperation of the dualism between hardware and software; specifically, the net separation between a technological sub-level and a thinking, people-based level.

This dualism has created a true gap to be filled. Technology has centered on applications, while organizational researchers have concentrated on the analysis of the process of knowledge creation. The former, by reducing knowledge to an object, have lost sight of the link between knowledge management and learning. The latter have simply lost sight of the applications and have not been able to build managerial systems and tools in support of learning management. No one is worried about the interface. Both have continued to consider machines and people as independent agents in some form of relationship, instead of considering the people/machine system as a whole, in which the relationship between individuals and technical artifact not necessarily assumes the forms of subordination (see Chapters IV and V of this book).

Conclusion: Knowledge Management in an Organizational Learning Perspective

In this text we will try to step into the no man's land that we have defined as a gap area in order to achieve the following objectives:

*   To propose a theory of knowledge creation in organizations that define clearly the theoretical assumptions of KM.
*   To propose a theory of organizational learning that clarifies the distinction between individual and collective learning: this distinction is central to the integration of knowledge management practices at the micro level (traditional KM) with policies at the macro level for governing the process of a collective learning.
*   To identify a methodological approach, applicable in the gap area that allows for the integration of formal hard approaches typically used by technology with soft ones which are typically the prerogative of action research.

We will try to pursue these objectives by abandoning certainties, as well as the rigidity of the IT-based approach, and attempt to propose a methodological approach, which try to fill the gap between the two subsystems.

With respect to the first point, we will demonstrate in the second part of the text that the distance can be reduced by adopting a form of representation of knowledge that is at the halfway point between explicit knowledge and the codified knowledge of "intelligent" machines, and the tacit and private knowledge of each individual. In Chapter VIII of this book we define this knowledge as *grey knowledge,* in that it is not obscure like tacit knowledge, nor is it completely transparent like explicit knowledge. We will also demonstrate how such knowledge is identifiable through an analysis of evaluation and decision-making processes made by organizational actors and the discourses that they use to "explain" the results of their learning to others (Chapters VI-IX of this book).

The grey knowledge theory is the logical outcome of a *collective learning theory* and the creation of knowledge in organizations that we will present in Chapters II through V. This theory is built upon concepts of action and collective memory. In Chapters II through V we will specify how an organizations "acts," "remembers" and "learns." We propose a model in which the memory of an organization is not a simple metaphorical extension of individual memory, but the documentable set of explicit values, formal rules and managerial tools through which an organization coordinates the actions of its members and carries out the regular functioning of its own operations.

*We claim that an organization learns when a **documentable** and **lasting** change in its memory takes place through a change in its values of reference, its rules or its coordination instruments.* This change begins with individual initiative but becomes organizational when the individual "discoveries" are included in the collective memory.

In the second part of the volume, we perform an in-depth analysis of the mechanisms that can spark the creation of new knowledge of organizations (Chapters VI-IX of this book). In particular, in Chapter IX we present a model that describes our learning theory and the relationship between individual and collective learning (MEP model – memory, experience, project). The opportunity to learn begins when a member of an organization (actor) along with other members (clients) tries to respond to a need or request within a given time. When the request is not standard, the actor must give a nonstandard response by assembling resources and individual and collective capacities for action; they must explore individual and collective memories to find possible solutions. At the end of this phase, the actor presents a response to the clients and explains why it is a satisfactory response.

The explanation of the resulting action is fundamental to collective learning. It comes about in two steps: (1) The clients recognize that the explanation is convincing and the actor has provided an original solution to a new problem; (2) the procedures and the tools that the actor has used are in some way encoded and "published" in organizational memory. Neither the first nor the second step is trivial and there are various obstacles that can prevent the process from being carried out. Of the two, the second step is the one that comes about with the most difficulty. The model explains why individual learning is a relatively frequent event in organizations, while organizational learning is much less so.

Finally, in the third and fourth part of the volume, we describe a methodological approach that thanks to the integration of qualitative methods of action research[10] and the quantitative methods taken from advanced computation allow us to identify grey knowledge and to construct managerial tools for managing collective learning.

References

Blackler, F. (2002). Knowledge, knowledge work and organizations. In C. W. Choo & N. Bontis (Eds.), *The strategic management of intellectual capital and organizational knowledge*. Oxford: Oxford University Press.

Boisot, M. (2002). The creation and sharing of knowledge. In C. W. Choo & N. Bontis (Eds.), *The strategic management of intellectual capital and organizational knowledge*. Oxford: Oxford University Press.

Choo, C. W. (1998). *The knowing organization*. Oxford: Oxford University Press.

Drucker, P. (1993). *Post-capitalist society*. London: Butterworth Heinemann.

Foss, N., & Foss, K. (1999). *The knowledge-based approach and organizational economics: How much do they really differ? And how does it matter?* Working Paper Series, Department of Industrial Economics & Strategy, Copenhagen Business School. Retrieved from http://swopec.hhs.se/iivswp/abs/iivswp99-1.htm

Fransman, M. (1994). Information, knowledge, vision and theories of the firm. *Industrial and Corporate Change, 3*(2), 1-45.

Gouldner, A. W. (1954). *Patterns of industrial bureaucracy*. Glencoe, Il: Free Press.

Lewin, K. (1951). *Field theory in the social science: Selected theoretical papers*. New York: Harper & Row.

Martin B., Subramanian, G., & Yaverbaum, G. (1996). Benefits from expert systems: An exploratory investigations. *Expert Systems with applications, 11*(1), 53-58.

Morgan, G. (1997). *Images of organizations*. Thousands Oaks, CA: Sage.

Nonaka, I., & Takeuchi, H. (1995). *The knowledge creating company*. Oxford: Oxford University Press.

Polanyi, M. (1958). *Personal knowledge: Towards a post-critical philosophy*. London: Routledge.

Polanyi, M. (1966). The logic of tacit inference. *Philosophy, 41*, 1-18.

Reason, P., & Bradbury, H. (2001). Inquiry and participation in search of a world worthy of human aspiration. In P. Reason & H. Bradbury (Eds.), *Handbook of action research*. Oxford: Oxford University Press.

Reich, R. (1991). *The work of nations: Preparing ourselves to the 21ˢᵗ century capitalism*. London: Simon and Schuster.

Rifkin, J. (2000). *The age of access: The new culture of hypercapitalism, where all of life is a paid-for experience*. New York: Tarcher/Putnam.

Rubenstein-Montano, B., Liebowitz, J., Buchwalter, J., McCaw, D., Newman, B., & Rebeck, K. (2001). A system thinking framework for knowledge management. *Decision Support Systems, 31*, 5-16.

Satyadas, A., Harigopal, U., & Cassaigne, N.P. (2001). Knowledge management tutorial: An editorial overview. *IEEE Transactions on Systems, Man and Cybernetics. Part C, Special Issue on Knowledge Management, 31*(4), 429-437.

Schein, E. (1987). *Process consultation: Its role in organization development.* Reading, MA: Addison Wesley.

Simon, H. A. (1981). *Sciences of artificial.* Cambridge, MA: MIT Press.

Smith, D. E. (2000). *Knowledge, groupware and the internet.* London: Butterworth Heinemann.

Sveiby, K. (1997). *The new organizational wealth: Managing and measuring knowledge-based assett.* San Francisco: Berret Koehler.

Turing, A. M. (1936). On computable numbers with an application to the entscheidungsproblem. *Proceedings of the London Mathematical Society, 2*(42), 230-265.

Turing, A. M. (1950). Computing machinery and intelligence. *Mind, 59*, 433-460.

Von Neumann, J., & Morgestern, O. (1944). *Theory of games and economic behavior.* Princeton, NJ: Princeton University Press.

Weick, K. E. (1979). *The social psychology of organization* (2nd ed.). Reading, MA: Addison Wesley.

Wenger, E. (1999). *Communities of practice: Learning, meaning and identity.* Boston: Cambridge University Press.

Wiener, N. (1948). *Cybernetics or control and communication in the animal and in the machine.* Cambridge, MA: MIT Press.

Wiig, K. (1993). *Knowledge management foundations.* Arlington: Schema Press.

Endnotes

[1]   Speech made at the 80th Anniversary Award dinner of the Conference Board, New York, October 16, 1996 (quoted from Rifkin, 2000).

[2]   The most important mechanism in the logic of propositions is logical inference. Given the degree of truth in the assumptions, it is possible to "calculate" the degree of truth in the conclusions. For example, given that "all men are mortals" and that "Socrates is a man," we can deduce that "Socrates is a mortal." Propositional calculations such as this can be made by logical circuits that are programmed to do so.

3   In reality this vision is only theoretical. In practice, Tayloristic and bureaucratic organizational models end up generating many dysfunctions due to the
conflicting tension between the worker and the control production system, as
demonstrated in various studies (Gouldner, 1954). The worker's lack of power
in every task that is not reduced to pure execution of orders and standard
operations was also the object of Marxist criticism on alienation. According
to this criticism, the capitalists did not only take material advantage of the
workers, but they also took away the sense of their own work, reducing them
to automatons.

4   In simplistic terms, this metaphor makes reference to the well known concept
in organizational literature of organizations as sociotechnical systems.

5   A neologism invented to indicate the supply of individual knowledge, or grey
matter.

6   On a theoretical level, the knowledge factor and the relationship between
knowledge and organizations has been widely treated in a series of studies
starting in the 1950s (Grant, March, Nelson, & Winter, Penrose, Simon, Wil-
liamson, etc. for a review see Fransman, 1994, Foss & Foss, 1999). Although
the results provided by these contributions are outstanding, on a theoretical and
conceptual level above all, they do not shed light upon managerial practices
and tools, but are restricted to the arena of scientific debate.

7   Wiig himself, not long afterward, almost apologized for not having come up
with a better expression than "knowledge management" to give a name to the
new discipline.

8   A third school of thought came from Europe, in Sweden, with the research
of Karl Sveiby. After a series of studies carried out in service companies, the
Swedish school delineated the concept of KM in terms of intellectual capital
management. The most important contribution of this school is above all in
the development of theories and methodologies for the evaluation of intangible capital in companies (Sveiby, 1997). It is well known that the traditional
accounting is conceived to evaluate companies in terms of physical and fi-
nancial capital, but not in terms of *intellectual capital*. It is also true that the
capitalization of companies with high knowledge intensity, such as service
companies or computer companies, in many cases can be the same or higher
than traditional companies. Comparing high tech companies such as Microsoft
and IBM, Rifkin (2000) observed that in November, 1996, the capitalization
of Microsoft was $85.5 billion against the $70.7 billion of IBM, even though
IBM had fixed assets valued at $16.6 billion and Microsoft had "just" $930
million.

9   The analysis of the knowledge process human experts develop in the execution of a given task is actually the main job of the knowledge engineer when
creating expert systems. But this type of analysis is carried out at the individual

level and does not take into consideration the social-organizational aspects relative to the transmission and elaboration of knowledge.

[10]   At the very base of the action research approach is the consideration that a real organizational change cannot be obtained only through a diagnosis performed by an external expert, but it requires the adoption of a "generative style" aimed at "helping others to help themselves" (Lewin, 1951; Reasons & Bradbury, 2001; Schein, 1987). Consequently, organizational analysts need to achieve an adequate level of understanding of the organizational context through frequent interaction with it and its members. For this reason action research usually involves the use of qualitative methodologies aimed at performing an in-depth analysis of the context such as case studies, ethnography, interview methods and mapping methods (for more details see Chapter XVIII of this book).

Chapter II

Complexity as a Resource

—Perhaps it hasn't one [a moral]—Alice ventured to remark—'Tut, tut, child! Said the Duchess.—Everything's got a moral, if only you can find it.' [...]—How fond she is of finding morals in things!—Alice thought to herself.

~ Lewis Carrol, *Alice in Wonderland*

Abstract

Before moving on to a more rigorous and systematic discussion in the following chapters, through diverse suggestions and references, this chapter intends to offer the reader a key to the theme of learning in organizations. We consider learning in organizations as an individual and collective response to the complexity that comes out of the encounter between the organization and its environment. We show that in this perspective, learning cannot be governed through the usual managerial logic based on control, standardization and planning, but requires new approaches and instruments. It is found in sense-making, meaning the capacity of individuals to reduce the ambiguity through the construction of plausible hypotheses and the production of convincing explanatory discourses, the starting point for the analysis of the process of organizational learning and the construction of new managerial tools.

The Experience of Complexity

A voyage that is exemplary in its complexity began on December 26, 1541. That was the day that Francisco de Orellana left the expedition headed by Gonzalo Pizarro, who was bogged down in the Peruvian Forest along with 60 men, and began to float down the Coca River in search of food (Toribio Medina, 1988). He never turned back, but following the River Coca and then the Napo, he finally reached the Amazon River, upon which he traveled for eight months using improvised rafts, all the way to the river mouth.

The detailed account of the adventurous voyage on the river written by the Dominican Friar Gaspar de Carvajal is a description of events that are repeated with few variations. The sounds that emerge from the dark forest: *"... some of our companions seemed to hear indio drums ..." " they clearly heard drums from very far away ..."* The obsessive hunger: *"... we were forced to eat leather, belts, and the soles of shoes ..."*, *"we ate some wild roots ..."* and then, encounters with indios, skirmishes to get food, stopping to rest, the immense river that drags on, villages that suddenly appear and finally, the wonderful details of things that were more imaginary than real, the gold, the Amazons. Every attempt to make overall sense of that new and marvelous world was in vain. The account is a sequence of events lined up along an endless river.

There is no better metaphor for the experience of the complexity of a voyage through an unknown territory.

Traveling along the vein of water, the Amazon River, is a small community with its own small boat full of stories, ambitions, tools, and prejudices. All around them, there is an unknown universe that is explored in points and segments. The experience of complexity is realized in a set of encounters unconnected by any causal relationship, an accumulation of details, impossible to place within the framework of a general structure. The experience is additive and cannot be synthesized. There is no underlying structure, no believable simplification, and no summary is possible. The external world does not allow itself to be captured, it never takes form, a precise meaning is never stabilized, and thus it generates contradictory feelings. The explorers of Orellana each time experience a chaotic succession of a sense of mystery, of uncertainty, a feeling of being lost, inebriation, euphoria, anxiety, paralysis, or frantic action, as if it were a universe where opposites are brought together with confusion, confronting each other without mediation.

One needs not live through an adventure like Orellana's to experience complexity. Complexity threatens everyday experience from quite nearby; it is just beyond the thin canvas that covers the objects of our existence. Just a few small cuts in the canvas are enough to cause us to experience complexity. Mr. Palomar, in the book by Italo Calvino (1985), discovers it in the field surrounding his house, as soon as he stops to observe it with scrupulous precision. His analytical eye cuts through the canvas of visual habit and discovers a universe of infinite details, which are not able to completely describe the experience:

The lawn is composed of dichondra, darnel, and lover. This mixture, in equal parts, was scattered over the ground at sowing time. The dichondra, dwarfed and creeping, promptly got the upper hand: Its carpet of soft little round leaves spreads everywhere, pleasing to the foot and to the eye. But the lawn is given its thickness by the sharp spears of darnel, if they are not too sparse and if you do not allow them to grow too much before cutting them. The lover sprouts irregularly, some clumps here, nothing there, and farther on a whole sea of it; it grows exuberantly until it slumps, because the helix of the leaf becomes top-heavy and bends the tender stalk.

[...]

But counting the blades of grass is futile: You would never learn their number. A lawn does not have precise boundaries; there is a border where the grass stops growing, but still a few scattered blades sprout farther on, then a thick green clod, then a sparser stretch: are they still part of the lawn, or not? Elsewhere the underbrush enters the lawn: You cannot tell what is lawn and what is bush. But even where there is nothing but grass, you never know at what point you can stop counting: Between one little plant and the next there is always a tiny sprouting leaf that barely emerges from the earth, its root a white wisp hardly perceptible; a moment ago it might have been overlooked, but soon it, too, will have to be counted. Meanwhile, two other shoots that just now seemed barely a shade yellowish have definitively withered and must be erased from the count. Then there are the fractions of blades of grass, cut in half, or shorn to the round or split along the nervation, the little leaves that have lost one lobe...The decimals, added up, do not make an integer; they remain a minute grassy devastation, in part still alive in part already pulp food for other plants, humus. (Calvino, 1985, pp. 29-33)

Sometimes complexity takes other forms that are quite different from the infinite lawns of Palomar. In Norman Rockwell's picture, "The Connoisseur," the painting explodes in swirling squiggles of colors that the conventional middle class man tries in vain to decipher. Or it assumes the dramatic aspect of short circuits that paralyze reason and action, as in the poetry by the father of anti-psychiatry, R.D. Laing (from *Knots*, 1974, p. 1):

They are playing a game. They are playing at not playing a game. If I show them I see they are, I shall break the rules and they will punish me. I must play their game of not seeing I see the game.

Complexity appears on the horizon of life every time the canvas of memory and reason that covers and forms experience is lacerated, every time that the past does not help to give a name to the present, every time the course of events pushes us outside the narrow trail of habit. It is enough to alter the structure of experience even a little to meet up with complexity.

When looking at Monet's "Water Lilies" (Figure 1), we experience complexity. In the pond full of water lilies, Monet pushes impressionism to the limit and trusts in the accuracy of the eye and the movement of the paintbrush to capture the infinite variety of atmospheric effects, in the end destroying the same forms in a dusting of colorful light.

Figure 1. Monet water lilies

Note: *According to Hughes (1980), "the water lilies would be still among the supreme of vision in western art. The pond was a slice of infinity. To size the indefinite, to fix what is unstable, to give form and location to sights so evanescent and complex they hardly be named—these were basic ambitions of modernism and they went against the smug view of determined reality that materialism and positivism give us" (Hughes, 1980, p. 124).*

Box 1. Learning theory (by Teresa Cucciniello)

Hillgard and Bower (1981) define learning as long-term behavior modification as an effect of experience, excluding both temporary changes due to occasional, isolated or traumatic events, and changes resulting from innate factors. Most of the considerations about the argument share this definition. Generally speaking, there are three fundamental approaches to learning:

a. Behaviorism theory (emphasis on behavior)

b. Cognitivist theory (emphasis on mental processes and structures that regulate learning)

c. Humanistic theory (emphasis on the motivations and the social function of learning)

We will present a brief summary of these three theories that highlights the most important points. We will then briefly point out the most significant works: Piaget's Adaptivity and Bateson's Learning to Learn.

Behaviorism. As a positivist approach, behaviorism refuses every form of introspection and reference to the "consciousness" of the subject, focusing research on animal and human behavior in its attempt to explain the phenomenon of learning as precisely as possible. The basic principle of these theories is the association between a stimulus 'S' coming from the environment and a response 'A' on the part of the subject, according to the pattern "S-A." The emphasis is on the 'environment-subject' relationship, as in the procedures of classic conditioning, also called 'responsive' or 'Pavlovian.' Pavlov, at the beginning of the 20th century, observed and studied the phenomenon with the famous experiment in which a dog learns to associate a stimulus S (a ringing bell) with the appearance of food, giving an observable response (salivation) The law of reinforcement is based on this experiment, where the organism 'repeats' the rewarded behavior (Thorndyke, 1913; Skinner, 1938). According to behaviorism, natural associative mechanisms are at the base of all learning; even the most complex forms.

Cognitivism. With the studies of Ulric Neisser (1967, after a long history beginning with W. James and passing through the work of Bruner, Chomsky, Gardner, Minsky) the cognitivist approach focalizes attention on the cognitive functions that regulate the learning process (attention, perception, thought, memory, language patterns, representation, etc.) instead of as the result of behavioral change. Central to the concept of representation, is the act of reproducing a perceptive experience introspectively without sensory stimulation. Acquiring new knowledge or abilities implies the transformation of a preexisting representation in another more adequate one, according to the well-known theories of the Gestalt school.

The behavioural approach had conceived the learning subject as a passive receiver of information coming from the surrounding environment. Cognitivism disagrees with a mechanistic interpretation of learning and conceives the mind as an active and selective processor of environmental stimulation, which filters the information and self-corrects, modifying its own structure, its own models, in a continuous verification of congruency between the structure itself and the existing objective conditions. In this process, memory plays a fundamental role, both in the acquisition and the real-time processing of information (short-term memory) and in the reorganization of knowledge (long-term memory). Another key concept is that high-level cognitive activities can be broken down into a hierarchy of elementary processes (Minsky, 1988).

Cognitivist research has taken particular advantage of the new technologies (cybernetics, informatics) that have allowed it to elaborate functional models of the mind, as well as take more control of experimental situations (ex. Measuring the reaction times as indicators of underlying elementary operations). The computer metaphor created by Atkinson and Shiffrin (1968) view the mind as a complex system that is able to process and choose incoming information (input), while transforming and making decisions about them (output).

Humanism. Learning theories in the field of humanistic approach link learning to the need for personality growth that restructures itself globally while in the midst of the act of learning. In this perspective, learning affects the entire personality, not only at the behavioural or cognitive level, but also the level of emotions, affections, and values. Maslow (1974) and Rogers (1976), underline the need for self-realization and self-esteem as motives for every action. In particular, Maslow elaborates a model of learning-development based on a scale of motivations that follow a precise hierarchical order, from the primary needs (food) to self-realization. The pathway to learning–development is done through "peak experiences," crucial moments of reorganization of personality structures.

continued on following page

Box 1. continued

The adaption of Piaget: Jean Piaget's theory begins with the following principle: learning is the search for better forms of adaptation by an organism. It matures thanks to the transformation of simple operative structures into more complex ones. The construction of cognitive structures is the result of two processes: assimilation of new aspects of reality and accommodation of mental maps-frameworks already existing in the subject.
Bateson's Learning to Learn. Gregory Bateson (1972) elaborates a learning theory that sees mental processes as making up a system into which the subject is inserted. The mind is intended as a complex system, which is a subsystem of the larger ecosystem, made up of a group of interacting regenerative and conservative components. Bateson defines information as "a difference that produces a difference." Using Kant's definition, for Bateson the idea-difference is a choice of a fact that becomes information. In the learning process, the mind receives the 'differences, it regenerates and transforms them, building and rebuilding its mental maps, at the same way that we build geographical maps, showing only the differences in relief (altitude, surface, vegetation).
Learning is therefore a process of acquiring information, according to a hierarchical framework that begins at the simplest level ('zero learning', summarized as a simple recognition of a difference, 'one' corresponding to the capacity to distinguish the context and correct the response) to arrive at more complex.

Experiencing Complexity: The Paradoxes

We need to learn to experience complexity if we want to cope with it adequately. Sometimes we must evoke it when habit brings us to a *cul-de-sac* without any answer. We need to learn to enter it, just as we need to learn to come out of it, without allowing ourselves to become ensnared in its endlessness or be trapped in its labyrinths. That is the only way that complexity ceases to be a threat and becomes a resource. Entering complexity means experiencing something new, placing yourself at the edge of habitual experience, in an area where personal experience does not yet have a social existence, where the collectivity is not able to sustain itself with words, concepts categories and adequate examples. Morin (1985) identifies eight different ways to experience complexity, and all of them derive from a conscious act of recognizing it:

1. **Randomness:** Recognize and accept the chance event without trying to bring it back to a preestablished order

2. **Singularity:** Recognize the specificity of a single event, without prematurely killing its individuality by classifying it into a case that is already known

3. **Complication:** Accept the entanglement of interactions that characterize the biological and social world without producing hurried simplifications

4. **Complementarity:** Recognize the unsolvable, and in some ways mysterious relationship that ties opposing properties, without destroying it in favor of another in search of abstract coherence

5. **Organization:** Recognize the emerging qualities in the entire organization, without necessarily going back from the quality of the whole to the quality of its parts

6. **Hologram:** Recognize that in each part of an organization is reflected in the propriety of the whole without reducing the part to simple building blocks

7. **Ambiguity:** Recognize the lack of certain limits between things, recognize the existence of ambivalent meaning, without hurrying to circumscribe and define the experience

8. **Observer:** Consider the observer as part of the observation, recognizing that each point of view and every observation is partial, without the pretence of wanting to produce a complete description of the world from an absolute point of view

Who will be able to navigate in complexity? It is no news that literature sometimes offers simple ways to answer complex questions. Literary texts are a mirror in which possibilities, dreams, and fears that a collectivity expresses are represented in a condensed form. So, in order to answer our question, we must turn to Alice, the heroine that Charles Lutwidge Dodgson, alias Lewis Carroll, created in 1872.

Alice is a curious little girl who at first follows a rabbit, and then by entering a mirror, falls into Wonderland. It is a strange place. There are no fairies, or gnomes, nor even men, but individual characters that do and say incomprehensible things continuously challenging common sense.

During the entire voyage, our heroine is forced to do some intense intellectual work to make sense of the experiences that she is having. Nothing is taken for granted in Wonderland: Every experience, every meeting, every character is an enigma that operates according to his own logic, which Alice has difficulty penetrating and accepting. Every experience challenges Alice to knit together a meaning that is continuously lost along a thousand pathways. Sometimes Alice would like to give up: 'Perhaps it hasn't one [a moral]' Alice ventured to remark. «Tut, Tut, child!» said the Duchess. 'Everything's got a moral, if only you can find it.' [...] 'How fond she is of finding morals in things!' Alice thought to herself. Alice, the first modern traveler ever to go to Wonderland (alias *The Reign of Complexity*) discovers at a great cost to herself the biggest danger that surrounds her: the slippery, treacherous, and omnipresent existence of the *Destruction of Sense*.

The only chance that Alice has for avoiding submission to the *Destruction of Sense* is to follow the advice of the Duchess: find a moral. It may seem crazy at first, but in reality it is the only weapon that Alice can use to preserve her identity. And so Alice, with great difficulty, weaves together the rules of the past with the strange experiences of the present.

Sometimes the mix works well. Sometimes she is forced to suspend the discourse because she has gone into a blind alley. Sometimes she has to interrupt the experience abruptly so as not to be overwhelmed by it. Sometimes she is helped by chance, sometimes by reason. Sometimes she has to backtrack, confused. Sometimes she has to deform the memory to adapt it to the present evidence. One thing appears certain: she is forced to go ahead in her search for sense. You can get out of Wonderland only if you give form to experience. The *Destruction of Sense* in Wonderland is the destruction of form, the subversion of the order of things, or at least the order that we expect to recognize.

It is no surprise that an enterprise, or more in general an organization, can be transformed into the reign of complexity. Several organizational researchers in recent decades have identified some paradoxical characteristics of effective organizations: (1) loose-coupling as well as tight-coupling; (2) high specialization of roles as well as high generality of roles; (3) continuity of leadership as well as infusion of new leaders. Cameron (1981, 1986) reported on research carried out on colleges and universities, where he argued that organizational effectiveness is inherently paradoxical, and, to be effective, an organization must possess attributes that are simultaneously contradictory, even mutually exclusive. He discovered competitive organizational features such as: (1) innovative actions along with conservative mechanisms; (2) openness to environmental opportunities along with concentration on internal human resources; (3) attention to symbols along with attention to substance; (4) domain defense along with domain offense; (5) culture preservation along with innovation and creative activities.

Organizational paradoxes emerge when contradictory and mutually exclusive issues are present and operate at the same time (Poole & Van de Ven, 1989). They occur more frequently when environmental complexity and turbulence increase.

Because complex environments are characterized by very complex interactions among several elements (individuals, firms, institutions, markets, purposes, objectives, etc.), it is impossible to construct a complete and coherent representation of what is going on. Consequently, any representation magnifies only a part of the system, and as different representations interact, then conflict, contradictions and paradoxes arise. Furthermore, turbulent environments, characterized by rapid changes in technology, markets, and competition, continuously interrupt the unstable coexistence between antagonistic issues, with the consequence that paradoxical situations could be considered a normal situation, instead of an exceptional one.

To emphasize paradoxical organizational features, Quinn and Cameron (1983) and Rohrbaugh (1981) developed a model of organizational effectiveness, named *competing values model*, based on couples of opposite indicators of effectiveness arranged in two relevant dimensions (decentralization/centralization and internal focus/external focus). This model claimed that, in order to understand the effectiveness of business organizations, opposing requirements should be held together.

Only the balance and tension between opposites can propel the organization toward excellence.

Coping with Paradoxes Through Learning and Language

The *tolerance of opposites* prevents the organization from paralysis and transforms a collection of individuals into a new entity, capable of new ways of understanding and new actions. We understand also that language and communication play a very central role in this.

Because any integration with formal procedures is made impossible because of the many apparent paradoxes they would contain, the task of coordination and integration can be effectively performed only through the use of natural language, whose vagueness tolerates the presence of opposites.

About 30 years ago, Pondy and Mitroff (1979) urged organizational theorists to look beyond mechanistic and organic models of organization and develop language-based organizational models. According to this point of view, organization is seen as a *collective storytelling system*, where the story is defined as an oral or written performance involving two or more people interpreting past or anticipated experiences (Boje, 1991). Through stories, organizational members exchange their individual memories, solve conflicts, coordinate their activities, modify their categories, reproduce their social system and update their institutional memory.

Daft and Wintington (1979) express a similar point of view as follows:

Planning, reflection, and control based upon formal information systems implicitly assume a well understood and stable organizational system. But most human systems, although stable in many respects, tend to be only vaguely understood. Further, destabilizing events can erupt at any time: dissatisfied workers might decide to lead a walk-out; a valued employee may decide to accept an offer from another company; or perhaps delivery of an urgent order for a large customer may fall behind schedule. Because of this instability, the manager must continually sense various parts of the system, test the implicit model against what is found, incorporate new information, and either revises the cognitive model and/or send signals for system adjustments. The ongoing state of the system and system adjustments are communicated in meetings, telephone conversations, and through rumors and gossip. This high variety information can capture the subtleties and nuances of behavior so that substantial meaning can be conveyed to and from the manager-controller.

(Daft & Wintington, 1979, p. 184)

The authors conclude that representations based on natural language may be more powerful than precise and quantitative models for understanding and describing the complexity and variety of many organizational processes. One of the most important results of the modern theory of organizational action is that natural language is an organizational tool.

However, managing paradoxes through natural language faces several important problems:

1. The efficiency of evaluation and decision processes is limited by face-to-face communications.
2. The Firm's competencies become more 'volatile,' being encoded mainly in human memory.
3. The firm's identity in time and space is partly loose, as decision processes and evaluation criteria become more and more dependent on local cultures.
4. Organization is partly opaque to the top management.
5. Communication skills become excessively important compared to professional skills and technical competencies.
6. As the time and cost of language-based coordination are high, the firm tends to decentralize evaluations and decisions, which leads to the formation of separate entities (divisions, functions, groups) within a larger organization.

To overcome these problems, companies usually try to reduce the ambiguity arising from the intensive use of natural language and develop alternative approaches to neutralize problems raised by organizational paradoxes. This way, they can increase the degree of their control over the internal and external environment (Poole & Van de Ven, 1989):

1. **A 'space' approach:** By separating contradictory organizational requisites through levels and functions.
2. **A 'time' approach:** By separating opposites in time, by pushing groups to focus on differing requirements at different times.
3. **A 'formal' approach:** By creating procedures that specify which data are relevant for evaluation and decision making, and how organizational members should collect, codify and process them.

Even if the separation of differing requirements in space or in time and the formalization of group interactions are the most common deliberate strategies used in dealing with organizational paradoxes, those approaches face bureaucracy, complications and perpetual conflicts as complexity increases. They also create the illusion that the complexity related to group dynamics and learning can be controlled and governed through traditional top-down approaches.

To overcome these problems, organizational procedures and routines should be designed in a new way: While from the traditional point of view procedures and routines were designed to separate differing requirements and eliminate paradoxes, from the new point of view procedures and routines should tolerate differing requirements and paradoxes.

The learning process occurs when paradoxes are somehow solved through sense-making. Such a process cannot be planned, measured, or controlled. Managers can only try to trigger it and become careful observers of how their people frame the world and solve problems. They should allow for a higher than usual degree of autonomy and involvement and encourage self-organization and emergence.

The manager's attitude must change because the type of work has changed. The worker becomes a "cognitive" worker who is occupied most of the time with reducing ambiguity by producing acceptable interpretations of events through the construction of explanations. The construction of explanations through the proposal of hypotheses is defined as abductive logic. Abduction is the logic, though irreplaceable and imperfect, of cognitive work. Learning can be reduced to the process of producing new hypotheses and revising those that have already been decided upon.

Learning as the Explanation of Complexity

It is easy to get lost in complexity because a complex world is a world without form. The only way to escape is to attempt to stabilize it by overlapping the tangle of events with a form by constructing hypotheses, choosing between possible interpretations and taking action. It is the construction of the sequence of hypothesis-choice-action that breaks the infinite production of descriptions and interrupts the interminable cycles of reasoning. On the other hand, it is not a contemplative activity, but a cycle immersed in the flow of events triggered by action.

An event can be created through action, and the act of searching for information and points of reference can be called sense-making. Actions give meaning and form to experience because it is through action that the individual introduces experience into a flow of events and therefore takes at least partial control.

Orellana was able to escape from the Amazon River because on many occasions when faced with the unknown world in which he found himself, he decided what to do and with the prejudices and the brutality of the conquistadores, took action. Calvino's Mr. Palomar has no other solution for interrupting the description of the infinite lawn than to place himself within the flow of events that generate and transform the lawn by starting to mow it; Rockwell's Connoisseur can lessen his discomfort only by moving on to observe the next painting; Laing's tormented man can break the cycle of his reasoning by starting to play along with the others.

The building cycle of hypothesis-choice-action allows individuals to trigger learning and to escape complexity. Individual sense-making becomes an accessible reality for others if it is articulated through a discourse that is able to describe the reasons of the speaker in comprehensible and convincing terms to a community of interlocutors. The discourse has the form of an explanation and has the goal of connecting and attributing meaning to a set of facts. This meaning can be communicated, discussed, confirmed, and corrected through other discourses.

Not all observers can deliver all discourses. Not all of the facts can be incorporated into discourses. Not all discourses have the same form. But the essential fact is that the meaning of experience can be individually and collectively studied and that this meaning can be used as a point of reference for creating new actions and future discourses.

What has been said thus far is summarized by a definition by Brandom (2000) of rationality: "*The general idea is that the rationality that qualifies us as reasoning (and not purely sentient) beings can be identified as the participation in the social, implicitly prescriptive game, of offering and evaluating, producing and consuming reasons*" (Brandom, 2002, p. 85). This is the point of view of this book:

Individual actions in organizations are rational by virtue of the existence of explanatory discourses that make reference to categories of judgment and shared interpretations. Organization as a whole is rational by virtue of the existence of a storyline of discourses and the schema and categories of shared thought that are needed in order to understand them.

Learning is interpretation, a process of discovery that leads toward a new awareness of the actions carried out by oneself and others and a new awareness of the world in which that action takes place. Nonetheless, not all of the processes of interpretation can lead to the generation of new awareness and they do not necessarily all work in the same way. Peirce (1935-1966, 2.623), using the famous example of the beans, underlines how in any inferential process, three types of propositions are involved:

- RULE: All the beans in that sack are white.
- CASE: These beans are from that sack.
- RESULT: These beans are white.

The three propositions can be ordered in six different ways. The first two terms constitute the premise of the inference, while the third is the consequence. Because the order of the first two terms is not significant, we would have three just three sequences of order that correspond to the three inferential methods of:

a. **_Deduction_** (RULE, CASE / RESULT)
b. **_Induction_** (CASE, RESULT / RULE)
c. **_Abduction_** (RESULT, RULE / CASE)

In the case of *deduction*, the observer can establish the rule as a possible link connecting two facts (the case and the result). In the case of abduction (see Box 2), the observer can establish a result, outline a possible rule to explain it and prove a plausible explanation. In this way he answers the question: *Where do these beans come from?* Peirce's conclusion (1935-1966, 5.145) is that "Induction can never produce a new idea. Neither can deduction. All of the ideas in science come to science through abduction."

Abduction consists in studying the facts and thinking of a theory to explain them. But where does the RULE come from that the observer uses to explain? Bonfantini (1987) distinguishes between three types of abduction, ordered in terms of their growing innovation:

1. **First type:** The rule is given in a biding and automatic way, and the observer is forced to use it
2. **Second type:** The rule is made through some mechanisms of search or recognition within the available rules
3. **Third type:** The rule is constructed *ex novo*

This last case is particularly interesting. A rule can emerge as an extension of an already existing rule in another semantic field, such as disassembling and reassembling the available rules, mediating between concurrent rules, or overcoming a conflict between, generating, or particularizing current rules (Figure 2).

Conclusion

The experience of complexity, and how to enter into it and escape from it, assumes a critical value for organizations. In the study of economics and management, one

Box 2. Abduction

Aristotle considered a third form alongside the better known forms of deductive inference, induction and deduction, called απαγωγη. Peirce renamed this form of reasoning as abduction with a clear reference to its retrospective nature. The objective of abduction is, in fact, to identify a possible explanation of a given observation through the ex-novo creation or the recovery and adaptation of a suitable rule. In more formal terms, the result of an observation A is the identification of a rule "If B then A" that explains the occurrence of A as a consequence of a premise B. It differs from induction and deduction in the process through which a conclusion is reached, which is not transparent nor necessarily valid. Actually, there may be more than one plausible explanation for the same fact.

Identifying a rule aimed at explaining a fact is a creative act; instead, deduction and induction necessarily lead to valid conclusions and come out of the application of rules within a preexisting logical system just as in mathematics, where from a set of axioms it is possible to deduct a series of theorems.

Abduction was considered by Thagard (1992) as one of the main mechanisms in the process of scientific discovery. The observation of natural phenomena is the basis upon which scientists formulate plausible hypotheses aimed at explaining the phenomena they have observed.

The same phenomenon can be explained through diverse, sometimes contrasting, hypotheses; for example, both geocentric and heliocentric systems allow us to predict the movements of the planets correctly. Nevertheless, Thagard says, even though abductive reasoning is used in both cases, we can say that one explanation is better than another when it (a) allows for the explanation of more phenomena; (b) allows us to formulate simpler explanations; (c) leads to the construction of conceptual systems that present a limited number of inconsistencies.

In other cases, the higher level of adequacy of an explanation can be shown empirically. For example, the theory of oxygen formulated by Lavoisier to explain some phenomena of oxidation was originally based on a conjecture that anticipated the presence of a substance in the air, oxygen, as a determining cause for triggering the processes of oxidation. Lavoisier's theory went against the dominant theory which assumed instead that a substance which played a similar role, phlogiston, was contained in objects that presented oxidation phenomena. However, it was only much later that scientists could do what Lavoisier, with the techniques of that era, had not been able to do: isolate oxygen and demonstrate its existence.

In other words, before its discovery, oxygen was only a conjecture. Abduction, therefore, begins with an attentive observation of the facts; it is a process of discovery in which random and unpredictable factors often play a crucial role (as in the famous anecdote of Archimedes who, immersed in the bath, discover the law that regulates the behavior of bodies immersed in fluid); it is retrospective; it presupposes that the observer has an adequate level of experience and knowledge that allows him to notice details that others find insignificant and to formulate adequate abductive hypotheses; it is a conjecture whose validity must find empirical evidence, or, in ist absence, must be evaluated in terms of explicative efficiency and effectiveness with respect to concurrent hypotheses.

Figure 2. The creation of new forms through violation of common sense

Note: The birth of a new rule is the creation of a new form. It is a creative process that is not dissimilar to methods with which great artists have invented their own forms to express their perception of the world visually. Magritte, for example, enjoyed creating new rules through the unexpected juxtaposition of objects Braque and the cubist painters destroyed the objects only to recompose the fragments according to a new visual logic. Medieval artists created fantastic creatures such as the "cricket" in this figure, by combining human and animal traits. The entire history of the visual arts suggests numerous methods from which new rules can be invented visually.

Box 3. Organizational learning

Organizational learning (OL) has been the subject of many studies starting from the 1960s thanks to the diffusion of the evolutionary economics theories according to which also companies, like organisms, are involved in natural selection and adaptation (Burns & Stalker, 1978; Herriot et al., 1975; Nelson & Winter, 1982). But it was the work by Argyris and Schön (1978) that at the end of the 1970s moves the debate from the relationship with the environment to the organizational level and learning process within the organization.

In their seminal book *Organizational Learning. A Theory of Action Perspective* Argyris and Schön (1978) develop for the first time a theory of OL. Starting from such a contribution, OL has received remarkable attention by managers and scholars. The latter focuses on the meaning of collective learning, on the relationship between individual and collective learning, and on how an organization can learn. The former are interested in how OL theories can improve organizational and business performance.

Generally speaking, the supporters of OL claim that OL is something more than the sum of the learning of all employees and that organizations, like individuals, can learn to better adapt to their environment. According to the definition provided by the American Society for Training & Development (ASTD) OL is how an organization uses its collective ability to make sense of and respond to its surroundings. It includes individual learning as employees interact with the external environment or experiment to create new information or knowledge, the integration of new information or knowledge, the relation and collective interpretation of all available information, and action based on the interpretation (Dixon, 1995).

According to Argyris and Schön (1978), any organization builds its own theory of action describable in terms of the rules its members follow (or violate) to execute tasks. In any organization it is possible to find an official theory (espoused theory) promoted from the top and many private tacit theories (theories-in-use) that actually guide individual everyday action from the bottom. The espoused theory and the theories-in-use can be incoherent between them and in conflict.

According to Argyris and Schön (1978), organizations learn only if they are able to update their theories of action. This can happen at two different levels (Bateson, 1972): the single-loop learning, when action is corrected to improve adaptation in a given context, and the double-loop learning, when action is directed to change the context (the so-called "think-out-of-the-box, Figure 3).

Argyris and Schön (1978) attribute a main role in OL to what they call "defensive reasoning." Defensive reasoning arises when individuals do not want confront their opinions with other people because they are afraid of change and possible conflicts. The fear of conflict prevents individuals to question existing theories of actions, even when they become inadequate or obsolete. Then, weakening defensive reasoning is a premise to spark OL.

Peter Senge (1990), in its book *The Fifth Discipline*, made OL a popular subject for managers and consultants. In particular Senge refers to concepts borrowed from System Dynamics such as the concept of feedback to describe how an organization can be transformed into a Learning Organization whose members are able to learn how to learn.

In the late '90s, OL has been framed in a knowledge management perspective (see Chapter I). Nonaka and Takeuchi (1995) attribute a key role to the transformation of individual tacit knowledge into explicit-organizational knowledge. Tacit knowledge is more relevant if it is not confined at the local level as well as explicit knowledge is more valuable if individuals are able to reframe and interiorize it. The conversion from tacit to explicit and vice versa creates OL through four main processes: socialization (tacit/tacit), externalization (tacit/explicit), combination (explicit/explicit), and interiorization (explicit/tacit).

Figure 3. Single and double loop learning

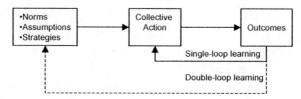

More recently Edgar Schein in an interview with the Harvard Business Review (2002) has introduced the themem of the anxiety of learning. According to Schein, individuals learn only when they are forced to do so, specifically when the following condition is satisfied:

continued on following page

Box 3. continued

Necessity for change > anxiety of learning

Consequently, organizations can foster OL in two different ways: Either by increasing stress and pressure to augment the perception of the need for change or by reducing the anxiety of learning by favoring exchange, openness, and internal discussion.

Most OL theories question the obsession for control of traditional management and claim that learning processes can not be "managed" since they are ongoing, spontaneous and self-regulated by individuals who ask for more and more discretionary power, autonomy and motivation.

---

repeatedly hears that "*The enterprise is being forced to confront a turbulent and complex environment.*" Apart from the tiresome rituality of the commonplace, there are some aspects of this statement which we reject. First, it hints that complexity is a property of the world outside the enterprise, something which the enterprise is *forced* to take into account. So the fact that complexity exists within the sphere of organizational experience is hidden, along with the fact that it is the result of the interaction between the organization and the outside world. What the statement really means is that this encounter produces the experience of complexity so often that it becomes objectified and attributed to the outside world. But, we can equally attribute it to the organization, and ask ourselves how and why it constructs the experience of complexity so frequently and involuntarily, and how it can be transformed from an involuntary to a voluntary experience.

Second, the statement contains an implicitly negative judgment of complexity. It is seen as a threat, something that questions the activity and its organization. Actually, this can be true only for those organizations that do not want to learn from or experience complexity, nor to use it as an inexhaustible resource where even unpredictable answers can be found to current questions.

Third, the phrase is often followed by advice and suggestions on how to disaggregate and put up with complexity, that is, how to take it apart and manage it through the usual logic based on the obsession for control.

The point of view based on the theories, the models and the methods that we will illustrate in this book assumes instead that complexity is a challenge and that it can turn out to be a resource under two conditions: (1) a change in the dominant image of organizations as machines to control and maintain, (2) the development of methodologies and tools with the appropriate characteristics to describe and analyze the processes of sense-making.

If, as outlined above, on the one hand, paradoxes and language play a special role in the experience of complexity and the relationship between excellence and paradoxes is an intrinsic aspect of innovative organizations, then, on the other hand, the use of natural language as a management tool to solve organizational paradoxes is not immune to negative consequences. As the firm relaxes formalization and develops methods based on natural language, it faces problems of coordination and efficiency. To overcome this problem a practical solution usually consists in achieving a sort of balance between the informal side of the organization (represented by individual behaviors and dialogues), and the formal side (represented by structures and proce-dures), as set out by many contributions in the theory of organizational learning.

Our point of view is quite different. We do not see any necessary separation between the informal world of individuals and the formal world of the administration. Instead of conceiving these worlds as antagonistic or complementary, we argue that, given appropriate conditions, such worlds can communicate and reinforce each other, and that organizational learning happens only in this latter case (see in particular Chapters III, IV, and V of this book).

We claim that managers are very often too conditioned by inappropriate organiza-tional theories and, consequently, they design procedures under the influence of old paradigms that are no longer valid in the era of cognitive workers. The main problem of traditional approaches to coordination based on hierarchy, planning, and control and inspired by dated ideas of rational behavior is that they do not permit the full exploitation and development of the cognitive abilities of individuals.

These arguments are developed in detail in the rest of the book. In the first two parts of the book, we describe a theory of organizational learning and knowledge creation, and in the third part we propose new methods aimed at managing learning and knowledge through language, based on a mixture of qualitative and quantitative techniques, such as fuzzy logic. In the final part of the book, we outline the implica-tions for researchers and for managers arising from our approach.

References

Argyris C., & Schon, D.A. (1978). *Organizational learning. A theory of action perspective.* Reading, MA: Addison-Wesley.

Atkinson, R.C., & Shiffrin, R. M. (1968). Human memory: A proposed system and its control processes. In K. W. Spence & J. T. Spence (Eds.), *The psychology of learning and motivation* (Vol. II, pp. 89-195). New York: Academy Press.

Bateson, G. (1972). *Step to an ecology of mind.* Chandler.

Boje, D. (1991). The storytelling organization: A study of storytelling performance in an office supply firm. *Administrative Science Quarterly, 36*, 106-126.

Bonfantini, M. A. (1987). *La semiosi e l'abduzione.* Milano: Bompiani.

Bower, G. H., & Hilgard, E. R. (1981). *Theories of learning.* Englewood Cliffs, NJ: Prentice-Hall

Brandom, R. B. (2002). *Articulating reasons: An introduction to inferentialism .* Cambridge: Havard University Press.

Burns, T., & Stalker, G. M. (1978). *The management of innovation.* London: Tavistock.

Calvino, I. (1985). *Mr. Palomar.* Orlando: Harcourt Brace & company

Cameron, K. S. (1981). Domains of organizational effectiveness in colleges and universities. *Academy of Management Journal, 24*, 25-47.

Cameron, K. S. (1986). Effectiveness as paradox. *Management Science, 32*, 539-53.

Daft, R. L., & Wintington, J. C. (1979). Language and organizations. *Academy of Management Review, 4*, 179-191.

Dixon, N. (1995). A practical model for organizational learning. *Issues and Observations, 15*(2), 1-11.

Gardner, H. (1985). *The mind's new science: A history of the cognitive revolution.* New York: Basic Books.

Herriot, S. R., Levinthal, D., & March, J.G. (1975). Learning from experience in organizations. *American Economic Review, 75*, 298-302.

Hughes, R. (1980). *The shock of the new.* McGraw-Hill.

Laing, R. D. (1974). *Knots.* Harmondsworth: Penguin Books.

Maslow, A. (1954). *Motivation and personality.* Harper & Row: New York.

Minsky, M. (1988). *The society of mind.* New York: Simon & Schuster.

Morin, E. (1985) *On the definition of complexity.* In S. Aida (Ed.), *The science and praxis of complexity.* United Nations University.

Neisser, U. (1967). *Cognitive psycology.* Englewood Cliffs, NJ: Prentice Hall.

Nelson, R. R., & Winter, S. G. (1982). *An evolutionary theory of economic change.* Cambridge, MA: The Belknap Press of Harvard University Press.

Peirce, C. S. (1935-1966). *Collected papers of Charles Sanders Peirce.* (Ed. C. Hartschorne, P. Weiss, & A. W. Burks). Cambridge, MA: Harvard University Press.

Piaget, J. (1969). *The psychology of the child.* Basic Books.

Pondy, L. R., & Mitroff, I. I. (1979). Beyond open systems models of organization. In L. Cummings & B. Staw (Eds.), *Research in organizational behavior.* Greenwich, CN: JAI Press.

Poole, M. S., & Van de Ven, A. (1989). Using paradox to build management and organization theories. *Academy of Management Review, 14,* 562-578.

Quinn, R. E., & Cameron, K. S (1983). Organizational life cycles and shifting criteria and effectiveness. *Management Science, 9,* 33-51.

Rohrbaugh, J. (1981). Operationalizing the competing values approach. *Public Productivity Review, 5,* 141-59.

Schein, E. (2002). The anxiety of learning: An interview with Edgar Schein. *Harvard Business Review.*

Skinner, B. F. (1938). *The behavior of organism: An experimental analysis.* Appleton Century Crofts: New York.

Thagard, P. (1992). *Conceptual revolution.* Princeton: Princeton University Press.

Toribio-Medina, J. (1988). *The discover of the Amazon.* New York: Dover.

Thorndyke, E. L. (1913). *Educational psycology II: The psycology of learning.* Teachers College: New York.

Chapter III

Organizational Action:
Persistence and Change

But in vain I set out to visit the city: Forced to remain motionless and always the same in order to be more easily remembered, Zora has languished, disintegrated, disappeared.

Each city recreates its form from the desert it opposes.

~ Italo Calvino, Invisible cities

Abstract

Do organizations act? How can we describe collective action? How does such an action come about? The aim of this chapter is to provide the reader with a review of the various perspectives and to propose a definition of collective action as an attempt by the organization to maintain stability and regularity, and create an externally recognizable identity.

Organizational Action

Organizations exist in order to accomplish tasks that a single individual would not be able to do or would have a difficult time doing alone. It follows that organizations are created primarily as tools for the coordination and integration of actions of a group of individuals.

Therefore, organizational action can be understood as the result of the coordination and integration of individual actions (see Box 1 for a review of the main points of view in the literature on the concept of organizational action). If we imagine the actions of a group of individuals as vectors of different intensities and directions, collective action can be seen as the composition of these forces (Figure 1).

According to the vector metaphor, an organization must possess the following characteristics[1] in order to "do" something:

a.   A **group of individuals**

b.   A **task** to carry out through the contribution of several individuals

c.   Rules for the **composition** of individual actions

d.   Rules for the **evaluation** of benefits derived from their cooperation

Box 1. Some formulations of the concept of organizational action

---

In organizational literature, organizations are commonly defined as systems of collective action, which means systems that through the coordination of individual actions accomplish tasks that a single person would not be able to do alone or would accomplish less effectively and efficiently. For example, here are some definitions of organization:

a.   The ways in which the division of labor is broken down into distinct tasks and the coordination of these tasks (Mintzberg, 1979).

b.   The number of roles that single employees have to play and the relationships between them whose coordination will permit the achievement of company goals (Aldrich, 1979).

c.   The rational coordination of activities of a certain number of people in order to reach a common and explicit goal through the division of labor and through the creation of a hierarchy (Schein, 1985).

d.   A complex system of people charged with carrying out a common goal, who divide the tasks among themselves according to certain rules, establishing roles connected in a hierarchy and in a dynamic relationship with the external environment (Bernardi, 1989).

e.   A social entity guided by objectives and planned as a system of activities that are deliberately structured and coordinated to interact with the external environment (Daft, 2001).

Some scholars have characterized the concept of organizational action in detail, with the objective of specifying in what sense it is possible to affirm that an organization acts (see the review by Maggi & Albano, 1999).

---

continued on following page

Box 1. continued

For Weber (1922), organizational action is a meaningful form of social action; it is intersubjectively comprehensible, characterized by intentional rationality, based on the means/end calculation, and oriented toward a defined goal according to expectations and individual interests.

Recognizing the same characteristics of organizational action proposed by Weber, Barnard (1938) underlines the role of authority, intended as the capacity to influence other people's decisions instead of as a hierarchical prerogative, and the interaction between the formal and informal components of an organization.

Starting with Herbert Simon's theory of limited rationality (1947), Thompson (1967) considers the tension toward the reduction of uncertainty when structuring processes and building the environment as a consequence of the choices made in the construction of organizational processes.

For Argyris and Schön (1978) organizations always and only act through their members. Nevertheless, an action becomes organizational when shared procedures for making decisions are available and someone is delegated to act in the name of or on behalf of the collectivity.

March (1988) identified six perspectives for interpreting organizational action:

1.   **Adherence to the norm:** The action is the outcome of the application of procedures and rules in appropriate situations.

2.   **Solution to the problem:** The action is the response to the resolution of a specific problem.

3.   **Learning:** The action is the consequence of knowledge acquired through experience.

4.   **Conflicts:** The action is the result of a conflict between people with divergent interests.

5.   **Contagion:** The action can be thought of as an event that spreads from one organization to another.

6.   **Regeneration:** Turnover introduces new members to the organization and therefore new attitudes, abilities and aims.

An organizational action can have various connotations according to the point of view of the observer and the effects that it produces. Therefore it can be political action, coordination, interaction, reaction, etc. The fundamental attribute, in any case, is the fact that it is a collective action, whose occurrence requires the involvement of several individuals sharing common beliefs and plans.

Figure 1. Organizational action as the result of individual actions

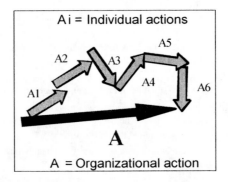

Note: Organizational action can be thought of as the composition of individual actions. In the "vector" metaphor, the different directions and intensities of the vectors represent the variety of individuals and the need to redirect this variety toward an orderly and coherent plan. In traditional organizational analysis, this task is achieved through preconstituted roles and procedures. By reversing this perspective, is a paradigm admissible in which organizational action emerges as a result of the bottom-up integration of individual actions?

It is not strictly necessary to assume that the pursuit of goals shared among individuals is a fundamental reason for an organization to exist. Instead, it is more realistic to think that the members of an organization converge more on the means rather than on its ends. Cooperation is perceived by members of a group as being advantageous for reaching their own personal objectives. The convergence on shared means is the main reason for a collective structure to exist (Weick, 1979).[2]

It is quite common for people to think of organizations as machines (see Chapter I of this book). All things considered, a machine is also a system that coordinates the actions of its single elements, such as the levers and gears of a clock, or the subroutines and modules of software programs. At any rate, organizational thought has long since reached the conclusion that organizations cannot be compared to machines, and that the machine is only a captivating metaphor (Morgan, 1997).

There are at least four reasons that make it problematic to think of organizations as machines:

a. **Degree of participation:** Gears, devices and levers are certainly parts of a machine; contrarily, individuals often belong to an organization voluntarily and they only belong partially. Generally, individuals are members of more than one organization at a time: work, family, friends, associations, etc. It is more useful to speak of the degree to which individuals belong to the organization. It follows that the recognition of the organizational boarders is often problematic.

b. **Predictability of action:** Gears and levers complete predetermined tasks. Instead, individuals in organizations are called upon to evaluate the alternative courses of action in conditions of ambiguity and uncertainty. The possibility to choose inevitably produces a deviation from the predicted sequence.

c. **Coordination:** The hierarchical relationships between the single gears and the parts of a machine are specified unambiguously, once and for all. This is not true when the parts of the "machine" are people.

d. **Continuity of action:** A machine works in a regular and predictable way when predefined conditions are met. Instead, organizations require both controls and systems of incentives that assure the regularity and reproducibility of an action as well as its outcomes.

Nothing is automatic when dealing with human organizations. The composition of individual actions requires a set of rules, procedures and tools that must continually reproduce a sense of belonging in people, as well as the predictability, coordination and continuity of organizational action. *A group of individuals that adopt rules, procedures and tools with the goal of reproducing the collective action is an organization.*

Moreover, the composition of individual actions includes a political dimension, in that the mechanisms that regulate collective action must take into account questions concerning authority and hierarchy, as well as the distribution of power and negotiation (Crozier & Friedberg, 1977). Thanks to these political mechanisms, the organization can also operate by means of just one of its members, who act on behalf of the rest of the group. In this case, a single person act on behalf of everyone by authority or delegation.

More generally, we will say that an organization *acts*:

a.   **Through the integration of individual actions:** In other words, when the results are the fruit of the composition of the individual actions with respect to the preestablished ways of regulating membership, predictability, coordination and continuity of action.

b.   **Through authority:** When one of its members is authorized to act in the name of, and for, the organization (Argyris & Schön, 1978).

The Persistence of Organizational Action

Organizational literature has given wide attention to the problem of the composition of individual actions, particularly with respect to the production of decisions and coordination. Yet, little space is given to the problem of *the continuity of organizational action*. Nevertheless, the objective of the composition of individual actions is to articulate the tempo and rhythms of organizational life with regularity, to guarantee their normal development: In other words, to *simplify* and reconstruct them so that they are always identical.[3]

It is the dedication to *simplification and reconstruction* that assures the convergence of the means (for example, through standardization), the continuity of the performances, and the predictability of the outcomes. It is in the simplification and continuous reconstruction of actions that the essence of organizing can be seen. Nevertheless, the continuity and regularity of collective action cannot be taken for granted.

The metaphors of the organization as a machine, organism or computer (Morgan, 1997) all of them, in essence, inspired by a mechanistic vision of the organization, have one defect: They do not take into account that the organization ceases to exist every evening, when its members leave their offices and factories and go home.

As a consequence, the coherence of organizational systems must be *reconstructed and reestablished every day*, through coordination, support for task completion, incentives and motivation. It is matter of systems being designed to restrain indi-

Figure 2. Organizations and Penelope's web

Note: Organizations are not machines, but, like machines, they must guarantee the standardization, regularity and predictability of their actions and products. Organizational actions must be weaved and reweaved every day. Just as Penelope weaved and reweaved her web, not only as an excuse to put off her wedding, but as a way to give some meaning to her long wait, reminding herself that she was still married.

vidual actions, just as the loom restrains the actions of Penelope, as well as the plot of her web (Figure 2).

Organizational action is essentially demonstrated in the process of reconstruction and maintenance of collective action that must be repeated the same way each time. It is the continuity of action in time that shapes the identity of the organization. This identity becomes externally recognizable because it is connected to the action, and continues as such even after some members have abandoned the organization.

Therefore, it can be affirmed that *organizations do not exist, but persist in time*. It is the continuous reconstruction and maintenance of the *collective identity through the repetition of action* that allows for the recognition of stable organizations such as schools, hospitals, companies, and public administrations by fleeting or destructured aggregations, such as opinion groups, or groups of friends.[4]

In practice, the persistence of organizations is obtained through *the definition and updating of rules and tools*. The rules establish the ways actions will be carried out, which roles will be played and by whom, who will have the decisional power, how power will be delegated, etc. The tools are needed to implement the action in certain ways and are developed to support and shape individual actions. Rules and tools, in other words, identify the domain and the limits of organizational action.

It is nevertheless important to observe that the link between the rules and the tools is characterized by a certain amount of ambiguity. Tools are shaped through "interpretations" of the rules, creating a particular version for a specific social and cultural context. For example, the top management of a company can decide to carry out a procedure for personnel evaluation and define a set of values and rules to follow in the evaluation. A group of experts compiles a list of items to evaluate. The middle managers then use this evaluation form to evaluate their own collaborators. Between the initial decision to establish the rules to follow in the evaluation, the definition of the tool (the form), and its concrete use by the people, there is a loose connection that allows a great deal of freedom (usually higher than expected). For instance:

1. The evaluation of the rules established by managers can be ambiguous
2. Many possible forms acknowledging such rules can be designed
3. Evaluation items can be interpreted in many different ways when the form is actually used by different managers

Any social group can be defined as an organization when it makes up a set of rules and tools that some of its members can use in order to act "in the interest" of the organization. For example, a group of friends that loves the mountains can create an association for the protection of the natural mountain environment. The association has a series of material, social and symbolic artifacts such as the internal statutes and rules, procedures for the election of a board of directors or a president, identification cards that demonstrate membership, roles for the execution of specific tasks, a logo, real and virtual meeting places, etc.

The most interesting aspect of such artifacts is that they can survive the members of the group and become concrete elements that sustain the continuity of action of the association. The artifacts transform the association into an organization.[5]

The set of rules and tools that sustain the continuity of organizational action, once they are shared and made explicit, form a true *technical apparatus of persistence* in organizational action.

Organizational Change

In practice, every organization constructs its own particular apparatus of persistence made up of specific systems aimed at gathering and controlling data and information, inspection procedures, incentive programs, norms for evaluating performances, rules of behavior, organizational charts, job descriptions, etc.

The specific characteristics of any apparatus of persistence are based on (and justified through) explicit or unspoken ways of thinking that guide organizational action, all of which Argyris and Schön (1978) attribute to the denomination of theories of organizational action. For example, a supplier evaluation form is based on a theory of action that a certain organization might develop with respect to something that must be meant by "good supplier," the characteristics that a "good supplier" must have, on how to measure them, on how to use the results of the evaluation, etc.

Returning to Argyris and Schön (1978), an *espoused theory of action* is meant as an explicit theory of action that guides a given pattern of activities and is usually describable in terms of rules, such as "If A then do B." The espoused theory of action is therefore fully demonstrated in the characteristics of the technical apparatus of persistence (for example in a system of evaluation for a supplier with certain characteristics, etc.). The use of the apparatus of persistence should, in turn, contribute to reinforce the theory.

This action of reinforcement is not completely taken for granted. On the contrary, various degrees of misalignment between the espoused theory and its practical application can often be found in organizations. Parallel to the declared theory, individuals tend to develop *theories-in-use*, i.e., theories relative to the concrete implementation of the pattern of conduct supplied by the technical apparatus. The concrete implementation of a particular rule of conduct is the result of a contextualization through a *subjective interpretation* of the espoused theory. Theoretically the same espoused theory can therefore create multiple interpretations, i.e., multiple theories-in-use that are not necessarily coherent amongst themselves, nor with the espoused theory that generated them.

The emergence of a theory-in-use that is partially inconsistent with the espoused theory may be due to various causes such as: (1) political conflict, (2) interpretative disagreement, (3) communication problems, and often, (4) a need to adapt, that is, a partial recognition of the inadequacy of the espoused theory in the resolution of unexpected events or contingent problems.

Returning to the example of the evaluation of a supplier, inconsistency can be due, respectively, to: (1) an evaluator being prejudicially hostile to the procedure because his/her adversary gains an advantage from its application, (2) a different interpretation about what should be meant by "good supplier," (3) to erroneous communication by management about the purpose of the method, and (4) the need to "adjust" the evaluation to unforeseen situations.

Persistence of action is an objective that organizational action tries to achieve. Being made up of individuals and not inanimate mechanisms, organizations can inadvertently cause a reaction to the imposition or inadequacy of persistence. Organizational conflict is nothing more than the act of questioning the current systems of control, power, relationships, rewards, and so forth, within the organization in question.

It is necessary to underline that the explicit theory and the attached apparatus of the persistence of action are structurally incomplete, in the sense that they are not able to control all of the information the organization uses. Instead, the dissimilar, ambiguous, weak and neglected information is revised by individuals, who can form new theories or adapt existing ones to unexpected situations or to emerging problems. In most cases it is a matter of individual learning, even though they are due to "organizational" causes. This is the condition needed for organizational learning. In order for the organization to learn, it is necessary that individual learning be propagated and incorporated into an eventual revision of the espoused theory. It is only when persistence is questioned, and its technical apparatus is changed, that organizational learning may occur.

If individual learning is not put into a system through its incorporation into the espoused theory, the advantages derived from it, although potentially significant, are fleeting. In fact, the contribution derived from individual learning can also be a great advantage for the organization, but it is, and always will be, the patrimony of the individual that has generated it since the organization is not always able to adopt it.

Organizational Macrocycles: Persistence and Change

Organizational action is constructed by a social group that has built an apparatus of persistence in order to guarantee continuity and the maintenance of a collective identity.

Espoused theories, which the apparatus makes reference to, can condition social actions by forcing them to follow the predefined rules of conduct. Individuals are called upon to act, as much as possible, in conformity with the espoused theories. The work they do is always, to a certain extent, "cognitive work," which tends to reduce the ambiguity of work situations and to make sense of an action within the framework of organizational rules. In this way, members of an organization feed a mechanism of reinforcement, defined here as a cycle of persistence (Figure 3).

However, as much as it is imagined to be articulate and pervasive, the apparatus of persistence is not able to exhaust all of the possible interpretations nor provide all of the necessary answers. In order to make the uncertainty disappear so the functioning of the organization can become more predictable, the apparatus, when trying to rationalize problems, creates in its turn uncertainties that can be used by

Figure 3. Organizations amidst persistence and change

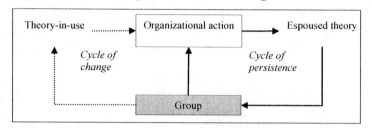

Note: Organizational action is the outcome of a social game within a group, resulting from two essential cycles: The cycle of persistence, that is shown through the attempt to reduce the entropy of social action within recognizable and stable forms, and the cycle of change through which individuals construct theories-in-use and create spaces of action for the achievement of individual advantages.

members of the organization to construct theories-in-use, which are useful for attaining instrumental advantages (Friedberg, 2001).[6]

The theory-in-use is not necessarily a reaction to formalization, but a natural product of organizational action. According to Friedberg, "*The positive functions that explain the need for conventions, norms and rules must never allow us to forget the strategic and primarily political nature of human interaction. This interaction leads to the erosion of conventions, norms and rules, as soon as they are created, blurring the context and making room for opportunism [...] Therefore, the actual role of the formal characteristics of an organization is not to determine behaviors, but to create spaces for negotiations between the actors*" (Friedberg, 2001, p. 106). In other words, to establish the rules of the social game.

The construction of theories-in-use is aimed at guiding individual actions in the spaces the apparatus leaves uncovered. Therefore, theories-in-use also fully contribute to form organizational action, at times filling the spaces left open by espoused theories, at other times instrumentally bending the technical apparatus to achieve individual advantages, or in the end, openly opposing the espoused theories by creating "malfunctions," "deviations," or "nonconformities." In all cases, the cognitive worker is expected to create new explicative hypotheses and new ideas for action. Next to the cycle of persistence, organizational action, through the social game, contains within itself the conditions for bringing about a cycle of change (Figure 3).

As we have already shown, individuals play a central role in the process of organizational learning thanks to their ability to construct theories-in-use. But these "private" theories are only rarely translated into changes in the espoused theory, for various reasons largely explored in organizational literature:

a.   Individuals often bring about defensive ways of thinking to avoid conflict (Argyris & Schön, 1978), meaning that they avoid exposing themselves and challenging the dominant points of view.

b.   Changes question the existing balance of power (Crozier & Friedberg, 1977).

c.   The uncritical repetition of what has worked well in the past produces excessive confidence in what is already known and inertia in exploring possible alternatives (competency traps, March, 2001; prejudices and cognitive biases, Nisbett & Ross, 1980; Tversky & Kahneman, 1973, 1974, 1978).

d.   Changes generate real learning anxiety in people, tied to the fear of change and the effort of unlearning which is now useless but is already known (Schein, 2002).

Conclusion

In this chapter, we have described collective action as a mechanism to ensure the continuity and predictability, but also the continuity and predictability of the outcome and of individual and organizational behavior.

Resistance to change in organizations is therefore the natural outcome of systems designed to last. The consolidation of practices, procedures, and rules over time reinforce the set of rules and tools that form *the apparatus of persistence*. In the end, it becomes a patrimony that the organization preserves and maintains which obliges the action to be deployed in one or just a few possible ways.

Organizations often become prisoners of their own apparatus and prejudices. In the end, they pretend to believe that their existence is developing in the best of all possible ways. In that case, the apparatus of persistence ends up being part of a mask through which the organization maintains the image it has of itself and the identity that it has constructed, at times hiding, mostly from itself, the wrinkles and marks of time. In a certain way, it is possible to affirm that the technical apparatus of persistence can be considered as an important part of the "memory" of an organization. In the next chapter, we will analyze the concept of collective memory and will propose a coherent model along with the concept of organizational action presented in this chapter.

References

Aldrich, H. (1979). *Organizations and environment.* Englewood Cliffs, NJ: Prentice Hall.

Argyris, C., & Schön, D.A. (1978). *Organizational learning: A theory of action perspective.* Reading, MA: Addison-Wesley.

Berger, P. L., & Luckmann, T. (1966). *The social construction of reality: A treatise in the sociology of knowledge.* New York: Doubleday.

Bernardi, G. (1989). *Sistemi organizzativi aziendali.* Padova: Edizioni Libreria progetto.

Crozier, M., & Fiedberg, E. (1977). *L'acteur et le système.* Paris: Editions du Seuil.

Daft, R. L. (2001). *Organization theory and design.* Cincinnati, OH: South Western College Publishing.

Friedberg, E. (2001). Le quattro dimensioni dell'azione organizzativa. In A. Fanelli (Ed.), *Le organizzazioni che apprendono,* special issue of *Sviluppoe Organizzazione* (pp. 103-118).

Kay, R. (2001). Are organizations autopoietic? A call for a new debate. *Systems Research and Behavioral Science, 18,* 461-477.

Luhmann, N. (1995). *Social systems.* Stanford: Stanford University Press.

Maggi, B., & Albano, R. (1996). La Teoria dell'Azione Organizzativa. In R. C. D. Nacamulli & G. Costa (Eds.), *Manuale di organizzazione aziendale.* Torino: UTET.

Maturana, H., & Varela, F. (1980). *Autopoiesis and cognition: The realization of living.* London: Reidl.

Mintzberg, H. (1979). *The structuring of organization.* Englewood Cliffs, NJ: Prentice Hall.

Morgan, G. (1997). *Images of organizations.* Thousands Oaks, CA: Sage.

Schein, E. (1985). *Organizational culture and leadership.* San Francisco: Jossey Bass.

Nisbett, R., & Ross, L. (1980). *Human inference: Strategies and shortcomings of social judgement.* Englewood Cliffs, NJ: Prentice Hall.

Schein, E. (2002). The anxiety of learning. *Harvard Business Review, 80*(3). Interview with D. Coutu.

Simon, H. A. (1947). *Administrative behavior.* New York: Macmillan.

Thompson, J. D. (1967). *Organizations in actions.* New York: McGraw Hill.

Tversky, A., & Kahneman, D. (1973). Availability: A heuristic for judging frequency and probability. *Cognitive Psychology, 5*, 207-232.

Tversky, A., & Kahneman, D. (1974). Judgement under uncertainty. Heuristics and biases. *Science, 185*, 1124-1131.

Tversky, A., & Kahneman, D. (1978). Causal schemata in judging under uncertainty. In M. Fishbein (Ed.), *Progress in social psychology*. Hillsdale, NJ: Lawrence Erlbaum.

Weber, M. (1922). *Wirtschaft und gesellschaft*. Tubinga (Germany): Mohr.

Weick, K. E. (1979). *The social psychology of organization*. Reading, MA: Addison Wesley.

Endnotes

[1]   The term organization does not always necessarily refer to organized social collectives, but it can be attributed to many systems, such as machines and living beings. Maturana and Varela (1980) define an organization as a group of relationships that must exist between the components of something so that it can be considered as a member of a particular class. The fundamental idea is that an organization is made up of elementary parts that interact through stable and recognizable relationships and patterns.

[2]   Incidentally, this view of organizations that is built around the means instead of the ends appears to probably make more sense in a postindustrial social-economic context, where individuals share common means, but different goals under the umbrella of institutional aims.

[3]   Persistence as a characteristic trait of organized social systems can also be explained through the theory of autopoietic systems (Maturana & Varela, 1980). An autopoietic system reproduces itself continually through the maintenance of its limits and its individuality, meant, at the most elementary level, as the ability to distinguish itself form the external environment. Proposals to extend the autopoietic theory from living systems to social ones have been made repeatedly, in particular in the work of Luhmann (1995). Nevertheless, both the legitimacy of such an extension, as the theory of autopoiesis *tout-court* have often been criticized at an epistemological level (for a summary of the debate see Kay, 2001).

[4]   The concept of persistence should not be confused with that of formalization, the latter being just one possible way of guaranteeing persistence (by far one of the most common). According to Friedberg (2001) all organizations can be

placed on a continuum made up of four variables: the level of formalization of the regulation, the degree of awareness or consciousness of the regulation by members of the organization, the degree of finalization of the regulation and the degree of delegation made explicit in the regulation. It follows that organizations exist, and are weak or strong according to the intensity of the level of each of the four variables. Thus, a group of friends and a bureaucratic organization are only two extremes of a continuum.

[5]   The mechanism through which a group creates a stable social community that survives its founding members is *institutionalization*, thoroughly analyzed by Berger e Luckmann (1966, see also Chapter VI of this book).

[6]   The problem can be reformulated in a more theoretical way by affirming that every determination of meaning inevitably creates more vagueness or ambiguities (see Chapter IV of this book). The meaning, intended as a "surplus" of references to further possibilities of making experiences and doing things" (Luhmann, 1995) is not able to overcome its own redundancy, and incessantly creates other meanings. The proliferation of meaning can be limited, discouraged, or even prevented, but never suppressed.

Chapter IV

Collective Memory

Le group humain se comporte dans la nature comme un organisme vivant; de même que l'animal ou la plante, pour qui les produits naturels ne sont pas immédiatement assimilables, mais exigent le jeu d'organes qui en préparent les éléments, le groupe humain assimile son milieu à travers un rideau d'objets (outils ou instruments) [...] les techniques sont implicitement contenues dans le jeu de deux milieux: le milieu extérieur et le milieu intérieur du group humaine.[1]

(André Leroi-Gourhan,Milieu et techniques, 1973)

Abstract

In the previous chapter we focused on the concept of collective action. In the same spirit, this chapter investigates another fundamental component of learning, i.e., memory, and attempts to reformulate this concept at the collective level. Do organizations remember? In which sense it is possible to talk about collective memory? What is the nature of such a memory? The chapter presents a model of organizational memory which can not be reduced to a metaphor, nor to a mere extension or generalization of individual memory.

Organizational Memory: Artifacts and Culture

The term 'memory' has a number of meanings that are commonly used. Linguistic uses go beyond the conventional meaning of cognitive function. It is often used metaphorically in biology, computer science, history, and in the organizational and the social sciences. In computer science it corresponds to the concept of archives, and therefore it is regarded as a resource aimed at the passive and neutral conservation of information. Furthermore, in everyday language, the concept of memory is intended both as the product and process of remembering.

The extended use of memory refers to the idea of preserving, evoking, testifying, reconstructing, and reutilizing a corpus of knowledge, information, practices, habits, and patterns of behavior. The creative function of memory is demonstrated by the Greek myth in which the Muses, and therefore art, were conceived by the union between the goddess of memory, Mnémosyne, and Zeus.

Although the concept of memory is often used metaphorically, later in this chapter we will propose a model of organizational memory that is not referable to a simple metaphor, nor to any kind of generalization or extension of individual memory.

The introduction of the concept of organizational memory brings up two principle questions: (a) What are its main elements? (b) How is organizational action influenced by organizational memory?

The need for organizational memory can be explained through action theory. In the first place, organizations act through systems of rules and tools designed to guarantee the control and execution of tasks and the persistence of the organization itself. This system, defined as *apparatus of persistence*, must be preserved and maintained. It is the framework of organizational memory, without which the organization would be unable to act in an efficient and regular way. It would be forced to reinvent every day the procedures for the composition of individual actions.

The apparatus of persistence makes organizational action possible because it imposes behavioral restrictions on individuals. It influences the definition of objectives and priorities, structures the perception of events, directs interpretative and decisional processes. Finally, it supplies the tools and support needed to operate and communicate.

At first glance, the apparatus of persistence is a group of artifacts that incorporate the possibilities of limited actions. Some possibilities are apparent to everyone, while others are more subtle and ambiguous. So, a hammer incorporates the action of "driving nails," as everyone knows. However, for a Master Builder, under special conditions, it can also incorporate the action of "laying a plumb line." In action theory, "driving nails" is a strong theory of action, while "laying a plumb line" is a weak one.

Organizations act as systems for the maintenance, management and production of theories of collective action (knowledge for Grant, 1996; routine for Herriot, Levinthal, & March, 1975; Nelson & Winter, 1982) through the construction and the maintenance of such apparatuses. There are many artifacts that incorporate such theories. In practice, each material or immaterial element is repeatedly involved in the action. A list follows, though it is necessarily incomplete:

- *Maps*, such as organizational charts, job descriptions, and flow-charts
- *Archives*, such as databases and case-bases, project libraries, best practices, and written memoirs
- *Places*, such as offices, department lay-outs, and meeting rooms
- *Tools*, such as computer networks, computer software, forms, and badges
- *Routines and procedures*, like those that regulate the execution of productive activities and controls
- *Norms*, such as regulations, statutes, and quality control assumptions

Maps, archives, spaces, routines, procedures, and norms represent all of the rules and tools that support the composition of individual actions for the realization of organizational action.

Patterns of action and communicative formats, preserved in organizational memory in the form of knowledge and experience that the organization has accumulated, codified and systematized over time, assume particular relevance. These codifications are continuously invoked and put to good use by members of the organization in order to carry out specific tasks. But a pattern of action is not necessarily incorporated into a procedure or a norm. Often it is incorporated into speeches, stories, organizational myths, and values, whose effects are less direct and tangible. When dealing with such intangible artifacts, organizational action abandons the solid ground of technical artifacts and enters the unsettled world of organizational culture.

While the technical artifacts support and constraint *collective action*, organizational culture acts on the *individual interpretations* of the premises and the outcomes of the action. Organizations tend to stabilize individual interpretations through culture intended as system of shared references such as values, beliefs, preferences and taboos (see Box 1).

Artifacts and culture work together inextricably to make individual actions and interpretations coherent and effective. In other words, organizational memory is always the integration of:

a.   A set of technical artifacts aimed at constraining individual actions and stabilizing collective action

b.   An organizational culture aimed at constraining and stabilizing the various subjective interpretations around shared points of reference

Therefore, artifacts and culture interlace in order to reach a state of equilibrium characterized by artifact stability and cultural conformity. Nevertheless, artifacts and culture more often constitute a situation that is more or less intensely agitated by dialectical and political tension, shaken by contradictions and threatened by unexpected events coming from both inside and outside the organization.

Box 1. Schein and organizational culture

Edgar Schein (1985) developed and examined the concept of organizational culture closely as a result of his experiences with American prisoners of war during the conflict in Korea. By analyzing the behavior of ex-prisoners, Schein observed that the forms of collaboration with the enemy were only in rare cases dictated by the coercion practiced by Chinese soldiers. On the contrary, Schein affirms the Chinese were able to introduce a subtle form of psychological warfare through the manipulation of the group dynamics which had emerged among the prisoners in order to facilitate the growth of mutual distrust. Thanks to these practices, in the communities of American prisoners in Chinese camps, a social structure and a culture was developed that helped the Chinese not only to control the prisoners, but in some case to gain their explicit support.

For Schein culture is:

1.   A set of shared basic assumptions

2.   Invented, discovered or developed by a group

3.   In an attempt to resolve the twofold problem of external adaptation and internal integration

4.   That have worked reasonably well in the past in order to be considered valid and that therefore

5.   Must be taught to new members of the group as

6.   The correct way to perceive, think and feel in relation to certain specific problems

According to Schein's approach, culture is the way a group tries to reach a compromise between external adaptation and internal integration. It is directed at preserving the unity of the group and stopping conflicts that might threaten stability from arising. With respect to *external adaptation*, it is necessary for the group to establish a sufficient level of consent on the objectives and the strategies to follow. To guarantee *internal integration*, members of the group must develop common beliefs and language, criteria of inclusion/exclusion in and from the group, mechanisms of power distribution and the regulation of social interaction among members and with other groups.

Integration and adaptation are problematic and they come about in ambiguous conditions. The role of multiple interpretations therefore becomes central to the construction of beliefs and of the convergence on shared interpretations.

According to our view of collective memory, culture alone is not sufficient to guarantee the continuity and persistence of organizational action. A generic group (a stadium crowd, for example), does not necessarily need to guarantee the continuity and regularity of collective action. It is the need for persistence that transforms a group into an organization over time, making the latter an individual reality that is independent of its members. In the logic of persistence, organizational culture establishes the meaning of action and offers a kind of safe haven where members of an organization can anchor their own interpretations in reference to a value system, which is consolidated through experience and tradition.

However, the concrete and regular development of action is only possible through *instrumental conditioning*, i.e., by means of restrictions and support provided by organizational artifacts.

The Vestiges of Memory: Organizational Artifacts

Collective memory tends to be crystallized within *cognitive and material structures* characterized by a certain amount of stability that survives individuals turnover. According to Pierre Nora (1978), *"Collective memory is what remains of the past in group experiences, or **what these groups make of the past**"* (1978, quoted in Le Goff, 2003, p. 56, emphasis added).

Collective memory can be investigated from various points of view:

a.   That of the *archaeologist*, through an investigation that begins with traces of action and collective experience (handmade articles, tools, remains, traces, etc.)

b.   That of the *historian*, by means of analyses and interpretations of the most important events of the past

c.   That of the *anthropologist*, through the study of rites, traditions, customs, and taboos that make up culture

d.   That of the *psychologist*, through the analysis of individual choices, archetypes, and the cognitive processes of behavior

Each investigation will produce some vestiges of collective memory, constructions of the human group produced in order to guarantee the persistence of collective action beyond the biological cycle of the members of the group. We call such constructions *organizational artifacts*. Artifacts are above all cognitive products resulting from thought. They possess the following characteristics[2]:

a.   **Documentation:** The artifact lends itself to an intersubjective description that can be recorded by means of an operation of "registration" (through writing, drawing, filming, etc.)[3].

b.   **Use:** The artifact refers to an action theory. An individual who has the right knowledge will be able to reconstruct the use of the artifact in terms of functions, uses, and adaptations to the context (Simon, 1981).

c.   **Restriction:** The artifact restricts the execution of the action (Conte, 2002).

d.   **Social recognition:** The artifact and the action theory it refers to are socially well-known.

e.   **Access:** Artifacts are accessible to members of an organization.

f.   **Habit:** The artifact is used frequently by members of the organization, or it has been used in the past.

Additional, though unnecessary, properties of the artifact are:

g. **Evocation:** Symbolic meaning are associated to the artifact.

h. **Imitation:** Artifacts can imitate the real (Simon, 1981).

i. **Structure:** Artifacts are characterized by a recognizable order.

Therefore, organizational artifacts are tools for carrying out organizational action. Typical organizational artifacts are: tools, projects, marketing plans, reports, manuals, procedures, notices, regulations, labels, glossaries, images, software programs, missions, Web sites, uniforms and clothing, training materials, purchase notes, contracts, etc.

Apart from these official elements, members of an organization also use informal elements as artifacts: Stories, speeches, rumors, myths, coffee machines, images and status symbols. In other words, some artifacts do not refer to espoused action theories. In more general terms, artifacts can be seen as a message that suggests possible, though limited, courses of action. This message naturally implies the existence of a receiver who is able to interpret it.[4]

Organizational memory is populated by artifacts. It is referable to the concept of artificial memory proposed by André Leroi-Gourhan (1964, p. 260):

Memory [...] is not a characteristic of intelligence, but the base, whatever it may be, upon which a series of actions is recorded. At this point we can speak of "specific memory," to define the set of behaviors in animal species, of an "ethnic" memory, that insures the reproduction of behaviors in human society, as well as an "artificial" memory, "electronic" in its most recent form, that allows for the reproduction of sequential mechanical acts without having to use instinct or reflection.

Organizational artifacts guarantee *the reproduction of sequential mechanical acts* that do not necessarily need to refer to intuition or reflection. Organization artifacts, in other words, incorporate grammars of use founded upon shared theories of action. The set of official and informal artifacts make up an interface, or a technical shell through which the individual can interact with the organizational environment (Figure 1). Actually, even the most prescriptive of the artifacts can be put to unexpected uses (alternative, creative or improper) but the task of the artifact is always to simplify the world and provide a direction for action.

The artifact *par excellence* of the artificial memory of organizations is the map. It is no accident that organizations are well-supplied with maps of all types, beginning with the organizational chart that is often associated with the very concept of

Figure 1. Organizational artifacts as intermediaries in the interaction between the individual and organizational reality

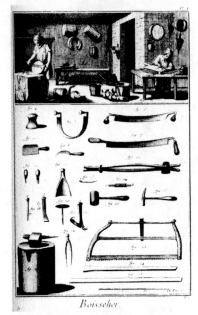

For André Leroi-Gourhan (1973), human groups assimilate their environments through a set of objects (tools). The techniques are implicitly contained in the interaction that occurs between two areas: The external physical realm and the internal social sphere. The tools and techniques drive the procedures and rules that organize not only what is done but social interaction as well. In organizations, individuals are surrounded by artifacts, as in this representation of the wood-turner workshop from the Diderot and D'Alembert Encyclopédie. Artifacts are the instruments through which members of an organization come into contact and explore the world of organizational reality. Just as tools allowed Robinson Crusoe to reconstruct an outpost of civilization on a desert island, so too do organizational artifacts allow for the regulation of social action, subtracting it from arbitrariness and improvisation.

organization. As we know, the objective of a map is not to imitate reality, but to guide whoever consults it in a certain direction and for a certain reason toward the perception and interpretation of reality and action.

The effect produced by a map on the action can be paradoxical. Karl Weick quoted an intriguing anecdote (Huff, 1990): During the first World War a group of soldiers in the Austro-Hungarian army was lost during a war operation in the Alps. Thanks to an old map of the region found in their supplies, the group was able to find its way back to the base. The group leader said that it had not been an easy journey, since the map was very old, almost unreadable and not updated. His surprise turned to wonder when someone told him that what they had used was actually a map of the Pyranees!

Although the soldiers had used the wrong map, it had channeled their capacity to make sense of the situation. Without the false map, perhaps they would never have found their way.

So, organizational artifacts are the *trait d'union* between memory and organizational action. They are:

a.   Part of organizational memory because they are the products of knowledge that the organization has accumulated and consolidated through experience.

b.   Part of organizational action since they allow for a fast and effective composition of individual actions.

It is in this quality of belonging to memory and action that artifacts find their justification in organizations and in social life. As we will see later, belonging to both memory and action allows artifacts to play a decisive role in organizational learning processes.

Memory and Action

Organizational memory is a set of artifacts that are amalgamated by organizational culture. Culture is made up of often tacit values and beliefs shared by member of an organization (Bettis & Prahalad, 1995; Martin, 1992; Schein, 1985).

Artifacts supply actors with "external" points of reference for the production of action. Culture provides the same actors with "internal" references for action: Motivations, meanings, interpretations, values. Culture and artifacts are related through a circular relationship (Figure 2).

Artifacts have their own instrumental identity. That is, they are a means for action. Like every means, an artifact can only allow some actions and not others. However, to think of artifacts only as a means is limiting and false. Because artifacts are constantly being used, they often assume a symbolic function and are associated to stories and values.[5] These symbols, stories, and values have their own independent existence; they circulate in an organization and contribute to the construction of a universe of reference where members of an organization live. This universe of symbols and values is organizational culture. It is like a fluid that surrounds the action and the tools that support it.

Figure 2 shows the idea of a strong connection between cultural system and artifacts: The modification of artifacts is a consequence of cultural change. In some cases individuals can develop theories in use that cause them to modify the way they use

Figure 2. Memory and organizational experience

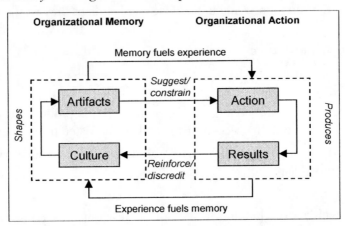

The set of shared beliefs and values underlying organizational culture influence the design of and reinforce the use of organizational artifacts, which support and restrict individual actions. Therefore, the observation and the interpretation of outcomes of an action by members of an organization condition and, at the same time, are conditioned by organizational memory.

the artifacts or to create new ones. But the new ways of using new artifacts cannot be considered "organizational" until their use is legitimized through their inclusion in the apparatus of persistence.

An example related to personnel evaluation systems can help clarify this point of view.

The organizational culture shapes the design of the artifacts for personnel evaluation, such as forms, assessment scales, procedures for the interpretation and use of results, etc. In particular, the criteria used in an explicit evaluation are a clear reflection of the official organizational culture, with reference to questions such as, "*What does it mean to work well in our organization?*"; "*What are the characteristics of our best employees?*"; "*What are some useful/productive/rewarding behaviors?,*" etc. Evaluation results reward those behaviors that are coherent with the organizational culture (even if such a reinforcement is not taken for granted).

Alongside evaluation models that are characterized by the espoused theory, managers tend to develop theories-in-use that are not always coherent or compatible with the espoused theory relative to its evaluation criteria, to the profile of the ideal candidate, or to the scales. As a result, many times managers use artifacts for evaluation instrumentally to reward those candidates that in reality had already been evaluated according to personal categories of judgment and models of their own theory in use.

The most interesting aspect is that managers often consider theories-in-use as being more effective in the evaluation of their own collaborators than the espoused theory and its wealth of organizational artifacts. At any rate, managers are not authorized to

Box 2. An organizational memory model

Walsh and Ungson (1991) attribute a distributed design to organizational memory, without centralized control and constituted by a network of retention systems for information and knowledge belonging to one of the following categories (Figure 3):

a.   *Organizational structure*

b.   *Transformations,* which is a set of systems and rules for production through which an organization accomplishes its own output

c.   *Ecology,* that is the workplace and its activities

d.   *Culture,* that is the shared value and belief systems

e.   *Individuals,* as depositories of organizational knowledge

f.   *External archives,* which is the set of any archives that do not belong to the organization, but contain information about its past activities

Figure 3. The structure of organizational memory (our adaptation from Walsh & Ungson, 1991)

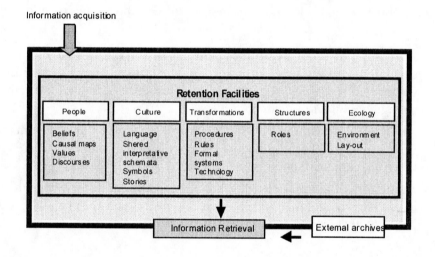

Unlike the model proposed by Walsh and Ungson, the formulation proposed in this text considers the relationship between organizational memory and individual action as a double bind (Bateson, 1972): individual action and organizational practice are activated, but at the same time constrained by the artifacts of organizational memory. On the other hand, it is the action itself that builds memory. The relationship between organizational and individual memory is furthermore considered as more problematic: The theories-in-use are not considered as part of organizational memory if they are not incorporated within artifacts belonging to the apparatus of persistence.

use different evaluation forms and measurement criteria. Even if they were to write their own evaluation forms, these could not be considered organizational artifacts because they are not included in the apparatus of persistence.

Organizational Memory as a System of Weak Links: The Role of Ambiguity

The model in Figure 2 introduces the concepts of organizational artifacts and culture within a classic learning framework for adaptation, in which experience potentially leads to a revision of previous beliefs. Yet, adaptation happens with much more difficulty than the framework in Figure 2 would have us believe. As March, Schulz and Zhou (2003) point out, the link between collective memory (history), actions and action theories (*rules*) is *weakly specified*, because of three types of ambiguity:

a. **Ambiguity of implementation:** How can action theories be translated into concrete action and behavior in specific situations and unique circumstances, without sufficient information and in the presence of limited rationality and ambiguity in the formulation of rules?

b. **Ambiguity of history:** Which actions will be chosen among the many and will become part of the collective memory (history) and what meanings will be given, ex-post, to these actions?

c. **Ambiguity of adaptation:** How are the teachings of history generalized and handed down, and then transformed into instructions or even into codes of behavior, that is, into action theories?

Ambiguity results from the presence of multiple interpretations of the same fact and the impossibility to reduce this multiplicity into a single dominant interpretation, except by force or explicit consensus. The result is that the ties of influence between variables that can be seen in the model of Figure 2 are weak links that create the potential for different possible evolution of the cycle of Figure 2. For example:

a. In the culture-artifacts cycle, there can be several possible ways to "incorporate" values and cultural meanings into artifacts. For instance, it is possible to design many different evaluation forms that acknowledge the cultural values of an organization.

b. In the artifact-action cycle, there can be several ways in which the artifacts condition the action, in that they can be used in "improper" or creative ways.

For instance, a manager can use the evaluation form to reward only the collaborators s/he likes.

c. In the action-results cycle, the same outcome can be considered satisfactory or not, according to multiple factors, such as the level and type of initial expectations, the consent/dissent that it can rise, the unforeseen consequences that it produces, etc. The action will be modified one way or another according to how the ambiguous outcome is interpreted. For instance an ambiguous evaluation can trigger unexpected reactions by collaborators and a change in the evaluator behavior to prevent conflict.

d. In the result-culture cycle, a powerful group can use actual evaluation results either to reinforce or to modify organizational culture. For instance, the dominant group in the top management team can use evaluation results to reward only those people that behave conformingly to the existing culture.

Conclusion

The culture artifacts-action-outcome relationship, with its feedback cycles, is, in the end, a mechanism for the construction of pattern of action. Nevertheless, the process of the creation of meaning is fueled by the same ambiguity that it tries to reduce.[6]

The presence of ambiguity according to March and Olsen (1976) produces incomplete cycles of learning in which one or more of the links are weak. This can actually make the process of change in organizations more complex and difficult, but it is a formidable mechanism for the generation of variety.

Ambiguity generates a number of possible worlds and many possible ways to control them. It allows organizations to construct their own environment instead of reacting passively to external stimuli. And this variety, if it is not inhibited and repressed, is the main condition for the process of organizational learning. In other words, if the social group has the chance to elaborate new theories of action and to begin cycles of learning, it is due to the inevitable presence of a certain dose of ambiguity in organizational memory.

Ambiguity determines what we call *the paradox of organizational learning* that will be described in the next chapter. *The paradox states that organizational learning is produced and blocked by organizational memory.* In the next chapter, we will illustrate that in order to deal with such a paradox, organizations need to manage and exploit ambiguity by building a kind of memory that is able to balance the structuring of action and the exploration of different courses of actions.

References

Akrich, M., & Latour, B. (1992). A summary of a convenient vocabulary for the semiotics of human and nonhuman assemblies. In W. E. Bijker & J. Law (Eds.), *Shaping technology/building society.* Cambridge, MA: MIT Press.

Bateson, G. (1972). *Step to an ecology of mind.* Chandler.

Bettis, R.A., & Prahalad, C.K. (1995). The dominant logic: Retrospective and extension. *Strategic Management Journal, 16,* 5-14.

Conte, R. (2002). Scienze sociali e scienza cognitiva. *Sistemi intelligenti, 15*(1), 7-31.

Grant, R.M. (1996). Toward a knowledge-based theory of the firm. *Strategic Management Journal, 17,* 109-122.

Herriot, S.R., Levinthal, D., & March, J.G. (1975). Learning from experience in organizations. *American Economic Review, 75,* 298-302.

Latour, B. (1992). Where are the missing masses? The sociology of a few mundane artifact. In W.E. Bijker & J. Law (Eds.), *Shaping technology/building society.* Cambridge, MA: MIT Press.

Le Goff, J. (2003). *Memoria.* Torino: Einaudi Piccola Biblioteca online, www. einaudi.it

Leroi-Gourhan, A. (1964). *Le geste et la parole. La mémoire e les rythmes.* Paris: Michel.

March, J. G.. & Olsen, J. P. (1976). Organizational learning and the ambiguity of the past. In J.G. March (Eds.), (1988). *Decision and organization.* Oxford: Blackwell.

March, J. G., Schulz, M., & Zhou, X. (2000). *The dynamics of rules: Change in written organizational codes.* Palo Alto,CA: Stanford University Press.

Martin, J. (1992). *Culture in organizations: Three perpsectives.* New York: Oxford University Press.

Nelson, R.R., & Winter, S.G. (1982). *An evolutionary theory of economic change.* Cambridge, MA: The Belknap Press of Harvard University Press.

Nora, P. (1978). In J. Le Goff & R. Chartier e J. Revel (Eds.). *La nouvelle histoire* (pp. 467-472). Paris: Retz.

Schein, E. (1985). *Organizational culture and leadership.* San Francisco: Jossey Bass.

Simon, H.A. (1981). *Sciences of artificial.* Cambridge, MA: MIT Press.

Walsh, J.P., & Ungson, G.R. (1991). Organizational memory. *Academy of Management Review, 16*(1), 57-91.

Weick (1990). In A. S. Huff (Ed.). *Mapping strategic thought.* Chirchester, UK: Wiley.

Endnotes

[1]   The human group behaves in nature like a living organism; just as the animal or the plant, for which the natural products are not immediately assimilable, but require the set of bodies which prepare the elements of them, the human group assimilates its environment through a curtain of objects (tools or instruments) [...] the techniques are implicitly contained in the interplay between two environments: the external environment and the environment internal to the human group.

[2]   Our concept of artifact has much in common with the one developed in the by Latour and Callon in the field of sociology of technology. The objective of the actor network theory is the relationship between technology and society and the sociological implications of technology use and development. We are more interested in the organizational aspects of artifacts and above all their power to coordinate individual action to achieve persistence.

[3]   According to our definition, texts can be considered as a particular kind of artifact to the extent that they are used to drive action. For instance, a manual can guide an individual to use a machine properly; a road sign may tell us to do or not do something; a poem can be used as a means to convince a girl of our love for her. A text can be simply used to describe the characteristics of an artifact.

[4]   See Latour (1992) and the vocabulary provided by Akrich and Latour (1992), which illustrates several properties of artifacts.

[5]   While both artifacts and symbols may be used to evoke a set of specific meanings, there is a major difference between these two concepts. An artifact is a tool; i.e., it can be used to act, or to perform a task while a symbol cannot.

[6]   We can say with Luhmann (1995) that "*the phenomenon of meaning always appears in the form of a surplus of references to other possibilities for attempting and acting [...] On the other hand, every meaning reformulates the need for selection that is always implicit in complexity, and a certain meaning is therefore affirmed, by favoring certain possibilities of connection and making other possibilities improbable, difficult, remote or (temporarily) excluded. Meaning [...] is a selection that, if it can be said this way, submits to a justification*" (p. 148).

Chapter V

The Paradox of Learning

Wonder is the beginning of knowledge; when we stop wondering, we also stop knowing.

(Ernst H. Gombrich, Art and Illusion, 1977)

Abstract

In this chapter we show that the nature of organizational learning is intrinsically paradoxical. According to the model of organizational memory proposed in the previous chapter, organizational learning is produced, and at the same time, inhibited by existing artifacts and culture. How can organizations enhance learning, and at the same time, structure collective action in order to ensure regularity and predictability? In this chapter we argue that organizations can manage this trade-off if they allow for a certain degree of "openness" when building their collective memory and, in particular, when constructing their artifacts.

Organizational Artifacts

The moment has come to analyze the relationship between artifacts and organizational learning more in depth.

We will begin with a group of studies that lead to *activity theory* (Blackler, 1999, 2002; Engström, 1991; Vygotsky, 1978). Underlying all of these contributions is the hypothesis of an indissoluble link between knowledge and action[1], and the idea that any process of knowledge creation and accumulation originates and develops from the interaction between a human being and the environment. Since organizations are social environments, it follows that learning in organizations is strongly influenced by interaction among its members.

Due to the intrinsic chaotic and unstructured nature of such interaction, learning is influenced by tension, ambiguity, and incoherence. Contrary to approaches based on individual knowledge and skill, activity theory emphasizes the *available resources that allow learning and action.* The cultural *infrastructure* that supports learning includes the concepts, the instruments and technologies shared by members of a community, as well as their division of labor and social rules (Blackler, 1999).

Figure 1. Role of artifacts in the mediation between the individual, the group, and the activity (Adapted from Blackler, 2002)

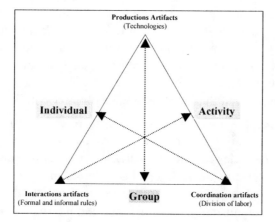

The role of artifacts in the mediation between the individual, the activity, and the group refers to:

a.   The relationship between the individual and the group through artifacts for social interaction (rules of behavior) or coordination artifacts.

b.   The relationship between the individual and the activities, through the use of production artifacts or coordination artifacts.

c.   The relationship between the activities and the group, through interaction artifacts and coordination artifacts.

The *available resources* and the cultural *infrastructure* for Blackler are what we call organizational artifacts and culture. The organizational system (Figure 1) is a system of tensions between the individual, activities, and group, which is mediated by artifacts. The resolution of these tensions and the reconfiguration of the action system require the abandonment of existing artifacts, their modification, the creation of new artifacts and new underlying cultural values.

A learning organization is able to control the tension by questioning existing artifacts, modifying them appropriately, and inventing new ones. An organization that does not renew its patrimony of artifacts does not learn. It can only survive in a stable environment that requires the organization to provide standard solutions to well-known problems.

It is here that the paradox of learning is evident. The artifacts and the culture are instruments for knowledge in that they enable action and direct knowledge. But, they are also potential obstacles to change because they restrict both the action (to one or few possible ways of carrying it out), and interpretation (through frameworks that can prevent us from looking at reality in a new way). On the other hand, an organization that has no artifacts and no culture is an organization that has difficulty in accumulating knowledge; it also maintains its own organizational identity in a highly approximate way. An organization without artifacts and without culture is a transient group and not a structured social system.

Organizational memory, which artifacts and culture are part of, creates a double bind for organizational learning (Figure 2)[2]. The past can get in the way of learning, a routine can become an inadequate response to a changing world (Nelson & Winter, 1982), and technical knowledge that is reinforced by use can create competency traps (March, 2001). On the other hand, creativity and invention cannot emerge in a vacuum. They are the products of the past, of the capacity to reinterpret and reevaluate an ambiguous and contradictory past with a critical eye, and of the capacity to accumulate knowledge, and the courage to have doubts about it.

The nature of organizational action is such that learning is intrinsically paradoxical. Learning and innovation are the natural products of systems that are able to balance opposing tendencies and allow contradictory requirements. In other words, they tolerate paradoxes and a certain level of internal incoherence. Many studies have demonstrated that excellent organizations have exactly these characteristics (see Box 1). In these organizations, incoherence and internal paradoxes are shown in the form of dilemmas such as:

a. Specialization vs. diversification
b. Continuity of leadership vs. a need for change
c. Centralization vs. decentralization of decisions

Figure 2. Paradoxes and learning

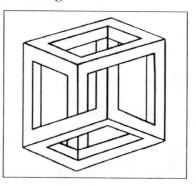

Learning, intended above all as discovery, takes place thanks to the emergence of paradoxes: Incoherent facts within a given system of knowledge. A logical leap opens new cognitive possibilities and can lead to the construction of new conceptual frameworks in which the paradox is resolved. Let us observe the ambiguity of this the three-dimensional representation on a plane constituted by the sheet of paper. Is the side of the cube internal or external? In three-dimensional space, the answer is clear; but in a two dimensional space the problem remains unsolved: both answers are possible.

d.   Attention to symbols vs. attention to their contents

e.   Preservation of organizational culture vs. the impulse toward creativity

If we look closely, organizational dilemmas are always referable to the paradox of learning, and to the more general dilemma between persistence and change.

Artifacts and Action

Artifacts are the central elements of organizational memory. They condition actions and carry explicit organizational theories. They are the means through which the processes of knowing and organizing intertwine; they are the rocks in a stream that regulate the flow of organizational action.

Taking up an observation made by Jacques Le Goff (2003), it is possible to affirm that *"the phenomena of memory, both in its biological and its psychological aspects is nothing other than the results of dynamic systems of organization, and it exists as long as the organization preserves and restores it"* (Le Goff, 2003, p. 2).

Organizing is the imposition of order upon the chaotic flow of social action. It is an attempt to reduce the disorder of a collective system through the imposition of codes of orderly and *"unnatural"* conduct. Organizing is therefore the act of giving a recognizable form to social action. When the action disappears over time, the persistence of artifacts contributes to making a memory out of the action that has effectively been carried out. An example from Eco (2000) can contribute to the clarification of this concept:

[...] in the general tendency toward disorder and therefore toward the uniformity of disposition that the winds create with the thousands of grains of sand that make up a beach, the sudden passage of a human creature that imprints its foot upon the surface of the sand represents a complex interaction of events that produces the statistically highly improbable configuration of a footprint. This configuration, that is a form, a fact of organization, will obviously tend to disappear beneath the action of the wind [...] Nevertheless, it happened within the environment of that system, precisely because of the lessening of elementary order and the onset of an order, of the relationship between cause and effect: the cause was the set of intervening facts that interacted with the grains of sand (read: human foot), and the effect is the resulting organization (read: footprint).

How can we stop the wind, and chance events, from erasing the footprint? How can we block external pressures and internal conflicts from dissolving the form of an organized social action? How can we defend it from everything that can contribute to its alteration or place it under discussion? By building a technical apparatus of persistence made up by artifacts and underlying culture.

It is clear that artifacts and organizational culture are the fundamental elements for the survival of organized action. Among artifacts, culture and organization, there is a continuous action of reinforcement. So:

a.   The purpose of artifacts and culture is to guide action theories constantly, and therefore perpetuate them.

b.   The purpose of organizing is to guarantee the continuity of organizational action.

c.   Organizing therefore means constructing artifacts and organizational culture in order to allow the organization to persist.

In other words, to guarantee its persistence, the organization endows individuals with artifacts. In simple terms, it can be said that organizations are groups of humans who are endowed with artifacts. Artifacts perpetuate the history, identity and organizational action, suggest interpretations of the facts, and remind members of an organization "how it is done."

The relationship between artifacts and individuals is complex. It is a cooperative relationship, but it is also full of tension, because artifacts are never under the

Box 1. Paradoxical organizations

Cameron and Whetten (1983), following the analysis of some of the models proposed in the literature explaining and evaluating the effectiveness of an organization (goal model, system resource model, internal process or maintenance model, strategic constituencies, legitimacy model) affirm that *"whereas each is valuable in its own right because it includes distinctions absent in the others, none has enough explanatory power to supersede other approaches"* (1983, pp. 7-8). The lack of completeness comes from the fact that such models are based on hypotheses of linearity and consistency. The models favor some aspects instead of others in an attempt to preserve their internal consistency. As a consequence, they only consider some of the variables that explain the performance of an organization.

In the past, a great number of studies identified paradoxical characteristics in the organizations that were characterized by excellent performance: (1) loose-coupling and centralized control systems; (2) hyper-specialization and de-specialization; (3) the continuity of leadership and the entry of new leaders.

Cameron (1981, 1986) illustrates some of the results obtained by research conducted in various types of organizations in order to show that they have coexisting contradictory characteristics. He cites some examples of mutually exclusive organizational characteristics, such as the coexistence of innovative actions and conservative mechanisms, the attention to symbols and substance, the defense and attack, the preservation of organizational culture and creative activities.

The probability that paradoxes will emerge is directly related to the level of complexity and turbulence in the external environment; because complex environments are characterized by a number of interactions between diverse elements (individuals, businesses, markets, institutions, etc.) it is impossible for the organization to have the available time necessary to analyze the environment and build up a coherent picture of the world. It follows that every picture hits upon just some aspects of the problem; the practical ways out for organizations are antithetical:

a.   Either reduce the complexity within a single dominant vision, suffocating other points of view.

b.   Favor the presence of more incomplete pictures.

On the one hand, in rapidly and continuously changing environments, it is highly improbable that the first option will turn out to be the winning one. On the other hand, the presence of conflicting pictures are at the origin of the emergence of organizational paradoxes.

Quinn and Cameron (1983) and Rohrbaugh (1981) have developed a model of organizational effectiveness based on the concept of paradox, the Competing Values Model, made up of opposing pairs described in terms of indicators of effectiveness classified according to two principle dimensions (centralization/decentralization and internal focus/external focus). The model is based on the assumption that the organizations must have opposing characteristics in order to reach high levels of effectiveness. Only balance and the tension between opposites allow the organization to proceed along the path to excellence.

---

complete command of individuals, and because artifacts compete with individuals for the power to direct the action. Artifacts can be classified along a continuum that shows, on the one hand, artifacts that obediently submit to the individual (supporting artifacts), and, on the other hand, artifacts that require the individual to follow his own rules of operation (governing artifacts).

Supporting artifacts are instruments that help the individual to carry out a task or to resolve a problem. Some possible examples of supporting artifacts may be the computer, memory, software, geographical maps, and texts.

Governing artifacts have the job of imposing patterns of conduct. In general, it comes in the form of rules (norms, regulations, roles, etc.). Governing artifacts reverse the relationship between producer and the product, giving the individual a complementary role with respect to the artifact.

The Abuse of Memory: Closed Artifacts

The paradox of learning lies in the double nature of the "servant" and the "master" that can be found in each artifact that presides over action. Artifacts are knowledge instruments because they allow the action to develop. At the same time, they are obstacles to change because they restrict the action to a limited number of possibilities.

The role played by "closed" artifacts is particularly problematic. A closed artifact refers directly and unequivocally to highly prescriptive action theories. Closed artifacts allow one or very few possible interpretations of the message that they are carrying. They curb the action and subordinate it to the artifact itself. Closed artifacts only allow specific uses, they are conceived in order to obtain specific objectives, they can anticipate forms of centralized control, and their access can be regulated. A traffic light, a sign prohibiting something, and a formal procedure are examples of closed artifacts.

The strict separation of executive and managerial tasks, rigid rules for the division of labor, prescriptive rules of execution and control, bureaucratic procedures, and formal job descriptions are examples of closed artifacts that an organization gives itself in the attempt to guarantee the coordination and regular development of processes and activities.

By intensifying their recourse to closed artifacts, organizations construct their identity to the detriment of individual identity *and sacrifice the subjectivity and creativity of their members in favor of persistence.* Closed artifacts are deliberately planned to limit individual interpretation and creativity, which is considered an unplanned, inconvenient variation, or as a kind of interference, a disturbance, or even a threat.

Closed artifacts exasperate an intrinsic characteristic of artifacts: They remind the individual that the know-how (how it should be done) is simply a reflection of how "*it has always been done.*" Artifacts allow users just a glimpse of the "reason why." The routine use of artifacts is the clearest expression of the division between the "how" and the "why" of action. Therefore, it should not be surprising that organizational action can easily become a tired repetition of "duties" and unconscious rites. The organization gives up learning and at best can survive idly in stable and nonproblematic environments.

We refer to this phenomenon as the *crystallization of organizational memory*. It is the outcome of a situation, in which there is a strong prevalence of positive feedback, as opposed to negative feedback, where the natural ambiguity of the world has been removed and sacrificed in favor of the stability of action.

Bureaucracies (all organizations, to some extent) are typical examples of the crystallization of memory. Bureaucracy is designed to increase efficiency, reduce arbitrariness and amplify administrative transparency. The logic of procedures dominates their intention, the "how" becomes more important than "why," action subordinates sense-building, and habits prevail over awareness. So the organization irresistibly drifts toward a situation in which bureaucracy preserves forms of action that are by now senseless and can often prevent the attainment of the goals they were designed to reach: To assure transparency and limit abuses due to arbitrariness.

The abuse[3] of organizational memory means freezing the action and its interpretation and reversing the relationship of dominance and control that individuals have over the instruments and the results of their actions. By sharing the means through which individuals pursue legitimate individual and reciprocally compatible objectives, organizations are transformed into communities of individuals who are enslaved to the collective logic of persistence. Is there a way to prevent an organization from drifting toward the natural rigidity of organizational action?

Open Artifacts and Grey Knowledge

While a closed artifact drastically reduces the individual interpretation to a pure recognition of forms and recipes for action, an open artifact requires the individual to have a highly executive and interpretative autonomy with regard to the objectives of the artifacts and their possible use.

Open artifacts generally have the following characteristics: They have many different uses (they are *multipurpose*), there is an absence of centralized control (in their use, access and level of participation), their structures are spread throughout the organization (in networks), they have a modular structure, and they contain the possibility of *upgrading*, personalization, interactivity, connectivity, universal interfacing, and mobility. Examples of open artifacts are open-source software codes, forums, web portals, computer networks, flexible software packages, open archives, digital libraries, knowledge bases, as well as communities, workshops, brainstorming sessions, multifunctional spaces, break rooms, templates for documents and presentations.

Open artifacts do not subordinate the action, even though they restrict it; instead, they solicit a contribution on the part of the user, who in the most interesting cases is both the user and the planner at the same time (just as in open-source software communities). Open artifacts induce a critical appropriation of the artifact itself on the part of the user, stimulate the interpretation and limit the risk of disunity between planning and use, reducing alienation and increasing individual involvement.

The concept of *"open works of art"* is the same proposed by Umberto Eco (2000) in his essay *The Open Work* in reference to the nondetermination of contemporary poetics. A work of art is considered to be open when the artist deliberately means to solicit interpretations of the meaning of the work itself, in that one asks the "user" (observer, reader, etc.) to contribute to the completion of the work, by making a critical and imaginative effort, but above all reelaborating the contents of the work within a vast field of interpretative possibilities. For Eco (2000), one the fundamental traits of contemporary art is the deliberate introduction of ambiguity into the work by the artist. Contemporary artists do not have answers, but questions; their works are deliberately ambiguous and incomplete and they cause the spectator to produce a critical and imaginative effort, to reelaborate the content of the work from a field of interpretative possibilities that is often quite vast.

The mind goes to a famous work by Norman Rockwell portraying a middle-class museum visitor looking at a painting by Jackson Pollock. Rockwell's painting leads us to imagine the expression of the visitor (in the painting it is not possible to see his face) when faced with the action-painting by Jackson Pollock. It is not difficult to imagine the rapt and perplexed expression that we often see on the faces of many visitors at contemporary art exhibits or museums. Is Rockwell's middle-class man searching within himself for answers, or is he waiting for the right answers to appear? Does he have the conceptual tools to analyze the work or would he prefer a guided visit?

Open artifacts do not impose a course of action but may suggest one from a field of possibilities that is not predetermined. They solicit and invite individuals to search for and build a primary meaning during and after they have been used.

Their openness requires a more sophisticated interpretative ability on the part of the user, as well as predisposition for facing indefiniteness, many possible courses of action and the ambiguity of situations. It is normal for an open artifact to generate anxiety, conflict, insecurity and confusion in the individual.

Openness can only apparently be ascribed to the objective characteristics of the artifact. Instead, it is a property of the *transaction* between subject and artifact (Dewey, 1934) and of the contingent situation in which the transaction takes place. The map of the Pyrenees used by Weick's soldiers does not seem at first to be an artifact that is characterized by a particularly high degree of openness, but the degree of openness turned out to be higher than expected in a situation where it was important above all to have *a map*—any map.

What counts is not only the structural properties of an organizational artifact, but the relationship between the artifact and its user. Knowledge itself is transactional; it is a difficult negotiation in which, after a first impression, the individual incorporates the memories of past perceptions into a current perception, and shapes the current experience in this way (Eco, 2000).

It is in the transaction between artifact and individual that the encounter between organizational memory and individual memory occurs. Meanings, beliefs, values, expectations, and theories contained in individual memory intertwine with the possibilities of action that the artifact suggests. Between the artifact and the individual there is a mute dialogue that progressively transforms the action. The indistinct knowledge that comes out of the transaction between the individual and the open artifact from now on will be called *grey knowledge*.

The name "grey" derives from the fact that such knowledge can be considered a form of intermediate knowledge between the obscurity and intangibility of tacit knowledge and the clarity and complete describability of explicit knowledge.[4] We will provide an in-depth analysis about grey knowledge in Chapter VIII. Here we will simply say that grey knowledge is characterized by a high degree of volatility, contradiction, opacity, and ambiguity. It is a metaphorical and fragmented knowledge in pieces that have not yet fused into a coherent form. It is knowledge that leaves the artifact open to many possibilities of use. It is knowledge that does not completely resolve the ambiguity of the situation the individual finds himself in. It is knowledge that asks questions and does not give solid answers. It is knowledge that is full of expectations and is open to discovery.

Conclusion

Grey knowledge disappears when the individual is incapable of discovering new uses for the artifact. This is how we should interpret Gömbrich's affirmation that *"Wonder is the beginning of knowledge, and when we cease to wonder, we cease to know"* (Gombrich, 1977, p. 21).

Grey knowledge is the knowledge that each of us can obtain when we contemplate a work of art. The form of contemplation depends on many factors, such as the first expectations, previous knowledge, degree of interest, momentary disposition, the context or the specific situation within which the transaction takes place.

It is not easy to make grey knowledge fully explicit, since it is so tightly connected to sensations and emotions. Every formal structure reduces the often chaotic richness of grey knowledge. The only sufficient, structured and plastic way to reelaborate and modify it while preserving its intrinsic ambiguity is through language.

The speeches, conversations, declarations, and dialogues that are developed in organizations are open artifacts *par excellence*. Verbal artifacts are better able to codify the complex cognitive and emotional relationship that has been established between the individual, organizational artifacts and the work situation. They become the point of departure for other verbal recodifications that could be codified in formal language. That is why verbal artifacts are the unit of analysis that we will use in the rest of the book for the analysis of the process of organizational learning.

In the next few chapters we will show how organizational memory is the result of an ongoing process of social construction in which language, and discourses in particular, play a major role.

References

Blackler, F. (1995). Knowledge, knowledge work and organizations: An overview and interpretation. *Organization Studies, 16*(6), 1021-1046.

Blackler, F. (2002). Knowledge, knowledge work and organizations. In C.W. Choo & N. Bontis (Eds.), *The strategic management of intellectual capital and organizational knowledge.* Oxford: Oxford University Press.

Cameron, K.S. (1981). Domains of organizational effectiveness in colleges and universities. *Academy of Management Journal, 24,* 25-47.

Cameron, K.S. (1986). Effectiveness as paradox. *Management Science, 32,* 539-53.

Cameron, K.S., & Quinn, R.E. (1988). Organizational paradox and transformation. In R.E. Quinn & K.S. Cameron (Eds.), *Paradox and transformation.* Cambridge, MA: Ballinger.

Cameron, K.S., & Whetten, D.A. (1983). *Organizational effectiveness.* New York: Academic Press.

Dewey, J. (1934). *Art as experience.* New York: Bolch and Company.

Eco, U. (2000). *The open work.* Cambridge, MA: Harvard University Press.

Engström, Y. (1991). Developmental work research: Reconstructing expertise through expansive learning. In M. Nurminem & G. Weir (Eds.), *Human job and computer interfaces.* Netherlands: Elsevier.

Gombrich, E.H. (1977). *Art as illusion a study in the psychology of pictorial representation* (5th ed.). London: Phaidon Press Limited.

Le Goff, J. (2003). *Memoria.* Torino: Einaudi Piccola Biblioteca online, from http://www.einaudi.it

March, J.B. (2001). The pursuit of intelligence in organizations. In K. T. Lant & Z. Shapira (Eds.), *Organizational cognition: Computation and interpretation.* Mawah, NJ: Lawrence Erlbaum Associate.

Nelson, R.R., & Winter, S.G. (1982). *An evolutionary theory of economic change.* Cambridge, MA: The Belknap Press of Harvard University Press.

Quinn, R.E., & Cameron, K.S. (1983). Organizational life cycles and shifting criteria and effectiveness. *Management Science, 9,* 33-51.

Rohrbaugh, J. (1981). Operationalizing the competing values approach. *Public Productivity Review, 5,* 141-59.

Vygotsky, L.S. (1978). *Mind in society.* Cambridge, MA: Harvard University Press.

Endnotes

[1]   The relationship between knowledge and action has been largely investigated by Piaget (1964. *Six etudes de psychologie.* Paris: Éditions Gonthier) in several studies about the cognitive development of children. Through such studies, he has demonstrated that the development of cognitive abilities in children, in particular in the early stages of life, is influenced by their ability to interact with the world.

[2]   The concept of the double bind has been proposed and largely investigated by Bateson (see Bateson, 1972). *Step to an ecology of mind.* Chandler.

[3]   The effective expression of "use and abuse of organizational memory" is quoted from Walsh & Ungson (1991). Organizational memory. *Academy of Management Review, 16*(1), 57-91.

[4]   The attribute "grey" has been introduced with reference to a similar concept developed by Sainsbury. (1995) *Paradoxes.* Cambridge: Cambridge University Press.

Section II

The Emergence of Organizational Learning

Chapter VI

The Construction of Shared World

The story goes that three umpires disagreed about the task of calling balls and strikes. The first one said "I call them as they is." The second one said "I call them as I see them." The third and cleverest umpire said, "They ain't nothin' till I call 'em."

(Simons 1976, p. 29 quoted in Weick, 1979)

Abstract

In the previous chapters we have introduced and analyzed the concept of organizational memory and examined how artifacts and culture influence organizational learning. In this chapter and the following three chapters we show that organizational memory is the product of an ongoing process of construction developed by organizational members in the course of action. This process starts from individual sense-making and develops until the organization is able to construct and maintain a shared world of meanings and a stable identity.

Memory and Organizational Identity

Organization is the attempt to achieve coordination through actions tending to guarantee persistence in time, as well as beliefs and behaviors that are deemed appropriate, functional, and coherent. The result of persistence is the stability of collective action and its recognizability. In other words, thanks to persistence, organizations can build their own identity.

Unlike machines, the systems that organizations are often compared to (and not only metaphorically), the link between the various components of an organization is loosely specified; organizations are loosely-coupled systems, in which, "*[...]both stability and adaptation are achieved with less interdependence, less consensus, less mutual responsiveness than we usually assume*" (Weick, 1979, p. 110). What is derived from the construction of organizational identity is in reality an exhaustive and uninterrupted maintenance of meaning and awareness.

A machine does not have identity problems: For the user it has a "functional" identity guaranteed by the constancy and reliability of performance. For the components of the machine, the problem of identity does not exist, because as an inanimate object it is not aware of itself and above all because the link between each unit is specified functionally, and can only be challenged by accidental external causes (Figure 1).

The stability of loosely-coupled systems is problematic, but sometimes they are more stable than it was expected to be. The reaction to an external disturbance can bring just a part, instead of the whole system, into play. The same signal can be "in-

Figure 1. Organizations and machines: The internal rack and pinion mechanism of an 18ᵗʰ century tower clock

Organizations are often compared to machines, as sets of related parts. In reality, organizations are loosely-coupled systems, systems in which, "both stability and adaptation are achieved with less interdependence, less consensus, less mutual responsiveness than we usually assume" (Weick, 1979, p. 110). Although the machine metaphor can sometimes be misleading, nevertheless it decisively conditions the way individuals perceive being in an organization.

terpreted" as an insignificant disturbance, or as a coherent message that is therefore more amplified. This ambivalence depends on how the disturbance is interpreted by the system, that is, which meanings are attributed to it.

Paradoxically, loosely-coupled systems can be so hyper-stable because they are able, within certain limits, to attenuate the "disturbances" and limit their propagation. They also can be hyper-unstable, in that they can amplify weak signals excessively, as can be seen in chaotic systems.

Organizations tend to underestimate their own potential for self-organization, elasticity, and flexibility that is typical of loosely-coupled systems. They tend toward creating prescribed mechanisms, in the vain hope of increasing the coherence of action and guaranteeing some control over its parts. The dominant movement is toward the establishment of meaning. An organization that evolves in a stable environment naturally tends toward "closure," so it becomes insensitive to external changes. It continually tries to resolve "unknown" situations by using "known" solutions.

Since they are not machines, but they act as if they were, organizations not only try to subordinate individual action to collective goals and objectives, but also try to establish systems of meaning that guide the actions of their members. The establishment of meaning is used by organizations as a lever to transform themselves from loosely-coupled systems into pseudo-machines.

The means most often used to condition meaning are organizational artifacts. A function of organizational artifacts (roles, norms, tools, organizational procedures, organizational charts, databases, etc.) is to contribute decisively to the maintenance of identity and organizational coherence, guaranteeing the persistence of collective action and its results.

Thanks to their capacity to conform individual action to their habitual and consolidated use, artifacts constitute the framework of organizational memory and contribute conclusively to the establishment of meaning.

The process of the establishment of meaning cannot be resolved simply through the imposition from above of an apparatus of rules and instruments to a group. Actually, it is a more articulated and complex process, that takes place over time, thanks to social interaction, the accumulation of experiences and shared meanings, the repetitive use of artifacts. It is a process of collective construction of knowledge that Berger and Luckmann (1966) define as "the social construction of reality."

The Stabilization of Meaning Through the Social Construction of Reality

Berger and Luckmann, in the incipit to their essay, entitled *The Social construction of reality*, affirm that "*reality is socially constructed and the sociology of knowledge must analyze the processes in which this occurs*" (Berger & Luckmann, 1966, p. 1)[1]. The reality they refer to is the daily reality of organizations: that flow of events in which the organizational actor recognizes the more or less independent existence of his or her will; a set of actions governed by the collective rites and procedures that tend to be repeated frequently and regularly.

This socially constructed reality is a collective representation, which is more or less shared, of what happens in an organization. It is a reality that is consolidated through experience and routine and it is the specific reality of the organization that created it. It is a reality that changes continuously and slowly, and evolves according to the changes that a collectivity experiences throughout its history.

The shared reality of an organization is an awareness that is unproblematic and taken for granted. It is the background upon which individuals project a meaning for their actions. It is a shared world, the common space of action in which it is possible for individuals to understand each other and interact.

The presence of a neutral and stable background allows individuals considerable advantages in terms of the reduction of anxiety and of cognitive economy. The background, as a matter of fact, guarantees stability and a point of reference. For this reason, it tends toward the stabilization of meaning, so the constructed reality cannot easily be questioned, because it has the function of clarifying and reassuring individuals.

Neutral backgrounds are often defined in terms of action protocols, which are taken for granted. When a client enters a restaurant, for example, both the client and the waiter follow a "script" (Schank, 1986). They define their expectations and wait for a confirmation of their actions from the interlocutor, according to a well-known sequence of action in the form of routine: Sitting down, looking at the menu, ordering, eating, asking for the bill, etc.[2]

The reality constructed within a sequence of expected actions is perceived as being objective. Organizational artifacts are the most effective vehicle for objectivization. An organizational chart becomes confused with the organizational structure, a role with an individual, a signature with the authority, etc. In general, artifacts are messages for action. These messages make sense if they make reference to a system of meanings and values that is shared and stable that configures a common interpretative code. Although it is a shared representation, organizational reality is continuously revised through the filter of subjectivity, through the processes of interpretation, in which the individual tries to construct a subjectively coherent world. Many interpretations of reality coexist under the umbrella of a shared representation. This, in order to be compatible with the subjective interpretations, must necessarily be ambiguous and blurred (Figure 2).

Figure 2. The ambiguity of rules in shared representations and the generation of paradoxes (Hogarth, False perspective, 1754)

The ambiguity of collective representations allows for a certain amount of overlapping and compatibility between the social reality (background) and subjective representation (foreground). This overlapping is possible as a consequence of an acceptance of the rules of the game and of the conventions at the base of the shared representation. The rules of perspective are an example of convention. But the unscrupulous or out of context use of shared representations can generate paradoxes and incongruities, such as in Hogarth's remarkable incision in which the author enjoys creating paradoxical effects through the violation of some drawing conventions.

Routines and Types: Living in a Taken-for-Granted World

Organizational memory operates actively to establish the meanings that circulate in an organization:

a. Through the commemoration and the exaltation of the founding values and principles of the tradition (values).

b. Through the imposition of models of conduct, that is through rules, roles, systems of authority ad delegation (interaction artifacts).

c. Supporting the execution of tasks according to frameworks of preestablished action (artifacts of production).

d. Facilitating the division of work (coordination artifacts).

Shared memory is reinforced through the daily actions of individuals (see Box 1).

Memory is not a passive archive, but a process of continuous maintenance and re-construction. The relationship between individual memory and collective memory is one of tight circularity and continuous support (Figure 3).

The two main mechanisms used to support memory are the proceduralization of activities and the typification of events. The procedure consolidates the present and the future within a known pathway. As in the restaurant script, the individual knows what to do at every moment, as well as what others are doing, and what will happen afterward. S/he is calmed by the fact of living in a world that s/he already knows. Typification and proceduralization are complementary concepts.

Typification means dividing variety in the world into a finite set of characteristic parts. Objects, people, phenomena, all are part of general categories characterized by well-defined properties.

Often, organizational types are defined explicitly, as in the case of a range of products, segments of the market, roles, etc. In other cases they correspond to tacit categories of interpretation, such as styles of leadership, behaviors, types of clients/bosses/col-leagues, typical places, furniture, and clothing.

The process that leads toward the production of procedures and types and to their institutionalization is traceable in any long-standing social group, as outlined by Berger and Luckmann (1966). It is the result of the establishment of habitual prac-tices after a transitory initial adjustment. The repetition of an action by an individual facilitates its description in terms of a fixed framework, applicable under the right circumstances when predicting the behavior of others.

Figure 3. The circularity and self-referencing of the processes of social construction

Contextual to the creation of an organization is the construction of a collective memory that contains values, models of conduct, instruments and procedures for the execution of tasks and the division of work. A relationship of tight circularity is established between the collective memory and the individual memory through a continuous process of reciprocal mirroring, validation and rewriting, as shown in this picture.

When an action is repetitive, human activity becomes more and more specialized and routine, which generates reciprocal typification over time. In other words, habits create the division of tasks. The tasks become the prerogative of specific individuals and are characterized by the ways and the places they are typically done, and, given enough time, typification gains the upper hand, and tasks, roles, activities and institutions become anonymous, impersonal and objective for the group that has produced them.

The price paid for a cognitive economy directed through the establishment of procedures and types is that of knowledge, which seems precise and reassuring, but is actually approximate and superficial. Knowledge, more often than one might believe, leads to errors of evaluation and prejudices (Nisbett & Ross, 1980; Tversky & Kahneman, 1977). It also creates a formidable obstacle to the processes of learning. The obvious advantage is the construction of an unproblematic world and a solid organizational and individual identity.

The entire community, through continuous collective validation, upholds its validity. This is possible as long as procedures and types make sense, and meaning is socially accepted and advantageous. In the taken-for-granted world *knowledge is a set of socially shared conventions about the world that are capable of producing patterns of conduct that are appropriate in typical situations.*

The degree of adequacy in behavior is not necessarily measured according to objective methods, but is based on *social consent.*

The fundamental advantage of the search for consent lies in providing adequate models of interpretation of reality and of social conduct to the individuals, together with the ability to predict the conduct of others. The second advantage lies in the division of work, thanks to coordination mechanisms offered by the organization.

Conclusion

The relationship individuals develop with organizational memory is two-sided. On the one hand, individuals use organizational memory as an interpretative umbrella under which they place the events of organizational life. On the other hand, they revise these events subjectively through interpretative processes that are conditioned by organizational memory and artifacts. The revising of the shared knowledge is a problematic act that is not done frequently in organizations, but it is absolutely necessary for triggering the processes of organizational learning.

As we show in the next chapter, natural language, in the form of dialogues, speeches, and written texts, is the fundamental means through which the shared representations contained in collective memory are communicated, discussed and revised.

Box 1. An example of social construction: the most photographed barn in America

The following excerpt is from the novel by Don DeLillo entitled *White Noise*. For us it represents a perfect example of social construction and the self-referencing of collective constructs.

Several days later Murray asked me about a tourist attraction known as the most photographed barn in America. We drove twenty-two miles into the country around Farmington. There were meadows and apple orchards. White fences trailed through the rolling fields. Soon the signs started appearing. THE MOST PHOTOGRAPHED BARN IN AMERICA. We counted five signs before we reached the site. There were forty cars and a tour bus in the makeshift lot. We walked along a cowpath to the slightly elevated spot set aside for viewing and photographing. All the people had cameras; some had tripods, telephoto lenses, filter kits. A man in a booth sold postcards and slides – pictures of the barn taken form the elevated spot. We stood near a grove of trees and watched the photographers. Murray maintained a prolonged silence, occasionally scrawling some notes in a little book.

"No one sees the barn" he said finally.

A long silence followed.

"Once you've seen the signs about the barn, it becomes impossible to see the barn".

He feel silent once more. People with cameras left the elevated site, replaced at once by others.

"We're not here to capture an image, we're here to maintain one. Every photograph reinforces the aura. Can you feel it, Jack? An Accumulation of nameless energies".

There was an extended silence. The man in the booth sold postcards and slides.

"Being here is a kind of spiritual surrender. We see only what the others see. The thousands who were here in the past, those who will come in the future. We've agreed to be part of a collective perception. This literally colors our vision. A religious experience in a way, like all tourism".

Another silence ensued.

"They are taking picture of taking picture" he said.

He did not speak for a while. We listened to the incessant clicking of shutter release buttons, the rustling crank of levers that advanced the film.

"What was the barn like before it was photographed?" he said. "What did it look like, how was it different from other barns? We can't answer these questions because we've read the signs, seen the people snapping the pictures. We can't get outside the aura. We're part of the aura. We're here, we're now".

He seemed immensely pleased by this.

(Don DeLillo, 1984, White Noise, Penguin Books, p. 12)

References

Berger, P.L., & Luckmann, T. (1966). *The social construction of reality: A treatise in the sociology of knowledge.* New York: Doubleday.

Galambos, R.P., Abelson, R.P., & Black, J.B. (Eds.). (n.d.). *Knowledge structure.* Hillsdale, NJ: Lawrence Erlbaum.

Johnson-Laird, P.N. (1983). *Mental models.* Cambridge, MA: Harvard University Press.

March, J.G.(1988). *Decision and organization.* Oxford: Blackwell.

Nisbett, R., & Ross, L. (1980). *Human inference: Strategies and shortcomings of social judgement.* Englewood Cliffs: Prentice Hall.

Schank, R.C., & Abelson, R.P. (1977). *Scripts, plans, goals and understanding, an inquiry into human knowledge structures.* Hillsdale, NJ: Lawrence Erlbaum.

Schank, R.C. (1986). *Explanation patterns: Understanding mechanically and creatively.* Hillsdale, NJ: Lawrence Erlbaum.

Tversky, A., & Kahneman, D. (1971). Belief in the law of small numbers. *Psychological Bullettin, 76,* 105-110.

Tversky, A., & Kahneman, D. (1973). Availability: A heuristic for judging frequency and probability. *Cognitive Psychology, 5,* 207-232.

Tversky, A., & Kahneman, D. (1974). Judgment under uncertainty. Heuristics and biases. *Science, 185,* 1124-1131.

Tversky, A., & Kahneman, D. (1978). Causal schemata in judging under uncertainty. In M. Fishbein (Ed.), *Progress in social psychology.* Hillsdale, NJ: Lawrence Erlbaum.

Endnotes

[1] With their essay, "*The social construction of reality,*" published in 1966, Berger and Luckmann founded a new line of research in the field of contemporary sociology, known as the sociology of knowledge. As the authors explain, the question, "What is reality?" is not an attempt at metaphysical philosophical investigation, but a sociological conception of reality that is found exactly halfway between the conception of the philosopher and that of the man on the street.

[2] The mechanism behind the construction of action protocols (*scripts*) may be condensed into a single rule such as: When faced with an event, maximize the internal coherence of your belief system by minimizing the cognitive effort that is necessary to frame the new event as something that is already known. The thing that is known is given by the set of structures of knowledge connecting the characteristics of the event to appropriate actions that have worked well in the past (Galambos et al., 1986; Schanck & Abelson, 1977). These structures correspond to *scripts,* or standard operational programs that are activated every time the individual finds a satisfying correspondence between the new situation and the prepackaged model in his memory. Among these preexisting structures we can also include the mental models of Johnsonn-Laird (1983). According to the supporters of the Yale school (Schanck, Abelson, Galambos, Black and

others), comprehension is a process that can be described as (Galambos et al., 1986):

- **Top-down:** Beginning with individual expectations and, searching for external confirmation, even if the reality must be distorted in order to find a correspondence between the expectation and objective reality

- **Content-specific:** There is a strong similarity between the characteristics of the cognitive schemes and those of the task involved

- **Functionally flexible:** The structures of knowledge are operative; they help us to understand, they organize memory, and guide the learning and abstraction processes

[3] The use of structures of knowledge can be extremely effective in some situations, but harmful when the framework is activated when the conditions are not ideal. The presence of frameworks explain both the mistakes and the cognitive traps into which human beings can fall (Nisbett & Ross, 1980; Tversky & Kahneman, 1973, 1974), and the phenomenon of decisional block in ambiguous situations (March, 1988). Operationally, a situation can be defined as ambiguous when the congruity of its characteristics and those of the usable mental models in that context are not high enough to trigger the application of just one of them.

Chapter VII

Constructing Explanations

I wanted to express everything. I thought, for example, that if I needed a sunset I should find the exact word for a sunset—or rather, the most surprising metaphor. Now I have come to the conclusion (and this conclusion may sound sad) that I no longer believe in expression: I believe only in allusion. After all, what are words? Words are symbols for shared memories.

Jorge Luis Borges, *This Craft of Verse*

Abstract

Organizations are systems designed to guarantee the regularity and continuity of collective actions through the standardization of patterns of action and the establishment of meaning. Artifacts direct theories of action and regulate the way in which the tasks are carried out. Organizations create stable and shared meanings through a process of social construction. But how concrete is such a process? In this chapter we will demonstrate how language, and in particular explanatory discourse, is a fundamental instrument both for the establishment of dominant systems, and for questioning and changing them.

The Role of Discourse in the Construction of Shared Meaning

In a world in which everything is taken for granted, contradictions emerge continuously and they must be dealt with.

Let's look again at the engraving by Hogarth (Figure 2, Chapter VI). Each part is coherent, and, to a hurried observer, the scene appears altogether possible. However, a closer look reveals that the interconnections between the single elements are absurd. The visible order seems to have been overturned. This violation of established order does not reassure us, and yet it seems to create the awareness that mixing up the cards may be the first step toward the emergence of a new order. Hogarth's ability lies in his use of a codified formal language in the laws of perspective to construct little absurdities.

Analogous things can be done with language. Absurdities such as "I am a liar" can be constructed. This is a phrase that everyone can understand, but if a logical analysis is done of the same proposition, it is contradictory. Because if the phrase P "I am a liar" is true, then I am really a liar. Since liars, by definition, do not tell the truth, then P is false. Vice versa, if P is false, then I would be telling the truth, and therefore I would be lying.

Obviously, when we hear the phrase, "I am a liar," we do not embark upon this sequence of logical deductions, but more simply we translate the phrase as follows: "Usually, I am a liar. This time, however, I am sincere and I am telling the truth." We do not know if this interpretation is correct, but it is enough to avoid interrupting the dialogue.

Because if its plasticity, of its ability to deal with incoherence, and prevent the interruption of action, language is considered as the most important means for the social construction of reality. Paradoxes, interpretative deformities, and logical contradictions can be resolved through the rhetorical use of language, communication, dialogue, conversations, and discourse. The intrinsic ambiguity of language on the one hand, allows for possible differences of opinion, while on the other hand, it tolerates the presence of diverse interpretations within a shared representation of reality, that is, within certain limits and by mutual consent.

In the processes of linguistic objectivation, the attribution of a verbal description to any product of human action (an idea, an action, a concept, a tool, etc.), contributes to making that product seems to ourselves and others as an object that exists independently of our own will, accessible to others as an element in a shared world. (Berger & Luckmann, 1966).

The production of artifacts provides yet another example of objectivation. Artifacts are none other than a means for making a theory of action accessible to another individual. Moreover, artifacts are objective, in that they are detached from the intention of the people who invented them when evoking their theories of action. Obviously, evoking does not mean describing. Only language can describe the theory of action associated to an artifact, with all of the nuances and implications connected to it. Each qualified member of an organization is able to describe more or less exhaustively how an artifact is made and how it is used. An organizational chart, a job description, or an assessment form are examples of easily described artifacts. When an organizational actor describes an artifact, s/he gives his own version of the facts, taking for granted that his version is shared by the other members of the organization.

Discourse connects the artifact to the action. It is possible to use discourse to explain the theory of action and the values it refers to so that they are made accessible to others. The discourse itself, particularly if it is reported in a textual form, is an artifact. Indeed, thanks to its ability to describe other artifacts, it is a meta-artifact.

Like all social artifacts, discourse is both a product and a constraint for human action. It allows an individual to construct categories in which it is possible to catalogue subjective experiences. However, the use of such categories in communication is only possible if they are shared by a social group.

At this point, we can understand what makes up the knowledge of reality on the part of a social actor and why this knowledge has such a tight rapport with language. Individual knowledge of a social reality is knowledge of the "logic" of social organizations. "*Language provides the fundamental superimposition of **logic** on the objectivated social world*" (Berger & Luckmann, 1966, p. 97). This logic is "*part of the socially available stock of knowledge an taken for granted as such*" (ibid., p. 97). It is incorporated into syntactic and semantic linguistic models, that continuously allow the individual to give form to experiences.

Obviously, the fundamental hypothesis at the base of the possibility to produce discourse is that the world of experience is a comprehensible world; a world in which the individual is able to *explain* how things work. That is why attempts to attribute meaning to our own actions and those of others can be done through linguistic explanations.

The objective of these explanations is "*to produce and consume them as reasons*" (Brandom, 2000, p. 190) in order to convince others or ourselves of the plausibility or the unacceptability of a phenomenon within the dominant social logic. This logic is formed by a set of statements that are generally regarded as true, whose validity is continuously confirmed through experience.

We like to think of explanations in terms of a special type of immune system, that preserves the cultural identity of the individual. When the world functions as expected, the relationship of the individual and the world runs as smoothly as the organs of a healthy human body. If that system is unexpectedly attacked by a virus, the immune system reacts. The unexpected event *must* be referred to the logic of the dominant cultural system. It must be made compatible with the set of propositions already known about the functioning of the world. It is here that the explanation begins: As an attempt to encapsulate the unexpected event in the same logic; as a defensive weapon of the cultural identity of the individual, his/her patrimony of knowledge and his history.

The Construction of Organizational Memory Through Explanatory Discourse

What is the connection between collective memory and discourse? The function of explanatory discourse is to contribute significantly to the system of shared meanings and shared theories of action that are part of collective memory.

Organizational memory, intended as a group of shared artifacts and values, can be seen as a background upon which the organizational members project their perceptions in order to give them a meaning. It is the "tool box" that provides interpretative structures and patterns of action. It is the *web* of admissible connections between events of the world. It is the clock that synchronizes individual behavior with the social system.

The contents of memory are traceable in the discourse with which the actors describe the theories of action. In order to guarantee its own persistence, organizations use a variety of tactics, tools, and practices for the establishment of meaning. They offer apparently stable and sometimes unquestionable worlds to their members, in order to direct conduct and coordinate individual behavior through shared meanings, theories of action, and artifacts. The taylorist organizational mechanism is an attempt to construct a strong functional identity.

Nevertheless, as soon as the real world is encountered, it produces blind spots, problematic situations, enigmas, and paradoxes. Actually, all constructed realities are problematic and ambiguous. The cognitive activity of individuals in organizational contexts is a continuous attempt to understand the meaning of one's own actions and those of others in any given situation (Daft & Weick, 1984; Weick, 1979).

The fundamental dimension of individual learning processes is the interpretation, through discourse, which reconstructs the meaning of an action. Through discourse, individuals reduce the ambiguity present in information coming from the environment and construct a representation of reality that maximizes the level of internal coherence, given certain secondary conditions: the level of ambiguity, interpretative capacity, availability of information, communicative ability, etc.

According to Weick, the information tied to events is always ambiguous. The reduction of ambiguity is done through the cycle of sense-making in three interrelated moments: *Enactment, selection,* and *retention* (Figure 1).

Individuals are not passive processors of information that exists independently from the subject. On the contrary, each subject has an active role from the very beginning of the process of interpretation. The interpretative process can be triggered by an accidental ecological change, but this change exists only if the individual reveals it as a *difference* or *variation* with respect to the given background knowledge. Just like Weick's umpire, who claimed that the balls "ain't nothin' till I call 'em" (see the quotation at the beginning of Chapter VI).

That is why the organizational actor does not *react* to the environment; instead s/he *enacts* it by isolating particular segments of the flow of experience and attributing meaning through verbal labels, linguistic categories, and heuristic rules. The output of enactment is raw data that are still ambiguous, which in later phases will flow together in the production of discourse for the creation of meanings and patterns of action. Through enactment, "*Managers construct, rearrange, single out, and demolish many 'objective' features of their surroundings. When people act, they unrandomize variables, insert vestiges of orderliness, and literally create their own constraints*" (Weick, 1979, p. 164).

The next phase of the process of sense-making is *selection*. During the process of selection, individuals actively search their memories for explanatory frameworks

Figure 1. The cycle of sense-making in organizations (Adapted from Weick, 1979)

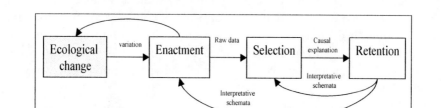

For Weick organizational reality is ambiguous and problematic. In the attempt to reduce the level of ambiguity, individuals observe the events and interpret them according to preexisting cognitive frameworks. These frameworks guide perception (enactment), impose structures on the otherwise chaotic flow of impressions, and confirm or modify sensory data to reduce the ambiguity of the information.

that help to reduce the ambiguity of the raw data produced by the enactment. These frameworks are the result of past experiences and can be explained, albeit in an approximate and ambiguous way, through the discourse of explanation. The goal of selection is to identify, from among several potential explanations, the one that most effectively minimizes the amount of ambiguity in the input by trying to transform the unknown elements into known/recognizable elements.

Finally, in the *retention* phase, the explanatory framework that turns out to be the most effective in the analyzed circumstances is archived in the memory. The entire process includes continuous feedback between the phases. The winning explanations will be those repeated most often, allowing for the creation of the *stimulus – explanation – action* routine. The winning interpretative frames will be those that will influence enactment the most in the future. These will become the cognitive background upon which the results of the rough selection of relevant events during enactment will be projected.

The fundamental character of the process of sense-making is that it is retrospective. Individuals can attempt to attribute a more complete meaning only after the action itself. In this process the *raison d'etre* of the organization is to provide stable frameworks of interpretation and action through artifacts and to construct a collective memory.

Organizations construct individual action because organizational memory conditions the actions of each person, as well as their value systems and perceptions. This conditioning poses the most serious threat to organizational learning: Hyper-stable meanings, the elimination of ambiguity, and closed artifacts crystallize the cycle of sense-making and obstruct change.

A world that is too stable does not welcome change. Learning anxiety prevails upon the need for change because in hyper-stable organizations individuals are not willing to explore other possibilities and the advantages of change.

It is rare for an organization to fail to perceive its own malaise. The metaphor of the frog in the pot of water, who does not notice the rising temperature of the water that will soon boil, is not convincing. Many times organizations pretend not to see the problem, or do not know how to define it, but they somehow sense that something is not right. It is no accident that in organizations that are having difficulty, the dominant feeling is not that of "blissful innocence" that continues without noticing the danger for the organization itself, but the presence of sometimes contrasting symptoms such as apathy and conflict, stasis or hyperactivity, concealment and open contrast.

Why risk casting doubt upon something that you know well? Why question consolidated systems of behavior and the balance of power, raising organizational conflicts? Hyper-stable organizations have this defect: They do not perfectly evaluate the cost/benefit relationship of learning, they hide or avoid conflicts, and they put off the solutions to problems.

Box 2. Sense-making and action painting

The following excerpt by Jackson Pollock is an excellent example of sense-making. In most cases, works of art are not the products of deliberate planning, but the retrospective recognition of the outcome of action. So action precedes knowledge, which is an epistemological perspective that is not very different from Piaget's (1964) in his studies on the psychological development of children. It is also similar to the presuppositions and auto-poiesis of Maturana and Varela (1980). Here is how Pollock explains his working methods:

My painting does not come from the easel. I hardly ever stretch the canvas before painting. I prefer to tack the unstretched canvas to the hard wall or the floor. I need the resistance of a hard surface. On the floor I am more at ease. I feel nearer, more part of the painting, since this way I can walk around it, work from the four sides and literally be in the painting. I continue to get further away from the usual painter's tools such as easel, palette, brushes, etc. I prefer sticks, trowels, knives and dripping fluid paint or a heavy impasto with sand, broken glass or other foreign matter added. When I am in my painting, I'm not aware of what I'm doing. It is only after a sort of 'get acquainted' period that I see what I have been about. I have no fear of making changes, destroying the image, etc., because the painting has a life of its own. I try to let it come through. It is only when I lose contact with the painting that the result is a mess. Otherwise there is pure harmony, an easy give and take, and the painting comes out well.

(Jackson Pollock, Quoted in Possibilities, winter 1947-1948)

Conclusion: Explanatory Discourse and the Emergence of Organizing

The stabilization of meaning and the maintenance of organizational identity are the result of two interdependent processes:

a. Social construction that determines shared meanings and codes of conduct through the institutionalization of practices, artifacts and values

b. Interpretative processes (sense-making) through which individuals actively elaborate events and information again, through the explanatory discourse

As a consequence, organizations present a mixture of knowledge from the composition of a large number of variables that are both codified, recognized and explained, and not formalized, localized and tacit (Boisot, 1995; Nonaka & Takeuchi, 1995). The world of dominant organizing, made up of rules, procedures, hierarchies, and the world of emerging organization, made up of behaviors, individual interpretations and discourses, are both complementary and antagonistic at the same time.

In tayloristic organizations and in bureaucracies the relationship is between action and reaction: The rigidity of the rules creates conflicts and produces contrasting actions on the part of individuals. Otherwise, the proliferation of deviant behavior exasperates the verification and conditioning (Gouldner, 1954).[1]

In post-taylorist organizations, tacit and explicit knowledge are in a tight complementary relationship, as shown in the studies and organizational models proposed by Nonaka and Takeuchi (1995).[2] According to these approaches the task of organizations is to construct favorable conditions for the production of new knowledge. The mechanisms of social interaction between members of an organization are at the base of the processes of exchange, sharing and the integration of individual knowledge. In the end, new knowledge is created only when organizations are able to create appropriate conditions for facilitating and reinforcing the mechanisms through which tacit individual knowledge is transformed into shared knowledge.

The main difference between a Taylorist organization and a post-taylorist organization lies in the fact that the first was founded upon antagonism and the conflict between tacit and explicit knowledge, while the second aspired to a productive synthesis between these two forms of knowledge.

The real question in post-taylorist organizations is not so much the problem of codifying and explaining knowledge, but in the ability of the organization to motivate people to be creative and transmit their knowledge to the organization.

A successful organization facilitates the processes involved in the transformation of knowledge from tacit to explicit and vice versa. Tacit knowledge is worth more if it is possible to avoid confining it to an individual or a group. In the same way, explicit knowledge is worth more if individuals are put in a position to make it their own through the process of internalization.[3]

Nevertheless, incentives for creativity, discretionary power, participation, and involvement are not enough for organizational learning to take place. It is necessary for the outcomes and discovery of individual initiative to become the patrimony of an organization through the modification of organizational memory, that is, through the introduction of new artifacts and new values.

In the next chapter we will conduct an in-depth analysis of explanatory discourse. We will show that it represents a very powerful tool for illuminating the black box of interpretative processes and for pointing out theories of action, the presuppositions and the values that are part of organizational memory.

References

Berger, P.L., & Luckmann, T. (1966). *The social construction of reality: A treatise in the sociology of knowledge*. New York: Doubleday.

Boisot, M. (1995). *Information space: A framework for learning in organizations, institutions, and cultures*. London: Routledge.

Borges, J.L. (2000). *This craft of verse*. Cambridge: Harvard University Press.

Brandom, R.B. (2000). A*rticulating reasons: An introduction to inferentialism*. Cambridge: Harvard University Press.

Daft, R.L., & Weick, K. (1984). Toward a model of organization as interpretation systems. *Academy of Management Review, 9*(2), 284-295.

Du Gay, P., & Salaman, G. (1992). The cult(ure) of the customers. *Journal of Management Studies, 29*, 615-633.

Focault, M. (1972). *The archeology of knowlegde*. London: Routledge.

Ford, J.D., & Ford, L.W. (1995). The role of conversations in producing intentional changes in organizations. *Academy of management Review, 20*, 541-570.

Giddens, A. (1993). *New rule of sociological method*. Stanford, CA: Stanford University Press.

Gouldner, A.W. (1954). *Patterns of industrial bureaucracy*. Glencoe, IL: Free Press.

Heracleous, L., & Barrett, M. (2001). Organizational change as discourse: Communicative actions and deep structures in the context of information technology implementation. *Academy of Management Journal, 44*(4), 755-778.

Knight, D., & Willmott, H. (1989). Power and subjectivity at work: From degradation to Subjugation in social relations. *Sociology, 23,* 535-558.

Maturana, H., & Varela, F. (1980). *Autopoiesis and cognition: The realization of living*. London: Reidl.

Nonaka, I., & Takeuchi, H. (1995). *The knowledge creating company*. Oxford: Oxford University Press.

Oswick, C., Keenoy, T., & Grant, D. (1997). Managerial discourses: Words speak louder than actions. *Journal of Applied Management Studies, 6*, 5-12.

Piaget, J. (1969). *The psychology of the child*. New York: Basic Books (originally published in French, 1966). La Psychologie de l'enfant. Paris: Universitaires Press.

Polanyi, M. (1958). *Personal knowledge: Towards a post-critical philosophy*. London: Routledge.

Polanyi, M. (1966). The logic of tacit inference, *Philosophy, 41,* 1-18.

Polanyi, M. (1967). *The tacit dimension*. New York: Doubleday.

Pondy, L.R. (1978). Leadership as a language game. In M.W. McCall Jr. & M.M. Lombardo (Eds.), *Leadership: Where else can we go?* Durham, NC: Duke University Press.

Pondy, L.R., & Mitroff, I.I. (1979). Beyond open systems models of organization. In L. Cummings & B. Staw (Eds.), *Research in organizational behavior* (pp. 3-39). Greenwich, CT: JAI Press.

Weber, M. (1991). The nature of social action. In W.C. Runciman (Ed.), *Weber: Selections in translations*. Cambridge, UK: Cambridge University Press.

Weick, K.E. (1979). *The social psychology of organization* (2nd ed.). Reading, MA: Addison Wesley.

Weick, K.E. (1977). Enactment process in organizations. In B. M. Staw & G. R. Salancik (Ed.), *New directions in organizational behaviour*. Chicago: St. Clair Press.

Wenstley, F., & Mintzberg, H. (1989). Visionary leadership and strategic management. *Strategic Management Journal, 10*, 17-32.

Endnotes

[1]   In a well-known study on the distortions inducted by an excess of verification and bureaucracy in organizations at a mining company, after observations directed to the field and analysis of data collected through interviews, Gouldner and his colleagues observed that when the use of bureaucratic rules and control were intensified, there was a corresponding rise in the level of hostility toward the superiors and a sharp fall in the level of productiveness in workers.

[2]   According to Polanyi (1958, 1966, 1967), tacit knowledge cannot be articulated. In every activity, it is possible to find two types of knowledge: *focal* knowledge, relative to the phenomenon or event that is at a certain point the object of specific attention, and *tacit* knowledge, meaning the knowledge that is used at the same time to sustain and improve focal knowledge. In other words, tacit knowledge is knowledge of the background that helps in finishing a certain job, whether it be manual or cognitive, without requiring the individual to pay conscious attention. For example, while he is reading a text, the individual concentrates on the meaning of the text and automatically applies syntactic rules.

[3]   According to Nonaka and his team, the conversion of tacit into explicit knowledge should feed a virtuous cycle that represents a continuous process of organizational learning. There are four types of conversion mechanisms:

a.   From tacit to tacit, or *socialization*

b.   From tacit to explicit, or *externalization*

c.   From explicit to explicit, or *combination*

d.   From explicit to tacit, or *internalization*

The process of *socialization* is the means through which individuals acquire new tacit knowledge through shared experiences and processes of imitation. *Externalization* is the process that allows the conversion of tacit knowledge into explicit, through various mechanisms such as the use of analogies and metaphors or formal encoding. *Internalization* is the process through which individuals appropriate explicit knowledge, as it happens, for example, through traditional training. Finally, *combination* is the process through which new explicit knowledge is generated through the combined use of a number of sources of explicit knowledge that has been acquired previously.

Chapter VIII

Constructing
Grey Knowledge

From the moment I wrote that page it became clear to me that my search for exactitude was branching out in two directions: On the one side, the reduction of secondary events to abstract patterns according to which one can carry out operations and demonstrate theorems; and on the other, the effort made by words to present the tangible aspect of things as precisely as possible.

Italo Calvino, Six Memos for the Next Millennium, 1988

Abstract

Through explanatory discourse people apply, construct and explain theories of action and attribute meaning to events and to their own actions and those of others. In this chapter we will conduct a detailed analysis of the structure of explanatory discourse and the character of its rationality. Through this analysis we will demonstrate (a) that the rationality of organizational actors is an argumentative rationality aimed at the construction of consensus and shared meanings; (b) that the knowledge contained in the explanations is both structured and opaque, (c) that this particular mix between opacity and structuring makes it possible to both accumulate past knowledge and construct new knowledge.

Maps, Finds, Oracles

Let us examine three artifacts and the relative cognitive work that the individual must carry out when he encounters them.

1. **The artifact is perfectly recognizable:** *The map.* The cognitive work consists in recovering "instructions for use" from the individual and collective memory. With a map, the individual only has to activate the theory "how to read a map" and its wealth of ideas, conventions, information, warnings, base knowledge, and "tricks right out of the book" (for example, by consulting the legend, verifying the scale and the orientation, recognizing points of reference in the landscape, etc.). Given this basic knowledge, the possible ambiguities can result from the correspondence between the model and reality (as in the story of the map of the Pyrenees in Chapter III).

2. **The artifact is not recognizable:** *The archeological find:* Cognitive work consists in starting a process of investigation by attempting to give answers to questions such as: Can the artifact be referred to a recognizable structure? How can it be used? What were the intentions of the person who created it? What meanings does it transmit? The most immediate example is that of an archeological find whose functions are not obvious, such as the Phaistos Disk (Figure 1): Was it a calendar? An abacus or more generally an "accounting" device? Was it a cult object? In cases such as these, the individual finds himself, at best, faced with a certain number of alternative explanations that are more or less plausible. He has no choice but to choose one, giving a full explanation as to why that choice is more acceptable than the others.

3. **The artifact is deliberately ambiguous:** *The oracle.* The artifact is intentionally open to a number of possible alternative interpretations. That is what happens with an oracle: An enigmatic phrase is uttered, representing the voice of God. Because there are many possible, even contradictory, interpretations for the meaning of the phrase, the questioner must choose one very carefully. The answer interpretation that Xerxes gave to the oracle of Delphi is famous: "*If you go to war you will destroy a powerful kingdom.*" Xerxes faithfully went to war. The result was the destruction of his/her kingdom.

Figure 1. The Phaistos Disk

The Phaistos Disk is an archeological find from Crete coming from the Minoan period. It is not clear what it represents and archeologists have put forward many theories explaining its function, from toy to calendar, to cult object. In the context of this book, the archeological question can be reformulated as follows: what is the theory of action that is associable to the Phaistos Disk?

What the three cases have in common is the relationship between the artifact and theories of action. Any well-known, unknown, or ambiguous artifact provokes processes of interpretation. It forces the individual to bring into play her/his own cultural patrimony into play, made up of memory, experience, and plans. The main difference lies in the fact that in the first situation, the individual applies a theory, in the second he evokes many possible theories, and in the third, s/he invents an *ad hoc* theory. It is clear that in all three cases there can be some innovation, but the probability that a creative act will result is surely more likely as we move from the second to the third case.

In particular, the logic of the oracle is to construct meaning. The idea of chance is a recent acquisition in the history of humanity. If nothing happens by chance, then everything must have meaning; things speak arcane languages that must be interpreted before taking action (Jaynes, 1984). As many scholars have recognized, the role of oracle in antiquity has strongly conditioned history, as in the case of geographical discoveries. Greek colonization had its energy source at Delphi and the messages of the prophets were interpreted in order to determine the routes and destinations of the ships.

In organizations as well, the patrimony of artifacts is made up of maps, finds, and oracles with which individuals apply, evoke, and construct mini-theories. This allows a certain logic to overlap the flow of organizational action, which would otherwise be indistinct and incoherent. Organizations inspired by the taylorist paradigm use many maps and have few finds. They carefully maintain their own apparatus of persistence with the aim of verification. They treat oracles with diffidence, or even contempt, unless they contain the rigor of strategic planning and forecasting. Organizations in transition instead make maps coexist with oracles, and they quickly fill up with finds. Because of the environmental turbulence, these organizations watch their own technologies, as well as their values, rapidly becoming obsolete. Oracles often assume the form of visions, missions, slogans, and values charts. Organizations in transition understand that maps and compasses are often useless, but they cannot free themselves from them completely.

Learning organizations revisit their own maps continuously. In other words, they are able to transform oracles into maps, and maps into finds, when they need to. For these organizations the use of grey knowledge represents a fundamental part of organizational life. Grey knowledge points out the daily reality of organizational life, the background upon which members of an organization project the meanings of their actions, the opaque world of the obvious and of taking things for granted. It also reveals new situations, which are still indistinct and fragmentary. In more concrete terms, analyzing grey knowledge means noting the system of beliefs and assumptions that are put to the test in the theories of action. It means, in other words, investigating organizational memory and building explanations in a partially enigmatic way. This is where the creative process can be seen. It is not limited to a reduction of the unknown to the known, but builds new paradigms (Kuhn, 1962), metaphors (Morgan, 1997), models of explanation (Schanck, 1977), interpretations and meanings (Daft & Weick, 1984), and resolves paradoxes (Quinn & Cameron, 1988).

Grey Knowledge

Explanations are attempts to describe both espoused theories and theories-in-use in a structured way. Through explanatory discourse individuals can, though only in a partial and incomplete way, produce the reasons underlying their own behavior, the categories of judgment, models of interpretation that have influenced the choices, the resources used to complete a task, and the role of artifacts in the action. Explanations guide the wealth of grey knowledge in a sufficiently accessible form.

The fundamental characteristic of grey knowledge is the fact that it is a form of knowledge that is on some point of the *continuum* which separates the clarity of explicit knowledge from the opacity of tacit knowledge. It is a form of knowledge that is neither completely tacit, as it is socially shared and expressed through speech, nor totally explicit because it is more or less ambiguous and imprecise. Yet, grey knowledge, precisely as an intermediate form between explicit and tacit knowledge, plays an important role in the processes of organizational learning. Speeches are an example of grey knowledge. They are open artifacts that are sufficiently structured and ambiguous at the same time. The intrinsic ambiguity of speeches force organizational actors to reformulate the information provoking multiple interpretations.

Language is a tool that increases our ability to perceive and construct reality. What we call the ambiguity of language (the inability to describe an object, a state of mind or an event in objective, in unequivocal terms) is in reality a form of *openness to the world,* underlying its outstanding plasticity. Clearly, it is anything but inability: Ambiguity is a characteristic that allows for the expressive power of a linguistic system while maintaining a *parsimony of signs* (Eco, 1997).

According to Berger and Luckmann (1966), and Maturana and Varela (1980), the word is not only a label that indicates an object, *it is the object itself.* The correspondence between the label and the object is therefore problematic and its identification is an act of knowledge inasmuch as it presides over the complex activity of the formation of concepts. We can affirm that the ambiguity of language is also its power. Words can condition individual action for the simple fact of having a relevant evocative power, as happens in many forms of artistic expression such as poetry, but also in daily and organizational life.

Words do not function according to a stimulus/response type of logic; quite the opposite, language differs from the elementary forms of communication because of the weak correspondence between verbal terminology and meaning, and the possibility of continuously reconfiguring this relationship.

In other words, the ambiguity of language is at the base of its evocative power and the evocative power of words can be, if not a mechanism of creation of knowledge in itself, a powerful triggering agent for the cognitive process. Although memory is not reducible to a linguistically indexed archive, nor language is a prerequisite for thinking (Pinker, 1994), it is still undeniable that the conscious processes of reflection, the reconstruction of past or creative events adopt mechanisms of linguistic association in which the concepts are represented through webs of dynamic meanings.

The interpretation of the organizational facts contained in speeches and the act of clarifying through convincing arguments, represent the spark that potentially starts modifying collective memory and therefore organizational learning.

The theory that is sustained here is that the analysis of explanatory discourse is fundamental to the study of the processes of organizational learning. In order to reach that objective, we must:

a.   Note and describe theories of action in use in a structured way.

b.   Utilize the output of these analyses to identify obstacles to learning and to make due allowances for the implementation of processes of *organizational change*.

c.   When possible, incorporate grey knowledge into tools and management systems characterized by principles of openness, such as in the construction of tools for the support of decisions made in specific tasks or knowledge bases.

All things considered, in a theory of organization where the differences matter (Nelson & Winter, 1982), what distinguishes a successful organization from the rest is in the distinctive vision of the world that it has been able to build through its members, and in its ability to be aware of it, analyze it, question it, and modify it, whenever necessary.

Characteristics of Grey Knowledge

When considering any human institution one realizes that it is primarily made up of words: statutes, laws, regulations, procedures, documents, speeches, memories, contracts, and job descriptions.

Here we will add that organizations are primarily made up of *explanations*. Explanations are necessary for describing not only the formal functions of an organization, but also its informal and tacit aspects, such as socially convenient or acceptable conduct/behavior, beliefs and prejudices, systems of social relationships, gossip and opinions.

It is important to observe that the ability to argue, that is, to effectively sustain the necessity and advantages of a point of view, is not only a fundamental competency of cognitive work, but also a prerequisite for innovations to move ahead in organizations through the transfer of knowledge from the individual to the organizational memory.

What are the characteristics of the knowledge contained in explanatory discourse, which is *grey knowledge*? Grey knowledge is found on some point of the continuum that separates the opacity of tacit knowledge from the transparency of explicit knowledge. We can describe grey knowledge as:

* Knowledge that is not formalized but conscious
* Knowledge that is not institutionalized, but locally shared
* Knowledge that is unstable enough to be continuously reappraised and modified, but sufficiently consolidated to be taken for granted
* Knowledge that is sufficiently far from automatic and instinctive action, but constructed through action, in particular in the process of social interaction
* Knowledge that is not unfathomable, nor objectively measurable and describable
* Knowledge that is not obscure to the person who possesses it, but characterized by intrinsic ambiguity

In the tacit\explicit *continuum,* organizations are particularly interested in procedural knowledge, the theories of "how to do" and "how to act" that are not "questioned," but simply "put into practice." It is the knowledge of the taken-for-granted world, made up of values and beliefs, as well as procedures, routines, and socially acceptable behavior which is applied almost automatically or unconsciously. The social acceptance and the seeming obviousness of these forms of knowledge are due to the fact that it is strongly shared in the social context.

The knowledge contained in speeches allows for the construction of "light" theories that are imprecise but usually simple and sufficiently flexible. Table 1 reviews some differences between tacit, grey and explicit knowledge with respect to some dimensions.

Tacit knowledge is created through learning-on-the-job. The experience is internalized at the subconscious level. Knowledge is learned and transmitted above all through practice and imitation. It is localized in individuals and it is not explicitly describable, if not through heuristic techniques of automatic learning.[1] It is usually relative to the practice of manual or artistic ability and assumes ways of thinking that are difficult to articulate or even unconscious.

On the contrary, explicit knowledge is created through an operation of formal codification. It is learned through traditional methods. It can be transmitted through the proper channels without altering its content, except when there are distortions due to the channels through which it is transmitted. It is localized on physical supports; it is completely formalized; it is inclined toward the manipulation of symbols; and its processes of reasoning are based on mechanisms of logical inference.

Grey knowledge is situated between these two opposites. It shares many aspects with tacit knowledge and explicit knowledge. It comes from experience and socializa-

Table 1. The tacit/explicit continuum

Knowledge Type Aspect	Tacit	Grey	Explicit
Creation	On the job learning through action and experience	Routines, objectivation institutionalization	Codification, formal representation
Learning	Learning by doing, imitation, internalization	Socialization, speeches	Traditional training
Transmission	Examples, action, metaphors, association of ideas	Routine, traditions, informal communication	Channels of transmission
Localization	Individual	Social group	Tangible support
Explicit description	Impossible, or to a limited degree through heuristics	Partial, through speeches and texts	Formal descriptions
Elaboration	Manual and artistic ability	Argumentation	Symbolic manipulation

tion, and produces elements that can become part of routines or codes of conduct. However, there are broken, incomplete, or temporary forms that acquire meaning in the situations where they are generated and in the specific social dynamic that sustains them. We find grey knowledge in the transcripts of telephone conversations, in recordings of meetings, in notebooks full of notes, and in sketches.

A more articulated and structured form of grey knowledge is transmitted in speeches. In particular, explanations, in which the speaker attempts to weave together facts from experience into patterns of coherent reasoning, in trying to make a meaning, an objective, or an intention clear. For each explanation, others will be added and set against it. Each one will follow its own course, and will have its own existence. It can respond to or generate conflict, it can generate new speeches, or it can coexist with other speeches, juxtaposed. Often, one of the two conflicting speeches will assume a dominant position while the other takes a subordinate position.

Persuasive speeches incorporate and help grey knowledge to circulate in an organization. The wealth of syntactic structures in a language, the broad system of connotative and denotative reference that each word and every proposition contains, the multiplicity of rhetorical figures that it is possible to create, the possibility to entertain a variety of linguistic games, all of these properties of natural language allow organizations to hold together a set of weak, controversial and secondary facts. This wealth is the most important tool that individuals have to understand the complexity of the world.

The Collective Logic of Grey Knowledge

In socially constructed reality, *"language provides the fundamental superimposition of logic on the objectivated social world. The edifice of legitimations is built upon language and uses language as its principal instrumentality. The «logic» thus attributed to the institutional order is part of the socially available stock of knowledge and taken for granted as such. Since the well-socialized individual «knows» that his/her social world is a consistent whole, he will be constrained to explain both its functioning and malfunctioning in terms of this «knowledge»"* (Berger & Luckmann, 1966, p. 64).

This excerpt reminds us of the self-referencing character of socially constructed knowledge and its ties with the individual processes of the elaboration of knowledge. Moreover, it allows us to see that the *imposition of a certain logic* to socially constructed knowledge comes through language, through explanation. Explanation represents a way of structuring that is particularly effective for organizing, transmitting and elaborating knowledge.

Organizational literature has recognized the potential of the processes of argumentation for organizational analysis for quite some time (Fletcher & Huff, 1990; Mason & Mitroff, 1983; Sillince, 2001). Argumentation is traditionally considered in rhetoric

Box 1. Explanation in the cognitive sciences

Thagard (1992) classifies explanations according to the type of approach (deductive, statistical, schematic, analogical, causal, linguistic/pragmatic) and the branch of learning in which they were done (philosophy and artificial intelligence), as illustrated in the following table.

Approach	Philosophy	Artificial Intelligence
Deductive	Hempel (1965)	Mitchell et al. (1986)
Statistical	Salmon (1970)	Pearl (1988)
Schematic	Kitcher (1981)	Schank and Abelson (1977)
Analogical	Campbell (1957)	Kolodner (1993) Schank (1986) Thagard (1989)
Causal	Salmon (1984)	Pearl (1988) Peng e Reggia (1990)

According to Hempel's nomological-deductive model, explanation is a rational process in which the premise is a general law and the explanandum follows the premise through deductive inference. According to this approach, an explanation *x because a* can be transformed into a rule, *If a then x*. Nevertheless, many philosophers and scholars have claimed that deduction is not, in general, a necessary condition, nor is it sufficient for, explanation. A weak version of the nomological approach is that of the statistical explanation. Salmon (1970) describes the explanation of an event as a description of the factors that are statistically relevant to the occurrence itself. For example, the statistical incidence of smoking on the possibility of contracting lung cancer gives an explanation of the link between smoking and illness without being able to predict whether a given smoker will die of cancer, which should result when applying a process of pure deduction.

Followers of the schematic approach affirm that comprehension is mediated by structures of knowledge (schemata, scripts, etc.). For Schank and Abelson (1977) explaining a new event means applying an appropriate pattern in order to respond adequately, and, at a more sophisticated level (creative explanation) create a new pattern.

In the analogical approach, the explanation is the outcome of the application of similarities between known and new events (A is to B as C is to D) to understand the characteristics of the new event. Indeed, every familiar event is associated to an explanation that can be activated to explain an entire class of analogous events. In artificial intelligence, this approach led to systems of Case-based Reasoning (Kolodner, 1993).

In causal theories of explanation, explaining means putting events into a causal representation of the world (Salmon, 1984) by identifying and building causal relationships among events. The question of what might be a cause and how people perceive relationships of causality is an argument around which an enormous debate has developed, both at the philosophical level and at the psychological-cognitive level. Limiting ourselves to this field, there are two fundamental approaches in the literature: a) Kelley's covariation (1967), who asserts that the basic mechanism through which people detect cause-effect relationships is to observe phenomena that vary simultaneously; and b) the approach based on the causal mechanism (Ahn and Bailenson, 1996), in which a fundamental role is played by the background knowledge and by the capacity to build mental maps of plausible causal mechanisms, whose existence often pushes us to use the observation of facts as a confirmation of our prejudgments.

For Thagard (1989, 1992) explanation is an abduction (Peirce, 1935-1966) through which individuals build hypotheses to explain new phenomena (see Box 1, Chapter II).

as the heart of persuasive discourse through which the orator tries to convince an individual or an audience of his/her own opinions. It is therefore a particular type of explanation that has the persuasion of others as its direct objective rather than individual comprehension of a phenomenon. The social dimension of argumentation is therefore clear.

The conviction of others must necessarily be based on plausible arguments, in an atmosphere of shared rationality. The speaker must know the characteristics of this rationality and must make good use of rhetorical and linguistic expedients to increase the effectiveness of his/her reasoning. In the attempt to make his/her ideas convincing, the speaker wisely unveils the rationality of his/her reasoning, which means the set of hypotheses and mechanisms of reasoning the assumption of which will bring the listener to the same conclusion.

This attempt to convince others is what makes explanatory speeches extremely interesting for the study of organizational learning. As a matter of fact, the reconstruction of the rationality of organizational actors through discourse analysis is an attempt to detect *structures of knowledge* that are hidden behind the artifact and the values that constitute organizational memory, particularly in the form of theories of action. The analysis of such structures is the place to start when analyzing collective memory and for planning actions of organizational change.

The Ambiguity of Explanations

One of the strengths of language that makes it extremely flexible lies in the weak and ambiguous correlation between its sign system and meanings, and in the capacity of language to operate recursively. These two characteristics allow for the generation of a communicative repertoire that is practically unlimited. Natural language allows the individual to take contradictory events into consideration, to resolve paradoxes and to generate many possible explanations.

For researchers, the analysis of explanations contained in speech can be a tool for highlighting the interpretative categories used by the organizational actors and for identifying the hidden rationality of the organization. Indeed, if the dialectical and/or political conflict is a constant aspect of organizational life, more than one explanation of the same phenomenon coexists at every moment and at times they may be contradictory. Moreover, the explanations are not stable.

The reconstruction of meaning always comes after the fact, and therefore the discourse is modified while the action is being carried out. In addition, it is modified on the basis of the temporal distance from the events to be explained, the expectations, and the level of attention (March, 1988). That is how, for example, the failure in launching a new product can be interpreted as the result of an erroneous launch strategy, or of an unsatisfactory analysis of the buying habits of the target consumer, or of errors in the operational phase of the launch, or of changed external conditions (market, economic trends, technology, etc.)

The flexibility and ambiguity of the language can be used to accommodate conflicting explanations, such as when trying to reconcile apparently contrasting explanations, whose synthesis favors a more complete comprehension of the problem, or for pure and simple contractual objectives.

Precisely because of the flexibility of language, the analysis of speech can contribute to the discovery of grey knowledge that it is not detectable through the analysis of codified knowledge.

In a study on the cognitive categories activated by managers in personnel evaluation, remarkable discrepancies have emerged between formal evaluation protocols and interpretative content in explanatory speech (Capaldo & Zollo, 2001). It turns out that evaluations are the result of situated knowledge, made up of mental prototypes relative to standard candidates, and activated in specific work situations. Although the evaluators use central and recurrent evaluative categories, they evaluate with respect to subjective points of view, contingent factors, emergent characteristics, weak signals, incoherent behavior (*weak facts*), described thanks to the flexibility and the wealth of natural language.

The analysis of evaluation activities underlines the unstructured and nonsystematic nature of activities of sense-making by individuals. This process, nevertheless, requires a certain level of codification and systematization at the organizational level. A process of codification that is too rigid would implicate a lack of flexibility in the evaluation in terms of ability to interpret ambiguous data. The verbal explanation is the means that has all of the characteristics for managing the double bind of adequacy to the situation and of formalization.

Actually, all processes of sense-making promoted by individuals in organizations have a structured base and are adaptive at the same time. Attempts to encapsulate them into formal procedures and schedules risk not capturing the essential characteristics of the process. Formalization entails a filter, which cuts through an important amount of information by eliminating the interference caused by the ambiguity and the natural fragmentary nature of the process.

Meaning and Consensus: Organizational Rhetoric

We will now assume *explanatory speech* as our unit of analysis for the study of organizational memory (from this point forward referred to simply as speech). More precisely, *we define speech as any verbal declaration, expressed in written or oral form, which has the objective of explaining a judgment or an intention.*

For example, with judgment, we are referring to an expression such as: "*The market share has dropped considerably during the past year*"; and with argumentative speech, we mean a series of affirmations like "... *the decrease of the market share is mainly due to insufficient marketing ... In spite of the quality and the originality of the product, sales have dropped because of an erroneous promotional campaign that did not adequately identify its target ...*"

Speeches like this contain rules of reasoning (if x then y), hypotheses and assumption that are often implicit (enthymemes), opinions and evaluations ("*In spite of the quality and originality of the product*"), and facts ("*the market share has dropped considerably during the past year*").

What makes argumentative speech particularly interesting is its characteristic, highlighted by the first Greek rhetors, Anaximander, and Gorgias, of being similar to logical reasoning.

However, this takes advantage of the ambiguity and the flexibility of natural language in order to bend the rigidity of logic to the objectives of the rhetor, using the strength of conviction of rational argumentation, the evocative power of words, and the system of meanings and socially constructed conventions, which are behind them.[2]

Toulmin (1959) maintains that the argumentation is a kind of working logic that people use when they want to persuade others to accept their own convictions. The rules of argumentation, however, are closer to those used by rhetors and lawyers than to those used in formal logic. Indeed, as Perelman and Olbrechts-Tyteca (1966) claim, it is within the nature of argumentation and deliberation to oppose necessity and what is obvious, since no one deliberates when a solution is necessarily determined or questions what is obvious. The realm of argumentation is the credible, the plausible and the probable inasmuch as the latter does not require calculation.

In Table 2 the differences between argumentation and logical demonstration are highlighted.

Words and phrases constitute the raw material of argumentation. The ambiguity of the relationship between the sign and the meaning in natural language and the evocative power of words are weapons at the disposition of the orator for making his/her hypothesis more convincing. The premises of argumentative discourse are often tacit, both because they are obvious or unquestionable in the social context in which the argumentation was created, and because they are purposely omitted, especially when their truthfulness is not taken for granted or can be questioned. They are also unconsciously activated by the orator, in that they correspond to assumptions belonging to his/her background knowledge.

Argumentative techniques are the set of tools and rhetorical artifices that the orator has at his/her disposition or can use in order to support the argumentation.[3] The

Table 2. Argumentation and demonstration

	Argumentation	Logical demonstration
Elaborated objects	Words (ambiguity between sign and meaning)	Sign systems and unambiguous notations
Premises	Partially explicit, tacit (enthymemes), ambiguous, inferred by abduction	Explicit and elaborated through formal inference mechanisms (deduction, induction, syllogisms)
Techniques	Argumentative techniques (Perelman & Olbrecths-Tyteca, 1966): • Quasi-logical arguments • Arguments based on the structure of the real • Arguments intended to establish the structure of the real	Techniques of inference: • Modus ponens • Modus tollens • Syllogism
Knowledge base	Belief systems, social conventions, opinions and data	Axiom, theorems, and data
Measured validity with respect to	Strength Verisimilitude Plausibility	Internal consistency (non contradiction)

argumentation is spurred by the knowledge placed upon a shared and socially constructed *knowledge base*. Its effectiveness cannot be measured by objective criteria of noncontradiction, but in terms of persuasive strength and compatibility between the related facts in the speech (Thagard, 1992).

Conclusion:
Explanation and Organizational Learning

It is interesting to note how argumentation is configured not as logical, but as *plausible* discourse that is expressed through quasi-logical means, and the logical discourse can be considered, in some ways, as a particular case of argumentation. Argumentative discourse has a particularly interesting set of characteristics for the analysis of the rationality of organizational actors:

a. It has recognizable structure inasmuch as it is possible to identify the premises, the reasoning flow through arguments chain, and the conclusions

b. Such a structure aims at reaching plausibility

c. It is triggered on a system of beliefs and values that are shared by the audience and the orator

d.   The coherence of the argumentation depends not only of the correct application of argumentation techniques, but also on the ambiguity of the relationship
between sign and meaning

Thanks to such characteristics, explanatory discourse constitutes an essential tool
for triggering processes of learning at the individual level. Explanations are given an
internal logical structure that guides comprehension, but they also have an intrinsic
flexibility due to the ambiguity of language that allows us to avoid being trapped
in patterns that are too rigid.

But how important is explanatory discourse at the organizational level? We will
answer this question in the next chapter where the role of discourse in the processes
of collective learning will be analyzed through the presentation of the MEP model
(memory-experience-project).

The MEP model allows for the description of the collective learning process and the
role that the various elements analyzed have within it: collective action, memory,
paradoxes, social constructions, language and explanatory discourse.

References

Ahn, W.K., & Bailenson, J. (1996). Causal attribution as a search for underlying
mechanism: An explanation of the conjunction fallacy and the discounting
principle. *Cognitive Psychology, 31*, 82-123.

Berger, P.L., & Luckmann, T. (1966). *The social construction of reality: A treatise
in the sociology of knowledge*. New York: Doubleday.

Calvino, I. (1988). *Six memos for the next millenium*. New York: Vintage Books.

Campbell, N. (1957). *Foundations of science*. Collected papers of Charles Sanders
Peirce. New York: Dover.

Capaldo, G., & Zollo, G. (2001). Applying fuzzy logic to personnel assessment: A
case study. *Omega, 29*, 585-597.

Daft, R.L., & Weick, K. (1984). Toward a model of organization as interpretation
systems. *Academy of Management Review, 9*(2), 284-295.

Eco, U. (1997). *Kant e l'ornitorinco*. Milano: Bompiani.

Fletcher, K.E., & Huff, A.S. (1990). Argument mapping. In A. S. Huff (Ed.), *Mapping strategic thought*. Chirchester, UK: Wiley.

Hempel, C. (1965). *Aspects of scientific explanation*. New York: Free Press.

Jaynes, J. (1976). *The origin of consciousness in the breakdown of the bicameral mind.* New York: Houghton Mifflin Company

Kelley, H.H. (1967). Attribution theory in social psychology. In D. Levine (Ed.), *Nebraska symposium on motivation.* Lincoln: University of Nebraska Press.

Kitcher, P (1981). Explanatory unification. *Philosophy of Science, 48,* 507-531.

Kolodner, J. (1993). *Case-based reasoning.* San Mateo, CA: Morgan Kaufman.

Kosko, B.(1997). *Fuzzy engineering.* Englewood Cliffs: Prentice Hall.

Kuhn, T.S. (1962). *The structure of scientific revolutions.* Chicago: The University of Chicago Press.

March, J.G.(1988). *Decision and organization.* Oxford: Blackwell.

Masoff, R.O., & Mitroff, I.L. (1983). A teleological power-oriented theory of strategy. In R. Lamb (Ed.), *Advances in strategic management* (Vol. 2, pp. 31-41). Grenwich: JAY Press.

Maturana, H., &Varela, F. (1980). *Autopoiesis and cognition: The realization of living.* London: Reidl.

Mitchell, T., Keller, R., & Kedar-Cabelli, S. (1986). Explanation-based generalization: A unifying view. *Machine Learning, 1,* 47-70.

Morgan, G (1997). *Images of organizations* (2nd ed.). Thousands Oaks, CA: Sage.

Nelson, R.R., & Winter, S.G. (1982). *An evolutionary theory of economic change.* Cambridge, MA: The Belknap Press, Harvard University Press.

Pearl, J. (1988). *Probabilistic reasoning in intelligent systems.* San Mateo, CA: Morgan Kaufman.

Peirce, C.S. (1935-1966). Collected papers of Charles Sanders Peirce, C. Hartschorne, Paul Weiss & A. W. Burks (Eds.). Cambridge, MA: Harvard University Press.

Peng, Y., & Reggia, J. (1990). *Abductive inference models for diagnostic problem solving.* New York: Springer-Verlag.

Perelman, C., & Olbrechts-Tyteca, L. (1969). *The new rhetoric: A treatise on argumentation.* Notre Dame, IN: University of Notre Dame Press.

Pinker, S. (1994). *The language instinct.* William Morrow and Company.

Cameron, K.S., & Quinn, R.E. (1988). Organizational paradox and transformation. In R.E. Quinn & K.S. Cameron (Eds.), *Paradox and transformation.* Cambridge, MA: Ballinger.

Salmon, W. (1970). Statistical explanation. In R. Colodny (Ed.), *The nature and the function of scientific theories* (pp. 173-231). Pittsburgh: Pittsburgh University Press.

Salmon, W. (1984). *Scientific explanation and causal structure of the world.* Princeton: Princeton University Press.

Schank, R.C., & Abelson, R.P. (1977). *Scripts, plans, goals and understanding, an inquiry into human knowledge structures.* Hillsdale, NJ: Lawrence Erlbaum.

Schank, R.C. (1986). *Explanation patterns: Understanding mechanically and creatively.* Hillsdale, NJ: Lawrence Erlbaum.

Sillince, A. (2001). A model of strength and appropriateness of argumentation in organizations. *Journal of Management studies, 39*(5), 585-618.

Thagard, P. (1989). Explanatory coherence. *Behavioral and Brain Science, 12,* 435-467.

Thagard, P. (1992). *Conceptual revolution.* Princeton: Princeton University Press.

Toulmin, S.E. (1959). *The uses of arguments.* Cambridge, MA: Cambridge University Press.

Endnotes

[1]   Kosko (1997) proposes an algorithm, based on the joint use of neural networks and fuzzy logic, which allows a computer to drive a truck that is in reverse. Algorithms are "intelligent" in the sense that they gather data, in this case a set of trajectory examples done by human drivers. Indeed, algorithms approximate a mathematical function describing the input/output relationship and translating the guidelines. This function can be considered as a description of the rules for driving a truck in reverse.

[2]   It is precisely this characteristic that causes Plato's hate for the Sophists. For Plato, rhetoric is an art, and, like all arts, it can only represent the appearance of truth and not absolute truth. Rhetoric is therefore a mystification of logic, like painting, representing the appearance of an object, and not of the "idea" of itself, is a mystification of reality. Hence, Plato's invective against the Sophists, in particular in the *Gorgia*.

[3]   Among these, proposing the classification of Perelman and Olbrechts-Tyteca (1966) we remember the quasi-logical arguments, the arguments based on the structure of the real and the arguments aiming at establishing the structure of the real.

Chapter IX

The Emergence of Organizational Learning

The perceived object [...], in the present case, a wooden jigsaw puzzle—is not a sum of elements to be distinguished from each other and analyzed discreetly, but a pattern, that is to say a form, a structure: The element's existence does not proceed the existence of the whole, it comes neither before or after it, for the parts do not determine the pattern, but the pattern determines the parts:

Knowledge of the pattern and of its laws, of the set and its structure, could not possibly be derived from discrete knowledge of the elements that compose it. That means that you can look at a piece of a puzzle for three whole days, you can believe that you know all there is to know about its colouring and shape, and be no further on than when you started. The only thing that counts is the ability to link this piece to other pieces [...] The pieces are readable, take on a sense, only when assembled; in isolation, a puzzle piece means nothing.

Georges Perec, *Life: A User's Manual*

Abstract

In this chapter we present a model of organizational learning that ties together the conceptual elements described in Chapters II, III, IV and V with the process of organizational memory construction analyzed throughout Chapters VI, VII and VIII. This chapter also concludes the theoretical part of the book. In the MEP (memory – experience – plan) model organizational learning emerges from three basic coordinates: the coordinate of past knowledge (memory), the coordinate of current interaction (experience), the coordinate of intention and anticipation (plan). In this three-dimensional space, learning emerges out of actions and explanations. Organizational learning emerges from the bottom through the construction of a new explanation and its incorporation into organizational memory.

The Starting Point: Explanatory Discourse

In the preceding chapters we have seen that organizational members, during sense-making activities, select and interpret the various cues coming from the outside world and make evaluations and decisions through action. Sense-making is strongly influenced by shared memory and artifacts that individuals use in their daily activities.

Sense-making activities implicate the activation of a continuous process of selection and modify the interpretative framework in order to lead the variations and anomalies noted during the enactment phase back to known cognitive patterns.

The successful patterns, those that most often survive the selection process, tend to be memorized as models of explanation and applied repetitively by individuals in attempting to interpret ambiguous situations. The explanation the individual creates tends to refer back to something known.

According to Schank (1986, p. 227), *"An explanation is considered in the common sense as a set of words that a person can say to another in order to make understandable what is not."* Explanations, moreover, tend to be carried out according to cognitive processes established by "standard" phases:

1.   Identify the anomaly
2.   Establish the objectives of the explanation and the relevant questions that must be answered
3.   Identify a coherent explanation[1] from among the known explanations referred to by the questions

4.   Evaluate its appropriateness; change the pattern, when appropriate, if the explanation is insufficient

It is fairly easy to check the correspondence between this sequence and that of the enactment, selection and retention cycle in Weick's sense-making processes (1979, see Chapter VI). The entire process takes place through natural language, both when the explanation is made in order to convince other people, and when it is used to "convince oneself."

What interests us here is the time period during which the sense-making process is carried out within an organization. In this case, the system of individual beliefs, for the most part, is a product of the social reality and therefore partially overlapped by a collective belief system made up of shared typification (cultural conditioning, values, rules and codes of conduct, prejudices, etc.) belonging to organizational memory. At the individual level, the repeated application of strongly shared explanation can be considered as an evidence of the existence of a collective memory.[2]

In the following section, you will find a model of how individuals develop the construction of meaning in work situations and elaborate the consequent explanatory discourse. The model is called MEP: memory – experience – plan.[3]

Figure 1. The MEP model: Memory – experience – plan

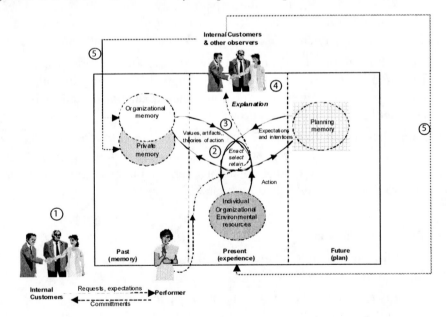

The MEP Model

The MEP model describes both the attribution of meaning to events, and the formation of consensus, which is the construction of a shared interpretation of the same event. This process is centered on the action that ties the individual to the situation. This action has a complex relationship with time. The present is not a fleeting instant; it lasts as long as the action. In this "continuous present" the situation appears in the consciousness of the individual as a space for action, in which the actor can have access to a collection of resources. This is a problematic collection that is open to interpretation. Even the past, as well as the future, become the present in situations with memory and expectations. In the concentrated space and time of the situation, the individual constructs the world through action. At the same time, they make sense of the world for themselves and for the community. The most surprising thing is that the unexpected, emergent result of the entire process is organizational learning. The process comes about in five steps:

- **Step 1. Enter the work situation:** The first step of the process is the social construction of the plan. The intentions that move the action are not previously given, but are built socially through processes of communication and negotiation. The definition of reciprocal responsibilities and obligations is partly implicit, and partly explicit. From the point of view of the individual (who will be called the "actor" from this point on) organizational life is a set of situations that one enters, like the rooms of an apartment, to carry out a series of actions. Different rooms can be traversed during the same day, just as they can be during an entire career. One can cross the same room at different periods of time while remaining more or less in the same place. The important thing is that the actor, before entering into a situation, will have assumed tacit or explicit responsibility with a fairly wide range of internal customers (bosses, colleagues, clients, subordinates), to whom one will be called upon to answer. These responsibilities do not necessarily form a coherent and explicit whole. This set of responsibilities define the future coordinate in the temporal structure within which the cognitive worker is placed.

- **Step 2. Build facts by activating resources:** In work situations, the actor uses some typologies of resources: Personal, organizational, and environmental. His/her problem is to recognize and use these resources appropriately in order to build actions and get results for his/her customers. Organizational memory provides the actor with values, artifacts, and theories of action. Individual memory provides additional resources for integration, correction and modification of the organizational memory. By putting together the available resources with the shared and private interpretative categories, the actor makes sense of a continuous back and forth of events that need to be interpreted.

- **Step 3. Leave the situation while building an explanation of the results:** When the actor has produced a sufficient number of facts that can be interpreted as results, then s/he leaves the situation using explanatory discourse. S/he will try to illustrate to what degree the results produced are coherent with the customer's expectations, how they were reached through the use of the available resources, and within which constraints and conditions it was conducted. If the customers were coherent and unambiguous, if the available resources were perfectly accessible and coherent with the expected outcome, if the organizational memory was highly prescriptive, then the actor should have had no problems producing the action (by following a kind of "algorithm") or explaining the final outcome (by explaining the algorithm s/he used). The explanation becomes more complex if the customers are not coherent amongst themselves, if the values and theories of action in the organizational memory are inadequate, or if the resources are opaque and not perfectly accessible. In this case not only does the production of the action become more complex, but the explanation becomes more difficult to build. In order to explain the results obtained, the actor must not only call upon the constructs of the organizational memory, but also his/her own personal convictions, point of view, reference criteria, way of acting, previous experience and s/he will have to justify his/her courses of action and his/her use of resources and artifacts that are not yet present in organizational memory.

- **Step 4. Explain the reasons for the outcome:** Customers are privileged observers that have an interest in both the outcome and the "how" and "why" it was produced. Customers and observers also produce their own evaluations on the basis of the evaluations received and their own direct and indirect experience of what has happened in the situation. In the hypothesis, in which the final facts are perfectly coherent with the expectations, the customers will not need to ask for evaluations, because what happened is obvious. The case of unexpected results, where "unexpected" means unexplainable through the only interpretative categories offered by the organizational memory is by far more interesting. In that case, the performer can construct a more articulate explanation, perhaps "inventing" new interpretative categories and new ways of doing things through the construction of new theories of action. The new explanation will begin its journey in the organization.

- **Step 5. Create new resources:** If the theories of action described in the new explanation are accepted by the other members and incorporated somehow into organizational artifacts, a tangible change will be produced in organizational memory. The creation of new artifacts and/or of new shared value are the outcomes of organizational learning. Without this transition, organizations do not incorporate the innovations introduced by their members, which remain confined to the informal, tacit level, or are spread to just some parts of the organizational system. When the theories of action contained in a new explanation are incorporated in artifacts or "encoded" into new values, new resources are created for the organization. Fundamentally, when organizational memory is modified, what is updated is a new way to interpret events and utilize resources. At the end of the cycle, organizational learning will come about if the production and diffusion of pertinent evaluations produced by individual actors is successful. It will be incorporated into new artifacts and therefore will have increased the patrimony of resources that are available to the organization.

The MEP Model in Action: A Case Study

The Company and the Problem

In this paragraph we will illustrate one application of the MEP model in an action research experience in an Italian public services company.[4]

ACI (Automobile Club d'Italia) is an Italian public nonprofit organization whose main institutional aims are to provide services to motorists and to safeguard their interests. It is, by far, the largest and most important Italian organization for motorist assistance, with more than 2,200 employees and 100 offices located in each major Italian town all over the whole national territory. Among ACI services, there are road assistance services, road educational programs, information, and assistance to Italian and foreign motorists through media such as magazines, radio, the World Wide Web and television. A relevant part of ACI activities concerns the management of the Italian Public Register of Motor Vehicles (PRA). PRA offices are in charge of providing all administrative and bureaucratic services related to motor vehicles (taxes payment, changes of property, demolition, etc.).

In the last few years, the social and economical context in which ACI operates has undergone a major transformation characterized by the passage from a monopolistic into a competitive market in which customers may choose among a wide range of services from different operators. Moreover, a deep reorganization in the PRA organization took place in the last few years through process reengineering because of the increasing automation of several administrative tasks.

As a consequence of such deep changes, ACI is transforming from a hierarchical organization strongly focused on the accomplishment of administrative tasks and rigid procedures into a modern, flexible service provider in which each employee is required to know the whole job process and to pay attention to internal/external customers needs.

To cope with such transformation, ACI top management undertook a project of a deep renovation of its current human resources (HR) management practices. Despite large investments in training, the HR director was not completely satisfied with the results produced by such actions, perceived by managers and employees as "imposed" from the top, and designed without the availability of reliable information related to training needs and critical competencies to be developed.

In order to cope with such issues, the HR director decided to develop a new and more effective personnel management system, based on an updated and more detailed picture of the jobs performed by several professional roles in ACI's offices. The aim of the new personnel management system was to contribute to support the strategic changes above outlined through the development and redesign of these roles toward quality, customer satisfaction, market competitiveness. Consequently, from the very beginning the new management system was targeted to meet organizational development needs. It was thus decided to develop a competencies management system in order to:

a. Develop a *map of the competencies* currently held by the organization and by a number of areas characterized by a high interaction with customers

b. *Develop a competencies management system of nonexecutive staff,* which would facilitate the identification of the training needs of a large share of the company's employees through an analysis of their points of strength and weakness

c. *Developing managerial tools and procedures* which would constantly and dynamically support HR management in identifying competencies and evaluating training needs

d. Achieving *better co-ordination* between HR management department and the peripheral offices scattered all over Italy

The MEP Approach to Building a Human Resources Management System

In order to reach the objectives outlined above, a research group, in which the authors took part, carried out a field study guided by the logic of the MEP model. The underlying assumptions were as follows:

a. Explicit knowledge is contained in the espoused theory and is incorporated into artifacts and values belonging to the organizational memory.

b.   Organizations know more than they think they do. There are often latent, tacit or emerging competencies. These competencies unfold in theories of action in use belonging to the private memory of the individuals.

c.   The use of dictionaries and standard competency profiles does not allow us to capture the specific and situational characteristics of competencies, especially in organizations experiencing major changes. In the language of this text we can affirm that these dictionaries, often used by consultants, are an extraneous element to the memory of the organization and its members.

d.   Given the enormous impact that a new personnel management system can have on the work life of the individual, it is preferable that it be constructed with a strong involvement of the people at all levels of the organizational chart. This should be continually developed with the existing system and through the search from consensus.

ACI was an organization in deep transformation, where it was possible to observe or prompt the process of organizational learning. It was the perfect natural laboratory for seeing the MEP model in action. Our objective was to analyze the memory of the organization to identify the declared competencies and describe the theories in use in order to map the tacit or emerging competencies.

In our approach (Capaldo et al., 2006), competence is an individual ability or characteristic that is activated by a worker together with personal, organizational or environmental resources to cope successfully with specific work situations. Individual abilities and characteristics are personal attributes such as skills, know-how, traits. Resources are the means for action such as tools, facilities, relationships with other people, archives, knowledge repositories etc., that are made available by the individual, the organization or the external environment as a whole. Job situations are perceived by individuals as prototypical spaces of action characterized by a certain combination of expected behaviors and results.

Competencies come about in two ways. First, when the performance of an expected behavior is considered by an internal or external client to be above average (expected competence), and second, when surprising or unexpected results are obtained in the course of action (emerging competence).

In other words the competency does not only coincide with the acquired knowledge, the capacity to solve problems, or the personal characteristics of an individual, but represents a complex concept that revolves around some fundamental dimensions.

Consider the example shown in Figure 2, where the MEP model can be seen in action. The work situation can be described as *"customer asking for a certificate."* Suppose that it is not a standard request. The main expectation the client has in such situations is that s/he be provided with a quick and accurate response.

The front-office employee tries to satisfy the request either implicitly or explicitly within the given time limit and in such a way that the certificate will satisfy the legal requirements. Since it is a nonstandard request, our performer must begin doing some research in order to find the necessary information. Their sources are the organizational memory (e.g., the procedures and the company's information systems, etc.), private memory (e.g., personal contacts, background, etc.) the resources available to the organization (e.g., documents, colleagues with more experience, etc.). When the research phase is finished either the performer will produce the requested output, or not. In both cases an explanation must be provided to the client or the manager.

In both cases, the explanation will contain an articulate report of an experience and a detailed report of why the request was (or was not) satisfied. The set of the performer's characteristics that allowed him/her to obtain the results are competencies; among these, we find the ability to search for information, knowledge of the pertinent legislation, the ability to listen to the client, and so on.

If the competencies emerge from the way that individuals manage critical or unusual work situations, then the identification and the analysis of the competencies in an organization must also: (a) begin with the daily work and activities that the individual effectively carries out; (b) involve the protagonists in any given work situation: clients, colleagues, managers, and obviously, the performer.

How can we identify the dimensions of the competencies? According to the MEP model we must analyze the explanatory discourses that the performer and the re-

Figure 2. The dimensions of competence according to the MEP model

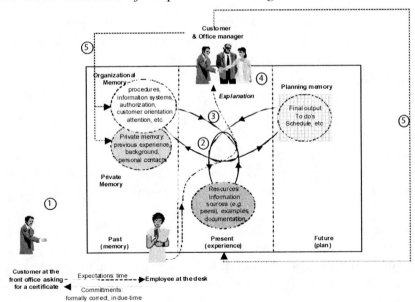

ceiver construct in order to justify why a performer is seen as being particularly competent in a given work situation.

In other words, the individuals formulate value judgments on the performance of others (e.g., John is an excellent project manager). When asked to provide arguments for judgments like this, people construct explanations. In order to be convincing, such explanations must refer to shared beliefs and values or must be enriched with new plausible arguments.

According to the MEP model, when individuals construct explanations they ideally move between the three knowledge-bases: the knowledge of the past, of the present, and of the future, depicted in Figure 2. They refer to the available resources and the ways in which they have been used, they recall values, artifacts, and explicit and tacit theories of action, compare the actual results with the expected ones and the intentions of the performer, and make explicit references to real life examples drawn from concrete job situations.

Furthermore, by collecting the explanations offered by different observers and performers with reference to a same job situation it is possible to elicit different points of views, ambiguities, multiple interpretations, as well as shared beliefs and values.[5]

Through appropriate identification techniques (see Chapters X and XI) the analysis of discourses allows us to highlight individual competencies in diverse work situations as they are perceived by the members of an organization. Moreover, it is possible to identify conflicting explanations and verify the degree of overlapping between organizational and private memory.

Since we are dealing with a descriptive analysis, it is not necessarily true that the constructs identified are real competencies, meaning knowledge and abilities causally related to a superior performance (Boyatzis, 1982). However, the peer-review mechanism inherent to the identification techniques increases the probability that the relationship is significant and, in any case, it is easy to check later if the relationship exists through statistical analysis.

Moreover, it is not necessarily true that the competencies identified are those that the organization needs and it may be that some competencies are lacking. At any rate, the analysis of training gaps and the interventions aimed at strengthening some critical competencies would be more effective if there were this kind of up-to-date x-ray of the current competencies and their links to organizational memory.

Updating Organizational Memory

The construction of a competencies map was the first step and the cornerstone needed to build a new integrated competence-based HRM system. A competencies assessment tool was designed by considering the usual aspects such as the structure of the evaluation form, the development of suitable metrics, the way to determine aggregated judgements. An information system was designed for archiving the data gathered in the evaluation sessions held in the ACI offices all around the nation. Finally, a computer-based managerial dashboard was implemented for the analysis of data in order to support the human resources central headquarters in planning organizational development interventions. The introduction of the system was preceded by various phases of experimentation and accompanied by training sessions and information packets aimed at illustrating the structure, its goals, and how to use the new system.

Thanks to the analysis of explanatory discourses, the organizational memory was updated with new artifacts, the most important of which is the map of competen-

Box 1. The movement of competencies

The so-called "movement of competencies" began to take hold in the 1960s with the pioneering studies done by McClelland and his associates (1978). These studies demonstrated that work performances are, if the conditions are the same, determined by individual characteristics which are describable in terms of knowledge and capacity (competencies). The most interesting result that emerged from such research was that the competencies were transversal with respect to gender, ethnicity and religion; the primary effect provoked by McClelland's studies was to make methods of evaluation and selection available to Human Resources managers that were less discriminatory toward cultural conditioning with respect to methods based on traits, behaviors or testing methodologies such as the classic IQ test, which was found to overestimate the actual performance of workers.

Later on, other authors, such as Boyatzis (1982) and Spencer and Spencer (1993), systematized both the theoretical and the methodological aspects of approaching competencies and their implications for managing Human Resources. In particular, for Boyatzis, competency is "an intrinsic characteristic of the individual tied to a superior work performance with respect to the average." Spencer and Spencer, through studies on very large samples of managers in various countries, compiled competency dictionaries, finding that "the intrinsic characteristics" of Boyatzis were recurrent, in particular at the intermediate management levels. Examples of the competencies found in the Spencer and Spencer dictionary are the following: achievement, leadership, problem solving, analytical thinking, concern for order and accuracy, customer focus, etc. Another important contribution of the Spencer and Spencer method is the proposal of competencies assessment scales.

The Boyatzis and Spencer and Spencer approach is known in the literature as a deductive-rationalist approach (Sandberg, 2000), in that it tends to make the meaning and the content of the competencies objective and transversal with respect to the specific characteristics of the organization, business or context. In other words, regardless of the specific business in which the managers operate, and of the religious, ethnic or gender group, the managerial competency profiles are similar.

Alternative approaches, classified as situational, emphasize instead the dependence on the characteristics of the competencies from specific and idiosyncratic factors tied to the individual biographies of the workers (Le Boterf, 2001: Levy-Leboyer, 1996), to the work situations in which the competencies are expressed (Capaldo & Zollo, 2001), to the sense and the specific way in which individuals interpret their own work and role in organizations (Sandberg, 2000).

Regardless of the advantyages and disadvantyages of each point of view, what counts is that the competencies based approach gives rise to a real Copernican revolution in the management of human resources, and more generally, in organizational planning.

On a purely organizational level, in fact, the competency approach puts the basic assumptions of the mechanistic-tayloristic conception of organizational planning in a critical position. According to that conception, the independent variable is the set of duties and activities of a given role, and the job of organizational analysts is to identify the subjects whose characteristics bests match the predefined roles.

cies. Some tacit, emerging or unrecognized competencies were included in the map. The method was transferred to the ACI human resources department who can autonomously update the map over time. With the introduction of new artifacts, the learning process is complete.

In reality, the case study demonstrates a general approach to the construction of a management system in an organization through the following steps:

1. Identification of the problem
2. Analysis of the organizational and private memory through explanatory discourses aimed at identifying the espoused and implicit action theories that the organizational actors develop when confronted with a problem, as well as the eventual discrepancies between the various theories and the different interpretations of the problem
3. Construction of new artifacts that exploit and/or integrate and/or revise the dominant action theories through the involvement of the organizational actors and experts
4. Introduction of new artifacts in the organization

Conclusion

Potentially, then, every explanation is an organizational act that is capable of making a profound change in an organization. Sense-making and explanation are the fundamental mechanisms for the continuous reconstruction of organizational reality. They are the heart of organizational learning. According to the logic of the MEP model any collective learning has a bottom-up genesis. Being a process emerging from ambiguity and individual creativity and motivation, it can not be governed with a top-down approach, which is it can not be controlled, planned and measured against possible standards. What an organization can do is to leave room for ambiguity, redundancy, loosely-coupling, autonomy, motivation and willing to accept alternative or emerging points of view. Also, the temporal aspect of the process can not be scheduled since learning has its own time.

The MEP model is not only descriptive but suggests implications for practice. The first recommendation is that managing organizational learning means being capable to observe how the processes described in the MEP model develop. Since explanation is at the heart of learning and represents the trait-d'union between individual and collective learning, it can be considered as a relevant unit of investigation to observe the development of such processes. In the third part of the book (Chapters X to XIV) we describe a methodological approach and a set of tools that can be utilized to collect, analyze and model explanations. We also show through several examples that this methodological approach can be used for several purposes, such as organizational analysis, knowledge modeling and management, development of decision support tools.

References

Boyatzis, R.E. (1982). *The competent manager: A model for effective performance.* New York: Wiley.

Capaldo, G., & Zollo, G. (1994). Modelling individual knowledge in personnel evaluation process. In J.R. Meindl, J.F. Porac, & C. Stubbart (Eds.), *Advances in managerial cognition and organizational information processing.* Greenwhich: Jai Press.

Capaldo, G., & Zollo, G. (2001). Applying fuzzy logic to personnel assessment: A case study. *Omega, 29,* 585-597.

Capaldo, G., Iandoli, L., & Zollo, G. (2006). A situationalist perspective to competencies management. *Human Resource Management, 45*(3), 429-448.

Morgan, G. (1997). *Images of organizations* (2nd ed.). Thousands Oaks, CA: Sage.

Perec, G. (2003). *Life: A user's manual.* London: Vintage Books.

Le Boterf, G. (2000). *Ingenierìa de las comptencias.* Barcelona: Gestion.

Levy-Leboyer, C. (1996). *La gestion des compétences.* Paris: Les éditions d'organisation.

McClelland, D.C. (1978). *Guide to behavioral event interviewing.* Boston: McBer.

Nelson, R.R., & Winter, S.G. (1982). *An evolutionary theory of economic change.* MA: Cambridge. The Belknap Press of Harvard University Press.

Polanyi, M. (1966). The logic of tacit inference. *Philosophy, 41,* 1-18.

Sandberg, J. (2000). Understanding human competence at work: An interpretative approach. *Academy of Management Journal, 43*(1), 9-25.

Spencer, L.M., & Spencer, S. M. (1993). *Competence at work. Models for superior performance.* New York: Wiley.

Schank, R.C. (1986). *Explanation patterns: Understanding mechanically and creatively.* Hillsdale, NJ: Lawrence Erlbaum.

Thagard, P. (1992). *Conceptual revolution.* Princeton: Princeton University Press.

Toulmin, S.E. (1959). *The uses of arguments*. Cambridge. MA: Cambridge University Press.

Toulmin, S.E., Rieke, R., & Janik, A. (1979). *An introduction to reasoning*. New York: MacMillan.

Tversky, A., & Kahneman, D. (1974). Judgment under uncertainty. Heuristics and biases. *Science, 185*, 1124-1131.

Weick, K.E. (1979). *The social psychology of organization* (2nd ed.). Reading, MA: Addison Wesley.

Endnotes

[1]   A coherent explanation is not necessarily correct for at least three essential reasons. In the first place, the processes of selection of the necessary information and inference are influenced by decisional heuristics and cognitive biases (Tversky & Kanheman, 1974) that can, in some cases, bring about considerable errors. In the second place, the assumptions upon which the explanation is developed are profoundly rooted in the beliefs system of the individual and therefore the validity of the explanation depends of the correctness of this system. Finally, as demonstrated in Chapter VIII, the process of explanation does not follow the rules of logical reasoning, but is developed according to an *argumentative logic* that uses the patterns and devices of rhetorical reasoning (Toulmin, 1959; Toulmin et al., 1979).

In the process of sense-making, the individuals are continuously searching for plausible and coherent connections that tie the interpretative patterns to events. The appropriateness of an explanation is evaluated on the basis of two factors (Thagard, 1992):

a.   The coherence of the explanation with respect to subjectively valid criteria

b.   The degree to which the explanation is acceptable to other members of a social community of reference

The use of rhetorical devices can contribute to reaching the second objective, but this can not be achieved if the explanation is not verbally *articulated* in the language of the organization that inevitably refers to interpretative categories and typification contained in a shared belief system.

[2]   The reflection of shared interpretations in individual memory is at the base of the holographic principle according to which members of the organization partly reflect the organization as a whole (Morgan, 1997).

[3]   Previous versions of this model have been published by Capaldo and Zollo (1994, 2001) as the *Knotting model*. The formulation proposed in the book can be considered a generalization of the knotting model and introduce some relevant new elements such as the temporal dimension and a substantial revision of the concept of organizational memory.

[4]   This case study has been adapted from Capaldo, G., Iandoli, & G. Zollo (2006).

[5]   In addition to being the result of the particular way that individuals interpret "external" stimuli through the cycle of enactment, selection, and retention (Weick, 1979), compentency is also a social construct. For Polanyi (1966), an individual is *competent in a tradition*, meaning that competency exists when there is a process of social construction of the meaning of the competency itself and of the evaluation criteria that establish when an individual is competent in a given social and temporal context. For this reason, Boyatzis' traditional definition (1982), which states that *competency is an intrinsic characteristic of the individual connected to superior performance* is incomplete, since it only considers the psychological dimensions of the competency without taking into account its social and organizational dimensions. If competency is both a social and an individual construct, then it cannot be characterized by simply observing the behavior of the individual. Because the criteria of validity and acceptability of a performance is socially constructed, it is necessary to reconstruct the network of organizational interlocutors who, as observers, have certain expectations and establish *when* and *why* an individual is competent on the basis of a system of socially constructed beliefs.

Section III

Methods and Tools for the Learning Organization

Chapter X

Eliciting Organizational Discourse

A single mind can not study itself, but a collective of minds can certainly study the collective mind.

(Edoardo Boncinelli, 2005)

Abstract

Beginning with this chapter we will describe a methodological approach to identify, represent and model explanatory discourses. In the first part of this chapter we will present the overall methodological framework while in the second part we will focus on the first step of the methodology, that is, the identification and acquisition of explanatory discourses. An interview technique is presented to elicit explanations followed by a detailed example and practical advice.

Investigating Organizational Memory Through Explanatory Discourse

It is time to proceed from theory to practice.

Before confronting the methodological aspects relative to the analysis of explanatory discourses, it is appropriate to sum up the theoretical considerations that have caused us to consider analyzing explanations in organizations from a privileged point of view in order to study the processes of organizational learning. The conceptual pathway followed up to this point can be summarized in the following steps:

a. Organizational memory is made up of a group of *artifacts*, which form the skeleton of the apparatus of persistence, through which organizations make an effort to insure the necessary coordination of individual actions and the achievement of shared objectives. The processes of organizational learning come about when organizations are able to question and to effectively modify organizational memory (Chapters III, IV, and V).

b. By following a constructionist approach, we have analyzed the processes involved in building organizational memory. We have examined the role of organizational actors and explanatory discourse in the *building of collective memory* using the MEP model (Chapters VI, VII, VIII, and IX).

c. We have characterized the "verbal" knowledge contained in explanatory discourse as *grey knowledge*. Individuals construct explanations when they illustrate their discoveries, or, more modestly, justify the outcomes of their actions, both to themselves and to the organizational customers for whom they have acted. The logic of grey knowledge is the logic of argumentation and persuasive discourse (Chapter VIII).

Artifacts, resources, and individual capabilities are the means through which organizational members construct "solutions" for their organizational customers. The rationality of the organizational actors inevitably refer to the constructs of collective memory and to the artifacts, and is consequently reflected in the discourses that organizational actors make in order to justify to themselves and their organizational customers the reasons behind their behavior and that of others.

Therefore, in this and later chapters, we intend to show how the analysis of explanatory discourse can be carried out in practice and used as a tool for observation, analysis, monitoring and management or organizational learning.

A Methodological Proposal for the Analysis of Discourse

In this paragraph we describe a protocol for the elicitation, representation and modeling of explanatory discourse. From the brief summary presented in the preceding paragraphs, some very important methodological indications emerge.

The MEP model (Chapter IX) outlines three temporal coordinates for action: results of past action (memory), current information (experience), intentions (plans). Any explanation will refer to these three coordinates. Furthermore, any of these three temporal dimensions can be referred to both the individual level (my time) and the collective level (others' or organizational time). Consequently all of the three coordinates of action should be analyzed by considering the inevitable overlapping of subjective and collective elements (Figure 1).

According to the logic of the MEP model we need to acknowledge some relevant methodological implications.

In the first place, it will be necessary to point out the experience of the organizational members. Experience is by definition the information coming from the ex-post revision that an individual does in a process of self-observation, in the light of the plan, motivations and memory frames.

In the second place, the constructs of organizational memory should be identified as elements of shared knowledge. Consequently, the analysis must necessarily be

Figure 1. The methodological implications of the MEP model for the elicitation of explanatory discourse

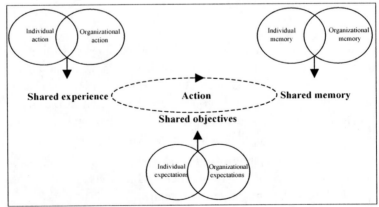

An explanation given by a member of an organization has value for the analysis of organizational memory if it possesses three requirements: (1) It refers to concrete experiences as a result of the comparison between individual and organizational action, (2) assumes an intersection between the expectations of the performer/customers and map (3) it turns to interpretative categories belonging to the collective memory in explaining the facts.

done on a large scale. It is necessary to observe that a necessary condition of the existence of a shared memory is the existence of a shared experience. In terms of methodology, this means taking into account in the identification phase the interactions between the performer and "typical" customers, through the analysis of the minimum web of the most frequent interactions in typical work situations.

In the third place, given that language represents one of the fundamental mechanisms for the construction of shared memory, it represents for us, as well, the fundamental instrument of analysis through the lens of explanatory discourse. From the whole of these elements we obtain four methodological requisites, which will guide us in the procedure of elicitation and representation of discourses:

- Discourses should be identified from among a *sample* of individuals in the organization that is *as expressive as possible* with respect to the specific task or organizational process that is being investigated (the selection of suppliers, for example).

- Discourses are pertinent to the *ways in which the members of an organization explain* their own behavior and that of others (When is a choice successful? What are the criteria for a "good choice"?, What is meant by "good supplier"?, etc.).

- It is important to identify the explanations made by most of the interlocutors that are part of the *minimum web of interaction* for each of the organizational performer included in the sample in order to identify their shared experiences. In other words, the network of the internal customers should be identified (Who is involved in the selection process? With whom do they interact and why? Who are the typical interlocutors to deal with in the selection process? Who are the customers and the observers of the actions?).

- Discourses should be identified with the *strong involvement of members of the organization*, both in the identification and in the interpretation of the information.

Keeping these assumptions in mind, the methodology is articulated in three phases (Figure 2):

a. **Eliciting explanatory discourses:** Pertinent to the organizational task/process that is being analyzed. The objective is to induce the actors to tell about their significant experiences, asking them in particular to defend the choices made by themselves or others in the realization of specific actions and in pursuing particular objectives.

Figure 2. A methodological proposal for discourse analysis

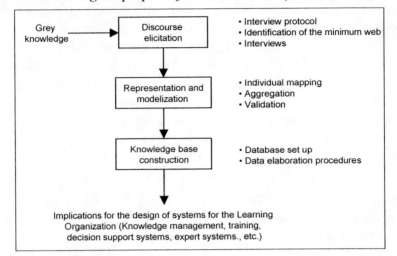

According to the proposed methodological framework, the analysis of explanation is articulated in three main steps: Elicitation, representation and modeling, and knowledge base construction. The input of the process is the grey knowledge contained in discourse. Each step is in turn articulated in other minor steps. For each step we will provide suggestions about the methodological tools to be used.

b.   **Representation and modeling explanatory discourse:** Through content analysis techniques and graphic representation of discourse that are typical of qualitative research.

c.   **Construction of the knowledge base:** After validation, discourse models can be archived within a knowledge base that can serve as a starting point for the construction of *support systems for the management of a learning organization* such as, for example, support systems for decisions, knowledge management platforms, and expert systems. Other uses of such knowledge can have to do with training and in general the support for organizational change.

Eliciting Explanatory Discourse

Critical Aspects of the Elicitation of Discourses

In the cases in which the sources are made up of written discourse contained within company documents, the problem of the elicitation of discourse does not appear at all, and it is possible to ignore this phase and go directly to the phases of representation and modeling. Instead, in cases in which it is necessary to isolate discourses, it is possible to use one of the many instruments among those available in the field of qualitative research methodologies for analyzing the belief systems of the actors, both in written and oral forms.[1]

Setting aside the specific technique and the field of application, the objective in any case refers to the attempt to analyze and represent the rationality of the organizational actor, intended as a group of categories of judgment, values, motivations, frameworks, and mental models that guide choices and social behavior.

In the first place, choosing the elicitation depends on considerations of suitability and coherence between the theoretical framework and the methodological instrument used. The choice may also depend on many practical factors, such as the specific goal of the analysis, the characteristics of the organizational context in which the analysis is carried out together with the research approach, the operative constraints, and the costs involved. The management of the trade-off between the depth of analysis and the scale of the investigation is a critical factor in this type of research. Indeed, a common characteristic of the methods based on an interpretative approach is that of being extremely time-consuming and hard to standardize. Moreover, such an approach requires an intense level of involvement and interaction between the researchers and the context. This inevitably creates problems for the management of the research and requires a careful cost/benefit analysis, especially in cases in which the field research must be done on a large scale.

A compromise might be to precede large scale with a pretest phase on a smaller sample, and use the results to plan more structured and standard tools, such as questionnaires and interview protocols to be used on a large scale for the sake of efficiency.

Because grey knowledge is socially constructed, the unit of analysis is not an isolated individual but the *minimum web of organizational interlocutors* who, as observers or customers, are able to describe alternative points of view with respect to the task being analyzed.

Determining an appropriate elicitation protocol can be done by looking at the specific characteristics of the application context, without causing the methodology to lose itself in generalities. For example, for the purpose of application, it is indifferent which sources are used, as long as they involve explanatory discourse. Nevertheless, in general, it is necessary to determine a protocol that can be extended to the different cases of application.

Protocol and Interview Strategies for the Identification of Explanations

It is necessary to create an interview protocol[2] for the elicitation of discourses. The interviews should be done in small teams of two or three analysts to improve the accuracy of the identification and interpretation of the results in the next phase of analysis.

The team of interviewers must interview the entire network that makes up the minimum web of interactions for the performer and his customers (the individual in self-evaluation, direct supervisor, colleagues, clients, etc.).

The interview must be a highly detailed report on the activities actually carried out by the subject in the execution of specific, possibly repeated or typical tasks. The description of the activities will be reinforced and generally more precise if examples are included. It is appropriate to prepare forms containing a questions checklist of the actions to carry out in order to conduct the interview effectively (setting) and possibly, typical questions (framing questions). The form is to be considered a kind of draft that can be adopted in a process that is mostly informal and unstructured.

The general structure of the interview takes shape in the few questions through which the interviewer tries to induce the interviewee to explain the reasons for past choices s/he has made (self-evaluation) or others have made (hetero-evaluation), or the reasons behind a particular evaluation or judgment he has made during the interview. If we call p any evaluative proposition (a judgment made to forecast the future such as *"The current unfavorable economic trend will continue until the end of the year."*), very general examples of framing questions are *"Why do you say that p is true?"*, *"What made you say that p?"*, *"What induced you to sustain that p?"* *"Can you give me an example showing that p?"*, *"What causes p?"*, etc.

The interview continues dynamically according to the answers given by the interviewee. The task of the interviewer is to attempt to go as deep as possible into the motivations and the rationality behind the explanatory discourse until reaching a satisfactory level (see Box 1 for a practical example).

Eliciting Explanatory Discourse Through Interviews: A Practical Example

A first analysis of the interview presented Box 1 allows us to make some observations:

1.   In the first place, the process of interviewing is clearly in the hands of the interviewer, who nevertheless limits himself to soliciting the interlocutor to provide convincing arguments for his/her own evaluations. In other words, to the question "Why r?", where r is any proposition contained in any subjective, unobvious evaluative judgment (*explanandum*) the interviewee can answer by producing possible reasons r1, r2 …rn, (*explanans*) to which the

Box 1. The elicitation of explanatory discourse through interviewing: A practical example

The following text is an excerpt from an interview conducted by one of the authors during a field study, in which an organizational actor was asked to evaluate his own work performance and to justify his evaluation. It is a concrete example of the use of the interview in eliciting explanatory discourse. The aim of the interview was to elicit the theories in use applied by members of an organization in the evaluation of individual competencies for personnel evaluation purpose (see the case study presented in Chapter IX).

Q: All things considered, if you had to express your opinion on how satisfied you are of your own performance, how would you judge yourself?

A: I am generally satisfied, conscious of having strengths and weaknesses that I am obviously trying to work on, and I believe that especially in the past year I have been able to improve.

Q: Can you explain what you mean by strengths and weaknesses? What do you base your evaluation of strengths and weaknesses on?

A: My strengths come from my long experience in the Personnel Office and so they refer to the consistent results I am able to obtain regarding certain circumstances at work. By now I have accumulated a historic memory of my past performances that have produced certain outcomes and confirmation from colleagues I work closely with and the ones I don't work with everyday, but fairly frequently, such as in the provincial offices, which have given me positive feedback regarding my efficiency at work [...]

Q: About feedback, can you illustrate how internal and external contacts in the company have shown their approval? What types of things have they mentioned in particular? You can give me examples, if you would like.

A: Both from my current director and the ones I have worked with in the past, since I began doing my new job in the personnel office, because I entered as an administrative employee, and later when Personnel Development Unit was set up, I was immediately involved in it with the current director. Then from union representatives in the management of some situations in reference to single dependents, colleagues or groups of employees, because I was involved in the evaluation of the professional performance for the career advancement and on that occasion I received positive feedback from the union on how I dealt with colleagues.

Q: What aspects of your work do you think have been particularly appreciated, for example by the union representatives?

A: Well, certainly the objectivity that I don't think they expected from a representative of the personnel office, because, in practice, shall we say, we are on opposite sides. Objectivity and fast answers when my colleagues needed them. These are the two main factors: the importance that I gave to their requests and the care I gave in providing a response. So, even when the answer was no, they were appreciative in that they accepted the reasons for the refusal and didn't consider them as being specious, or a simple contradiction to their position, because the response was the result of careful, in-depth research done to determine the validity of the colleagues' observation in contrast with a first decision that was made by the administration.

Q: When you speak of careful research, what type of research do you mean? What informational channels do you usually use, for example?

A: I use very few channels of information, because we haven't computerized our personnel records yet, and so all of the information we have is on paper. I think I have a good technique for finding information, especially because I know where to find it and I use my experience and historical memory for this.

Q: How long have you had your current job?

A: Actually, I have done my current job for about five years, even though I have also held other positions in the same company. I think I can say that in some ways I have become a point of reference within the company, in that many colleagues contact me, even informally, to ask me for information or advice. One of my strengths is certainly my ability to provide the needed information quickly, that is based on my memory of past events, episodes, precedents, data retrieval and rules...In addition to the ability to find information, another strength is in my ability to get to the heart of the problem and provide a response.

continued on following page

Box 1. continued

Q: It seems as if this ability comes above all from experience...or has it also been developed through specific training?

A: I think, in the first place, that it is a personal characteristic that has been developed in the field with experience supported only partially by training. Obviously, I tend to be quick but at the same time, analytical. I never stop at the first thing I see; I always check for the possibility of more confirmation. I always try to dig a little. Generally, the main complaint among colleagues in the local offices is that they feel cut off from the central office, when they call they are not satisfied because they get evasive responses. Instead, if they deal with me they are generally satisfied. So I have a sort of internal visibility that makes me happy, even though I have always experienced it not at the personal level but as visibility for the work we have done - that is what made me feel satisfied. Visibility that came from all the activities that we have been involved with in the past few years, of the sensibility that we are trying to instill in this company with respect to questions of development and professional growth, of competencies, and then perhaps cemented in the ability to provide effective answers to management and organizational problems that these changes have inevitably brought about. We have made the effort to contextualize and put into action, operationally so that there is an effective process of change in the company, discourses and projects that otherwise both the top management and lower level employees would think of as a marketing ploy.

Q: Looking back over our interview and returning to your strengths, other than the meticulousness, depth, precision and rapidity with which you do your research, being exhaustive when someone comes to you with a problem, correct me if I have misunderstood what you said, which other positive characteristics do you have, perhaps making reference, if you wish, to particular circumstances at work?

A: I could say that one of my personal characteristics, which is also a strength, is my intuition. That's what I call it, anyway, I don't know if there is a more appropriate term...

Q: Can you try to explain what you mean by intuition, in detail?

A: I would try to translate it like this. It often happens that new facts presented themselves that we have to deal with, for example, a new rule or problem with the management of contracts, etc.. Often they are problems that we did not notice in time, for example during the conception phase before starting a project. Intuition, for me, is anticipating these problems, understanding beforehand where they might lead. I am, perhaps with respect to my other colleagues, better able to anticipate unexpected consequences. This characteristic probably comes from a capacity for connecting several aspects of the life of the company, that in its turn is the result of more knowledge about the company's activities thanks to my previous experience, so that, when it is time to write a report, a document, a memorandum, I think I am better at evaluating what will be the positive or negative impact of what we are writing. My weak point is that I am not able to manage the other side of this ability. Which is a limit. As a matter of fact, I tend to radicalize my position because of an excess of confidence, and I don't accept that others are not able to see it or that I need to tolerate some inefficiencies that there may be for political motives or opportunities at a given moment. Sometimes my reaction is to become too rigid when something cannot be done the way it should be.

---

interviewer can respond with more questions like "Why r1?", "Can you give me an example in which r1?", etc. The *explanans* are in their turn evaluative judgments that, in the eyes of the interviewee, are acceptable reasons sustaining his own argument. Naturally, some of the *explanans* r1, r2 ...rn, can represent for the interviewer reasons that are not obvious, that must be justified by more detailed explanations. The level of depth is discretional, in the sense that the optimum level is the one that is sufficient for the interviewer to affirm that s/he *has understood* the reasons given by the interviewee.

2.   Through the analysis of the relationships between explanandum/explanans it is possible to describe theories of action (theories-in-use, see Chapter III) identified through the interview both in the form of rules such as:

If r1, r2 ...rn then r

If r11, r12 ...rn1 then r1

and in the form of "indemonstrable" propositions, or those that do not need to be demonstrated, which assume for the interviewee the value of "axioms," "laws," points of reference," "fundamental values," rules of thumb," etc.

For example, from the excerpt of the interview in the box, it is possible to identify some rules:

- The positive evaluation of own capabilities depends on the availability of objective feedback from other organizational actors.

- The negative response to a request is accepted if it is the result of meticulous and documented research.

- The ability to find useful information is the result of "historical memory," the ability to analyze, and speed in providing accurate answers.

Naturally, these rules reflect personal opinions and convictions, so they are not necessarily shared, normatively correct or generalizable.

3.   Interviewees find it very natural to make reference to specific and concrete "work situations" and to organizational artifacts and values in order to argue in favor of their judgment, possibly giving examples relative to past events often in the form of anecdotes and stories; it is the job of the interviewer to explore this type of construct and analyze it in depth both during the interview, and later in the mapping of the content (see Chapter XI).

4.   Behavior and events should be described with respect to concrete situations and the activities that an individual carries out in these situations in order to satisfy the expectations of someone, who assumes the role of customer and behaves as an organizational observer. The number of customers and observers may require the elicitation of all the explanatory discourse made by all of the individuals involved in the same object of investigation. The analysis of discourses developed by the individuals that are part of the same microweb of organizational relationships allows us to identify the presence of constructs and shared interpretative categories, as well as the possible cognitive discrepancies and categories between the actors. These webs also often contain references to resources which are accessible to members of the web and organizational artifacts that mediate the relationships between the members.

5.   The style of the interviewee is almost always retrospective; behavior and events are interpreted again as the result of experience rather than described in objective terms and remote from the context and from the circumstances in which they took place; often the interviewee dwells upon critical episodes in her own working life. The observer must examine these "critical incidents" closely (Flanagan, 1954; McClelland, 1971), noting behaviors and theories of action carried out in those circumstances.

Conclusion

These considerations, together with the example reported in Box 1, offer some practical suggestions to the reader for the identification of explanatory discourse through interviews. After the interview, the available output is given by the meticulous transcription of the interview itself and by the collection of notes and observations in the field.

There is a wealth of informational material, but it is still rough and unformed. In the next chapter we will describe some techniques for the systematic analysis and mapping of the content of the interview. By 'mapping the interview' we mean following a procedure for representing the synthesis of the content, in a graphic representation (maps), through which it is possible to highlight the most relevant concepts and the relationships between them contained in the interview.

References

Boncinelli, E. (2005). La mente esplora se stessa. In *Come alla corte di Federico II, ovvero parlando e riparlando di scienza*. Napoli: COINOR.

Bougon, M.G. (1983). Uncovering cognitive maps: The self-q interview. In G. Morgan (Ed.), *Beyond the method: Strategies for social research*. Thousands Oaks, CA: Sage.

Coffey, A., & Atkinson, P. (1996). *Making sense of qualitative data*. Thousands Oaks, CA: Sage.

Denzin, N.K., & Lincoln, Y. S. (2005). *Handbook of qualitative research*. Thousands Oaks, CA: Sage.

Eco, U. (1979). *A theory of semiotics*. Bloomington, IN: University of Indiana Press.

Erdner, C.B., & Dunn, C.P. (1990). Content analysis. In A. S. Huff (Ed.), *Mapping strategic thought* (pp. 291-300). New York: John Wiley & Sons.

Flanagan, J.C. (1954). The critical incident technique. *Psychological Bullettin, 51,* 327-358.

Huff, A.S (Ed.). (1990). *Mapping strategic thought.* Chirchester: Wiley.

Kelly, G. (1955). *The psychology of personal constructs.* New York: Norton.

McClelland, D.C. (1978, 4-9 August). *Guide to behavioral event interviewing.* Boston: McBer.

Wright, R., Simon, L., & Gilbert, W. (2000). *Cognitive maps of appraisal system effectiveness in Honk Kong: A comparison between human resources and the line.* Academy of Management meeting, Toronto.

Endnotes

[1] Among possible techniques that can be used to elicit individual belief systems there are *content analysis* techniques (Erdner & Dunn, 1990), the *repertory grid technique* (Kelly, 1955), interview techniques such as the *Self Q* (Bougon, 1983), *Focus Group*, the *Critical Incident Iinterview* (Flanagan, 1954), the *Behavioral Event Interview* (McClelland, 1978), narrative methods and *Semiotic Analysis* (Eco, 1979). Such techniques, originally developed in sociological and psychological research, have been largely applied in organizational and management studies (Coffey & Atkinson, 1996; Huff, 1990; Wright et al., 2000). A comprehensive book on qualitative research methods is the one edited by Lincoln and Denzin (2005).

[2] Here we will provide a set of coherent methodological indications for the methodology presented in this volume. For the more operational aspects and more in-depth methodological studies the reader can refer to one of the many available manuals available for conducting qualitative research in companies (Denzin & Lincoln, 2005).

Chapter XI

Mapping Discourses

La tua loquela ti fa manifesto.[1]

(Dante, Inferno, X, 25)

Abstract

This chapter deals with the issue of discourse representation. A possible way to represent discourse is by mapping its contents (concepts) and its structure (i.e., showing the relationships between concepts). In particular, we give a detailed presentation of the argument analysis technique, a mapping approach developed to elicit and represent argumentative discourse. Later in the chapter we also provide some references to a wider set of techniques that can be used to build cognitive maps, which is a way of represent the belief systems of an individual through which he/she interprets a specific problem or situation.

Analyzing and Modeling Explanatory Discourse

The objective of representing discourses collected through interviews is to arrive at a semi-formal representation of their contents and structure. These maps allow us to underline the essential elements of discourse and to represent the system of shared beliefs and meanings contained in discourses. (Eden & Ackerman, 1992; Huff, 1990; Weick, 1979). The structured nature of explanatory discourse facilitates both the process of analyzing the content of discourse and representing it.

The representation of explanatory discourses is accomplished in three phases: *mapping, aggregation and validation* (Coffey & Atkinson, 1996; Huberman & Miles, 1994).

The operation of mapping usually consists in the construction of a graphic representation of discourse. According to the approach described in Chapter X, Figure 2, the mapping step is usually preceded by an analysis of the contents of the discourse, in which recurrent terms, key expressions, and significant declarations are highlighted. To point out the internal structure of explanations a technique called *argument analysis is proposed* (Fletcher & Huff, 1990; Toulmin, 1957; Toulmin et al., 1979).

Explanatory discourse is intrinsically structured. It consists of a set of interrelated arguments, statements and facts provided by a speaker to persuade others about the validity of a nonobvious claim (see Chapter VIII). Many approaches have been proposed to describe the characteristics of such a structure, beginning with the rhetorical and ending with the applications found in organizational and managerial literature (Fletcher & Huff, 1990; Mason & Mitroff, 1983; Sillince, 2001).

Among the various approaches, *argument analysis* seems particularly appropriate because of its congruence with the theoretical assumptions of the methodological approach proposed in this book and for practical reasons tied to the relative ease of application. According to Toulmin (1959), Toulmin, Rieke, and Janik (1979), an argumentation is a sequence of interconnected affirmations (*claim*) that establish the content and the strength of the position of the orator. As a consequence, explanatory discourse can be broken down into a series of claims. The claims can be *designative* (they establish the existence of an event), *definitory* (they define the characteristics of an event), *evaluative* (they assign value to a given event), or *invocative* (they invoke the execution of an action). Claims can be classified into the following categories, with respect to the functions that they have in the discourse:

1.   The *key claim*, or conclusion of an argumentation.

2.   *Common claims* corresponding to facts, common sense, and the opinions of influential people.

3. The *grounds*, meaning the facts offered to support a claim. In argument analysis, the ground maybe: (a) shared and personal opinions offered as facts; (b) objective data.

4. *Warrants*, meaning the rules that demonstrate how the *grounds* support the *claims*; they can be *substantive* (justified through logic), *authoritative* (justified through authority), and *motivational* (justified through values).

5. *Qualifiers*, expressions or terms that limit the validity of the claims, such as "usually," "rarely," "according to what we know," etc.

In addition to these fundamental components, we need to consider the *subclaims*, that is the set of claims through which the interviewee articulates analytically a key claim and two basic rhetorical mechanisms: *reiteration*, and *elaboration*. Reiteration is the technique through which the interviewee reproposes a claim (or warrant or grounds), for example, at the beginning and at the end through a summary. Elaboration is a kind of parentheses of the discourse in which the interviewee dwells upon the illustration of a claim through examples, often in the attempt to circumstantiate and limit the field of reasoning, rather than as a communicative expedient.

The logic underlying argumentative reasoning is abductive (see Box 1 in Chapter II). It can explain an outcome, support a decision, and sustain an evaluation. It begins with the conclusion and goes back along a kind of logical chain until it finds plausible causes, like a tree develops from the top to its roots. When the tree of explanation is complete, then it is reversed. Through this reversion, the speaker can present his argument as if it were a logical argument by using the classic model of logical deduction (*modus ponens*): given the condition A, and given the rule *if A then B*, then B.

For example this is the technique that the famous character in Sir Conan Doyle's novels, the detective Sherlock Holmes, uses to solve his puzzling cases. But what Holmes defines as a chain of deduction[2] is actually a mix of deductive and abductive reasoning. The main difference between these two kinds of reasoning is that in deductive reasoning the consequence B necessarily comes from the rule *if A then B* and the acceptance of the assumption A; while in abduction, given B, for example from the observation of available evidence, Holmes finds a possible explanation in the form of a rule: *If A then B*, and concludes that it must (or at least could) be A. So there is no necessity in abductive argumentation but only knowledge in the form of wit or commonsense, and an explanation can rich of observations and objective facts but also of assumptions that are taken for granted, implicit or instrumental, which would have no place in the kingdom of traditional logic.

Apart from this clarification about the starting assumptions, the argumentative reasoning can develop similarly to a deductive reasoning. The mechanism that links claims, warrants and grounds is demonstrated in the following example (Fletcher & Huff, 1990):

GROUND	(GIVEN THAT) *The barometric pressure has decreased and the wind has begun to blow in the past hour.*
WARRANT	(AND BECAUSE) *Usually, decreasing barometric pressure and an increasing intensity of wind can signal the arrival of a low pressure system that will bring rain.*
CLAIM	(I AFFIRM THAT) *It will probably rain.*

In the example above, qualifiers such as *usually* and *probably* are immediately identifiable. Moreover, there is no difference between the ground and claim from the syntactical point of view. Both are assertions, but the claim is by nature potentially more controversial than the ground, which instead is offered by those who explain it as an acceptable fact supporting a Claim. Warrants, in the end, link the grounds and the claim through a quasi-logic reasoning.

The example cited above, as simple and uncomplicated as it seems, in which it is otherwise possible to take objective measure of the variables in question, underlines that in cases like this, language can be deeply ambiguous and inaccurate. How much does the pressure have to decrease? How hard does the wind have to blow? How much do the qualifiers such as *usually* and *probably* weaken the conclusion? How willing are we to bet that it will rain if we only have the information contained in the example?

Mapping Explanatory Discourse

A map is a graphic representation of concepts revealing the contents of discourse and their reciprocal relationships. The objective of mapping is to represent the relationships between the concepts through graphics and some formal rules.[3]

The characteristic of explanatory discourse of having a "rational" structure with the aim of persuading the interlocutor and the possibility, through argument analysis, of separating discourse into constitutive elements, greatly facilitates the identification of a graphic representation of the structure of discourse in which the principle components of the argumentation and their reciprocal relationships are easily recognizable (Figure 1).

It is clear that mapping loses some of the wealth of meaning through the reduction of ambiguity contained in discourse. For this reason, the operation of mapping should be done with the utmost care and the knowledge that "*the map is not the territory.*"

Box 1 and Figure 3 describe the application of argument analysis to the example interview reported in Chapter X.

Figure 1. Example of a graphic representation of explanatory discourse

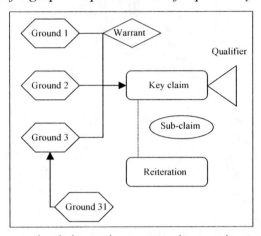

Argument analysis allows us to classify the speech acts contained in an explanation analytically according to their function in the context of the discourse. The graphic representation shown here is the visual representation of the structure of the discourse.

Figure 2. An example of a causal map (Adapted from Kosko, 1992)

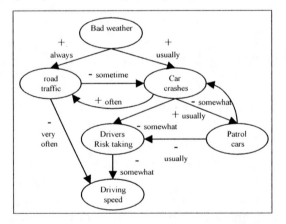

This figure contains an example of a cognitive (causal) map representing the theory of action of the driver of a car in bad driving conditions. Maps are a set of nodes (concepts) and arcs (relationships). In causal maps, the sign "+" and "-" between nodes i and j Mean, respectively, positive and negative causal links betweens the connected concepts.

Box 1. Analysis of content and mapping

In Figure 4 an example is shown of the mapping process relative to the interview reported in Chapter X in which the interviewee is asked to evaluate his own work performance and his own level of professional development.

Step 1: Analyzing the content, compiling the dictionary of concepts, codifying the relationships between concepts.

The transcription of the interview reported in Chapter X was analyzed through the technique of argument analysis. The objective is to identify and isolate the various components of explanatory discourse, and to assemble them so that they reproduce the structure of an argument. To facilitate the analysis it is helpful to have a coding sheet available, like the one in Figure 3, which shows a subset of the elements the have come out of the interview.

With reference to the codes used in Figure 3, CG stands for Ground Claim, meaning a claim used as a ground by an interviewee, for which the interviewer usually asks further justification. The simple ground is instead a fact that supports a claim in a way that is obvious to both the interlocutors. Warrants are also not reported when they are obvious. For each ground it is necessary to show the line of text in which it appears, the type (evaluative, designative, etc.) and a progressive code for identification. (n°).

The self-evaluation shown in the text of the tree in Figure 3 ("I am fairly satisfied..") is explained on the base of two subclaims (SC1: knowledge of his own strengths, and SC2; knowledge of his own weaknesses). The evaluation relative to his strengths is justified on the basis of a series of further affirmations, classifiable as ground-claims (GC), such as: "By now I have accumulated a historic memory of my past performances […]", "that have produced certain outcomes and confirmation from colleagues I work closely with and the ones I don't work with everyday, but fairly frequently, such as in the provincial offices, who have given me positive feedback regarding my efficiency at work", etc.

Step 2: Plotting the Map. The objective of mapping is to represent the structure of the argumentation through a graphic description. In this example, the form of representation used is that of a tree; the interviews are conducted so that the discourse assumes an almost hierarchical structure. Nevertheless, it is not a pure hierarchy because of the presence of horizontal relationships between the variables such as feedback, interactions and returns of various types. Therefore, we will speak in general of the tree of explanations even though it will actually be an oriented graph. In Figure 4 a map relative to the interview extract in Chapter X is shown.

The results of the discourse analysis should be used appropriately in the mapping phase. Indeed, the literature on qualitative research methodologies recognizes that the two typologies of techniques (content analysis and mapping) must be used in a substantially complementary way in order to avoid a situation in which the operation of synthesis that is obtained through mapping becomes excessively reductive. The phases illustrated in Chapter X Figure 2 should be implemented regardless of the specific technique of analysis of the content and mapping used. As the example also demonstrates, in the cases in which argument analysis is used, it is necessary to take into account the following ulterior indications:

In the text analysis phase, the results of the argument analysis must be taken into account through the identification not only of the relationships and concepts, but also the role of the concept in the discourse, specifying, for example, if a given affirmation is a claim (that is, a relationship that will be "demonstrated"), a ground (that

Figure 3. Example of a coding sheet

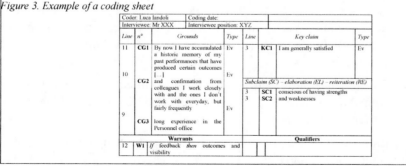

continued on following page

Box 1. continued

is, a "demonstrated or demonstrable affirmation or one that will be demonstrated as promised"), or a warrant (that is, a rule of acceptable inference), as shown in Figure 3. Moreover, in argumentative discourses the rules can be made only partially explicit, in particular this is often true for the premises. It is necessary, finally, to try and point out the use of possible artificial rhetoric with which the interviewee has used to particularly underline certain aspects or to define the environment and the validity of his reasoning (elaborations, reiterations).

In the phase in which relationships are codified, it is important to avoid limiting the process to the identification of cause and effect relationships, and to find information on the intensity and the limitations expressed by the interviewee regarding these relationships, such as "A has a positive influence on B", A makes it possible for B to happen", A facilitates B", etc. Moreover, it is also important to point out relationships that are of a different nature to cause/effect, such as "A is (is not) the equivalent of B", "A is (is not) an example of/belongs to/ a member of B", etc. For each type of relationship, it is important to show the relationships in the table that are possible qualifiers that limit the validity of the relationships, such as "often", "a fair amount", "always", "in most cases", etc.

Maps that are made to represent a system of beliefs of an individual are known as cognitive maps and there are various methodologies and approaches for information gathering and map construction. In Figure 2 an example of a causal cognitive map is shown. Causal maps are represented through graphs made up of nodes (concepts) and arcs (causal relationships). An arc is a bridge between two concepts, A and B in the direction of A toward B occurrence.

Further and more detailed examples of cognitive and causal maps will be provided in Chapters XIV and XV. Regardless of the specific technique used in the graphic representation, the methodology for the graphic representation of a discourse through mapping is articulated in six phases:

a.   **Analysis of the content:** It is necessary to reread the transcription of the interview carefully in order to identify the most relevant passages, the salient concepts present in the discourse, marking them directly on the original document (*documentary coding method*, Wrightson, 1976);

b.   **Composition of a "dictionary" of concepts:** A list of relevant concepts must be written as well as the meaning ascribed to them by the interviewee, assigning a code to each concept and trying to eliminate possible redundancies. In this phase, it is important to note the shades of meaning that are behind the labels used by the interviewee that will be used as names of concepts, paying particular attention to the frequency with which the most important terms are used in the text.

c.   **Codification of the relationships between the concepts:** In this step a list of the relationships between the concepts is created. The list should report the kind of relationship and the position in the text.[4]

d.   **Composition of the map:** Finally, the list of relationships and concepts is assembled into visual map.

Figure 4. An example of mapping of explanatory discourse through argument analysis approach

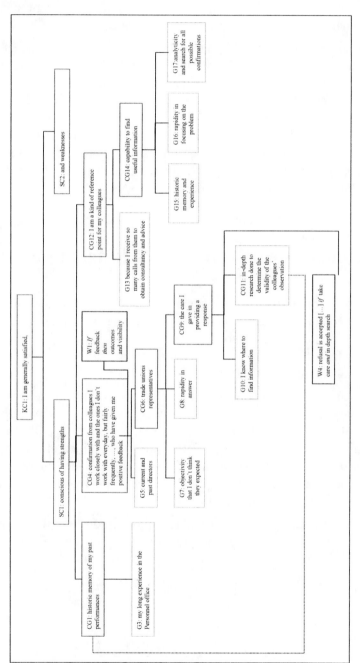

e.   **Aggregation:** Given a collection of individual maps, it is possible, if needed, to obtain a group map by merging the single maps. An alternative option is to building the collective map directly, together with the group members in ad hoc meeting.

f.   **Validation:** Validating the map consists of reaching a satisfactory level of reliability in the output of the interview data, considering that it will grow with the level of interpretative convergence between the analysts and the interviewee. The analysts must reach an adequate level of agreement in the interpretation of data and the information contained in the discourses. This agreement must include both the concepts (their identification and meaning) and the relationships between them. It is highly important that the interviewee confirm the results, by "recognizing himself in the map." We will analyze the validity issue in depth in Chapter XVI.

Conclusion: Toward Modeling Discourses

The representation of discourses is an attempt to capture and to structure the grey knowledge contained in explanation. This allows us to investigate and identify shared belief systems, mental models used by organizational members that influence choices and behavior, and possible changes that such cognitive systems undergo in the processes of organizational learning.

The proposed methodology constitutes just a first step toward a modeling of discourses, meaning the construction of formal systems that allow for the true elaboration of discourses through logical-mathematic models. This attempt, still at he embryonic stage, aims at the simulation of decisional models contained in discourses through appropriate algorithms. Which techniques can help us to reach our objectives? What use can be derived for the organization from the availability of "verbal machines" that implement formal models of discourse?"

The next two chapters will be dedicated to exploring some possible answers. These are complementary to the present chapter. They are meant to supply another methodological instrument for organizational analysts who intend to make an in-depth study of discourse modeling.

References

Coffey, A., & Atkinson, P. (1996). *Making sense of qualitative data.* Thousands Oaks, CA: Sage.

Eden, C., & Ackermann, F. (1992). The analysis of causal map. *International Journal of Management Studies, 29*(3), 310-324.

Fletcher, K.E., & Huff, A.S. (1990). Argument mapping. In A.S. Huff (Ed.), *Mapping strategic thought*. Chirchester: Wiley.

Huberman, A.M., & Miles, M.B. (1994). Data management and analysis method. In N.K. Denzin & Y.S. Lincoln (Eds.), *Handbook of qualitative research* (pp. 428-444). Thousands Oaks, CA: Sage.

Huff, A.S. (Ed.). (1990). *Mapping strategic thought*. Chirchester: Wiley.

Kosko, B. (1992). *Neural networks and fuzzy systems*. Englewood Cliffs, NJ: Prentice Hall.

Masoff, R.O., & Mitroff, I.L. (1983). A teleological power-oriented theory of strategy. In R. Lamb (Ed.), *Advances in strategic management* (pp. 31-41). Greenwich: JAY Press.

Sillince, A. (2001). A model of strength and appropriateness of argumentation in organizations. *Journal of Management studies, 39*(5), 585-618.

Toulmin, S.E. (1959). *The uses of arguments*. Cambridge, MA: Cambridge University Press.

Toulmin, S.E., Rieke R., & Janik, A. (1979). *An introduction to reasoning*. New York: MacMillan.

Weick, K.E. (1979). *The social psychology of organization* (2nd ed.). Reading, MA: Addison Wesley.

Wrightson, M.T. (1976). The documentary coding method. In R. Axelrod (Ed.), *Structure of decisions*. Princeton, NJ: Princeton University Press.

Endnotes

[1]   Thy mode of speaking makes thee manifest.

[2]   See the second chapter, "The science of deduction," in "A study in scarlet," the first Sherlock Holmes novel published in 1887.

[3]   Mapping the concepts and rules expressed in natural language through formal systems of representation has been widely used in some artificial intelligence applications, in particular in the development of expert (computer) systems that, by reproducing the reasoning of a human expert, are used to support the analysis and diagnosis of complex problems, the diagnosis and more generally support for decisions. The development of techniques for identifying and mapping the knowledge of experts is the objective of the so-called "knowledge engineering." In this field, the "reliability" of the representation has a strong

impact on the reliability and on the performance of the system. The approach to mapping proposed in this book, though methodologically similar to that of knowledge engineering, differs in that the aims are above all descriptive. The objective of the map is not, at least for now, to support diagnoses and decisions, but to identify the constructs of organizational memory in order to describe action theories in use, tacit constructs, and promote more awareness and wider knowledge of the organization in organizational actors.

[4]   A taxonomy of the typologies of relationships is effectively described in Huff (1990).

Chapter XII

Modeling Discourses

Marcel Benabou (Un aphorisme peut en cacher un autre, Bibliotèque Oulipienne, n.13, 1980) has designed a machine to create aphorismes. It is made up by two parts: A grammar and a lexicon. The grammar is formed by a certain number of general rules that are used by most of the aphorisms; such as: A is the shortest way from B to C, A is another way of doing B, the little A's make the important B's, A would not be A if there were not B, Happiness is in A and not in B, A is a sickness that can be treated with B, etc. The lexicon contains couples (or tuples) of words that can be false synonyms (love/friendness, word/language), antonyms (life/death, form/content, memory/oblivion), words with similar spelling, words used often together (crime/punishment, sickle/hammer, science/life), etc. The injection of the lexicon into the grammar produces ad libitum a series almost infinite of aphorisms, all sense makers, some more than others. A computer program created by Paul Braffort is able to produce on demand several dozens in a few seconds: Memory is a sickness that can be treated with oblivion; memory would not be memory if it were not oblivion [...].

(Georges Perec, Penser/Classer)

Abstract

In this chapter we introduce the concept of verbal model. A verbal model is a mathematical modeling of the variables contained in a discourse and of the relationships among them. A discourse may contain linguistic variables, i.e., variables assuming linguistic values. For instance the variable "performance" can assume values such as poor, satisfying, above average, excellent, etc. Verbal models can accept linguistic inputs as well as quantitative variables and can be implemented starting from the discourse map through fuzzy logic algorithms. Such algorithms can simulate to a certain degree the theories of action contained in explanations. This chapter presents an introduction to fuzzy logic and to some possible ways of constructing verbal models, while we provide several examples in Chapters XIII and XIV.

Systems for Learning Organizations: Rhetoric Machines

A logical machine can be thought of as of a device able to produce conclusions given some input by carrying out a process of logical reasoning. Personal computers are examples of logical machines. A logical machine can be very efficient and it produces objective and often unquestionable results. Let us consider a different kind of reasoning machine, a machine that is capable of producing (sometimes involuntarily) new meanings like the one described by Perec at the beginning of this chapter.

The *experiment* cited by Perec shows how it is possible to create meaning involuntarily through very simple, formal algorithms. Naturally, the meaning does not lie in the algorithm, but in those who interpret the aphorisms that are generated automatically. Benabou's machine is an example of an open artifact. An important part of the memory of a learning organization should be made up of the artifacts with the capacity to generate scenarios that have multiple or unexpected meanings.

As outlined in Chapter IV, one of the most common ways for an organization to guarantee the continuity of action is to transform itself into a machine through the adoption of closed artifacts that imply impersonal and prescriptive theories of action. This way, the organization can be compared to a software program, made up of libraries and programs, functions, databases, protocols, mass memory, and events of synchronization. The technical apparatus of persistence of an organization machine, consisting of procedures, bureaucracy, planning, and control systems, has many defects, which are often highlighted by organizational literature and recalled in this text (an excess of optimism, inertia to change, reductionism, etc.) but it has one positive aspect. For better or worse, it never stops working until someone, or something stops the engine. This is enough to keep managers occupied and placate their anxiety (and, rest assured, that is no small thing).

However, as we have discussed in Chapter V, a closed memory can prevent the organization from learning by revising its memory.

What systems should replace the procedures and closed artifacts of the organization machine? The problem for the learning organization is not to do without the artifacts in the name of a destructuralization of organizational processes. The problem is how to obtain open artifacts that support and structure action but at the same time are able to tolerate and solicit various interpretations, creativity, and a multiplicity of uses.

One possible suggestion is to build verbal models, through which it is possible to elaborate the information contained in the discourse, in order to simulate the theories of action described in the discourse itself.

Verbal models are an example of *rhetoric machines*. While the logic machines such as calculators, automatons, or more generally, algorithms (see Box 1), aim at resolving, through logic or computation, specific problems efficiently and quickly, rhetoric machines simulate the possible effects of theories of action contained in discourses, preserving the adaptability and the imprecision of verbal expressions.

Rhetoric machines, however, are still formal systems. The challenge is to build such formal systems overcoming the rigidity of algorithms and traditional machines. To do so we must use a new kind of logic.

Box 1. A very brief history of logic machines

The creation of "thinking" machines, those capable of imitating man and possibly replacing him in carrying out complex tasks that require the ability to reason, has been the goal of scientists and scholars over the centuries, not to mention the literary inventions of the same type: Praga's Golem, Asimov's robots, the humanoids of Blade Runner, by Philip Dick, and Kubrick's HAL, the super-computer in 2001: A Space Odyssey.

Aristotelian logic comes from an attempt to describe human reasoning in a formal way. The first attempts to assign a computational base to human thought were brought forward by Descartes and then by Leibniz. However, it was not until the 19th century that the first calculating machines began to be widely used. These machines included the mechanical calculator invented in England by the Babbages, who attempted, among other things, to commercialize it, without success. Mechanical calculators finally gained commercial success between the end of 19th and the first half of the twentieth century. Among the most surprising models was the Curta (http://www.vcalc.net/cu.htm), a formidable example of a pocket-sized mechanical calculator (Figure 1).

Mechanical calculators have two major limits: The first is that they are complex machines that are cumbersome and very expensive to make, since they are made up of complicated metallic parts; the second is that the functioning logic of these machines is incorporated into their physical structure. In other words, mechanical calculators are invented and built in order to carry out a few operations and they are only slightly reconfigurable or, as we would say today, programmable.

There are two fundamental innovations underlying all of the current "thinking" machines: a mathematical logic (Boolean logic) and a new technology (electronic circuits). Boolean logic uses mathematical formalism to describe logical operations of propositional logic through mathematical logical functions that assume true

continued on following page

Box 1. continued

or false values (0 and 1 in the binary system). The Turing machine (1950), made up of a memory-tape and a reading and writing system of binary data that allows for the implementation of formal algorithms and contains the logical framework upon which all computers are now based.

Fundamentally, it was Claude Shannon, as a PhD student at MIT in Boston in the 1930s, who understood intuitively that an electronic circuit could be used to physically carry out the logical operations that are typical of all the existing machines that process digital information.

As outlined in Chapter 1, Shannon's circuits and the Cybernetics revolutionized the concept of machine and gave birth to the era of the intelligent devices.

Figure 1. Assembly of the Curta, a pocket-sized mechanical calculator . http://www.vcalc.net/cu.htm

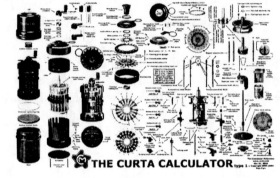

From Discourses to Rhetoric Machines

The techniques identified in Chapters X and XI allow us to describe the contents and the structure of an explanation as a static picture. The goal of the verbal model is to provide a dynamic model of a discourse in order to derive the consequences contained within it. Our point of view is that of simulation, which produce scenarios as result of the theory of action described by the verbal model. Our questions are: What are the consequences of our verbal model? What are the effects?

Usually, the operation of formalizing an explanatory discourse is a *reduction,* in which the ambiguity of the natural language is sacrificed in favor of the consistency of internal logic. Even the example presented in this chapter is a simplified representation of the complexity of discourse. Nevertheless, verbal models try to keep the loss of information due to formalization to a minimum. Verbal models reproduce the structure of the argumentation by turning to a set of mathematical techniques that allow us to model the ambiguity of linguistic expressions (Bonissone, 1980; Chen & Hwang, 1991; Herrera et al., 2000; Saaty, 1979; Wenstøp, 1975a, b; Zadeh, 1973).[1]

There are three assumptions underlying this approach:

a.   The first, theoretical in nature, according to which preserving the ambiguity of discourses contributes to the growth of flexibility and the degree of openness of organizational systems.

b.   The second, methodological in nature, according to which the verbal knowledge, though ambiguous, may contain useful information that should not be considered as noise.

c.   The third, applicative in nature, according to which, in all the cases where it is necessary to evaluate qualitative variables, nor is there any effective or low-cost proxy, it is appropriate to elaborate directly linguistic information.

Now is the time to define what we mean by *linguistic information*. Chen and Hwang (1992) suggest that we consider *linguistic* when dealing with the information characterized by at least one of the following attributes:

a.   **Unquantifiable information:** Intrinsically qualitative variable for which there are no reliable proxies or it is costly/arbitrary to identify them (e.g., the comfort of a vehicle is usually expressed in linguistic terms such as good, fair, poor, etc. They are qualitative data).

b.   **Incomplete information:** The information is approximate and the precision of the instrument is unknown (e.g., that car was going "*about 50 miles per hour*").

c.   **Unobtainable information:** An evaluation is possible but data are not available, so it is necessary to make estimates indirectly and qualitatively (e.g., an individual's bank account or age, if it is not to be revealed; in these cases one can estimate wealth or age by evaluating lifestyle choices or appearance).

d.   **Partial ignorance:** Imprecision can be derived from an awareness of an intrinsic ignorance of the phenomenon being described, due to the impossibility of gathering the necessary information (e.g., "*It is plausible that the stock market will not rise significantly in a short time.*").

It is not difficult to recognize the presence of such characteristics in the information that organizational actors face every day when taking action and making decisions.

Codifying the Uncertainty and the Ambiguity of Verbal Language Through Fuzzy Logic

The theory of fuzzy sets[2] (Zadeh, 1965) allows us to represent the ambiguity contained in linguistic information. The original paper on fuzzy logic encountered skepticism and occasional hostility. Forty years later many international journals have been published which include the word "fuzzy" in their title and thousands of patents have been applied. By 1973, Zadeh had stated the principle of incompatibility on which the fuzzy approach is based: *"As the complexity of a system increases, our ability to make precise and significant statements about its behavior diminishes until a threshold is reached beyond which precision and significance (or relevance) become almost mutually exclusive characteristics. It is in this sense that precise quantitative analyses of the behavior of humanistic systems are not likely to have much relevance to the real world societal, political, economic, and other types of problems which involve humans either as individuals or in groups"* [Zadeh, 1973].

The most important concept of the fuzzy sets theory is the partial belonging in a set, whose power is clearly illustrated by the following example: Say you park your car in a parking lot with 100 painted parking spaces. The probability approach assumes you park in one parking space and each space has some probability that you will park in it. All these parking space probabilities add up to 100%. If the parking lot is full, there is zero probability that you will park in it. If there is only one empty parking space, say the thirty-fourth space, you will park there with 100% probability. If the parking lot is empty, and if we know nothing else about the parking lot, you have the same slim chance, 1%, of parking in any one of the parking spaces.

The probability approach assumes parking in a space is a neat and bivalent affair. You park in the space or not, all or none, in or out. A walk through a real parking lot shows otherwise. Cars crowd into narrow spaces and at angles. One car hogs a space and a half and sets a precedent for the cars that follow. To apply the probability model we have to round off and say one car per space.

Up close things are fuzzy. Borders are inexact and things coexist with nothings. You may park your car 90% in the 34th space and 10% in the space to the right of it, the 35th space. Then the statement *"I parked in the 34th parking space"* is not all true and the statement *"I did not park in the 34th parking space"* is not all false. To a large degree you parked in the 34th space and to a lesser degree you did not. To some degree you parked in all the spaces. But, most of those were zero degrees. This claim is fuzzy and yet more accurate. It better approximates the "fact" that *"you parked in the 34th parking space"* [Kosko, 1993, pp. 12-13].

The partial belonging in a fuzzy set is represented in mathematical terms by the *membership function*. The following is the mathematical definition of a fuzzy set:

Given a universe of the discourse U, a fuzzy set A in U is defined by a membership function that assigns to each element u in U a value between 0 and 1. When a value 0 is assigned to u then u does not belong with the set A. When it assumes the value 1 then it completely belongs to set A. When it has an intermediate value between 0 and 1 then the element will partially belong to A.

Many phenomena can be effectively represented through the membership function. Practically all phenomena where there is a variable graduality and intensity. Moreover, dynamic phenomena can be grouped, with values that change over time. Finally, ambiguous phenomena, which can belong to two or more interpretative categories.

For instance, U is the universe of discourse of admissible values of height for an adult person (e.g., [140 cm, 200 cm]) and A is the set of "tall people" that naturally constitutes a sub-set of U.

The set, "tall people" does not have well-defined borders; it is a fuzzy set, with a gradual passage between belonging and not belonging to the set. A dividing line at 180 cm that separates tall people from people who are not tall is unnatural. There is no justification for the exclusion of people with a height of 179 cm from the set of tall people. The membership function reproduced in Figure 2(a) is therefore far from common sense and not ideal for reproducing verbal judgments.

However, we could also think of it in a different way. We can distinguish between individuals that certainly belong to the set of tall people A (for example people taller than 180 cm), individuals that do not belong at all (for example people shorter than 160 cm and individuals that only partly belong (all individuals with a height between 160 ad 180 cm). This produces the membership function in Figure 2(b) that foresees a diagonal line that allows us to represent the concept of "more or less tall." Moreover, the degree of membership of the individual u in the set A can be interpreted as the degree of truth of the proposition "The individual u is tall."

For example, for u = 130 cm the degree of membership of u in A is zero. This implies that truth of the proposition "the individual u is tall" is zero. That is, the proposition is false. For u = 190 cm the membership degree of u in A is one. Then the truth of the proposition "the individual u is tall" is one, meaning the proposition is true. The most interesting case is with u = 170 cm. In this case the membership of u in A is 0.5. Thus, the truth-value of the proposition "the individual u is tall" is 0.5. We can interpret this result as 'u is *neither* tall *nor* short.

Thanks to the possibility of applying fuzzy theory to already existing models and methodologies, fuzzy logic has provided significant innovative contributions in the field of automatic controls, advanced calculus, artificial intelligence and support for decisions.[3] The enormous potential offered by fuzzy logic can be found in the fascinating possibility to use the rigor of logic and mathematics in modeling

Figure 2. An example of membership functions for a fuzzy set and a canonical set

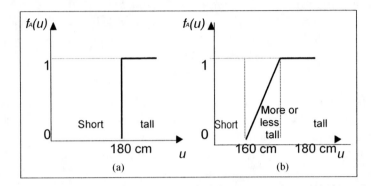

(a)   (b)

In the case of the canonic set, illustrated in the figure on the left, it is easy to distinguish objects that belong to the set from those that do not, through the introduction of an arbitrary limit (1,8 m). In the fuzzy case, it is impossible to draw a net line between the set and the external context. One possible way to consider this characteristic is to associate to different elements different intensities of membership in the fuzzy set. The people of medium height belong and do not belong to the set of tall people; the passage from being tall to not being tall is smooth.

linguistic expressions and forms of approximate reasoning. To represent, therefore, knowledge in many areas in which the complexity of phenomena allows above all for the imprecise linguistic descriptions, in particular for those systems that Zadeh (1973) defines as *humanistic systems*, setting them against inanimate of the natural sciences and engineering (*mechanistic systems*).

Zadeh states that the two main motivations that cause researcher to turn to this type of computational techniques are:

In the first place, computing with words can be a necessity when available informa-tion is too imprecise to justify the use of numbers, and, second, when a certain level of imprecision can be tolerated and exploited to achieve computational efficiency, robustness, low cost solutions, and a better correspondence with reality. (Zadeh, 1996, p. 105)

Zadeh's intuition comes out of the fact that individuals, when effectively completing even very complex tasks seem to tolerate acceptable levels of imprecision, thanks to their ability to describe a task in an approximate way, that is *linguistically*. In other words, in the execution of a task, individuals do not rely upon precise analytical models, like mathematical, but upon imprecise but adequate verbal models in the various situations they are involved in.

Methods for "computing with words" have been developed through concepts such as *linguistic variables, fuzzy relations, approximate reasoning, linguistic qualifiers, and linguistic modifiers*. More recently, the entire set of these techniques applied in the field of decisional support have been classified under the label of *linguistic decision analysis* (LDA) (Herrera & Herrera-Viedma, 2000).

In this approach, the concept of linguistic variables (i.e., variables assuming verbal values) is central assume linguistic values. For example, the variable "height" can assume a value of the set {very short, short, medium height, tall, very tall}. LDA provides a set of techniques for the representation, combination and aggregation of linguistic variables. It can be understood as a kind of linguistic arithmetic, in which the input of certain fundamental operations are not whole or real numbers, but linguistic expressions represented through fuzzy sets.

Although fuzzy logic is not in itself sufficient to represent the complexity and the shades of meaning contained in linguistic expressions, it is undeniable that it allows us to model many characteristics of these expressions; first of all, their fuzziness and their ambiguity, as we will explain through examples shown in the next two chapters.

Components of a Verbal Model

Usually, to obtain a model of a verbal discourse, we need to reduce it to a set of logical propositions and apply the inference mechanism to these in order to logically deduct the consequences of given assumptions.

Alternatively, verbal models can be transformed into a mathematical form. In this case as well, a reduction of the variables and the relationships between them is carried out to define measurable approximations (indicators) and a model, as a set of equations. The limits of both attempts at modeling the discourse are immediately apparent. Both the logical model and the algebraic model drastically reduce the shades of meaning and the wealth of information contained in the discourse. An example of logical and algebraic modeling is shown in Table 1.

Regarding the ability to effectively simulate the results of reasoning, the logical model, at least in the ingenuous representation in Table 1 is not stable in that, assuming the initial values of knowledge = 1 and forgetting = 0, the model fluctuates.

The incapacity of two-valued logic to take the intensity of the variables into account is in some ways resolved by the algebraic formulation of the model. But there is a price to pay, since one must identify: (a) procedures for the measurement of the variables (e.g., amount of learning, amount of forgetting, etc.); (b) meanings of parameters, often determined heuristically, but that do not have clear correspondence in the discourse (coefficients α, β e δ).

Fuzzy logic allows for a further way to implement a verbal model, since it provides the operative tools for "computing with words."

To illustrate some of the possible ways to represent and manipulate linguistic variables and connectives within *verbal model*, we will refer to the general model of the argumentative discourse shown in Chapter XI described according to the rules of argument analysis. In this model, we see the following fundamental components:

1.   **Verbal judgments:** In this category we include any verbal assertion that is classifiable as a *key claim* (conclusion of an argumentation), a *sub claim* (judgment in which the claim is articulated), *common claim* (facts, common sense, opinions of influential people), *ground* (facts offered in support of the claim).

2.   **The rules of argumentation:** In this category we group all of the rules of reasoning through which an individual "deduces" conclusions beginning with certain judgments used as premises; *warrants* (rules that demonstrate how the grounds support the claim) belong in this category.

3.   **Linguistic connectives** such as *qualifiers*, that limit the validity of the claim.

Modeling an explanatory discourse means having a methodology that allows for the formal representation of these three fundamental components.

In the following, we will show how it is possible to reach this objective through the computational and technical methods of *linguistic decision analysis*. We show how such methods allow us to attenuate the problem of meaning reductions that are typical of the formal modeling process with respect to the use of traditional quantitative techniques for the representation of verbal judgments.

Table 1. Example of modeling a discourse (Our adaptation from Wenstøp, 1975b)

Discourse
"Learning is based on reading good books, added to the ability to assimilate and not forget what has been read. Knowledge grows and is nourished by proper reading and by the knowledge itself. Unfortunately, it is also natural for human beings to forget more if too many things are learned at the same time and as the amount of knowledge accumulates, although it is more difficult to forget what is truly known."

Logical Model
If you read a lot and *do not* forget *then* you learn *If* you know *and* you learn *then* you increase what you know *If* you know *and* you learn *then* you tend to forget

Algebraic Model
Knowledge = Knowledge – forgetting Knowledge = Knowledge + learning Forgetting = $\delta \exp (\beta \text{ learning}) + \alpha \text{ knowledge}$

Fuzzy Reasoning

One of the main uses of fuzzy logic is the modeling of so-called *approximate reasoning*. For approximate reasoning we mean the reasoning described through linguistic rules such as *if...then*, as in the following example:

If the price of petroleum rises a lot, the rate of inflation tends to increase.

If inflation is high, there will probably be an increase in social conflict due to the rise in the cost of living.

It is well known that the first attempt to model reasoning was Aristotelian or bivalent logic. In Aristotelian logic, the basic rules of inference are *modus ponens, the modus tollens and syllogism,* which can be expressed in the following way:

If *a* and (*a* implies *b*) then *b*	(modus ponens)
If *not* (*b*) and (*a* implies *b*) then *not* (*a*)	(modus tollens)
If (*a* implies *b*) *and* (*b* implies *c*) then (*a* implies *c*)	(syllogism)

where *a, b* and *c* are propositions. The rule of *modus ponens* has been extended to fuzzy logic through the *compositional rule of inference* introduced by Zadeh (1973), in which the classic *modus ponens* makes up the particular case in which the logical values assumed in the propositions are limited to *true* and *false*.

The compositional rule of inference is based on the fundamental idea that a speech act, such as '*if x is A, then y is B*' (in which *A* and *B* are generally two linguistic labels) is the expression of a fuzzy link between the fuzzy sets *A* and *B*. In fuzzy terms, *A* and *B* are verbal labels that correspond to values of the linguistic variables x and y. Through speech acts, we define fuzzy functions, for example in table form (see Table 2), where A_i and B_i are labels that identify the values assumed by the linguistic variables x and y. It follows that speech acts of this type describe a relationship between two fuzzy variables. For example, the speech act "*If x is tall, y is heavy*" identifies the relationship between the variable *height* and *weight*.

What distinguishes the compositional rules of inference from the *modus ponens* of classical logic is in the fact that, given the rule *If A then B* and given the observation *A'*, different from *A*, the compositional rule of inference allows us to infer a conclusion *B,'* similar to *B, from A'* similar to *A*. While with classical logic it is not possible to deduce anything. For example, given the rule *If a tomato is red then it is ripe*, and given the observation that a *given tomato* is *more or less red*, the compositional rule of inference produces a fuzzy label B' next to *ripe*, that we can call *more or less ripe*. The choice of an appropriate operator for fuzzy implication also guarantees that other intuitive properties of reasoning are satisfied (Baldwin & Pilsworth, 1980; Fukami et al., 1980; Klir & Yuan, 1995).[4]

Thanks to the fact that the compositional rules of inference satisfy intuitive properties and that linguistic labels can be given to assumptions and conclusions, we can define systems of rules in verbal form.[5] Although there is no direct proof of the fact that a human being reasons effectively in a fuzzy way, nevertheless the simplicity of the method, if nothing else, leads us to make a hypothesis: when faced with complex tasks, human beings "simplify" the problem, tolerating acceptable levels of uncertainty and accepting an approximate, but satisfying execution of a task that can be improved with experience.[6]

Fuzzy Multiattribute Techniques

In problems where the number of variables is high, a fuzzy system of rule-based system becomes computationally inefficient. In such cases, or when simpler solutions are needed for the problem of aggregation of n fuzzy verbal judgments, it is possible to turn to fuzzy multiattribute techniques of aggregation.

Often, classic multiattribute techniques and the fuzzy set theory are used jointly (in such case it is also said that a preexisting method has been fuzzified). For example, it is possible to define fuzzy linear programming models (Zimmermann, 1991), in which constraints and objectives are defined in fuzzy of linguistic forms, or fuzzy models of regression in which the variables and the weights are fuzzy functions instead of simple numbers. In all cases, in which fuzzification has been done, normally there are computational complications as the object of the elaborations are not simple numeric values, but memberships functions.[7]

In general, for a multiattribute decision-making problem, a formulation can be done in the following way. A finite set of alternatives is considered $R = \{R_1, R_2, ..., R_m\}$, (for example, m candidates for a job interview), a set of finite criteria or attributes that such alternatives must satisfy $C = \{C_1, C_2, ..., C_n\}$ (for example, education,

Table 2. An example of linguistic function

X (height)	=>	y (weight)
A_1 = very short	=>	B_1 = very light
A_2 = short	=>	B_2 = light
A_3 = tall	=>	B_3 = heavy
A_4 = very tall	=>	B_4 = very heavy

Box 2. Linguistic decision analysis

The algorithms of fuzzy approximate reasoning are the foundation of the commercial success of fuzzy logic, which has been usefully employed in the resolution of problems of nonlinear system control with a very low cost/performance ratio.

Fuzzy technologies are largely employed in the construction of intelligent mechanisms incorporated into consumer products in which it is not necessary to achieve elevated levels of precision: Washing machines, automatic transmissions, and focus mechanisms in cameras and movie cameras. The control systems of these mechanisms use algorithms based on *If-then* rules such as *If the air cool then slow down the air conditioner*.

By translating verbal rules into mathematical models, fuzzy rule systems can simulate verbal discourses. This is the specific area of *linguistic decision analysis*.

While in the field of automatic controls there is a vast amount of literature in the area of linguistic decision analysis we can say that the problem is still on the forefront. Nevertheless, it is highly relevant to a series of applicative areas, generally tied to the interaction between man and machines. Pushed by the enormous success in the filed of automatic controls, fuzzy logic has partly abandoned that which, in the intentions of its inventor Lotfi Zadeh was supposed to be its primary objective: To identify a new way to model natural language that allows us to "compute with words" (Zadeh, 1996).

In recent years, scholars of fuzzy decision-making have given new energy to the research (Godo & Torra, 2000; Herrera & Herrera-Viedma, 1996, 2000; Torra, 1997; Yager, 1998; Zadeh, 2002). In any case, these studies focus on a formal and mathematical level and ignore interactions with linguistics and cognitive psychology. The sensation of many scholars is that it would be necessary to investigate more closely the possibility that fuzzy logic may have some cognitive foundations[7].

experience, motivation, technical competence, etc.). We can assign to each alternative R_i n scores x_{ij}, each expressing the degree to which the alternative R_i satisfies the criterion C_j (for instance, the x_{ij}'s could be the assessment of education level for the j-th candidate). In Chapter XIV we will discuss a fuzzy rule-based verbal model to analyze organizational behavior.

The problem is to identify, among the *m* available, the best alternative, which satisfies the criteria most closely. The process of determining the best alternative can be described in the following phases:

a.   **Scoring:** Assign a value x_{ij} to each couple (R_i, C_j)

b.   **Weighting:** Assign to each criteria C_j a weight w_j that represents its importance

c.   **Criteria Aggregation:** Calculate for every R_i an overall score $x_i = f_c(x_{i1}, x_{i2}, ..., x_{in}, w_1, ..., w_n)$ that represents the global score achieved by R_i through an appropriate function of multiattribute aggregation f_c

d.   **Ranking:** Given the set of points X = $\{x_1, x_2, ..., x_m\}$, choose the alternative that corresponds to the highest number of points

In order to resolve the problem of determining the global score for each alternative, starting with *n* elementary evaluations, it is necessary to establish how to represent the values x_{ij}, how to estimate the weights w_i, how to choose f and how to order the values x_i.

For each of these steps, many solutions have been proposed in the literature (Chen & Hwang, 1991), and there is a general consensus around the fact that a perfect solution, in general, does not exist, but that the choice of the method must be made according to the characteristics of the problem to be resolved.

In a fuzzy multiple attribute decision making (MADM) problem the values x_{ij}, x_i, w_i and the functions of aggregation f_c and f_p can be fuzzy, or expressable through linguistic labels. Therefore, in the presence of linguistic information, the MADM method, with respect to approximate reasoning models, allows us to "compute with words," although in a less transparent way. It can be said the fuzzy MADM method allows us to model very simple reasoning, such as:

If the attribute of C_1 of R_i has a value V_{i1}, ..., and the attribute C_m has a value V_{im}, and taking into account that C_1 has an importance of w_1 ... and C_m has an importance of w_m, then R_i has a value of V_i,

where V_{ij}, w_i and V_i are linguistic values that are representable through fuzzy sets.

An Example of a Linguistic Connective: The Fuzzy Quantifier

In classic logic two quantifiers are introduced, existential quantifiers of x (*there is at least one x*), and the universal quantifiers of x (*for every x*). For example, it can be said that a given property is true for all of the elements of a certain set or for at least one element of a given set. Sometimes, in daily language we use logic quantifiers imprecisely, such as when we say that *all birds fly*, while it would be more correct to say that *most* birds fly. Traditional logic does not admit this type of compromise.

However, in daily language we often use imprecise quantifiers, such as *few, many, almost all*, etc. Fuzzy logic allows for the representation of these linguistic expressions, generalizing the classic concept of quantifier. It is possible to demonstrate that an unlimited number of quantifiers can be defined that fall between the two extreme cases of traditional logic.

Fuzzy quantifiers are classifiable into two categories: *Absolute* fuzzy quantifiers, defined in *R,* such as *around ten, at least five, more than one hundred,* and *relative* fuzzy quantifiers, defined in the interval [0,1], such as *almost all, about half, most,* etc.

Fuzzy quantifiers are actually fuzzy sets. They can be represented through a membership function Q defined on a numeric interval R, which associates to every element r a value $Q(r)$ between zero and one. In Figure 3 two representations of the absolute quantifier "*about ten*" are shown, as well as the one relative to "*most.*"

Fuzzy quantifiers can be used to represent the qualifiers (see Chapter XI), i.e., linguistic connectives that have the task of limiting or circumscribing the validity of a judgment in a discourse, as in the expression bad weather usually creates traffic jams.

In the applications, fuzzy quantifiers are used in the modeling of the rules of approximate reasoning (Zadeh, 1996) and in multicriteria and multiperson aggregation (Herrera et al., 1996; Yager, 1988, 1993). For example, given a number of criteria (for example, those used for personnel recruitment of a certain professional figure in a company) it is possible to identify those candidates that meet most of the criteria (or many of the criteria, at least half, etc.).

From Theory to Practice

Up to this point, a quick overview has been provided for the reader on the set of possible approaches for modeling the verbal information contained in discourses through fuzzy logic.

The joint use of fuzzy techniques, of qualitative research methodologies and discourse mapping represents a possible answer to the need for learning organizations to have "soft" models that do not sacrifice information to the meaning, precision to flexibility of use, certainty of results to the exploration of multiple scenarios. This last characteristic will be explained more clearly through applicative examples presented in the next chapters.

One of the new things that must characterize the methodological apparatus of the learning organization is in the heterogeneity of techniques, in the eclecticism of methods, and in the strength of synthesis to join the effectiveness of qualitative techniques to the rigor and efficiency of quantitative ones.

References

Baldwin, J.F., & Pilsworth, B.W. (1980). Axiomatic approach to implication for approximate reasoning with fuzzy logic. *Fuzzy Set and Systems, 3*, 193-219.

Figure 3. Absolute and relative fuzzy quantifiers

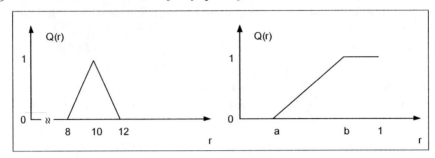

For a given number r, the value Q(r) represents the degree to which the value of r satisfies the concept expressed by the linguistic expression associated to Q. In the figure on the left we have the absolute quantifier about ten to which values between 8 and 12 units belong with a certain degree. On the right side we have the relative quantifier most, which is defined on the interval R = [0,1]. Here r is a percentage. If r = 60% we get Q(r) = 0.8, which means that a 60% percentage can be assumed to represent the concept most with a rather high degree of truth.

Black, M. (1937). Vagueness: An exercise in logical analysis. *Philosophy of Science, 4*, 427-455.

Bonissone, P.P. (1982). A fuzzy set based linguistic approach: Theory and applications. In M.M. Gupta & E. Sanchez (Eds.), *Approximate reasoning in decision analysis* (pp. 329-339). North Holland.

Chen, S.J., & Hwang, C. (1992). *Fuzzy multiple attribute decision making.* Berlin: Springer Verlag.

Fukami, S., Mizumoto, M., & Tanaka, K. (1980). Some considerations on fuzzy conditional inference. *Fuzzy Set and Systems, 4,* 243-273.

Godo, L., & Torra, V. (2000). On aggregation operators for ordinal qualitative information. *IEEE Transactions on Fuzzy Systems, 8*(2), 143-154.

Herrera, F., Herrera-Viedma, E., & Verdegay, J.L. (1996). Direct approach process in group decision making using linguistic OWA operators. *Fuzzy Set and Systems, 79,* 175-190.

Herrera, F., & Herrera-Viedma, E. (2000). Linguistic decision analysis: Steps for solving decision problems under linguistic information. *Fuzzy Sets and Systems, 115,* 67-82.

Klir, G.J., & Yuan, B. (1995). *Fuzzy set and fuzzy logic: Theory and applications.* Englewood Cliffs: Prentice Hall.

Kosko, B. (1993). *Fuzzy thinking: The new science of fuzzy logic.* Hyperion.

Saaty, T.L. (1978). Exploring the interface between hierarchies, multiple objectives and fuzzy sets. *Fuzzy Set and Systems, 1,* 57-68.

Tanaka, K. (1997). *An introduction to fuzzy logic for pratical applications.* New York: Springer-Verlag.

Torra, V. (1997). The weigthed OWA. *International Journal of Intelligent Systems, 12,* 153-166.

Turing, A.M. (1950). Computing machinery and intelligence. *Mind, 59,* 433-460.

Wenstøp, F. (1975a). *Application of linguistic variables in the analysis of organizations.* Doctoral dissertation, University Of California Berkley.

Wenstøp, F. (1975b). Deductive verbal model of organizations. *International Journal of Man Machine Studies, 8,* 301-357.

Yager, R.R. (1988). On ordered weighted averaging aggregation operators in multi-criteria decision making. *IEEE Transactions on Systems, Man and Cybernetics, 18*(1).

Yager, R.R. (1993). Families of OWA operators. *Fuzzy Sets and Systems, 59,* 125-148.

Yager, R.R. (1998). New modes of OWA information fusion. *International Journal of Intelligent Systems, 13,* 661-681.

Zadeh, L. (1965). Fuzzy sets. *Information and Control, 8,* 338-353.

Zadeh, L. (1973). Outline of a new approach to the analysis of complex systems and decision processes. *IEEE Transactions on Systems, Man and Cybernetics, 3*(1), 28-44.

Zadeh, L. (1996). Fuzzy logic = computing with words. *IEEE Transactions on Fuzzy Systems, 4*(2), 103-111.

Zadeh, L. (2001, September 18-20). Perception-based decision analysis. In *Proceedings of the VIII SIGEF Congress,* Naples, Italy.

Zimmermann, H.J. (1991). *Fuzzy sets and fuzzy logic: Theory and applications.* Norwell, MA: Kluwer Academic Publishers.

Endnotes

[1]   These techniques actually combine a set of tools (multiattribute and multiobjective decision making, fuzzy set theory) whose joint use represents an attempt to model the uncertainty contained in verbal expressions.

[2]   The attribute *fuzzy* was introduced by Lotfi Zadeh in his 1965 paper. It is synonymous with blurred, not clear, distinct or precise. However, none of these alternative connotations possess the provocative meaning deliberately introduced by Zadeh (1965). Previous attempts to formulate multivalues logic

were by Luckasiewicz in the thirties. The concept of vague set was introduced for the fisrt time by Max Black in 1937.

[3]   A bibliography of introduction to fuzzy logic, as important as it is, would be impossible given the huge corpus of pubblication on the subject. We will limit ourselves to suggesting two manuals that have been widely circulated as educational publications: Zimmermann (1991); Klir and Yuan (1995). Another interesting, though less rigorous, text is the one by Kosko (1993). For their historical importance, we suggest reading two articles by Zadeh (1965, 1973).

Many scientific magazines are dedicated to fuzzy logic, above all in the field of artificial intelligence and engineering. Among the more "general" ones we would like to remind the reader of *Fuzzy Sets and Systems, IEEE Transactions on Fuzzy Systems, Journal of Intelligent Systems*. Among the magazines dedicated to the application of fuzzy logic in the field of economics and managerial science we suggest the *Fuzzy Economic Review*.

[4]   Among the main properties that fuzzy inference must satisfy, we remind the reader of the following:

- **Fundamental property:** The consequence B' should never be more restrictive than the observation A' (for example, give the implication *x is tall -> y is heavy* and the observation *x is tall* it should not be possible to infer that *y is very heavy*).

- **Property of regularity:** More A implies more B;

- **Propagation of fuzziness:** In a chain of implications, the later inferences should be more and more vague; for example, considering the following chain of implications ' x is tall' -> 'y is heavy' -> 'z is obese' -> 'w is at risk for a heart attack' ->'v is at risk of a premature death,' given the observation 'x$_1$ is taller than 1.9m', it is clear that any consideration on the possibility of a premature death of x$_1$ should be much more vague on the inference on his weight.

- **Consistency:** Given the rule *if A then B* and given the observation A' = A (not B), the inference must produce the outcome B' = B (not A)

[5]   It is possible to demonstrate (Kosko, 1992) that a system like this is a *universal approximator* in the sense that it can approximate any continuous function defined or desired on a compact interval. The precision of the system grows with the number of rules adopted; the rules grow exponentially with the number of variables and the desired precision, which renders this type of model usable for smaller problems only (few variables, according to the precision required), unless the system that must be modeled does not admit a hierarchical decomposition. It is possible to demonstrate that given a function $f: R^n \rightarrow R^p$, a number of k^{n+p-1} rules are needed to approximate the function, where k is

the number of the fuzzy relationships necessary to "cover" the function f in a given hypercube.

[6]   And it is just that which is verified in hybrid systems obtained through the combination of fuzzy rules and neural networks in the operation of fine tuning the rules according to training data (Kosko, 1992).

[7]   Zadeh and Zimmermann, personal communication.

[8]   In quite simple terms, if it can be straightforward to say that $3 + 2 = 5$, it is not as easy to say that *more or less 3 + about 2= about 5*, because we have to add two functions (*more or less 3 + about 2*) to determine the shape of the function *about 5*.

Chapter XIII

Modeling
Verbal Judgements

Squareness may be succinctly and yet thoroughly defined as the inability to see quality before it's been intellectually defined, that is before it gets all chopped up into words ...We have proved that quality, though undefined, exists. Its existence can be seen empirically in the classroom, and can be demonstrated logically by showing that a world without it cannot exist as we know it. What remains to be seen, the thing to be analyzed, is not quality, but those peculiar habits of thought called 'squareness' that sometimes prevent us from seeing it.

(Robert M. Pirsig, *Zen and the Art of Motorcycle Maintenance: An Inquiry into Values*)

Abstract

In the previous chapter we have outlined the basic structure of a verbal model and its main components: Judgments, rules and qualifiers. This chapter proposes a model, called the dual truth model, to represent verbal judgments through fuzzy logic. Furthermore, the dual truth model permits us to examine more in depth and quantitatively assess the vagueness and ambiguity contained in a verbal judgment. An application of the model to the definition of assessment scale for personnel appraisal is also provided.

The Fuzziness of Verbal Judgments

One of the factors which makes natural language such a flexible and efficient tool is its inherent imprecision. It is surprising, in fact, how even a fairly limited vocabulary (it is estimated that the average educated person knows only a few thousand words) is enough to enable a person to carry out even very complex tasks.

The set of symbols which we use to denote events and circumstances is therefore relatively limited. It is also true that if there were enough symbols to allow for a one-to-one relationship with all possible events our brains would not be able to handle such a vast amount of information. How does a person manage to identify a potentially enormous number of events using a finite number of symbols?

Let's consider the example in Figure 1[1], where there are two sets: The set S of symbols {T, M, S} and the set O of objects {1, 2, 3, 4}. Let's assume, for example, that the symbols are three words {Tall, Medium, Short} and the objects are four different heights {180 cm, 170 cm, 160 cm, 150 cm}. The observer's task is to associate the symbols with the events. In a situation like this, one of the following three outcomes is possible:

1. *Uncertainty* (Figure 1a), where the observer is unable to identify a link between symbols and events because of lack of knowledge;
2. *Generalization* (Figure 1b), where the observer tries to use the same symbol to classify events which are different but in some way similar;
3. *Ambiguity* (Figure 1c), where the observer does not have the right symbol for the event so tries to use two others in combination to explain it.

With a given set of symbols whose total number is necessarily lower than that of possible events, the problem arises of how to deal with uncertainty, generalization and ambiguity. If we use the symbols as labels to denote objects it would be impossible to solve this problem, but fortunately language does not work like this. If we think, for example, of the adjective *tall* to indicate a person's height, we know that a person who measures 190 cm is definitely *tall* and that someone who is 150 cm definitely isn't, and also that someone who is about 170 cm is *tall* to a certain extent. At the same time we can still refer to someone of 160 cm as *tall* depending on the context, for example if we are talking about children or pygmies.

Figure 1. Uncertainty, ambiguity, vagueness, fuzziness

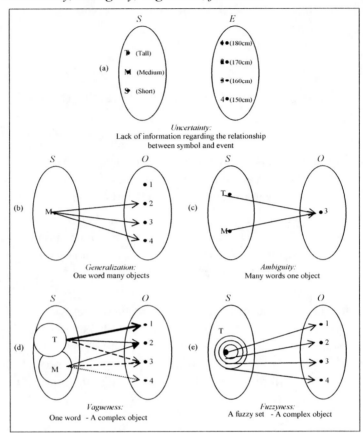

The concept of linguistic uncertainty derives from the difficulty in establishing a certain relationship between a limited number of verbal expressions and a large number of facts or events (Figure 1a). Generalization occurs when one word is used to indicate many things (Figure1b). Ambiguity instead results from using several different words to indicate the same thing (Figure 1c). The combination of generalization and ambiguity leads to vagueness (Figure 1d). In this case words are used in a rather indistinct way to denote categories of objects or events which partially overlap (vagueness). Fuzziness is a measure of the concept of vagueness, which we get by applying specific mathematical techniques (Figure 1e).

This example aims to show how we can use words as symbols of an uncertain significance and that it is this very uncertainty of language which enables us to adapt the same word to different events in different situations. As Russell reminds us, there are many possible facts which can go to prove a vague assertion.

In general, the vagueness of words, which is closely linked to the process of categorization of experience, means that many events can be labeled in the same way. The meaning which is then attached to the word is situated and socially constructed, making language use even more context-based and specific.

Language therefore enables us to adapt words to situations. Figure 1(d) represents the relationship between the imprecise word *tall* and four different values of height that can be applied to it, whereby the thickness of the line is proportional to how opportune or possible it is to use the word in each of the four cases. We could say that each of the four events can be thought of as elements belonging to a set which we can label *tall*, but each element belongs with a different intensity. Since height values only belong partially to the set *tall* we might think of these values as belonging to different sets simultaneously even if in varying degrees. For example, a person who is 175cm tall could be considered either *medium* or *tall*.

The fuzzy sets theory enables us to represent the vagueness of verbal expressions using a concept of partial membership. In other words, we can use a linguistic label to denote different events only if we accept that the boundaries of that label are not rigidly fixed.

A Model for the Representation of Verbal Judgment: Logical and Linguistic Truth

Usually, the representation of linguistic evaluations in a logical framework under-estimates how different the concept of truth is in linguistic and logical propositions (Strawson, 1952). Roughly speaking, the truth of a linguistic proposition is mainly a matter of social consensus, while the truth of a logical proposition is mainly a matter of coherence with other propositions. We are interested in two questions related to the relationship between these concepts of truth. First question: Given an event, what is the truth of a linguistic proposition describing that event? Second question: Given a true linguistic proposition, what is the logical truth, which corresponds to that linguistic proposition? In order to attempt to answer those questions we consider two cases. In the first case, we know that the height of John is 178 cm and we want to know the truth-value of the linguistic proposition "John is tall." In the second case, given the verbal proposition "John is tall," we want to know what the logical truth hidden in this proposition is, if no additional information is given. Let us look more closely at those two cases.

CASE A: What is the truth of the statement "John is tall," given that the height of John is 178 cm?

The proposition "The height of John is 178 cm" identifies a point in the interval [150 cm, 190 cm], while the term "tall" is an element of a set of terms used by the evaluator to explicit his or her evaluation. We can suppose that the term "tall" is the third term of the term set TS3 = {short, medium, tall}. According to the fuzzy set theory we can represent this term set as a family of membership functions, as represented in Figure 2. Thus, the truth of the proposition "John is tall" is given by the value of the membership function "tall" in the term set TS3. We can easily see that, for the value of height equal to 178, the value if tall is equal to 0.80. In formal terms:

truth ("John is tall" | (Height(John) = 178) AND TS3) = 0.80

CASE B: What is the truth of the statement "John is tall," no more information given?

In natural language the proposition "John is tall" means, for any possible listener, that in most situations John could be considered "tall" and only in few situations he could be considered short. Both for the speaker and the listener the word "tall" always includes the opposite concepts of TALLNESS and SHORTNESS. In other words we assume that the linguistic proposition "John is tall" can be broken down into two logical propositions, "John is SHORT" and "John is TALL," where ant-onyms TALL and SHORT (written in capital letters) denote "absolutely short" and "absolutely tall." Consequently, the truth of the linguistic proposition:

P = "John is tall"

Figure 2. The truth value of 'tall', given the height of 178 cm

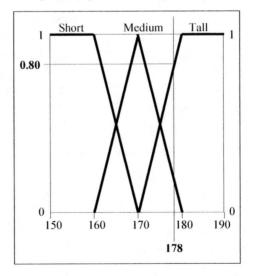

is broken down into the pair of truths related to propositions:

PL = "John is SHORT;"
PR = "John is TALL."

The linguistic proposition P = "John is tall" corresponds to a piece of information of the form "X is V," where the term X is a linguistic variable, and V is an element of the term set TS3 {short, medium, tall}. The terms of the term set are in an ordinal scale and each term V defines part of the universe of discourse whose extremes are the couple of antonyms SHORT and TALL. Figure 3 represents membership function of the term "tall" in the term set TS3.

In the same figure the functions of "SHORT" and "TALL" are represented. These functions correspond to the two diagonals of the square. Simply, they mean that the truth-value of TALL increases linearly from 0 to 1, and, vice-versa, the truth-value of SHORT decreases. Given these functions, the truth of the proposition P is equivalent to the determination of the degree of consistency (*cons*) of both the propositions PL and PR with P. If the evaluative sentence is the proposition:

P = "John is tall"

and the pair of related logical assertions is:

Figure 3. The truth value of 'tall', no more information given

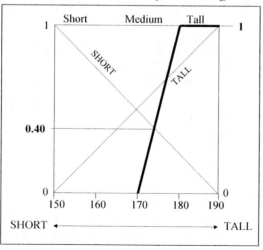

PL = "John is SHORT"

PR = "John is TALL"

the truth of the proposition P is a couple of values (a,b), such as:

truth ("John is tall") =

= (cons {"John is SHORT" | "John is tall"}, cons{"John is TALL" | "John is tall" }) =

= (sup {min(SHORT, tall)}, sup{min{TALL, tall)}}) = (a,b)

Table 1. Truth couples per term set varying from 1 to 11 values

Verbal values	number of verbal terms in the term set										
	1	2	3	4	5	6	7	8	9	10	11
VVL Very very low										0.92 0.17	0.92 0.15
VL Very low					0.86 0.29	0.88 0.25	0.89 0.22	0.9 0.2	0.91 0.18	0.83 0,25	0.85 0.23
L Low		0.75 0.5	0.8 0.4	0.83 0.33	0.71 0.43	0.75 0.38	0.78 0.33	0.8 0.3	0.82 0.27	0.75 0.33	0.77 0.31
MLL Moreless low							0.67 0.44	0.7 0.4	0.73 0.36	0.67 0.42	0.69 0.38
A⁻ Lower average				0.67 0.5		0.63 0.5		0.6 0.5	0.64 0.45	0.58 0.5	0.62 0.46
A Average	0.67 0.67		0.6 0.6		0.57 0.57		0.56 0.56		0.55 0.55		0.54 0.54
A⁺ Upper average				0.5 0.67		0.5 0.63		0.4 0.7	0.36 0.73	0.42 0.67	0.46 0.62
MLH Moreless high							0.44 0.67	0.4 0.7	0.36 0.73	0.42 0.67	0.38 0.69
H High		0.5 0.75	0.4 0.8	0.33 0.83	0.43 0.71	0.38 0.75	0.33 0.78	0.3 0.8	0.27 0.82	0.33 0.75	0.31 0.77
VH Very high					0.29 0.86	0.25 0.88	0.22 0.89	0.2 0.9	0.18 0.91	0.25 0.83	0.23 0.85
VVH Very very high										0.17 0.92	0.15 0.92

In the case depicted in Figure 3, the pair of truth-values of the proposition "John is tall" is (0.40, 1.00). The pair can be interpreted as answers to the following questions: "What is the possibility that John is considered absolutely short, knowing that someone said that he is tall? What is the possibility that John is considered absolutely tall, knowing that someone said that he is tall?" Or, more simply, "What is the truth degree of the assertion 'John is tall'? And what is its falsity degree?" The fuzzy model answers to those questions with a couple of values, which, according to the viewpoint of Sainsbury (1988), express the fact that the linguistic assertions are neither definitely true nor definitely false.

The pair of values represents a bridge between linguistic and logical propositions. We named as *dual truth model* this representation of how linguistic evaluations embody paradoxical truths.

We can generalize from this to calculate the truth couple per term set of any number of items. If we imagine that the items in a term set can be represented by triangular functions we get the truth couple (a, b) as shown in Table 1. The pairs show the following relationship:

$$a = (j + 2 - i)/(j + 2) \qquad b = (i + 1)/(j + 2)$$

where j is the number of verbal terms in the term set size and i the position the verbal values holds on the verbal scale.

It is interesting to note how as j increases, the two values tend to complement each other. Following this simple observation, it can easily be demonstrated that if j were infinite we would have no need to characterize the assessment P with a couple of values. One would be enough because each is the complement of the other (the negation, in the dual logic).

Properties of the Dual Truth Model

Although natural language is quite varied, we don't normally use many verbal terms to express our opinions. This means that they are often rather ambiguous. We ask a limited number of signs to represent a much larger number of events.

If we start with the truth couples we can find measures to assess precision, ambivalence and ambiguity in verbal judgments. The truth couples define a two-dimensional space known as the dual truth space as shown in Figure 4.

Any verbal judgment is represented by a point V whose coordinates are the values of the truth couple. A precision line can be identified in this plane. The proximity of the point to this precision line increases as the number of elements in the term set increases. The points which are actually on the line have the greatest degree of precision, just in this case we need a term set with infinite values. The point with coordinates (1,1) denotes a complete inability to express a judgment (degree of precision equals 0, e.g., an individual is tall and short at the same time with the highest degree of possibility).

The complement of precision is vagueness. For any given point on the plane we can find an associated measure of vagueness in the judgment which is defined as follows:

Vagueness = (right value + left value - 1)

The vagueness of V is proportional to its distance from the precision line.

The second diagonal in the dual truth space defines what is called an *ambivalence line*. Polarization is a measure to assess how sharp is a judgment. Ambivalence is the negation of polarization:

Polarization = abs(right value − left value)

Ambivalence = 1 − Polarization

Figure 4. Measures of precision, ambivalence and ambiguity in verbal evaluation

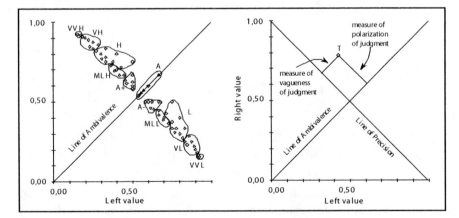

The verbal judgments shown in Table 1 can be positioned on a left value/right value plane thus determining how close they are to the lines of ambivalence and precision without actually being part of either (left side picture). The points are always located above the precision line. It is thus possible to introduce ambiguity measures into the judgement depending on its coordinates. On the right side figures, verbal judgments belonging to different term sets are shown.

where abs indicates the absolute value of the difference. The evaluation is more ambivalent the closer to the line of ambivalence it is. It is easy to prove that more polarized judgments like *very very low* or *very high* have low degrees of ambivalence whereas the term *average* has the highest degree of ambivalence. Even the measure of ambivalence, if the verbal judgment is equal, depends on the size of term set adopted.

We finally introduce the measure of ambiguity defined as:

$$Ambiguity = \frac{\sqrt{Vagueness^2 + Ambivalence^2}}{\sqrt{2}}$$

A judgment is ambiguous if it is vague and ambivalent. Once the term set is fixed, the most ambiguous judgment is *average*. However, as we might expect, the ambiguity related to *average* decreases as the number j of the elements in the term set increases.

The Representation of Judgment Through Fuzzy Scales

The dual truth model provides a framework for a more comprehensive use of the informational content of verbal judgment. It enables us to formulate an assessment scale whereby the assessor can choose the most suitable degree of precision for expressing his or her judgment.

The model presented below dispenses with the traditional concept of a scale as a successive ordinal scale of values each with its own label. The verbal scale is simply a bar with *n* number of boxes which represents a continuum going from a totally negative assessment to a totally positive one. There are no labels on the scale apart from those of the two opposites. The assessor can choose a box or a whole section of the continuum as illustrated in Figure 5.

The two antonyms, as well as representing the two opposite poles of an assessment, also represent two poles of meaning. For example, an assessment of the attention given to the customer is measured on a continuum from *evasive answer* to *documented answer*. The two poles thus act as a guide for interpreting the linguistic variable *attention to customer* within the context in which it is used and constructed. An answer like the one given in Figure 5 is the equivalent of a verbal assessment of the type: *"for the most part, X shows a high level of sensitivity to client needs."*

Figure 5. Uncertainty scale

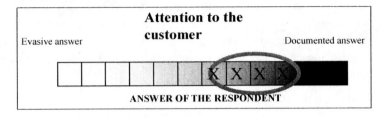

If we combine the scale model and the dual truth model we can measure the ambiguity inherent in the assessment, or give it a numerical value as shown in Figure 6.

If we divide the bar into *n* boxes a triangular function can be associated with the judgment expressed in anyone box. If the judgment is expressed in more than one box then it is vaguer and can be represented by associating a trapezoid membership function to it which is obtained by the convolution of the *m* triangles associated with the boxes.

Using the dual truth model we immediately associate a truth couple (*a*, *b*) to the fuzzy representation of the judgment which is obtained as shown in Figure 6. The result is (0.55, 0.82), according to the table in Figure 6. The following formula can be used to get a nonfuzzy reading:

V=(1-*a*+*b*)/2= (1-0.355+0.82)/2=0.635

Figure 6. Judgment represented using dual truth model and uncertainty scale

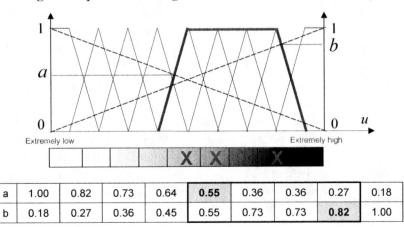

| a | 1.00 | 0.82 | 0.73 | 0.64 | **0.55** | 0.36 | 0.36 | 0.27 | 0.18 |
| b | 0.18 | 0.27 | 0.36 | 0.45 | 0.55 | 0.73 | 0.73 | **0.82** | 1.00 |

It is worth remembering that $(1 - a)$ expresses the *possibility* that the judgment may be "not negative" whereas b is the possibility that the judgment is positive. So V is a kind of average of the two possibilities[2].

The combined use of the dual truth model and the verbal scale gives us a powerful model for assessing verbal judgment. The main properties are the followings:

a. The problem of interpretation of labels on the part of the assessors is notably reduced as labels are replaced by two opposites which provide a more circumscribed and specific meaning for the judgment.

b. There are no arbitrary hypotheses regarding the values that the variable should assume like it happens with a predefined ordinal scale, since the fuzzy representation is a more direct representation of what the assessor actually said.

c. The assessor is free to express her/his uncertainty as s/he wishes because the scale enables them to vary the dose from *minimal uncertainty* (only one box) to *total ignorance,* by selecting the whole bar. When no answer is given, this can be interpreted as "don't know" and so represented by the closed pair $(1,1)$ which corresponds to a maximum level of ambiguity in the judgment.

d. The fuzzy scale enables us to identify a kind of naive variance within a judgment implicit in expressions like *"usually demonstrates a high level of attention to client needs," "her behavior is satisfactory in the majority of cases with some points of excellence,"* etc.

How to Aggregate Verbal Judgments

The dual truth model represents and combines in quantitative way the verbal judgments, while at the same time preserving vagueness, ambivalence and ambiguity of verbal sentences.

The following example regards multiple attribute decision making (MADM, see Chapter XII) when we have verbal or linguistic information available. Let's consider, for example, that we have to decide what evaluation to give a student essay, according the criteria *comprehensiveness, presentation, extensiveness of bibliography etc* (and let's call these criteria E_1, E_2, ..., E_{10}). Let's imagine that a teacher gave the following assessment for each criterion:

E_1: Very very high (7)	E_6: Very very low (9)
E_2: More or less high (7)	E_7: Low (5)
E_3: High (3)	E_8: Low (3)

E_4: Low (7) E_9: Medium (5)

E_5: Low (5) E_{10}: Very very low (9)

The numbers in brackets refers to the number of elements of the term set the judgment belongs to. The first step entails transforming the verbal labels into truth couples. Table 1. thus gives us:

Fuzzy judgement	V	Fuzzy judgement	V
E_1: Very very High (0.22, 0.89)	0.84	E_6: Very very Low (0.91, 0.18)	0.14
E_2: More or less High (0.44, 0.67)	0.62	E_7: Low (0.71, 0.43)	0.36
E_3: High (0.4, 0.8)	0.7	E_8: Low (0.80, 0.40)	0.3
E_4: Low (0.78, 0.33)	0.28	E_9: Average (0.57, 0.57)	0.5
E_5: Low (0.71, 0.43)	0.36	E_{10}: Very very low (0.91, 0.18)	0.14

The value $V = (1-a + b)/2$ represents the defuzzified value of the judgment, which is useful for successive combinations with fuzzy quantifiers. Let's imagine that we want to combine these evaluations in a global score that reflects that *the majority of the E_i criteria are met*. To do this we can use the fuzzy quantifier *most* (see Chapter XII and Box 1) which gives us a global evaluation in the form:

$(a, b) = F(V1, V2, …, V10) = (0.71, 0.43)$.

Still using Table 1, we can identify which verbal term is closest to the closed pair (0.71, 0.43). The pair (0.71, 0.43) corresponds to the judgment *Low* in a term set with a cardinality of 5.

Setting aside the technical details involved in the calculation, it is interesting to see that different quantifiers give us different results, as shown in Table 2. As we can see, the results are very different both for the fuzzy values as well as for the vagueness and ambiguity content.

Since the use or choice of a quantifier depends on the assessor, this kind of variability should not be seen as off-putting but, rather, as further proof of the variety of meaning and situation underlying verbal judgments.

The different ways in which judgments are combined can lead to different outputs. Examining the different scenarios, which are obtained using the different hypotheses, provide us with a multiplicity of options which can be used as the starting point for further in-depth analysis or used as a basis for comparison.

Table 2. Example of multicriteria combination using fuzzy quantifiers

Quantifier	Truth pair	Verbal judgement	Vagueness $v = (b + a - 1)$	Ambivalence $a = (1 - \|b - a\|)$	Ambiguity $\sqrt{(v^2 + a^2)/2}$	Defuzzied value x 100
Most	(0.71, 0.43)	*Low* (5)	0.14	0.72	0.52	36
Pure Average	(0.64, 0.49)	*More or less low* (7)	0.11	0.77	0.39	43
All	(0.91, 0.18)	*Very very low* (9)	0.09	0.27	0.14	14
At least one	(0.18, 0.91)	*Very very high* (9)	0.09	0.27	0.14	87
At least 70%	(0.8, 0.4)	*Low* (3)	0.2	0.6	0.32	30

Box 1. Aggregation of linguistic information through fuzzy quantifier

The aggregation of fuzzy judgments can be performed by a family of fuzzy operators called OWA (ordered weighted average). An OWA operator F of dimension n has an associated vector of weights $W = [w1, w2, …, wn]^T$ such that:

1) $w_i \varepsilon [0,1]$
2) $\Sigma_i w_i = 1$

Given n fuzzy judgments $a_1, a_2, …, a_n$ we can obtain an aggregated judgment in the following way:

$$F(a_1, a_2, …, a_n) = \Sigma_i w_i b_i$$

where b_i is the i-th largest of the a_i, hence an ordering is requested to perform the calculation. OWA operators have the basic properties of an averaging operator. The pure average is the OWA operator whose weighting vector is $W = [1/n, …, 1/n]$.

It is possible to demonstrate that for any OWA operator F we have:

$$min(a_i) < F(a_1, a_2, …, a_n) < Max(a_i)$$

i.e., OWA operators provides a gradual transition from the 'and' and the 'or' fuzzy logical connectives. Given an operator F with a weighting vector W it is possible to define the following orness measure:

$$orness(W) = \frac{1}{n-1} \sum_i ((n - i) w_i)$$

F is called an or-like (and-like) operator if orness(W) > 0.5 (< 0.5).

In our case we suppose that the value a_i represents the truth value of the proposition "The criterion E_i is satisfied" Consequently, the aggregation (max) yields the greatest available satisfaction level (i.e., the assessor is satisfied if at least one criterion is satisfied), which the *and* aggregation yields the lowest satisfaction level (i.e., the assessor is satisfied if all the criteria are satisfield). For this reason the orness measure is an optimism indi-

continued on next page

Box 1. continued

cator in the aggregation: any other operator would provide a certain degree of optimism ranging from absolute pessimism (orness(W) = 0) to absolute optimism (orness(W) = 1).

Yager (1991) shows that the calculation of the weighting vector W can be performed by means of fuzzy quantifiers: given a monotonically nondecreasing fuzzy quantifier Q(r) the weights w_i can be obtained through the following formula:

$$w_i = Q\left(\frac{i}{n}\right) - Q\left(\frac{i-1}{n}\right)$$

where n is the number of the criteria. Yager also demonstrates that the w_i can be interpreted as the additional satisfaction obtained if the i-th criterion is satisfied, provided the i-1 criteria are satisfied.

If the weights are calculated by means of a given fuzzy quantifier Q, it is possible to verify that the aggregated value can also be interpreted as the truth value of the proposition Q criteria are satisfied.

It is worth to note that by choosing a quantifier Q we also establish how we prefer to aggregate the judgements. For example, let's consider the quantifier most depicteed in Figure 3, Chapter XII: In this cases the aggregation performed through this quantifier is "*most* of the criteria should be satisfied." We could also find other ways to perform the aggregation by using different quantifiers, such as *all, a lot of, many, at least half,* and so on.

By calculating the weights for the fuzzy quantifier most with n=10, a=0.3, b=0.8 we have the following weight vectors:

Wmost =[0   0   0   0.2   0.2   0.2   0.2   0.2   0   0]$^\mathrm{T}$

In contrast with a pure averaging operation, the use of the OWA operators allows us to prevent from undesired compensation between positive and negative evaluation which eventually could shifts the group evaluation toward the value "average." For example, if we consider the quantifier *most*. We can observe that such a quantifier carries out an aggregation which does not keep into account the highest and the lowest available satisfaction level. The use of this quantifier entails an aggregation criteria according to which the group satisfaction we obtain is equal to zero if less than 30% of criteria are satisfied and the group incremental satisfaction gained by satisfying more than 80% of criteria is zero as well. Consequently, given a group of 100 criteria, because of the ordering, the overall evaluation will depend on the judgments belonging to the interval ranging from the 30th to the 80th best evaluation.

Conclusion

We have shown that with the combined use of the dual truth model, the uncertainty scale and fuzzy indicators we can hold the verbal ambiguity without too difficult computational effort. In more general terms, using fuzzy judgments has several concrete advantages:

a.   Enables us to limit the problem of reduction of meaning inherent whenever we formalize knowledge because fuzzy discourse models aim to represent the characteristics of verbal information as faithfully as possible.

b.   Assessor behavior in terms of attitude towards uncertainty is described more accurately. Using these uncertainty measures it is possible to ask oneself where the source of the uncertainty lies (In the assessor? In the situation? In the context? In the ambiguity with which the request was formulated? In the complexity of the task?).

It is important to remark that in fuzzy literature it is possible to find many other possible ways of representing judgments and that in general this is a very critical task when designing fuzzy systems. Rather than focusing on technical issues, through the dual truth model we wanted the readers focus their attention on some conceptual issues of judgment representation, in particular those arising from the ambiguity of verbal judgments and to which extent fuzzy logic can help to represent it. In the next chapter we turn our attention to possible approaches in modeling the second component of a verbal model, i.e., rules representation by providing several examples of verbal models.

References

Baldwin, J.F. (1986). Supporting logic programming. *International Journal of Intelligent Systems, 1*, 73-104.

Cannavacciuolo, A., Iandoli, L., & Zollo, G. (1999). The performance requirements analysis with fuzzy logic. *Fuzzy Economic Review, 4*(1), 35-73.

Chen S.J., & Hwang, C. (1992). *Fuzzy multiple attribute decision making.* Berlin: Springer Verlag.

Dubois, D., & Prade, H. (1980). *Fuzzy set and systems: Theory and applications.* New York: Academic Press.

Dubois, D., & Prade, H. (1982). The use of fuzzy numbers in decision analysis. In M.M. Gupta & E. Sanchez (Eds.), *Fuzzy set and possibility theory: Recent development* (pp. 309-321). Amsterdam: North-Holland.

Klir, G.J., & Yuan, B. (1995). *Fuzzy set and fuzzy logic: Theory and applications.* Englewood Cliffs: Prentice Hall.

Martin-Clouarie, R., & Prade, H. (1986). SPII-1: A simple inference engine capable of accomodating both imprecision and uncertainty. In G. Mitra (Ed.), *Computer assisted decision making.* Amsterdam: Elsevier Sciences Publishers.

Strawson, P.E. (1952). *Introduction to logical theory.* London: Methuen & Co.

Zollo, G. (1998, August). *Cognition, words and logic: How fuzzy logic can help us to design new organizational procedures.* Presented at the Academy of Management meeting. San Diego.

Endnotes

[1]   A previous version of this example as well as of the dual truth model has been discussed in Zollo (1998).

[2]   In more general terms, the formula is a defuzzification of V, that is, an operation which gives us a numerical value for V. See Klir and Yuan (1995) for a detailed study on possibility measures.

Chapter XIV

Modeling Rules

As the complexity of a system increases, our ability to make precise and yet significant statements about its behavior diminishes until a threshold is reached beyond which precision and significance become almost mutually exclusive characteristics.

(Lotfi Zadeh, 1973)

Abstract

In Chapter XII we outlined the basic structure of a verbal model and its main components: Judgments, rules and qualifiers. This chapter illustrates several approaches in representing the relationships among linguistic variables contained in a verbal model (rules). The description of the examples will skip technical details and it is mainly aimed at illustrating possible applications, finalities and advantages of verbal models.

Examples of Verbal Models

Let us take a look at some examples of verbal models, in order to complete the presentation of the methodological proposals outlined in this part of the book. This will allow us:

a.   To better understand the logic of construction and the function of verbal models.

b.   To highlight the potential applications and the managerial implications of their use.

It is useful to point out some particular characteristics of the methodological approach presented in this book before presenting few examples (Table 1).

The verbal models allow us to simulate the reasoning contained in the discourses that describe the theories of actions. It is, therefore, in principle, possible to predict the consequences of such theories through the simulation. Inputs of the simulation are made up of both qualitative and quantitative data and the fuzzy logic allows us to model the qualitative uncertainties in verbal opinions. Varying the inputs and some of the parameters that characterize the model, it is possible to analyze different scenarios that occur following different initial hypotheses (what-if analysis).

A Verbal Model for Organizational Analysis

Although it is possible to find numerous examples of the modeling of verbal discourses in fuzzy literature, they are, for the most part, relative to the attempts to model the discourses of human experts in order to create expert systems. In this paragraph, we will make reference to one of the few examples relative to the organizational applications of the concepts of verbal model proposed by Wenstøp (1975b).

Table 1. Characteristics of the proposed methodology (Adapted from Rosenhead & Mingers, 2001)

Scenarios for simulation and exploration of possible alternatives
Use of quantitative and qualitative data expressed in the form of verbal opinions
Ability to manage the uncertainties and ambiguities contained in the opinions of different individuals
Representation of the rules of reasoning and synthesis of the information contained in the discourses and in the theories of action

In order to illustrate the potential of the applications of verbal models to organizational science, Wenstøp applied a model of approximated reasoning to a well known case study of *organizational behavior* inherent to the analyses of organizational distortions caused by an excess of bureaucracy and control at a mining company (Gouldner, 1954).

From his direct on-site observations and the analysis of data collected during interviews, Gouldner and his colleagues noticed that an intensified use of bureaucratic rules and control corresponded to an elevated level of hostility towards superiors and a sharp fall in the level of workers' performance.

Based on these observations of empirical evidence, Gouldner described a model verbally to explain the events that he had observed and described. Although the meaning of the variables is intuitive, in a verbal form, such a representation cannot be easily translated in a analytic model. This verbal model does not provide any objective way of effectuating the measures of the variables in play. Furthermore, a systematic way to derive from its consequences and objectively test its ability to predict phenomena does not exist.

From an analysis of the text, Wenstøp first drew a graphical representation of the subject through a causal map. Then, he described it in the form of *if....then* rules, the cause-effect relationships contained in Gouldner's discourse. Eventually, he represented the variables and the relationships between them through linguistic variables

Figure 1. Structure of causal relationships in Gouldner's model (Adapted from Wenstøp, 1975b)

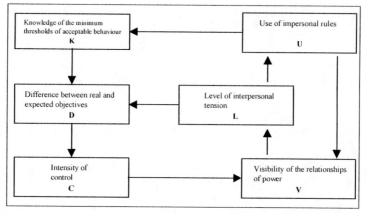

Gouldner's model highlights the consequences of excessive bureaucracy and control in organizations. The figure is easily assimilated to a causal map of the type presented in Chapter XI. The map is a graphical representation the argument in discussion through which Gouldner justifies the emergence of certain phenomena of poor organization reaching a climax of distrust between superiors and workers, an adjustment of workers to a minimum level of performance and the use of invasive techniques of control.

and fuzzy rules and simulated the discourse through the application of the fuzzy techniques of approximated reasoning. Figure 1 shows Wenstøp's causal map.

The verbal model, that represents the causal map in Figure 1 is based on fuzzy linguistic assertions, such as the ones contained in Table 2.

Linguistic variables (U_t, L_t, K_t, etc.) appear in the rules together with the values that they assume (*low, rather low, very high,* etc.), and where t is the instant of time in which the variable is measured. The relationships between the variable are expressed through *if ... then ...* rules or by similarity relationships (*is similar, is equal,* etc.). The model is a plain translation of Gouldner's reasoning into fuzzy rules.

The model establishes that the use of impersonal control rule (U_t) is the result of two consecutive periods during which the level of tension is high (L_{t-2}) and the level of bureaucratic control decreases when the level of conflict is low (Rule 1). Rule 2 states that the minimum level of adequate behavior of the workers' is closely tied to the current use of the bureaucratic control. Rule 3 implies that workers take ad-

Table 2. Fuzzy linguistic assertions

RULE 1	U_t is	Somewhat higher than	U_{t-1}	If L_{t-2} is *very high or quite high*
	Or			
	U_t is	Equal to	U_{t-1}	If L_{t-2} *it is not low or very high*
	Or			
	U_t is	*slightly lower*	U_{t-1}	If L_{t-2} it is *low or rather low*
RULE 2	K_t is	*very similar* to	U_t	
RULE 3	L_t is	*very similar* to	V_{t-1}	
RULE 4	D_t is	similar to	K_t	If L_t *it is not low*
	Or			
	D_t is	similar to	L_t	If L_t is *low or rather low*
RULE 5	C_t is	higher than	C_{t-1}	If D_t is higher than D_{t-1} and D_t is high
	Or			
	C_t is	Equal to	C_{t-1}	If D_t is high and D_t is not higher than D_{t-1}
	Or			
	C_t is	Equal to	C_{t-1}	If D_t is not high or low
	Or			
	C_t is	Slightly lower than	C_{t-1}	If D_t is low
RULE 6	V_t is	Equal to	V	If U_t is not higher than U_{t-1}
	Or			
	V_t is	Lower than	V	If U_t is higher than U_{t-1}

vantage of their knowledge of minimum acceptable behavior if the level of tension is not low, by restricting output. Rule 4 tells us that the workers limit themselves to doing the minimum necessary if the level of interpersonal tension is not low. Rule 5 expresses a typical management reaction pattern. Finally, Rule 6 says that the visibility of power relations is inversely related to U if supervision is low.

The fuzzy representation of the model allows Wenstøp to transform a discourse into an algorithm, and therefore it becomes possible to simulate the effects, given certain initial data. For example, if all variables assume the initial value *more or less high*, we can see that the model stabilizes after only two periods in the stable state (U, L, D, C) = (*very high, neither high nor low, very high*). In practice, it happens that if the use of bureaucracy is elevated, the level of conflict remains at an average level, the performance is poor and the control very intense.

Thanks to the simulation, the model can be used to effectuate analyses of the type *what-if*, for example, to test the opportunity of adopting certain policies of supervision and control. Running numerous simulations, Wenstøp demonstrated that:

a.   The verbal model seems to be in agreement with Gouldner's predictions

b.   Policies of intensification of supervision produce low performance and the growth of the bureaucracy

c.   There are no significant differences between the adoption of a supervision policy of an intensity *normal or low*, although it emerges that a low supervision is the only policy that can change a non favorable situation into a better one

d.   Given the structure of the system, there is no supervisory strategy which works well under all conditions and that permits to reach a desirable state of affairs characterized by good performance and low conflict

The Representation of Discourses Through a Fuzzy Causal Map

When the systems to be modeled contain an elevated number of variables and relationships, the use of the fuzzy rules becomes impractical from a computational point of view (Kosko, 1997). An alternative way of creating a verbal model is the integration of fuzzy logic and causal maps (Kosko, 1992).

Fuzzy causal maps are particularly suitable for representing systems, in which there are feedback relationships between the variables (causal cycles). An example of a causal cycle determined by the presence of feedback is the following: (a) An increase

Figure 2. An example of causal cycle

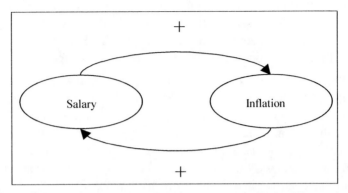

Fuzzy causal maps are similar to traditional causal maps as the one shown in Chapter XII, since they are oriented graphs expressing cause-effect relationships among concepts. There are, however, two important differences: each concept may be totally true, false or true to a certain intermediate degree. In addition, the intensity of strength of a causal relationship between two concepts can be fuzzy. For instance, we could say that an increase in salaries usually contributes to the growth of inflation.

in salaries can contribute to the growth of inflation; (b) an increase in inflation can generate the request for adequate salaries. Using the formal representation of the causal maps, such relationships are shown represented as in Figure 2. A causal map can contain many cycles composed of two or more concepts.

A map allows us to represent the causal ties explicitly contained in a discourse. In Figure 3 we show an example of a fuzzy causal map developed by Kosko (1992). The map is a representation of an explanation discourse proposed by a journalist in relation to the effects of the policies of investment in South Africa on the apartheid regime on the part of foreign states[1]. In the article, the author examines the consequences of a policy of reducing American investments in South Africa in order to weaken the apartheid regime. The maps are graphs composed of nodes (concepts such as "foreign investment," "black tribe unity," etc.) and arcs (causal relationships). An arc from a node A to a node B marked with a + signifies that a positive relationships between A and B. For example, the increase in foreign investments helps to develop the mining industry.

The map of Figure 3 is fuzzy in the sense that the relationships between the concepts can be more or less intense. For example, a growth in the mining industry brings about a *certain* growth in black work and contributes *decidedly* to the development of the mining industry. The concepts within in the nodes are also fuzzy as they can be absolutely true (logic value 1), absolutely false (logic value 0) or true o a certain degree (logic value ranging from 0 to 1).

If the sign is positive, the partial or total activation of a cause-node activates the effect-nodes to a certain extent. The extent to which a node is activated depends on

Figure 3. An example of a fuzzy causal map

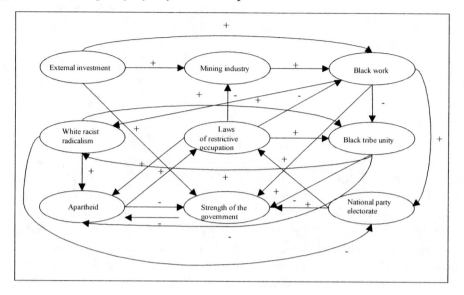

the number and the intensity of the previous active causes into which they merge. For example, the level of black tribe unity is influenced by the nodes; "radical white racist," "laws of restrictive occupation" and "black work". The node only starts to activate itself when the causal flow from the previous nodes is sufficiently intense and exceeds a prefixed threshold.

A certain configuration composed of the active and inactive nodes of a map in a given instant is known as the state of the system. Therefore, we can show the state of a map through a vector of values of as many elements as there are nodes, and the values of these correspond to the levels of activation of the map at a certain point. If the map is fuzzy, we will have vectors whose values belong to the interval [0, 1].

The evaluation of the levels of activation of the various nodes is not immediate due to the elevated number of relationships and feedback present in the map, but opportune algorithms have been developed and there are several software products available to implement them. The important thing to underline is that the map is a dynamic system whose evolution is influenced by the starting conditions that evolve and finally stabilize in a final configuration. There are three possible evolutions of a causal map:

a. **A fixed point:** A specific final state in which the map becomes stable

b. **A limit cycle:** A periodic oscillation between two or more states

c. **A chaotic attractor:** The map oscillates in a chaotic model, possibly remaining confined in certain areas of the space of all the possible states

The article to which the map in Figure 3 refers examines the theory claiming that a reduction in foreign investment in South Africa would have contributed to putting pressure on the local government and obtaining, in the long term, a substantial change in the apartheid government.

According to the author of the article, a reduction in investments would instead cause effects contrary to the intentions of its backers. To demonstrate this theory, the author put forward an explanation in which the map in Figure 3 is a sort of "graphic translation."

The fuzzy mathematical model allows us to test the coherence of the theory proposed in the article. By applying Kosko's algorithm (1992), it is possible to verify that if one starts from an initial condition in which only the "foreign investments" node is active, after several cycles, there is a convergence towards a fixed point in which the following nodes "foreign investments," "mining industry," "black work," "white racist radicalism," "government strength" and "national party electorate" are activated. The "apartheid" node and the others remain inactive. In other words, the presence of foreign investments contributes to strengthening the government and maintaining the status quo, but does not intensify the apartheid regime. This result confirms the theory of the article.

What happens if the foreign investments are suspended instead? To verify the effects of this policy, we need to start from a situation of equilibrium and deactivate the "foreign investments" node. Leaving the system to evolve, it moves towards a limited cycle composed of two states: In the first, only the two nodes "white racist radicalism" and "laws of restrictive occupation" are active; in the second, only the "black tribe unity" and "apartheid" nodes are active. In other words, noninvestment provokes a weakening of the government, negative relapses of occupation and a worsening of white radicalism to which follows a strengthening of black tribe unity and the consequent worsening in the regime of segregation.

The test confirms the theory of the article, but it is necessary to clarify that it is not a demonstration of the truth or falseness of the proposed theory. Rather, the map allows us to:

a. Describe the vision of the reality of the author of the discourse in terms of concepts and causal relationships between the concepts.

b. Verify that the predicted effects *coherently* follow the hypotheses and the network of causal relationships described in the explanation.

c. Individuate hidden schemes and other possible effects produced by the theory of the actions proposed in the discourse of the explanation.

In addition to describing and testing the internal coherence of a theory of the actions, the map can be used to modify existing theories of actions and simulate the effects produced by the modifications. For example, the addition of a node (concept) to an existing map, of an arrow (causal relationship), or even the simple modification to a relationship can drastically change the effects of initial hypotheses (see the examples reported in Weick, 1979, Chapter IV). Other methodologies also exist that allow us to build *collective* causal maps that are representative of the vision of reality expressed by a group of people (see Rosenhead & Mingers, 2001; Kirschner et al., 2003).

The maps can be also be used to highlight points of view and speed up innovative solutions through the comparison of multiple points of view.

Conclusion

We have shown that, through opportune techniques of mathematical modeling it is possible to model in analytical way both the verbal opinions contained in discourses and their aggregations.

Fuzzy models are a valid alternative for the representation and manipulations of linguistic information compared to traditional quantitative techniques. They allow us to represent several specific properties of complex organizational reality in a more articulate way. In general, the use of fuzzy operators complicates the elaboration process of linguistic information, as it introduces complications of a computational nature. It also has several advantages:

a.   It puts forward a further decision making support approach based on linguistic information which is potentially useful for both diagnostic and prognostic means in all the cases in which: (a) quantitative information is not available or it is too expensive to trace; (b) a certain level of imprecision in the output can be tolerated; (c) a weak level of characterization of the relationships between the variables of the model is acceptable.

b.   It is possible to simulate the discourses to produce multiple scenarios; therefore, in addition to being an instrument for the processing data, the verbal models are producers of meaning. Finally, they can perform a support function in the decision process.

References

Gouldner, A.W. (1954). *Patterns of industrial bureaucracy.* Glencoe, IL: Free Press.

Kirschner, P.A., Buckingham Shum, S. J., & Carr, C. S. (2003). *Visualizing argumentation: Software tools for collaborative and educational sense-making.* London: Springer Verlag.

Kosko, B. (1992). *Neural networks and fuzzy systems.* Englewood Cliffs, NJ: Prentice Hall.

Kosko, B. (1997). *Fuzzy engineering.* Englewood Cliffs: Prentice Hall.

Rosenhead, J., & Mingers, J. (2001). *Rational analysis for a probelmatic world revisited: Problem structuring method for uncertainty and conflict.* Chichester: John Wiley & Son.

Wenstøp, F. (1975b). Deductive verbal model of organizations. *International Journal of Man Machine Studies, 8,* 301-357.

Endnote

[1]   The map was created from the article by W. Williams, "South Africa is Changing" San Diego Union, 1986.

Chapter XV

The Management of Grey Knowledge Through Causal Maps:
A Field Example

Aboriginal creation myths tell of legendary totemic beings who had wandered over the continent in the Dreamtime, singing out the name of everything that crossed their path—birds, animals, plants, rocks, waterholes—and so singing the world into existence [...] By singing the world into existence the Ancestors had been poets in the original sense of poiesis, meaning creation. No Aboriginal could conceive that the created world was in anyway imperfect. His religious life had a single aim: to keep the land the way it was and should be. The man who went 'Walkabout' was making a ritual journey. He trod the footprints of his Ancestors. He sang the Ancestors' stanzas without changing a word or a note—and so recreated the Creation.

(Bruce Chatwin, The Songlines)

Abstract

In this chapter, through the description of concrete examples drawn from a field study,[1] our intention is to provide the reader with a detailed account of the application of the methodological approach presented in Chapter X. The example refers to knowledge management in software development. In particular, the aim of this chapter is to apply the methodology for the investigation and management of the grey knowledge created and elaborated by software development teams in the production of new software applications. The chapter focuses on the early stages of the process when development teams have to make a choice regarding the software life cycle model that best fits given constraints concerning ambiguity of the requirements, risks, costs evaluation and scheduling. A step-by-step application to a case-study of a software company is presented in order to illustrate the main critical methodological aspects.

Knowledge Management in Software Development Through Causal Maps

Typical knowledge management tasks, such as knowledge storing, elicitation, codification, and reuse have always been relevant issues in the management of projects of new software products. Managing knowledge within knowledge-intensive organizations, such as software firms, means providing companies with suitable methodologies and tools for each phase of the knowledge value chain.

Traditionally, knowledge management practices in software development and engineering have been focused mainly on knowledge sharing and maintenance, whereas less attention has been devoted to the elicitation issues. Actually, knowledge acquisition from internal sources, such as technicians and managers involved in the development of a new software product, is one of the most critical steps in the knowledge value chain. Being often situated, tacit, and idiosyncratic, grey knowledge is not easy to be captured and embedded into new organizational artifacts. According to the theoretical framework proposed in Chapters II to V of this book, this means that a large amount of knowledge incorporated into the theories in use does not become part of the organizational memory. This implies that especially knowledge-intensive organizations, such as software companies, actually risk missing the opportunity to activate organizational learning processes by neglecting the grey knowledge that software developers enact and share.

In this chapter, by developing further the methodological aspects illustrated in Chapters X and XI, we use causal mapping for the elicitation and mapping of grey knowledge created and elaborated by software development teams in the production of new software applications[2].

A causal map is a representation of causal beliefs though a network of causal relations embedded in an individual's explicit statements; they can be considered as an explicit representation of the deep-rooted cognitive maps of individuals (Huff, 1990; Nelson et al., 2000).

Causal mapping allows researchers and practitioners to investigate how people involved in the development process select and attribute meanings to variables, influencing the choice of a life cycle model. On the organizational side, information and individual knowledge represented through causal maps can be analyzed and discussed with the developers in order to increase their level of awareness and participation in the choice process. Furthermore, once elicited and structured through formal models, such as causal maps, grey knowledge can be embedded into organizational artifacts and so become part of the organizational memory.

In practice, eliciting and mapping grey knowledge in software development allows organizational analysts to:

1. *Identify critical factors* having impact on the success of new projects as perceived by team members.

2. *Compare different individual interpretations* represented through causal maps concerning the meaning and the importance of choice variables to verify the existence of overlapping perceptions and shared beliefs as well as of conflicting interpretations.

3. *Analyze individual knowledge* and use the results of such analysis for the design of more effective decision support tools for software life cycle selection.

Critical Issues in Formal Methodology Adoption for Software Development

Several studies have dealt with the issue of determining suitable methods for the selection of life cyle model for software applications (Boehm, 1981, 1988; Boehm et al., 2000; Bradac et al., 1994; Humphrey, 1989; McConnell, 1996; Putnam, 1992).

The life cycle of a software product begins with the idea formulation and the initial design and ends when the product is no longer available for further use. The life cycle model of a software product is a formal description of how the product should be developed, usually specifying development phases, deliverables, guidelines, and evaluation of intermediate and final results.[3]

The availability in the literature and in the professional practice of several proposals of life cycle models implies the problem of selecting the one that best fits the
development of a specific software application, given information usually concerning
requirements, level of perceived risks, more or less tight scheduling, etc. (Bohem,
1981; Matson et al., 1994; McConnell, 1996; Pressman, 2000; Putnam, 1992).

In order to support the choice of the best life cycle model, formal methodologies
are often employed in order to reduce risk, time to market, and development costs[4].
Despite these advantages, however, recent literature on software development has
investigated why software developers often show resistance against using formal
methodologies. Drawing up from previous researches (Davis, 1989; Moore &
Benbasat, 1991; Riemenshneider et al., 2002; Thompson et al., 1991) we classify
the determinants of the resistance against the adoption of formal methodologies in
software development in three main categories:

- *Individual factors* related to individual disposition and willingness as well as
  capability to employ formal methodologies and tools in software development
  (e.g., compatibility of the methodology with how developers perform their
  work, perceived usefulness, ease of use).
- *Organizational factors* related to the organizational support and incentive to
  the use of formal development methodologies (such as management commitment, facilitating conditions and tools, training, career consequences).
- *Social factors* related to the social acceptance of formal methodologies adoption (such as peers and supervisors opinions, social consensus, image and
  status).

What seems to emerge from such studies is that developers may perceive formal
methodologies as constraining, boring, and time-consuming instead of as effective
supports to software development. *By reframing this result in our theoretical framework we can say that formal rules and tools included into the persistence apparatus
constrains individual initiative and prevents people from learning.* The imposition
of a closed apparatus creates a misalignment between individual knowledge and
organizational memory. Closed artifacts are imposed from the top, but they are loosely
linked to theories in use. There is a missing connection between what people learn
and experience in their day by day work and the persistence apparatus made up by
formal tools and rules. How is it possible to build such link in order to, at the same
time, preserve repeatability and transparency and promote individual initiative?

As we have shown in Chapter V, this is another way to describe the organizational
learning paradox. A way to solve such a paradox is to activate the logic of the

MEP model, in other words to put grey knowledge in the circuits of organizational learning.

In this chapter it is argued that the adoption of formal methodologies in software development, and in particular in life cycle selection, represents an example in which such a misalignment occurs. We examine this problem through a deep analysis of the context structured in three main steps that will be discussed in the following: knowledge elicitation, knowledge mapping, and knowledge analysis for the construction of new artifacts.

The results of the analysis are obtained by analyzing developers' experiences and knowledge embedded in their cognitive constructs (frameworks, patterns of action, cognitive schemata, beliefs, etc.). Then, results can be discussed with the developers in order to help them to achieve deeper knowledge and awareness of the development process. In this way, a cognitive approach to the analysis of the life cycle model selection can help to increase the perceived usefulness of formal methodologies at the individual and at the organizational level by transforming them from standard "constraining" tools to learning and knowledge management procedures.

What actually happens is that traditional methodologies to support software development try to eliminate subjectivity through standardization and usually neglect social and human factors in software engineering (Pfleeger, 1999). In particular, their use does not allow us to take into account how people frame problems, select clues from the environment, attribute meanings to new events leveraging their knowledge and expertise to deal with ambiguity and novelty rising from new, poorly defined and unexpected situations.

In the following, we characterize the life cycle selection as a decision problem in which developers are expected to choose the best model with the given information on the project and constraints of time, cost and availability of human resources.

Explanations provided by software developers regarding the problem of choosing the best life cycle model in the early stages of a new software product development given information about situational constraints should permit to gain considerable and deep knowledge about theory in use and espoused theories evocated by individuals. In other words, following the logic of the MEP model (Chapter IX) we use explanations to shed light on organizational memory.

In the following section we describe step by step a methodology to elicit and map the theories of action that software developers activate when requested to choice a life/cycle model. This methodology is actually the same that has been described at a more general level at the beginning of Chapter X.

Eliciting and Mapping Theories of Action in the Life Cycle Selection through Causal Maps

The methodology was tested through a case study in an Italian software company producing software for accounting, management, office automation, and telecommunication systems; other activities of the company concern the outsourcing management of data elaboration centers. The company belongs to an important group with more than one thousands employees, half of which are software developers with a turnover of about 100 million euros in 2005. The proposed methodology develops according to the following steps:

1. **Sample selection and identification of the minimum web of interaction:** One or more development teams made up by experienced practitioners in software development are selected according to criteria: (1) *level of expertise*, as recognized by other experts or estimated from their position; (2) *variety*, in terms of roles, organizational positions, background (Calori, 2000). For the purpose of this specific case the team represents naturally the minimum web of interaction.

2. **Interview protocol definition:** A set of general *framing questions* concerning the main decision variables involved in the problem of choosing the "right" life cycle model is designed on the base of the literature analysis and through a first involvement of the developers.

3. **Interviews:** Framing questions are employed to *collect explanatory discourses* through interviews; explanatory discourses are analyzed to elicit *concepts and relationships* among them; relevant concept are described in details and reported into an interview's dictionary.

4. **Individual Mapping:** Individual causal maps are used to represent concepts and relationships between concepts and analyzed in order to identify input and output variables, most influential and relevant concepts.

5. **Aggregation:** Individual maps are confronted in order to identify similarities and differences in the framing of the life cycle selection problems across different individuals.

6. **Validation:** Is performed through intercoder reliability and feedback from interviewees.

7. **Knowledge base construction:** Once validated, the results emerging from causal maps analysis can be stored in archives such as data-bases and case-bases. Effective theories of actions can be incorporated into new artifacts, in order to complete the organizational learning cycle. If the new artifacts are designed with an adequate level of openness they will absolve to the double functions of driving actions and enabling learning.

Sample Selection and Identification of the Minimum Web of Interaction

The sample was selected according to the above mentioned criteria of level of expertise and variety. More specifically, a level of expertise was estimated through years of experience in software development, involvement in the development of large projects, peers' and managers' indications. Through such criteria it was not difficult to identify an experienced team. A satisfying degree of variety was ensured by the way the company makes development team usually made up by several developers with different roles (system analyst, programmers, network experts, etc.) and by one or more project managers. Of course team composition and duration depend on the characteristics of the project and may change during time. It is worth to note that the number of people to be involved into the field research may vary as well depending on the research purpose. For example, if one wants to build a very comprehensive collective knowledge base (Calori, 2000), it is necessary to interview a large number of experts in order to integrate as many as possible different points of view into representative and reliable descriptions. On the other hand, if the research purpose is to investigate in-depth a given organizational aspect through an action research approach (Argyris & Schon, 1978), the number of people to be involved may be sensibly lower than in the previous case.

Interview Protocol Definition

The aim of this step was to identify a set of general *framing questions* related to the main decision variables involved in the problem of choosing the "right" life cycle model needed to structure the interviews performed in the next step. The framing questions have been designed starting from a literature analysis. On this base a framework describing variables considered as relevant to the final choice of the life cycle has been constructed; this framework was then presented to some company's project managers and developers before being employed in the interview phase in order to be validated and integrated. Project managers and developers' suggestions were collected and used to refine the framework. Framework variables have been grouped in three main clusters:

a. *Organizational* variables concerning resources availability for the project, investments, managers and team commitment, leadership of the project managers, organizational culture.

b. *Customer-related* variables such as requirements, concerns for costs, quality, time, and visibility of changes, i.e., customer perception that his/her requests have been recognized and satisfied through actual changes in the product.

c. *Process* variables related to production as team competencies, maintenance, and relationships with the customers and possibility of further development.

Clusters have been obtained through two steps; in the first step an initial classification was proposed by us on the basis of the literature. The proposed classification was then refined through developers' observations and suggestions. Moreover, it emerged that each cluster represented a sort of dominant point of view shaping the way each interviewee perceives and looks at the problem; in other words, among the interviewees, some developers emphasized more the customer's cluster, others seemed more concerned about process, while a third group paid more attention to organizational constraints.

Interviews

The project manager and four team members were separately interviewed through on-site meetings during two months. Framing questions were used to structure the interview. Each interview, whose duration was in the average about two hours, was taped and transcribed.

Interviews were aimed at eliciting explanatory relations among concepts provided by software developers such as *concepts' explicitation* (e.g., "what does 'quality' mean for you?"), *causal relationship*: (e.g., "How individual and team competencies influence project development?"), *actions and/or decisions justification* (e.g., "How do you cope with high risk when choosing priorities?), *values and personal beliefs driving actions and choice* (How important is it for you to "have the control?"). Interviews developed dynamically through interaction; the interviewer asked to explain opinions and beliefs, to develop arguments until a satisfying detail was achieved.

Interviews were coded in two steps according to the documentary coding method (Wrightson, 1976): The assembly of a concepts dictionary and identification of explanatory relationships between concepts. This method was slightly modified and generalized in order to code explanatory relationships, which do not express solely causal influence but also justification and concepts clarification.

In the first step, relevant concepts were identified and listed; a detailed description of their meaning as emerging from the interview was provided for each concept. Examples of concept descriptions are the following:

- **Requirements:** Represent "what you need to do," what the company must deliver to the customer, and this may or not be always made explicit by the customer itself.

- **Requirements (ambiguity) reduction:** Is the possibility to reformulate customer's requests that is both able to satisfy his/her needs and technically clear and feasible. Sometimes reduction means requirements simplification, in other cases it may imply requirements dropping.
- **Etc.**

In the second step, the interview's text was carefully analyzed in order to identify and list explanatory relationships linking two or more concepts. For example, in one case, the interviewee underlined the importance of requirements understanding and specifications as follows:

Requirements are a fundamental variable: They represent "what you need to do" [...] If requirements are ambiguous, as is often the case, you need to create an effective channel to communicate and interact with the client. This usually means to spend money and time. A possible outcome of a successful interaction is the reduction of a requirement, that is a reformulation of the customer requests that is both able to satisfy his/her needs and technically clear and feasible [...]. A requirement reduction may imply success for a project. Summing up, understanding customer's needs has a definitive contribution on quality perception by the customer.

It is easy to recognize in this quotation the definition of some concepts such as "requirements," "requirement reduction," as well as several explanatory relationships that were coded in the following format A -> ex -> B, where ex stands for 'explain' and can be read as A explains B, B because A, A is a reasons for B to occur, A is (a better way) to say B, A (may) influence B, A (may) causes B. Examples contained in the quotation above can be the following:

Ambiguous requirements –ex–> Create a channel with the client

Create a channel with the client –ex-> Spending time and money

Successful interaction –ex-> requirement reduction

List of explanatory relationships can be reported on coding sheets analogous to the one illustrated in Chapter XI for argument analysis where additional information can be added concerning the localization in the text, notes aimed at further describing the relationships or reporting emphasis added by the interviewee, and links to other items of the list.

Individual Mapping

The mapping step may be carried out in a quite direct way from the interviews whenever text analysis and synthesis have been extensively and carefully performed. Mapping means essentially to assemble the several explanatory relationships emerged from the coding through the well-known graphical representation of causal maps, by eliminating redundant relationships and connecting those that are linked. It is important to remark that mapping concerns relationships such as A causes B, A influences, B, A has impact on B, and so on, i.e., explanatory relationships stating influence between two concepts.

In Figure 1 an example of causal map elicited from an interview excerpt is represented. The minus sign on the arches between two concepts represents negative influence. Observing the map in Figure 1 it is possible to recognize as input variables project dimension, team competencies, degree of access to technology, standardization (vs. customization) and degree of ambiguity of the requirements. These variables are perceived as sort of basic ingredients for the project success and as constraints usually beyond the scope of developers' control. On the other hand, control procedures and relationships with the client are considered the variables on which developers can actually have a certain degree of control to have positive impact on final results as delivery time, costs, and product's performance.

Through a software tool (Decision Explorer), a quantitative analysis of the concepts' relevance contained in the map of Figure 1 was performed. In particular, relevance was evaluated through *domain* and *centrality* analysis.

The domain analysis gives an indication of the complexity of linking around concepts. The centrality analysis gives an indication of the influence of a concept in the wider context of the map. The rationale behind domain analysis is that concepts

Figure 1. Examples of causal maps describing relationships

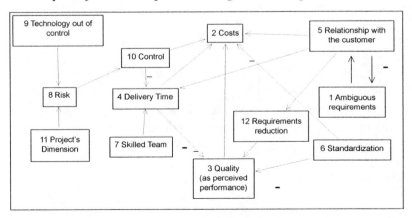

Table 1. Results of domain and centrality analysis of the causal map depicted in Figure 1

Top 4 concepts importance according to the priority declared by the interviewee	Top 4 concepts obtained from the domain analysis	Top 4 concepts obtained from the centrality analysis
Requirements Costs Delivery time Quality	(5 links around) Costs Delivery time Relationship with the customer (4 links around) Quality (as perceived performance)	Delivery time (7 from 11 concepts) Costs (7 from 11 concepts) Control (6 from 11 concepts) Relationship with the customer (6 from 9 concepts)

representing "key issues" will be highly elaborated; consequently the algorithm assigns to each key concept a high domain score equal to the number of incoming and outgoing links.

Centrality analysis is complementary to domain analysis in that it looks beyond the immediate environment around the concept and examines the complexity of links at a number of levels away from the center. In concrete, the centrality analysis evaluates the capability of a given concept C to influence other concepts belonging to the same map by calculating a score increasing with the number of other concepts directly and indirectly influenced by C.

The second and third column of Table 1 contains the results of domain and centrality analysis of the map in Figure 1; the first column contains the ranking of concepts importance as directed stated by the interviewee.

Aggregation

The same procedure of coding and mapping was applied to each interview collected in the field analysis. Centrality and domain analysis were performed for each map. The aim of this step was to compare and aggregate the individual perceptions of the problem in order to identify the consensus level among developers belonging to the same team. Consensus can be assessed with respect to three main aspects: Problem framing, meaning, and concepts relevance.

1. **Problem framing:** By examining the structure of the collected maps, a high degree of homogeneity appeared as concerns problem framing, in terms of overall map structure, input and output variables, and connections among concepts (of actions). Dominant and recurring issues are ambiguity of the requirements, team competencies, concerns for scheduling and delivery time, and project dimensions. Other concepts such as the client's role, and the need

to manage customer relationships appeared only in two maps out of five. The project manager's map appeared to be slightly more complex and rich in feedback and relationships between concepts. Customer-related concepts play a major role only in the project manager map, whereas the developer map appears to be more concerned about scheduling, project dimensions, and delivery time.

2. **Determining concept meaning:** By analyzing the concept dictionary attached to each map, it is possible to identify convergence and discrepancies in the meaning attached to each concept by different developers. In the case being considered, though a high level of consensus was achieved, relevant differences across the team members concerned concept meaning in some cases. Summing up, the main discrepancies in meaning as emerged from explanation analysis involve the following concepts: Quality for the customers, relationships with the customers, and requirements.

3. **Comparing concept relevance:** The main differences in the importance of variables, as emerging from centrality and domain analysis, concern delivery time and, again quality. Table 2 reports a comparison between the five

Table 2. Differences and similarities in concept relevance

	Interview A	Interview B	Interview C	Interview D	Interview E
Top relevant concepts as declared in the interview	-Requirements -Costs -Time -Quality	-Requirements -Time -Competencies -Costs -Quality	-Requirements -Time -Costs	-Requirements -Time	-Requirements -Time -Costs -Relationship with the customer -Competencies -Quality
Top relevant concepts as emerged from domain analysis	- Costs - Time - Quality (perceived performance) - Relationship with the customer - Control - Risk	-Time -Risk -Requirements -Quality -Competencies	- Budget flexibility - Risk - Team - Requirements - Time	-Requirements -Quality	-Requirements -Time -Costs -Quality -Project fragmentation -Competencies
Top relevant concepts as emerged from centrality analysis	- Time - Risk - Costs - Control	- Risk - Time - Requirements - Dimension - Competencies	- Budget flexibility - Risk - Requirements	-Requirements -Time	- Project fragmentation -Quality -Budget -Time -Requirements -Competencies

interviewees concerning concepts' relevance as obtained from interviewee's declaration, domain and centrality analysis.

Numeric weights can be assigned to concepts through an importance indicator calculated on the base of domain and centrality analysis according to the following rule: The importance of a given concept increases with (1) the score in centrality analysis, (2) the score in domain analysis; (3) the number of interviewees considering the given concept as relevant. After that the comparison of the individual maps at the three levels (framing, meaning, relevance) has been performed, it is possible to construct collective or group maps either through formal procedures and algorithms (Kosko, 1992) or by qualitative methodologies such as focus group.

Validation

The validation of the results was carried out in two steps. First, the coding and mapping steps were performed independently by each component of the research team for a same interview. Coding and mapping results then were compared, discussed and homogenized with the research team. A research report containing the results was sent to interviewees and discussed with each of them separately. The aim of the discussion was to verify if interviewees recognized in the map an adequate representation of their ideas. Also the concepts dictionary was validated in the same way.

Furthermore, a subsequent group discussion of the results was organized in order to construct a shared dictionary of the concepts in which each concept was defined trying to include or improve individual contributions.

Knowledge Base Construction

In this section we examine the issue of how to employ the results obtained from the previous steps to update organizational memory. According to the MEP model, an organization learns when new theories of use contained into explanations are elicited and incorporated into new organizational artifacts. This last step is crucial. As we have outlined in Chapters II to V organizational learning can not happen if the persistence apparatus is not revised or updated. Consequently, any analysis of this type should end with the revision of existing artifacts or the design of new artifacts.

In the example described in this chapter, the output of analysis of the explanations through causal maps was used to develop a simple decision support system (DSS) for the problem of life cycle selection. In particular, results emerging from the analysis were integrated into a DSS for life cycle selection based on the McConnell approach (McConnell, 1996). The McConnell approach is based on the definition of a selection matrix $S = [s_{ij}]$.

McConnell's table allows software project managers to compare a set of alternative development models reported in the matrix columns with respect to a set of evaluation criteria reported on the rows. Life cycle models that are reported in the table can be well-known models drawn from the literature such as the waterfall or the rapid prototyping model, or customized models developed by a company thanks to its know-how and past experience. The same applies for evaluation criteria whose list can be modified and integrated depending on the context of application.

The value s_{ij} is a verbal evaluation assessing the capability of the model j-th to satisfy the i-th criterion. Such evaluations are the results of the analysis of points of strength and weakness of each model. The set of judgments contained in each column can be considered as the description of the ideal case in which the corresponding life cycle model should be used. For example, one should use the spiral model if: (a) Requirements and architecture are very ambiguously defined, (b) excellence in reliability, a large growth envelope, and capability to manage risks is requested, (c) respect of extremely tight predefined schedule is not required, (d) overheads are low, (e) customer needs a excellent visibility on progress, etc.

Figure 2. Input output interface of a DSS for life cycle selection based on McConnell approach

Evaluation criterion	Evaluation	Weights
Works with poorly understood requirements	2	20%
Works with poorly understood architecture	2	5%
Produces highly reliable systems	5	15%
Produces system with large growth envelope	5	5%
Manages risks	5	8,0%
Can be constrained to a predefined schedule	5	2%
Has low overhead	4	14,0%
Allows for midcourse corrections	4	15,0%
Requires little management or developer	4	12,0%
Provides customer with progress	5	3%
Provides management with progress	5	1%

1= poor 2= poor to average 3= average 4= average to excellent 5= excellent

100%

Waterfall	Evolutionary	Spiral
1,92	1,65	1,24

On the basis of your judgements, the best life cycle model your project is	Spiral model

McConnell suggests that decision-makers evaluate a given project according to the criteria contained in the table and then to select the alternative that best fits the characteristics of the specific project.

The developed tool allows its users to define a selection matrix, to add life cycle models and evaluation criteria, to establish weights for evaluation criteria. The input and output interface of the DSS are illustrated in Figure 2.

In order to identify the best life cycle for a given project, users are asked to evaluate each criteria by assessing the characteristics of the projects through a Likert scale ranging from 1 to 5. In the example showed in Figure 2 the evaluator is saying that for the given project, the capability of the life cycle model to cope with poorly definition of requirements and architecture should be poor to average, the capability to ensure high reliability should be excellent, etc.

The user is also required to assign weights representing criteria importance expressed as a percentage and normalized. The algorithm then calculates a score for each model stored in the selection matrix representing the distance between the profile of the considered project described in terms of the evaluated criteria and the ideal profile corresponding to each model. Consequently, the model to which the lowest score is assigned should be selected as the best one for the given project. In the example shown in Figure 2, the numbers 1.92, 1.65 and 1.24 represent the distances between the profile of the given project described in the column 'evaluation' and the profiles of, respectively, the waterfall the evolutionary prototyping and the spiral model as contained in the selection matrix. On the base of such results the nearest is the spiral model.

Conclusion

The analysis of causal maps helps in improving the meaningfulness and the reliability of the DSS presented above. The in-depth analysis performed through causal maps can help companies to elicit unshared grey knowledge at the individual as well as at the team level that may be potentially useful. Such knowledge can be discussed and analyzed through the proposed methodology. Eventually, outputs of the analysis can be integrated in the decision support tools described above in the following way:

a. **Construction of better (i.e., richer and more complete) definition of evaluation criteria:** Concepts dictionary analysis and group discussion can help researchers to identify evaluation criteria on the base of the experience of developers through the integration of different points of view; existing criteria can be updated and new criteria can be added as new experience is gained.

b.   **Reduction of ambiguity in criteria meaning evaluation:** Comparison of individual maps and the dictionary can be used to identify possible discrepancies in meaning attribution to a same evaluation criterion by different developers; as shown above, this situation can be rather frequent. Through the explanations analysis those discrepancies can be elicited; different interpretations can be integrated into more comprehensive ones while incoherence and conflicts can be analyzed and discussed in depth. Analysis through discussion and self-reflection increases knowledge sharing, people involvement, and participation of team members in the decision-making process concerning project development.

c.   **Assessment of criteria relevance through the calculation of weights representing criteria importance:** Quantitative analysis of causal maps permits to estimate criteria importance through weights that are more reliable than weights expressed in a direct way since they keep into account concept relevance in the considered domain of analysis and causal patterns between them.

Evaluations can be expressed by the project manager or through a group discussion. It is also possible to implement multiperson aggregation algorithms to collect separately and aggregate opinions of different experts. Evaluation sessions can be stored in a database and reused in similar situations according to a case-based approach (Kolodner, 1991; Schanck, 1986), with ex-post comments about the validity of the choice made. Through time, the conjoint application of causal mapping and DSS can allow companies to store knowledge and past experiences that can be continuously revised and updated.

The participative way the DSS was built not only works toward the realization of a new artifact, but also ensures a certain degree of openness. Though the developed DSS is a formal tool, it has been developed without any top-down imposition of decision models and evaluation criteria, it can be updated in an absence of centralized control by allowing multiple access through a distributed architecture, and it has a modular structure since it allows the addition (or destruction) of pieces of knowledge without compromising the overall structure. While these and other attributes of openness depends mainly on the ways the system is implemented and used rather than on its intrinsic characteristics, on the other side the process the new artifact has been developed ensures a high degree of openness since it has been built:

a.   From the knowledge individuals use and develop daily

b.   Through their active involvement

c.   By using the language and experience of the organization

d.   By soliciting knowledge sharing and mutual learning

e.   By building systems that can be (and should be) updated and revised at any moment

A remarkable advantage offered by the approach proposed in this book is that knowledge elicitation and mapping is actually obtained through the strong involvement of employees and managers. This brings about many advantages such as:

a.   Their involvement may increase employees' motivation

b.   Companies gain more knowledge about how things are actually going in their organization, i.e., they can investigate the theory-in-use and detect possible discrepancies with the organizational espoused theory contained in formal procedures, documentation and organizational charts (Argyris & Schon, 1978)

c.   Divergent or conflicting interpretations can be elicited and analyzed

d.   Group discussions can allow team members to have a chance to reflect on their problem framing and to compare their opinions and cognitive schemata and attitude with other team members

e.   Implications for training and learning can be obtained

References

Argyris, C., & Schon, D.A. (1978) *Organizational learning: A theory of action perspective.* Reading, MA: Addison-Wesley.

Boehm, B. (1981) *Software engineering economics.* Englewood Cliffs, NJ: Prentice Hall.

Boehm, B. (1988). A spiral model for software development and enhancement. *Computer, 5,* 61-72.

Boehm, B., & Basili, V. (2000). Gaining intellectual control of software development. *IEEE Computer*, May, 27-33.

Bradac, M. D., Perry, & Votta, L. (1994). Prototyping a process monitoring experiment. IEEE Trans. *Software engineering, 10,* 774-784.

Calori, R. (2000). Ordinary theorists in mixed industries. *Organizational Studies, 6,* 1031-1057.

Davis, F. (1989). Perceived usefulness, perceived ease of use and user acceptance of information technology. *MIS Quarterly, 13,* 318-339.

Gainer, J. (2003). *Process improvement: The capability maturity model.* http://www. itmweb.com/f051098.htm

Huff A.S. (Ed.). (1990). *Mapping strategic thought.* Chirchester: Wiley.

Humphrey, W.S. (1989). *Managing the software process.* Addison-Wesley.

Kosko, B. (1992). *Neural networks and fuzzy systems.* Englewood Cliffs, NJ: Prentice Hall.

Matson, J., Barret, B., & Mellichamp, J. (1994). Software development cost estimation using function point. IEEE Trans. *Software Engineering, 4,* 275-287.

McConnell, S. (1996). *Rapid development: Taming wild software schedules.* Microsoft Press.

Nelson, K. M., Nadkarni, S., Narayanan, V. K., & Ghods, M. (2000). Understanding software operations support expertise: A causal mapping approach. *Management Information Systems Quarterly, 24,* 475-507.

Paulk, M. (1993). *Capability maturity model for software.* Software engineering institute at Carnegie Mellon University, Pittsburgh.

Pfleeger, S.L. (1999). Understanding and improving technology transfer in software engineering. *Journal of Systems and Software, 47,* 11-124.

Pressman, R.S. (2000). *Software engineering: A practitioner's approach* (5th ed.). McGraw-Hill Higher Education.

Putnam, L., & Myers, W. (1992). *Measures for excellence.* Yourdon Press.

Riemenshneider, C.K., Hardgrave, B.C., & Davis, F. (2002). Explaining software developer acceptance of methodologies: A comparison of five theoretical models. *IEEE Transactions on Software Engineering, 12,* 1135-1145.

Schank, R.C. (1986). *Explanation patterns: Understanding mechanically and creatively.* Hillsdale, NJ: Lawrence Erlbaum.

Wrightson, M.T. (1976). Documentary coding method. In Axelrod (Ed.), *Structure of decision. The cognitive amps of political elites.* Princeton, NJ: Princeton University Press.

Endnotes

[1] This appendix contains a revised and shortened version of the paper by L. Iandoli and G. Zollo, Knowledge at work in software development: a cognitive approach for sharing knowledge and creating decision support in lifecycle selection. In Narayanan, V.K. & Dr. D.J. Armstrong. (2004). *Causal mapping*

for information systems and technology research: Approaches, advances and illustrations. Hershey, PA: Idea Group Publishing. In particular this work has been completely revisited in the light of the theoretical and methodological approach presented in this book.

[2]   In this chapter, we do not report references to previous research on causal maps. Those, together with some examples, can be found in Chapter X.

[3]   Examples of life cycle models are the following:

Waterfall model, in which the development of software products is articulated into a linear sequence of phases (problem analysis, requirements analysis, development, integration, test, installation, and maintenance). The waterfall model is very simple and it can be useful in stable situations when the identification of the requirements is not problematic; major disadvantages concern limited interaction with the user (usually limited at the beginning and at the end of the product development), and lack of flexibility.

Prototyping model: In this model the design is carried out in order to develop a prototype of the product as soon as possible; the realization of the final product is seen as successive refinements of the first prototype in order to achieve a satisfying degree of convergence between user's needs and requirements, identification, and implementation. This model is particularly useful when user's needs are ambiguously defined.

Incremental delivery: Incremental models conceive the development of software products as set of stages, each one organized as a linear sequence of phases like in the waterfall model; at the end of each development stage the product presents new characteristics and improvements, i.e., it can be considered an evolution of the previous stage. This model can be used in case of big projects when available budget at the beginning of the project may be insufficient to ensure the development of the entire project or when it is important to gain flexibility and adaptation through incremental improvements.

[4]   The interest in the definition of suitable lifecycle models is clearly demonstrated by the capability maturity model (CMM) developed in the 1987 by the SEI (Software Engineering Institute, http://www.sei.cmu.edu/) for the evaluation of the maturity level achieved by software companies (Paulk et al., 1993). The CMM ranks software development organizations in a hierarchy of five levels, each with a progressively greater capability of producing quality software (Gainer, 2003). Each level is described as a level of maturity. To increase their own capability maturity level from Level 2 and Level 3, companies must adequately define the life cyle of all their projects. Furthermore, according to the well-known international normative ISO IEC 12207, regarding software

process management, in the software project planning the project manager must select activities and tasks of the development process and map them onto the appropriate lifecycle model.

5   The software tool employed in the simulation is Decision Explorer produced by Banxia software. It is possible to download from the web site www.banxia. com a free trial version capable to perform simulation of simple maps. It is an evolution of the previous software package Graphic cope developed by Frank Ackerman, Steve Cropper, and Colin Eden at the Deptartment of Management Science of the University of Strathclyde.

Section IV

Implications and Perspectives

Chapter XVI

Organizational Observers as Agents of Change

They are playing a game.

They are playing at not playing a game.

If I show them I see they are, I shall break the rules and they will punish me.

I must play their game of not seeing I see the game

(R.D.Laing, 1991)

Abstract

In this book we propose using verbal data such as discourses and speech as input for organizational analysis. One of the main differences between verbal data and traditional quantitative data is that the latter are objective whereas the former may give rise to multiple interpretations. In this chapter we deal with the issue of the reliability of discursive data and try to provide an answer to the following questions: How one can be sure the information contained in discourse has been correctly interpreted? Is there more than one admissible interpretation? When is an interpretation admissible? We show that in order to answer such questions the organizational analysts have to assume a mindset and research attitude that are rather different than the traditional objectivist point of view.

Three Problems

The methodological approach described in the preceding chapters assumes that discourses are used as input for the analysis of organizational memory and shared cognition. This kind of input is "problematic" and has quite different characteristics from the quantitative data traditionally used in empirical research.

The fundamental difference between numerical data and qualitative verbal data lies in the fact that while the first can be associated with objective meanings, the second can be attributed meaning only after a process of *subjective interpretation* of the data. For example, to affirm that "Today the outside temperature is 100°FC" is not the same thing as saying, "Today it is hot."

In particular, the question of the reliability of data brings up questions such as: How can we be reasonably sure that the information contained in the discourses is correctly interpreted by the analysts? When is an interpretation admissible? Is more than one interpretation admissible? Is it possible to find and evaluate interpretative errors?

In order to give satisfying answers to these kinds of questions we must consider a large set of epistemological and methodological aspects. However, we will limit our discussion to three fundamental questions:

a.   The problem of *distancing* between the researcher and the context of the study.

b.   The problem of *involvement* of the organizational actors.

c.   The problem of *reliability* of interpretation.

The Problem of Distancing:
The Organizational Analyst as an Agent of Change

In the study of organizational phenomena and in the social sciences in general, there are two opposing methodological positions that begin with very different epistemological assumptions: The interpretative/subjective approach and the positivist/objective approach (Sandberg, 2000).

The interpretative approaches assume a constructionist perspective that does not assume a sharp separation between what is being observed and the observer (see Chapter VI). Instead, the positivist approach is based on the dualism of the exact sciences in which the world of phenomena is an objective reality that is distinct from the subjectivity of the observer.

In the positivist empirical tradition the researcher must be a spectator, removed from the phenomena being studied, and must prevent, or at least limit, every disturbance of the context being observed. This position is usually not applicable to the problems we are dealing with in this book, for various reasons.

The object of the observation here is made up of social processes, interpersonal relations, theories that individuals develop while acting, and finally by concrete behavior and actions. When these phenomena are observed, it is impossible to guarantee some of the typical above requirements of laboratory experiments: The repeatability of the experiment, the possibility of isolating or neglecting the effects of some variables, the availability of methods for standardized and objective measurement techniques.

But, even when it succeeds through the development of sophisticated procedures of observation and identification, to guarantee that the requirements have been satisfied, the simple passive observation, as accurate as it is, would not allow us to fully comprehend the phenomena observed.

If the organized world is a socially constructed world, then the researcher must enter into the sphere of meaning that individuals have built through social action, meanings that are necessarily situated, in order to understand them.

How can a researcher comprehend the organization without interacting with it? How can this social reality, constructed on sense-making, be investigated? And, having to interact with the organizational actors to study the chosen object, how can the requirement of not disturbing the system be observed? Finally, how can the mere presence of the researcher, as careful and noninvasive as it may be, pass unobserved and not condition the object of the observation that, in the end, is the people's behavior?

If the interaction between researcher and context is necessary, if the goal is to comprehend and analyze the characteristics of a socially constructed world, and if it is impossible to prevent the disturbance from this interaction, then one of the main presuppositions of the use of positivist methodology has gone by the wayside.

Instead, by adopting an interpretative perspective, the researcher becomes aware that the social world is constructed. Above all, it must be understood that if the goal is to produce change in that world, the researcher cannot but enter the game and participate (perhaps pretending not to do so following Laing's suggestion quoted at the beginning of this chapter), while being aware of the effects that a foreign presence has upon the context.

Thus, the disturbance due to the interaction is not a "disturbing action" but becomes necessary for the production, or rather the induction of processes of organizational change.

The Problem of Involvement:
The Collective Inquiry and Organizational Investigators

If the turbulence caused by interaction between the analyst and the organizational context is not a disturbance, but a contribution to the flow of organizational action, then the mode of interaction between the researcher and the organizational actors becomes crucial. It is a two-way interaction: The organizational members are not "objects" being studied, nor passive receptors of management theories and tools, they are active subjects, they may be "investigators" of their organizational reality, and carriers of that form of situated knowledge that we have called organizational. All organizational members, perhaps with different intensities, behave like the performer of the MEP model (Chapter IX) by interacting with their customers, assuming commitments, constructing explanations and continually rebuilding the social world of meanings driving their actions and evaluating their outcomes.

If the goal of the research in the organization is finalized at producing change, or the simple observation of phenomena, then it becomes a true "social investigation" in which the involvement of the organizational members is fundamental:

a.   In the first place, because they are "carriers" of situated knowledge that the researchers/analysts have to learn and analyze with the support of the members themselves.

b.   In the second place, because the individuals, as subjects and not objects, tend to adopt those beliefs and organizational tools that they helped to develop and over which they have some kind of control (Lewin, 1951; Reasons & Bradbury, 2001; Schein, 1987).

In other words, the involvement and the transformation of the actors from objects of change to "organizational observers," and therefore to subjects of change, is one of the fundamental ingredients for building a learning organization. For Argyris and Schön, "*[...] organizational learning is a process activated by the members of an organization who operate alone or by interacting with others in the context of a unit of organizational investigation. The investigation becomes organizational when those individual investigate on the interest of an organization, within a community governed formally or informally through roles and rules*" (Argyris & Schön, 1978, p. 51).

So, the learning organization must have the right people, who will make the change within it. The researcher/consultant who shares this vision must then identify and assist the agents of change and become an agent of change himself. More concretely, the crucial role of the researcher/consultant lies in helping organizational members in uncovering the "hidden rationality," the shared belief systems, the prejudices and the routines, the patterns of organizational action, and the theories in use. In short, organizational members can be helped to observe with critical and fresh eyes the organizational world which is taken for granted.

The analysis of explanatory discourses is a true methodological tool through which the researcher/consultant can penetrate the constructed world and partly contribute to its discovery personally and with the other actors.

The Problem of Reliability:
The Shared Interpretation of Organizational Reality

How can we be sure that a methodology of analysis of explanatory discourses will give us a faithful representation of the constructed world?

It is important to point out immediately that, from a constructionist perspective, the concept of "faithfulness of representation" should be set apart. It makes no sense, in such a view, to speak of an objective reality of reference in comparison to the representation of the social reality obtained through discourse analysis.

The reality of reference is not objective. It is not a platonic, ideal world made up of incorruptible ideas in comparison to the imperfect events of social life. It is a socially constructed collective memory in continuous evolution, made up of conventions, agreements, beliefs, and values that are continuously being redefined. What emerges from the analysis of the discourses are forms of this constructed world. From the examination of such forms we can know how the social universe is "made." The universe of social forms is not the container of some objective content. There is no content to be discovered. Every comprehension of a social form is the reproposition of a new form.

For example, a conflict between two or more people does not exist in itself, at least not like the force of gravity or electromagnetic waves. It makes sense to speak of it because some members of the organization feel the conflict, i.e., *intentionally* experience a situation as marked by a conflict. It is not *useful* to ask if we have described the conflict "objectively." It may be important to ask if describing a situation as a conflict can help us to discover something more about the organization, and therefore change the situation.

We can substitute two requirements for the concept of faithfulness of representation: That of the *usefulness* of the representation in creating organizational change, and that of *consensus* around a representation that has been obtained (Bettoni, 1997).

So, instead of precise representations, the objective of the organizational analyst is to obtain plausible and useful representations aimed at increasing the depth of comprehension of the social reality and learning for the agents of change. In the final analysis, this is the recursive, paradoxical nature of learning: learning occurs when someone who is actively involved in the process of change *declares that learning has taken place and is able to explain in a convincing way what has been learned.*

If the problem of reliability can be resolved in a tendency toward the quality of the interpretation and in operative terms in following the requirements of usefulness and consensus (reliability of the process), it also invests the "sources" of the data, that is the discourses and the organizational members who pronounce them (reliability of input). Discourses, in fact, are the grey matter that is the object of interpretations by the agents of change.

It is possible to summarize some critical questions in order to verify the reliability of the input through the following questions:

a.   How well are people able to describe, through explanatory discourse, the theories of action that dictate their actions?

b.   To which extent are people able to actively reconstruct what has happened to benefit the observer?

c.   How can observers arrive at a consensual vision in relation to the content of a discourse?

d.   What restrictions and interests can block the activity of reflection on the past in terms of time, energy, and willingness to collaborate?

The organization, because of its political nature, is the natural place for divergent conflicts of interest (Cohen et al., 1972; Crozier & Friedberg, 1977; Mintzberg et al., 1976). The energies, the resources, and the attention that the organization dedicates to the various activities are necessarily limited. So, as to the fourth point, any attempt of change in organization will require to agents of change efforts to struggle for time, attention, collaboration and internal sponsorship.

Regarding the first point, that is, if the people are able to provide detailed enough explanations of the reasons for their actions, there are many scientific contributions that warn against the effective possibility of "articulating" verbally the knowledge and the motivations for actions, beginning with the well-known work by Polanyi (1967).

The problem, nevertheless, is not whether an optimum level of representation exists, but what is the satisfactory level of detail, and that depends on the objectives of the analysis, on the required level of depth of analysis, on the motivations of the interlocutors, and on the interpretative capacity of the organizational analyst, whether they are external researcher or internal members of the organization.

It is undoubtedly true, nonetheless, that explanatory discourse naturally allows for an analytical and detailed investigation of the determinants of action. The interaction between the observer and the observed should guarantee an adequate level of empathy and interpretative convergence with respect to how much is being revealed. Finally, after the identification of an interpretative discourse, a phase of feedback and joint reflection should be provided in which the speaker confirms what the observer has interpreted.

Let us consider point (b) relative to whether the people provide an "objective" explanatory account of something that is in their minds, or reinterpret and actively reconstruct what they have learned. What has been written up to this point confirms the second position. At any rate, it is possible to claim that this, far from being a limit, can be a point of strength in the analysis based on the language in the study in the processes of organizational change.

The reason that the analysis of discourses is important, particularly in the processes of organizational changes, lies in the fact that it allows the observer to analyze the implicit world of individual knowledge, the shared cultural values, and the widespread belief systems that are more or less liable to change. The analysis of explanatory discourses is to "force" the actors to reconstruct and structure, at least partially and ex-post, some elements of their own rationality and that of others.

The action of reconstruction of the language is fundamental because it opens a window on the tacit world of the organization on what is hidden under the point of the iceberg of the formal organization and of the explicit knowledge, a subterranean world which is often opaque to the organizational members themselves. The opaque world is almost always the world of the obvious and the taken for granted. Its opacity lies almost always in the automatic nature and the uncritical attitude with which it is activated.

Finally, regarding point (c), relative to how the observers can arrive at a consensual vision in relation to the content of a discourse, there are different methodologies in the field of interpretative research based on the concept of *interrater reliability.* Manuals on interpretative research methods can be of help (Denzin & Lincoln, 2005; Reason & Bradbury, 2001).

Underlying the *interrater reliability* is the tendency toward research of consensual interpretations obtained through the interaction and comparison of different researchers. The underlying hypothesis is that consensual interpretations independently obtained are more valid than divergent interpretations. So, it is necessary to reach, directly or indirectly, an adequate level of interpretative convergence in order to be able to increase the reliability of the data.

Naturally the problem of consensus involves other organizational actors as well, who are the "authors" of the explanations (or should we say coauthors?). Their "validation" of the interpretations given by the observers is fundamental.

Conclusion

If the organizational analyst (whether external or internal) has a robust methodology for analyzing discourses it will be possible to highlight a whole world of completely new facts.

These facts drive everyday interpretation and action of organizational members. Rebuilt facts, already incorporate the intentions of the performers and their tension toward the future. The facts that the analyst obtain from discourse analysis are arrows pointed towards the future.

Intertwining these new facts, understanding the directions where they point, driving them towards shared objectives are all tasks that the learning organization must be able to perform.

Thus, a good methodology for discourse analysis is an essential requirement for the learning organization. Such a methodology should allow organizational analysts to confront different opinions in a reasonable time.

The main objective of this book is to help the organizations to develop their own methodology for discourse analysis. A methodology for learning, with the same importance and dignity of methodologies developed for management of operations and strategy. In the next chapter we outline several implications for the management of the learning organization that can be derived from the theoretical and methodological approach presented in this book.

References

Argyris, C., & Schon, D.A. (1978). *Organizational learning. A theory of action perspective.* Reading, MA: Addison-Wesley.

Bettoni, M. (1997). Constructivist foundations of modeling: A Kantian perspective. *International Journal Of Intelligent Systems, 12,* 577-595.

Cohen, M.D., March, J.G., & Olsen, J.O. (1972). A garbage can model of organizational choice. *Administrative Science Quarterly, 17,* 1-25.

Crozier, M., & Fiedberg, E. (1977). *L'acteur et le système.* Paris: Editions du Seuil.

Denzin, N.K., & Lincoln, Y.S. (2005). *Handbook of qualitative research.* Thousands Oaks, CA: Sage.

Lewin, K. (1951). *Field theory in the social science: Selected theoretical papers.* New York: Harper & Row.

Mintzberg, H., Raisinghani, D., & Theoret, A. (1976). The structure of unstructured decision processes. *Administrative Science Quarterly, 25,* 465-499.

Polanyi, M. (1967). *The tacit dimension.* New York: Doubleday.

Reason, P., & Bradbury, H. (2001). *Handbook of action research.* Thousands Oaks, CA: Sage.

Sandberg, J. (2000). Understanding Human competence at work: An interpretative approach. *Academy of Management Journal, 43*(1), 9-25.

Schein, E. (1987). *Process consultation: Its role in organization development.* Reading, MA: Addison Wesley.

Chapter XVII

Managing in the Learning Organization

If you don't want a man unhappy politically, don't give him two sides to a question to worry him; give him one. Better yet, give him none. If the government is inefficient, topheavy, and tax-mad, better it be all those than that people worry over it. Peace, Montag. Give the people contests they win by remembering the words to more popular songs or the names of state capitals or how much corn Iowa grew last year. Cram them full of noncombustible data, shock them so damned full of 'facts' they feel stuffed, but absolutely 'brilliant' with information. Then they'll feel they're thinking, they'll get a sense of motion without moving. And they'll be happy, because facts of that sort don't change. Don't give them any slippery stuff like philosophy or sociology to tie things up with. That way lies melancholy.

(Ray Bradbury, *Fahrenheit 451*)

Abstract

In this chapter we provide several suggestions for managing cognitive work and learning organizations. We underline that managers should pay attention mainly to the processes through which learning develops and occurs within organizations rather than focusing their attention on outcomes and performance. Learning outcomes are not predictable, nor easy to evaluate and control. Learning may develop in unusual directions and produce unexpected outcomes. It is crucial to provide organizational members with adequate levels of autonomy and trust. This requires a deep change and a new attitude with respect to the management of time, place and work relations. Time, place and relations should be driven by creativity and innovation rather than by operations, hierarchy and efficiency.

Three Steps to Build a Learning Organizations

The construction of the learning organization requires some preconditions. Once such preconditions have been met, the learning organization needs to activate and maintain an ongoing process of continuous innovation and maintenance of its organizational memory. Such a process can be sparked and built upon a three layer structure, starting from the middle level (Figure 1):

- Investigating to find out about and describe the organizational memory in terms of awareness and shared values
- Planning and implementing open artifacts
- Creating a climate of consent by involving organizational members in the planning and implementation of the new artifacts

Forming project task force is a way of involving analysts, managers, testimonials or other stakeholders in the company by giving them a leading role as organizational investigators. In mixed task forces, both internal and external analysts have to work closely together during each stage of the investigation. This is especially true during the crucial on-site phases of interviews and interpretations of the results.

We also need to ask ourselves how it is possible to improve the degree of openness of artifacts, identifying multiple uses, reducing centralized control (of use, access and levels of participation), distributed architecture (network), modularity, and providing for possible upgrading, personalization, interaction, connectivity, universal interfaces and mobility.

Figure 1. Organizational learning pyramid

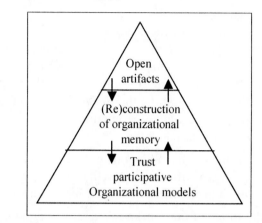

It is possible to identify three layers of organizational learning arranged within a hierarchical pyramid:

(a) Construction of open-ended artifacts

(b) Construction and updating of the organizational memory

(c) Climate of trust and organizational participation.

The hierarchy means that any intervention at one of the upper levels is useless if work on the level below has not been consolidated.

When new artifacts are introduced, parallel transfer activity is necessary, for example:

- Effective internal communication (before, during, and after intervention) to ensure people know about the aims and motivation behind the investigations and the results they produced.
- Intense training.
- Management of organizational follow-up after the introduction of the new system.

This last point is very important. Planning new artifacts necessarily leads to the production of collaterals such as:

- Updating the organizational memory by creating an archive of maps and knowledge.
- Developing a methodology for organizational investigation to support organizational inquiry.

Once the three layers have been made available, the learning process can start and grow.

It is important to stress that one of the crucial aspects of organizational learning processes is not so much getting definite results and specific outcomes as in the process itself. The results are difficult to predict and even harder to plan. The process of learning is not structured and is hard to control. It can take unexpected turns and give unhoped-for results. Its *serendipity*, that is the ability to find something new and interesting while we are searching for something else, is one of the features of learning processes (Merton & Barber, 2004).

If we are to change the emphasis from learning outcomes to learning processes we need to change the way organizational knowledge is traditionally managed, and create the conditions which make continuous learning possible.

One of the major limitations of current knowledge management systems is their lack of integration with organizational learning processes (Rubinstein-Montano et al., 2001). If knowledge management is to be integrated within learning processes then cyclical investigation needs to be carried out in order to ensure the updating and the maintenance of the collective knowledge stored in the organizational memory as shown in the cycle of Figure 2.

Essentially this cycle represents an attempt to create a system of organizational self-observation and self-diagnosis, where feedback and information exchange between the various people involved, as well as the use of open artifacts and participative policies, allows for organizational learning to take place.

Figure 2. System construction cycle in a learning organization

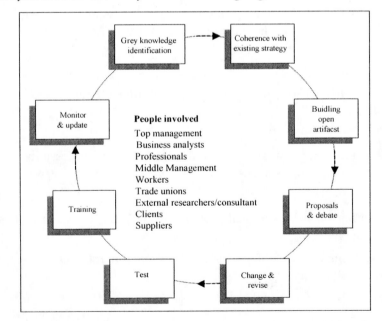

Suggestions for the Implementation of the Organizational Learning Cycle

The cycle of organizational learning depicted in Figure 2 can be supported in several ways. The most important are summarized in the list below, though it is by no means exhaustive:

1. Promote and institutionalize investigation within the organization

2. Create organizational models which encourage participation and involvement

3. Identify and analyze the theories in use to check for possible discrepancies between them and the espoused theories

4. Use descriptions of artifacts and shared values to identify and map out the organizational memory

5. Identify and describe interaction networks, including the major interlocutors and addressees, obtain sponsorship and commitment from the top

6. Create open artifacts and inform people about them and encourage their use

7. Tolerate redundancy

8. Place emphasis on identifying problems, putting forward solutions and gathering information

9. Identify hidden rationale and learning potential within the organization

10. Preserve diversity

These principles take account of accepted policy as regards information management within organizations (decentralization of decision-making, sharing, fast and low-cost access to knowledge base, work groups, etc.). However, the fact that information is available and people communicate does not, in themselves, guarantee that an organization can solve its problems.

We need something more to say that an organization has learned. First, an organization learns when it has the ability to set in motion, or at least not inhibit, processes of organizational investigation, in which organizational players are the protagonists and act as agents for change. Second, the results of individual learning become organizational when they are "encoded" into one or more new artifacts and/or values.

Learning often involves unlearning what you already know, rejecting certainties, and setting out on new routes and encountering new situations. And that, as Schein says (2002), can cause a real sense of learning anxiety.

On the other hand, organizations are also prey to a different kind of anxiety, which derives from the fact that they are functioning in a problematic and competitive field which constantly questions their existence. Schein states that learning can only occur if the following dis-equation is in place:

survival anxiety > learning anxiety

In other words, organizations, like people, only change if they have to. If this equation is true there are two ways in which organizational learning can be encouraged:

a.   Either increase survival anxiety by increasing control levels and encouraging internal competition and any of the other techniques belonging to the "carrot and stick" approach. The organizational machine can only learn when survival anxiety rises as a result of tough controls and there is a lot of external pressure.

b.   Or reduce learning anxiety, putting more emphasis on individual initiative and open artifacts.

The first approach is driven by the expected results: people *must* learn to achieve given performance objectives. The second approach is driven by learning itself: people *are willing* to learn for the sake of learning and because it can be useful and rewarding for them. The focus on the learning process rather than on the learning outcomes should induce managers to develop a new vision of the organization in which change is the result of an *ongoing dialectic process of discovery* instead of a product of internal conflict and external pressure.

To make sure that organizational learning becomes standard practice as opposed to something occasional, it is important to carry out periodic self-assessment in areas of knowledge that are hazy, so that the organization can monitor and update its knowledge map, identify the theories being applied and adapt them to the changing context and environment according to the cycle of Figure 2.

The objective is to actually to dig and uncover new knowledge; knowledge which *emerges* as a result of individuals, as well as the group, adapting to the environment as they work on their tasks. It must be remembered that the starting point for organizational learning is a continuous process of reinterpretation on the part of the players as they define their environment and role within it as well as their own way of operating in the organization. And this only happens if the individuals within the organization are actually learning persons, agents of change, and problem solvers rather than simply passive followers of orders.

The cycle starts with the analysis of the grey knowledge contained in explanations in order to identify the existing theories-in-use. Then the theories-in-use are compared with the existing strategy and espoused theory. The output of such a comparison can be potentially useful to build new artifacts or to augment the openness of existing artifacts. Once created, the new artifacts should be proposed and debated through the involvement of as many as possible organizational members in order to collect their points of views and suggestions and possibly revise and further improve the artifacts.

Once revised the new artifacts should be tested on the field and again revised. Finally organizational members should be informed and trained to use the artifacts and their use should be monitored and possibly improved through successive updates. In Figure 2, we also report a list of subjects that can be potentially involved in each phase. The actual list will of course depend on the specific case.

Organizational Learning as a Process of Discovery

In the first part of this book we maintained that organizations guide the collective action through apparatus based on shared "memories." This apparatus, which is based on values, artifacts and action theories, is necessary for ensuring that the collective action is coherent, reproducible and lasting.

Organizational learning, for organizational members, implies working their way through three consecutive stages where knowledge and impact progressively increase:

1. Find out about and use the apparatus in place to guarantee persistence
2. Question it if and when necessary
3. Make permanent changes to it to make sure individual learning becomes part of the collective heritage

Organizations are created to make collective action durable. Whether for a long or a short time does not matter. However brief their existence might be, organizations need any collective action to be regulated and regular.

As we have proposed in Chapter V, organizing can be seen as the imposition of (an) order on the chaos of social action, and therefore an attempt to make the collective system less indefinite by imposing ordered and "unnatural" ways of behavior. Organizing, therefore, implies giving recognizable form to social action.

The effort required to guarantee that action is regular is essentially what organization is about but, at the same time, it gives rise to a series of paradoxes, the first of which is the paradox of organizational learning.

The paradox lies in the double bind characterizing the organizational memory:

- Memory is a tool for attaining knowledge because it is a starting point and guide for any organizational change
- Memory is an obstacle to change because it encourages people to repeat their actions and makes for more rigid interpretation of action within consolidated structures

Traces of this paradox can be found in the dualism between process and structure which constrains the debate in organizational studies around two opposing visions of the concept of organization. One which favors a concept of equilibrium and one which stresses the idea of transformation and change (Hernes & Bakken, 2003).

For upholders of the equilibrium theory, *organizations are.* In other words, organizations exist, are made up of structures, norms, plans, organization charts, job descriptions, and the other things that go to make up the apparatus to ensure persistence. This consists of organizational artifacts and forms the scaffolding of the collective memory. Within this approach, the existence of an organization pans out along evolving pathways made up of equilibrium states, phases and life cycles marked by stable characteristics. According to the equilibrium approach, what characterizes organizations is the presence of roles (Katz & Kahn, 1978), available information (Simon, 1949), culture (Schein, 1985), adaptation to the environment (Lawrence & Lorsch, 1967), and institutions (Di Maggio & Powell, 1983; Scott, 1995).

What characterizes organizational equilibrium is a tendency to be impersonal in the sense that equilibrium tends to outlast the people who created it. Thus, an organization chart outlives the names appearing on it, a job description outlives the flesh and blood person actually doing the job and a procedure outlives the actions of the who carry it out.

For the "supporters" of the theories based on processes, organizations *do not exist but rather, they become.* In the concluding chapter of his famous work Weick (1979) maintains:

Although our focus throughout has been on processes and on the ways in which organizations unfold, it is possible for us to state where the organizations resides. The organizations consist of plans, recipes, rules, instructions, and programs for generating, interpreting, and governing behavior that are jointly managed by two or more people. If you want to find an organization and its static properties, then in terms of the organizing formulations you look at contents of the retention process, you identify the dominant assembly rules, you pinpoint the interpersonal cycles that tend to be most salient and incorporated into the largest number of processes, and you try to articulate the cause maps that recur in an organization's description of itself. These several properties constitute the stability, continuity and repetition that produces the impressions of similarity across time in the processes that occur. (Weick, 1979, p. 235)

According to the organizational approach, organizations are communities of practice (Wenger, 1999), double interaction assemblies (Weick, 1979), organized anarchies offering solutions in search of a problem (Cohen March & Olsen, 1972), social constructions (Nicolini & Meznar, 1995), interpretive systems (Daft & Weick, 1984), paradox systems (Cameron & Quinn, 1988), and discourses (Heracleous & Barret, 2001).

The third "way," which we have actually embraced in this book, takes organizations to be systems which constantly self-reproduce (autopoietics), in the sense that they continually redefine their borders, distinguishing themselves from a context which an observer would term their environment (Maturana and Varela, 1980; Luhmann, 1995; Kay, 2001).[1]

Autopoeisis develop as a dialectic tension between structure and process linked to the circular nature of the double bind: without a structure there is no process, without a process there is no structure. If we transfer this language to the organizational field we could say that without the organization there is nothing to organize but without organizing, the organization cannot exist.

If we manage to avoid the ideological temptation and organizational nihilism that the autopoietic approach has produced in organizational theory (Kay 2001), and more generally in social studies, it would seem a particularly apt way to describe the phenomena relating to processes of organizational learning, especially if these phenomena are described in concrete terms using artifacts belonging to the organizational memory.

In terms of organizational learning, structures mean the organizational artifacts and shared values, and processes refers to the individual reworking of the organizational memory (sense-making, decision-making, social construction, reasoning, and communication). The products of learning are new apparatus, which is new and consolidated memories.

They are the outcomes of a process of discovery which is at the same time enabled and constrained by the past.

Without apparatus and structure there can be no organization but without the ability and the strength to question the existing ones and create new ones there can be no learning. In other words, in contrast to theories of self-organization, self-management, and destructuralization of organizational processes and training, *we firmly believe that structure is necessary.* If only to contradict it. If only to reject it through reasoning and a search for consensus with a view to reworking the dominant rationale. If only as a starting point for the process of discovery.

But how can we stop the apparatus destroying the subjectivity which it ought to encourage? How can we avoid the trap of the organizational machine, the positivist illusion of rational, centralized control? And most of all, how can we replace good old Taylorism?

Critical Issues in the Management of Cognitive Work

As shown in the second part of this book, organizational explanations are central to setting up learning processes within organizations. In the MEP model, the creation of new explanations and legitimizing them means setting in motion processes for rewriting the organizational memory.

In organizations, where individual interpretation and organizational investigation are carried out and encouraged, the people are not just passively carrying out deeds or performing a routine but are active subjects who are required to make independent assessments, take decisions and find explanations for their organizational interlocutors (clients, colleagues, stakeholders, etc).

In an increasingly unpredictable and complex world, "knowing" how to reflect on your own job and the way you do it, as well as on the structural and organizational limitations within which you work, becomes a fundamental competence. Rediscovering subjectivity and the subject within work and organizations signals defeat for Taylorism and bureaucratic thought, and makes organizations face up to their new challenge: Managing cognitive work.

Using an existing definition (Cillario, 1990), what we mean by cognitive work is *work that is accompanied by reflection.* The cognitive worker reinterprets, and maybe even transforms, the organizational structure as well as the methods and procedures defining the job. In other words, cognitive work is the ability and the willingness on the part of the individual to reflect on and change organizational procedures relating to their job in terms of limits, methods, meanings, tools and outcomes.

Cognitive work is not the opposite of manual work, in fact it takes advantage of manuality in its broadest sense of practical ability, creativity, know-how and experience. The opposite of cognitive is more like routine, alienation, the expropriation of sense, the absence of participation and involvement, and the enslavement of individual action to the logic of the "machine," whether that be metaphorical or real.

Although we recognize there is a desirable evolution in moving from a taylorist-bureaucratic paradigm to a cognitive work one, we still need to be careful not to fall into the trap of the "wonderful, progressive future" kind of rhetoric, which organizational neo-humanism often goes in for. The reality of work is often very different. Although lip service is paid to the central role played by human resources in processes of values creation, when it comes to practice, even in the best-case scenario the principle is only partially adhered to and in the worst it is quite openly contradicted.

In reality, the management of cognitive work poses a series of challenges for both the organizations and the people within them which go well beyond traditional dilemmas of autonomy or control, hierarchy and market and the planning of adequate incentive systems.

Cognitive work is in fact necessary when the complexity of the environment is reflected in various situations at work. Thus, its very presence is an indicator that the organization and its people are operating in a context which is at least problematic if not critical.

As Ray Bradbury reminds us in its famous novel, *Fahrenheit 451*, people are not always able or willing to handle such high levels of complexity. "*Able and willing to handle*" means having the individual skills, the freedom to act, and sufficient levels of motivation, as well as an awareness of the constraints governing action. In other words, people may or may not have the skills necessary to deal with more complex situations, their actions may be hindered by external constraints, and they may not be sufficiently motivated or skilled to cope with the complexity because the incentives are not adequate or because they suffer from learning anxiety.

Substituting routine with creativity, or at least its poor relative "problem solving," creates a need for change because it forces individuals to question their own identity and professional stability, to revise and update their own professional knowledge base, to look at how they measure up against contradictions and paradoxes and to accept different roles and points of view thus bringing them into contact, as well as conflict, with other interlocutors. In conclusion, managing cognitive work and organizational learning processes requires a new work culture involving new approaches and competences on the part of the workers and managers as well as a new organizational paradigm.

Managing Cognitive Work within an Open Organization Paradigm

In Chapter V, we defined grey knowledge as transactional knowledge originating from interaction between individual and artifact. It is what results when the individual questions the artifact, and investigates how it can best be used, and defines it according to his or her own interpretive and creative ability. It is clear that this kind of knowledge is generated as a result of the relationship between an individual and any artifact whether it is open or closed. Even the most prescriptive of artifacts requires a certain amount of creative ability to decode the message and carry out an order. It is also obvious that the level and depth of analysis is both quantitatively and qualitatively much greater if the artifact is an open one.

Within post-Taylorist organizations, dealing with open artifacts before choice has become a necessity. For example, technology is becoming ever more complex and sophisticated. Products have multiple meanings and can be used in a variety of ways which even their designers are unaware of. We could say that artifacts have an increasing ability to bring out the interpretive potential in their users. In other words, artifacts can be used in numerous ways and they increasingly act as vehicles for an interpretive surplus, which it is up to the individual to identify and maybe even use.

How can organizations identify this *interpretive surplus*? How can they encourage its creation? How can they multiply its meanings, possible interpretations and connections?

What we maintain in this book is the potential for coordination and control offered by the organizational apparatus, the power of the organizational memory to condition interpretation, and the creation of meaning should not be sacrificed in favor of a complete destructuralization of the processes and a poorly-understood triumph on the part of subjectivity and individual autonomy. Learning processes emerge as a result of permanent tension between what organizations already know and what individuals bring to them, between the organizational memory and individual sense-making, between subject and object, between the individual and the collective with its rules and constraints. One aspect of the apparatus that does need to be abandoned is its closed nature which limits action and confines it to consolidated practice.

Here is a summary of some basic principles which, when implemented, could enable the organization to keep on the road of continuous learning:

- **Partial membership and fuzzy borders:** The organization interacts in different ways and with varying intensity with a large number of different people, work relations are increasingly versatile and flexible, relations with society and stakeholders are better-established and relevant to the organization's objectives, the competences that the organization needs no longer be found simply within the confines of the organization. The result is that there is a nucleus of competences and intrinsic resources at the heart of the company, then an outer area of varying competences and resources, which belongs only in part to the organization. It makes no sense to delineate any kind of boundary between these two areas.

Fuzzy organizational borders may facilitate the update of organizational memory through exchange with the external environment. On the other hand, excess of turnover prevents organizations from retaining what individual have learned (March, 1991; Miller et al., 2006).

- **Use of open artifacts and awareness of memory:** Open organizations have resources, infrastructures, and tool boxes, which are available for everyone to use, but they do not impose ready-made procedures or instructions for use. They prefer to ask their people to devise their own systems that work to the organization's advantage and benefit. An open organization encourages and develops cognitive work and resists any attempt at centralized control of these processes.

An open organization is aware of having a history and a memory, which it maintains, updates, codifies, and materializes in a set of organizational artifacts. The management of the awareness in organizations is more properly the management of memory. What distinguishes the organization inspired to openness from any traditional organization is not only the awareness and the consciousness of its own memory, but the ease with which individuals have access to this patrimony of knowledge, and they are able to question it and possibly modify it. Remember that modifying means *modifying for everyone* and that knowledge is organization when it has been incorporated into a new form of artifact or shared values.

- **Abolition of the principle of unity of time, place and action[2]:** Learning organizations are not obsessed with limiting the field of action of the individual, which, in organizations, means above all controlling work times and places. Cognitive work accompanies the individuals to their homes, private life, and working life weaving it together, and so creativity is not forced into logic of "times and methods." Creativity has its unpredictable schedules and is based on a structural redundancy of time, space and resources.

- **The absence of dualism from exploration and exploitation:** Open organizations do not distinguish between or separate innovation and new research from efficiency (March, 2001).

In the first place, even if it were possible, there would not be enough time. In the second place because it would be contrary to the logic of learning organizations, in that the tendency toward efficiency generates closure and closure generates obstacles to innovation. Open organizations live in an atmosphere of perennial research and experimentation and admits the redundancy of resources, *time* in particular. *Exploration* and *exploitation* are substituted by research and experimentation. This implies that open organizations do not alternate creative moments with productive moments, instead it pursues the two objectives at the same time.

Post-Taylorist organizations are similar to shops during the Renaissance, which were essentially places for learning and experimentation, and at the same time, production. In these productive contexts, creativity and productivity are synonyms: Being productive does not mean minimizing the consumption of material resources, but maximizing the effects coming from the use of cognitive resources, and this means creating more with apparently the same human capital, therefore freeing their potential. Actually knowledge is a strange kind of resource that is increased and not consumed when used.

In open organizations, the traditional objectives of efficiency, effectiveness and flexibility are secondary effects with respect to the primary objective: To innovate. The tendency toward innovation brings internal redundancy (organizational *slack*) as well as the capacity to anticipate tendencies, to knowingly elaborate "solutions in search of problems" (Cohen March & Olsen, 1972).

- **Emphasis on practice and experimentation:** In open organizations, the separation between knowledge and action, decision making and executive tasks, conceptual and operative work make less and less sense when in carrying out activities at an increased level of creativity: The person who makes the decisions must then carry them out, and whoever carries them out is deciding (think of an artist painting a picture). The objective is the sedimentation of experience, the construction of professionalism, the discovery and accumulation of knowledge through action and exploration.

- **Promotion of organizational inquiry through participation and involvement:** Open organizations promote and provide incentives for organizational investigation, motivating its members to transform themselves into organizational observers, or researchers, internal consultants, agents of change that explore the possibilities for innovation in the interest of the organization (Argyris & Schön, 1978). Open organizations adopt participatory organizational models in the search for innovation and substitutes participatory logic for antagonistic and contentious logic in the processes of managing Human Resources such as organizational development, training, and industrial relations (Baglioni, 2002; Volpe, 2002).

References

Argyris, C., & Schon, D.A. (1978). *Organizational learning. A theory of action perspective.* Reading, MA: Addison-Wesley.

Baglioni, G. (Ed.). (2002). Teoria della tutela della partecipazione. Special issue of *L'impresa al plurale*, n° 10.

Cameron, K.S., & Quinn, R.E., (1988). Organizational paradox and transformation. In R.E. Quinn & K.S. Cameron (Eds.) *Paradox and transformation*. Cambridge, MA: Ballinger.

Cillario, L. (1990). Il capitalismo cognitivo. Sapere, sfruttamento e accumulazione dopo la rivoluzione informatica. *Trasformazione e persistenza* (Saggi sulla storicità del capitalismo). Milano: F. Angeli.

Cohen, M.D., March, J.G., & Olsen, J.O. (1972). A garbage can model of organizational choice. *Administrative Science Quarterly, 17*, 1-25.

Daft, R.L., & Weick, K. (1984). Toward a model of organization as interpretation systems. *Academy of Management Review, 9*(2), 284-295.

Di Maggio, P.J., & Powell, W.W. (1983). The iron cage revisited: Institutional isomorphism and collective rationality in organizational fields. *American Sociological Review, 48*, 147-160.

Heracleous, L., & Barrett, M. (2001). Organizational change as discourse: Communicative actions and deep structures in the context of information technology implementation. *Academy of Management Journal, 44*(4), 755-778.

Hernes, T., & Bakken, T. (2003). Implications of self-reference: Niklas Luhmann's autopoiesis and organization theory. *Organization Studies, 24*(9), 1511-1535.

Katz, D., & Kahn, R.L. (1978). *The social psychology of organization*. New York: Wiley.

Kay, R. (2001). Are organizations autopoietic? A call for a new debate. *Systems Research and Behavioral Science, 18*, 461-477.

Lawrence, P.R., & Lorsch, J.W. (1967). *Organization and environment*. Boston: Harvard Business School Press.

Luhmann, N. (1995). *Social systems*. Stanford: Stanford University Press.

March, J. G. (1991). Exploration and exploitation in organizational learning. *Organization Science, 2*(1), 71-77.

March, J.B. (2001). The pursuit of intelligence in organizations. In K. T. Lant & Z. Shapira (Eds.), *Organizational cognition: Computation and interpretation*. Mawah, NJ: Lawrence Erlbaum Associate.

Maturana, H., & Varela, F. (1980). *Autopoiesis and cognition: The realization of living*. London: Reidl.

Merton, R.K., & Barber, L. (2004). *The travels and adventures of serendipity: A study in sociological semantics and the sociology of science*. Princeton, NJ: Princeton University Press.

Miller, K. D., Zhao, M., & Calantone, R. J. (2006). Adding inter-personal learning and tacit knowledge to March's exploration-exploitation model. *Academy of Management Journal, 49*(4), 709-722.

Nicolini, D., & Meznar, M.B. (1995). The social construction of organizational learning. *Human Relations 48*(7), 727-746.

Rubenstein-Montano, B., Liebowitz, J., Buchwalter, J., McCaw, D., Newman, B., & Rebeck, K. (2001). A system thinking framework for knowledge management. *Decision Support Systems, 31,* 5-16.

Schein, E. (1985). *Organizational culture and leadership.* San Francisco: Jossey Bass.

Schein, E. (2002). The anxiety of learning: An interview with Edgar Schein by D. Coutu. *Harvard Business Review.*

Scott, W.R. (1995). *Institutions and organizations.* Thousand Oaks, CA: Sage.

Simon, H.A. (1949). *Administrative behavior.* New York: Macmillan.

Volpe, V. (2002). Lavoro, soggettività e partecipazione nell'avvento post-industriale. *L'impresa al plurale, 9,* 225-235.

Wenger, E. (1999). *Communities of practice: Learning, meaning and identity.* Boston: Cambridge University Press.

Weick, K.E. (1979). *The social psychology of organization* (2nd ed.). Reading, MA: Addison Wesley.

Endnotes

[1] See Kay (2001) for an in depth review of the debate around the concept of autopoiesis in organizational science.

[2] This principle was invented by ancient Greek dramaturges. According to this rule, in the classic Greek tragedy the narrative plot would develop in the same place, within a clearly limited time frame, and it was centered around a single main character and his/her personal drama.

Chapter XVIII

Perspectives for Organizational Inquiry

Old paradigms fall from grace not because they are wrongs but because they are boring.

(Graham Astley, 1985)

Abstract

This chapter is dedicated to identifying future research perspectives for the methodological approach presented in this text. The methodological argument is taken up again from a wider perspective in order to propose a truly innovative computational approach to supporting organizational analysis. For each of the salient steps of the proposed approach, that is, the identification, mapping and modeling of discourses, the available or potential alternative methodologies are mentioned briefly and possible developments are outlined.

Organizational Decision as Unit of Analysis

The literature on organizational learning concentrates mainly on the psychological, cultural, and organizational obstacles that can inhibit learning, and much less on the methods and tools for conducting the research itself. It is widely acknowledged that the reduction of learning anxiety (Schein, 2002), the moderation of defensive ways of thinking (Argyris & Schön, 1978), the socialization of knowledge (Nonaka & Takeuchi, 1995) and more in general, the motivation to change are the inexorable requirements in triggering the dynamics of organizational learning. Without these, methodologies could not provide meaningful answers to organizational investigators. Nevertheless, once these conditions are acquired, it becomes necessary to turn to the problem of which methods and tools should support the organizational analysis.

In the second part of this book, a methodological approach based on the analysis of organizational explanations was presented, along with a set of instruments for identifying, analyzing and modeling discourses. Here it is appropriate to take up the methodological discourse from a wider perspective, in order to propose an *attitude regarding the method* that supports the organizations engaging in forms of organizational observation.

Before turning our attention to the methodological aspects let us briefly summarize the view of organizational learning we have proposed in this book:

a.   Organizations are systems that generate collective decisions and action

b.   The construction of actions and decisions is mediated by organizational memory, which is made up of shared artifacts and values

c.   Individual action is the result of the construction of meaning guided by the individual and organizational memory

d.   Theories of action are incorporated into explanatory discourses with which the organizational observers clarify the reasons for their own actions

This *schema* is applied as much to the clockwork organization (Chapter I) as to the organization inspired by the paradigm of openness (Chapter XVII), with an important and substantial difference: In the clockwork organization, the meaning of the information is taken for granted.

The clockwork organization tries to reduce the ambiguity associated to events and the discretionality of behavior to a minimum through the detailed definition of tasks and functions, the hierarchy, the repetition and the standardization of procedures and output. This means that collective action tends to produce certain and reliable data, which is suitable for quantitative elaboration.[1]

When the meaning of information becomes problematic, when it is the interpretation of events that make the difference, the quantitative methodologies that are at the base of forecasting, planning and socioeconomic analysis are found wanting (Rosenhead & Mingers, 2001).[2]

The Inadequacy of Traditional Methods for Studying Organizational Learning

Why do traditional quantitative methods, and more generally, the so-called positivist approach produce results that do not meet expectations? Although various scholars have provided different answers to this question,[3] in many cases, most of the observations can be traced back to *the problem of consensus*. There can be discordant interpretations of an organizational phenomenon that leads to different representations of the problem and to different courses of action that can all be equally legitimate.

In these cases, the problem of optimization makes no sense: While the search for a shared representation of the problem does.

Subjectivity is unavoidable. In many cases, there are no objective reasons for preferring one representation to another. The description itself of the problem is ambiguous, partial, and imprecise in that it is provided by agents characterized by a limited rationality and cognitive bias.

Subjectivity is, after all, at the heart of an organization. It is in the internal diversity of points of view, values, and interpretations that the organization can find answers when having to face tough competition.

If the production of choices is ambiguous, chaotic, and destructured, then, as we have demonstrated in the third part of this book, appropriate tools are needed to identify and describe them. Turning back to Rosenhead and Mingers (2001), *"The decision-making process in organizations can be seen as a process of mutual adaptation between independent agents in which agreement is not taken for granted by virtue of some higher order restrictions. The agents in question possess the capacity for judgement based on experience that cannot be reduced to numbers, can have diverse prospects and interests and do not have the talent for predicting reliably what the future holds for them"* (Rosenhead & Mingers, 2001, p. 11).

Sense-making and decision-making are developed in two macrophases: The first, oriented toward the creation of models and schematic representations of the reality (*mapping*); the second, in which the elaboration and problematic data are drawn up in the light of representations constructed in the first phase (*information processing*).[4]

What is interesting is that both the construction and the use of these maps is a collective phenomenon. Moreover, we can observe that the phases of *mapping* and *information processing* are not done sequentially, but are reciprocally influenced through a process of mutual adaptation, in the sense that mindsets can condition the way that reality is perceived, and the processing of information can (occasionally) require the revision of interpretative models. The interpretation of the novel situation is the result of a strategic adaptation to a preexisting interpretative scheme. *Reality, in other words, is always an "altered" reality depending on the cognitive patrimony of its interpreters.*

The proposal that emerges at the methodological level assumes that the mapping phase can be analyzed and described through typically qualitative or hybrid tools, common in the social and cognitive sciences, while the phase of information processing can be investigated through the use of methodologies used in the field of advanced computation and in particular of methods used in the so-called soft computing field (Figure 1).

On the right hand side of Figure 1 there are some possible methodologies that can be used for the study and analysis of the two macrophases in which the research has been articulated.

Methodologies for Mapping

In Chapter XVI, we presented the epistemological attitude that the organizational researcher must adhere to in the development of investigative methodologies that

Figure 1. A methodological approach in support of organizational research

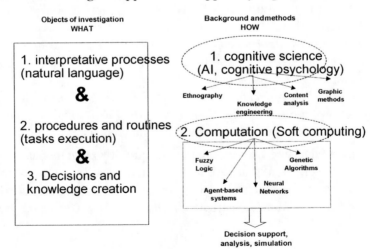

rely on techniques of qualitative and interpretative research. Moreover, we have indicated the numerous manuals that are available and can be consulted for the technical aspects of each method.

Here we are limited to a quick overview of the methods mentioned in Figure 1, referring to Chapter XI for the specific examination of the proposed method of analysis for explanatory discourses. In the following paragraph, the way in which these methods can be integrated with quantitative computational methodologies will be demonstrated.

We will classify a series of qualitative research techniques in the category of *ethnographic methods* that originate from the field of cultural anthropology. The aim of these methods is to identify and describe the organizational culture, usually through long and exhaustive research in the field. This requires an intense level of involvement and participation on the part of researchers who turn to protocols for observing organizational behaviors, as well as the use of interviews and the consultation of secondary sources.

The methods grouped in the category of *knowledge engineering* are made up of techniques developed in the field of artificial intelligence and computer science for the identification of the knowledge of human experts and its codification and representation within implementable formal systems and later in computer programs. All of the techniques used for the realization of so-called expert systems, meaning software able to simulate the behavior of a human expert in the field of a given domain, are part of this group. Among the best known are systems based on rules and case-based reasoning systems.

In *graphic methods* we will classify two associated methodologies which use representations based on oriented graphs: Cognitive mapping and social network analysis. Cognitive mapping is intended as the set of methodologies of mapping interpretative themes that individuals use in the interpretation of information. In general, such schemes are represented graphically in the form of maps showing concepts and relationships between concepts. Among the best known methodologies are causal maps (see also Chapters X and XI), repertory grid analysis (Kelly, 1955), and the SODA method (strategic options development and analysis, Eden & Ackermann, 2001). Regardless of the differences, a common objective of such methods is the representation of the belief system of the organizational actors, with the aim of providing a description, sharing, analysis and simulation, also through software tools, some of which are available commercially.

With their analogous spirit and techniques, the methods of *social network analysis* represent relationships between individuals within a work group or collectivity of various types. Unlike cognitive mapping, in this case they map people and information flow as well as different types and intensities of relationships between individuals instead of concepts and causal flows.

The category of *content analysis* methods refers to a set of techniques usually employed in the analysis of texts. In their simplest form, these tools, implemented through the use of software programs, are word processors that carry out statistical analyses of texts for the identification of structural and syntactic characteristics. In the more advanced applications, the challenge is to pass from a syntactic analysis to tools that support the semantic analysis of texts, particularly on the internet (semantic web). In addition to the methods of content analysis, which resort to computer science, in the same category we can include "paper and pencil" methods of analysis that are included in so-called narrative methods, for which the objective is to analyze the reports and the stories told by the organizational actors in order to identify the underlying structures of meaning, through methods developed in the field of language studies and literary texts (linguistics, semiotics, etc.).

Metodologies for Information Processing

Organizational members filter and process information through mental models and explanation frames belonging to both individual and collective memory. It is possible to conceive such representations as a set of "soft models" produced by individual sense-making and having the following characteristics:

a.   They are "verbal" models, contained within explanatory discourses, recipes, prescriptions, procedures, stories, dialogues, etc.

b.   They make use of *decisional heuristics* when aiming to reach a sort of cognitive economy that favors rapidity and efficiency while sacrificing completeness and precision.

c.   They are influenced by various types of *bias* (cultural, cognitive, etc.) at both the individual and organizational level.

Although it is controversial to affirm that the information processing done by individuals has a computational character (Newell & Simon, 1972), it is surely bolder to affirm that once the system of meaning has been established, it has an algorithmic-procedural approach. This means that rules and heuristics of reasoning, though they may be imprecise and rough, are applied within a semantic domain.

If we would like to reproduce the heuristic procedures that govern information processing of the organizational members, we must use modeling and computational techniques not included in the so-called hard modeling, such as systems of differential equations, systems theory, or formal logic. The models obtained through the application of such innovative techniques should possess some of the following characteristics. They should:

a.   Function according to heuristics

b.   Tolerate the use of imprecise information, both qualitative and quantitative

c.   Allow for the representation of nonlinear systems

d.   Be sufficiently flexible to adapt to a vast array of problems

e.   Allow for the representation of systems characterized by agents that work without centralized control

f.   Allow for the integration of different techniques within the same model, in that, often the combination of more than one technique succeeds when a signle methodology fails

These characteristics are part of a category of methods known as *soft computing* (Zadeh, 2001). The connotation of soft is relative to the capacity of such methodologies to process uncertain and approximate information, even though they are processed by algorithms that can be quite complex. The purpose of this algorithmic apparatus is not to find optimal solutions, but to simulate the scenarios and to discover emerging dynamics. The objective must be reached even when there is deficient information and a lack of "good quality" data. The idea is to reproduce the heuristics of human decision-makers, who, unlike machines, are able to carry out tasks and processes that are extraordinarily complex, using information that is lacking both on the qualitative and the quantitative level (see Chapter XII).

The reasons for implementing these algorithms can be many. Traditionally, they are used to implement prescriptive tools such as decisions support systems (DSS). Alternatively they can be used to analyze and simulate the dynamics of complex organizations by building virtual laboratory to perform *what-if* analysis.

In Figure 1 there are some methodological families that are traditionally classified in the field of soft computing.[5] As in the qualitative techniques, we will give a quick overview of these methodologies, referring to texts, manuals and specialistic studies for further study.

Fuzzy Logic

Fuzzy logic is a set of mathematical techniques that allow for the representation of uncertain and ambiguous information expressed in linguistic form. We will not dwell any longer upon the subject, given the ample space that it was allowed in Chapters XII, XIII and XIV. Here we will summarize some key concepts. As we said briefly in Chapters X, the operation of formalizing a verbal argument and its translation into a formal model (for example, an evaluation form) is actually a *reduction*, in which the ambiguity and the semantic richness of language are sacrificed in favor of the consistency of the internal logic. Any operation of formalization is not immune to this risk. Therefore, even fuzzy models produce a simplified and reduced representation of the complexity contained in the verbal information. Nevertheless, the techniques for "computing with words" (Zadeh, 1996) allow for a significant part of the informative wealth contained in the verbal information to be captured.

There are two convictions at the base of these approaches: The first is of a theoretical nature, in which uncertainty is not seen as background noise that should be eliminated in order to "clean up" the information from the undesirable disturbance, but is useful information for making decisions. The second is of a practical nature, in which in all cases where there is no direct and low-cost measure of qualitative information, it is a good idea to use such information directly in its linguistic form.

Chen and Hwang (1992) suggest that using the so-called linguistic information can be advantageous in each of the following cases:

a.   **Nonquantifiable information:** Intrinsically qualitative variables for which there are no reliable proxies or it is too expensive/arbitrary to identify them (e.g., the comfort of a car).

b.   **Incomplete information**: The information is identified in an approximate way and the precision of the tool is unknown (e.g., that car was going "about 90 miles per hour").

d.   **Unobtainable information:** A precise evaluation is possible and the data is theoretically available, but practically inaccessible. (e.g., an individual's bank account or age. In such cases it can be said that the person is rich or young).

e.   **Partial ignorance:** The imprecision can come from an awareness of partial ignorance of a phenomenon (e.g., "It is *plausible* that the stock market will not rise *significantly* in a brief period.").

In all of these cases, the information is available in linguistic terms. The question is: Can this type of information be used, when there is a lack of precise information? And which methodologies are most appropriate for representing and processing it? Fuzzy techniques give methodological answers to such questions, through the possiblity of modeling linguistic variables, verbal connectives and rules of approximate reasoning.

Neural Networks

Neural networks are like other algorithmic techniques in that they have been developed from "biological" metaphors. Neural networks, in particular come from an analogy with information processing in neurons within the human brain. The neurons are comparable to computational cells in which a given input, in the form of an electric signal, undergoes a specific process. The signal is then transmitted to one or more connected neurons in which it is processed again.

In the mathematical model, the neurons are represented through 'standard' functions, univocally identifiable by fixing certain parameters. A neural network is made up of a certain number of neurons organized in successive layers that connect n variables of input to m variables of output, where there is an unknown functional relationship, or at least it is hard to express analytically.

The most interesting characteristic of neural networks is that they are systems that are able to learn from real data. The network is initially calibrated through a set of training data that make up well-known couples of input/output. It calculates through attempts and errors according to the training data set, compares them with the desired output, and corrects some key parameters through numerous iterations until it is able to reproduce the desired behavior with a reasonable margin of error. Once the parameters have been set, in general the net works quite well when the input is similar to the training data. The combination of neural networks and fuzzy logic improves the performance of a network (Kosko, 1992).

Neural networks have the advantage of allowing the representation of nonlinear systems simply and efficiently when the number of inputs and outputs is not very high. They have one defect: The model determined by the neural network is not explicit, in the sense that its logic is still in a black box hidden in the network. This problem, however, can be overcome through fuzzy neural networks (Kosko, 1997). Fuzzy neural networks are able to identify rules from data: from instance, given a suitable number of observations of the actions and outcomes produced by a human expert, the network is able to identify the fuzzy rules describing the expert's behavior.

Neural networks can be used to reproduce and therefore simulate the effects of the evelation process done implicitly by organizational evaluators. For example, given a set of evaluations expressed by a decision maker in relation to the choice of suppliers, it is possible to reproduce the rules the decision makers apply in the choice by appropriately training a network (Albino & Garavelli, 1998). A more severe limitation of neural networks is that they function correctly only for input that is similar to training input, while they do not perform well for very different input.

Genetic Algorithms

Genetic algorithms come from an analogy with the evolution of organisms in nature[7]. According to the theory of evolution, a process of uninterrupted mutual reciprocal adaptation takes place between organisms and their environment. Following such processes, the genetic patrimony of the organisms continuously changes in order to find the appropriate evolutionary response to environmental changes. The basic mechanism is the selection of those who have adapted most successfully, who end up reproducing better with respect to those who have adapted less successfully, thus transmitting their improved genetic patrimony to successive generations.

Genetic algorithms are based on this type of mechanism. Let us suppose that we have a problem with a large number of possible solutions. Each solution is represented by a vector of information in which each element corresponds to a variable that assumes a more or less elevated number of values. Each of these elements represents, in the evolution metaphor, a *gene*. Suppose that it is possible to do a test for the effectiveness of any solution, for example, through a function that is called fitness function. The working mechanism of the algorithm is very simple and can be broken down into the following steps:

a. Identify a random sample of solutions (vectors)

b. Calculate the fitness for each solution

c. Rank solutions according to decreasing values of fitness

d. Choose a subset of solutions with the highest fitness

e. Mate the best individuals and generate a new "child" population of solutions

f. Evaluate the fitness level of the new population

g. Select a satisfactory solution, if it exists; otherwise repeat the cycle from steps a to f

To avoid a premature convergence and guarantee an adequate exploration of the search space, random mutations are introduced into the genetic patrimony of the solutions in every cycle, altering here and there one or more genes in each individual. This is the same as shuffling the cards and adding diversity to the system, that otherwise would have been excessively influenced by the choice of the initial population.

The use of genetic algorithms, typical of some operative research problems such as the identification of the best path in a graph, can be used to model organizational dynamics for which the evolution metaphor is appropriate. For example, think of any decision problem where a choice needs to be made when there are some restrictions, but the number of alternatives is unlimited. The modeling of a decisional problem through genetic algorithms can be a useful exercise for internal examination with the aim of organizational learning. It brings up many questions that the organizational investigators must face, such as: How can we model the search space? Why should we choose some dimensions (or variables) and not others? What criteria should be used in order to test fitness?

Moreover, the genetic algorithm, because of its intrinsic logical functioning, can generate unexpected, and therefore new, solutions.

Agent-Based Systems

Like neural networks and genetic algorithms, agent-based systems also come from an analogy to the natural world, in this case, with the structure and mechanisms of the functioning of social insects such as bees and ants. A beehive is, in effect, a collective entity that is born, grows, reproduces, and dies. These macrophenomena originate from the multiplicity of interactions between a high number of individuals that often carry out very simple procedures or behaviors and are not aware of their own contribution to the emergence of complex macrophenomena. It can be said that in these systems, the complexity of organizational action emerges from the unpredictable combination of even very simple behaviors and interactions.

The individual (agent) is not comparable to a gear that operates in a larger mechanism. The fundamental difference between a beehive and a machine is in the absence in the first case of any form of centralized control. Every machine is the result of a deduction, and contains within itself clearly codified rules that govern its behavior and each part of the machine contributes unambiguously to its functions.

If we destroy one lever, the whole machine will collapse. This does not happen with any complex system: a beehive continues its existence even if a number of bees die.

Instead, a beehive *emerges* from a multiplicity of interactions between simple but autonomous and heterogenous agents and their interactions. Moreover, these agents are, though in a limited way, capable of learning and adapting locally to changes in the environment. Once the microrules that specify the behavior of individuals and the interaction between them have been defined, the system is left to evolve and the behavior can be observed.

Any agents-based system can be constructed through the following steps:

- A context is defined (virtual space) characterized by certain properties and that represent the space of interaction between the agents (e.g., a road intersection).

- • A certain number of agents are defined (drivers, pedestrians, traffic policemen, etc.) as well as the microrules that guide their behavior (rules of right of way, opportunistic behaviors, etc.).

- • A virtual community is created: agents are left to interact and the eventual emergence of macrophenomena are observed (how does the intersection evolve at rush hour? What happens if a traffic light is installed? etc.).

The objective of a simulation is generally to verify whether certain microbehaviors of the agents are sufficient to explain the emergence of some regularities at the collective level, or whether the implementation of certain policies or the introduction of certain devices produces effects of some kind on the system, keeping in mind its structure of internal interrelations (Epstein & Axtell, 1996). For example, is the opportunistic behavior of drivers sufficient to explain a traffic jam? What happens if the intersection is regulated by a traffic light or a one-way street is changed? What changes if a system of incentives/punishment for behavior is introduced?

There are many applications for *social computation* in various fields: From demographics, to economics, and finally to organizational behavior (see appendix B). Today, there is an entire scientific community that works on the application of modeling based on agents for the simulation of social and organizational dynamics. This community has even built common platforms, which are often open-source, for processing the data, such as the NETLOGO software or the SWARM platform. SWARM is a series of programs written in C++ code or Java that allows for the construction of systems of simulation through the logic of object programming.

Beside the open platform solutions, other software tools have been developed that are less flexible but more user friendly, available for a fee, such as Agent-builder or Agentsheets.

Agent-based systems represent a powerful tool for analyzing complex social systems, whose complexity arises from the interaction of even simple individual behaviors, as organizations are. These are used to explain the emergence of collective behaviors of a limited set of individual behaviors and interactions between quasi-independent agents.

Conclusion: Toward a Social-Computational Approach to the Study of Organizations

The proposals contained in this chapter illustrate some possible research methods in the field of organizational investigations in the era of cognitive work. Organizations are transforming themselves from systems producing manufactured articles and standard services to systems for choosing and creating meaning; individuals are transforming themselves from makers of products and procedures into builders of evaluations and decisions, from managers of routines to problem solvers. Under these conditions, the organizational observer must obtain a methodological instrumentation that takes these transformations into account.

The units of analysis are the decisional and evaluative processes aimed at the evaluation and the choice of a structured collective environment in which the individual action is interaction mediated by artifacts, conditioned by shared values and various organizational restrictions (political, structural, economic, strategic, etc.).

Such a complex unit of analysis requires the adoption and integration of multiple theoretical perpectives and different methodological tools. It is necessary to realize both qualitative research, whose aim is identifying the meaning of consensual representations, and quantitative research, whose aim is measuring, operationalizing, implementing and simulating organizational processes.

In particular, the use of computational methodologies should be oriented not toward optimization, but toward the simulation of scenarios, to what-if analyses, to modeling organizational processes that are prevalently descriptive, but that allow for the production of a knowledge base for the discussion and comparison of alternatives.

References

Ackoff, R.L. (1979). The future of operational research is past. *J Opl Res Soc*, *30*(2), 93-104.

Albino, V., & Garavelli, A.C. (1998). A neural network application for subcontracting rating in construction firms. *International Journal of Project Management*, *11*, 107-122.

Argyris, C., & Schön, D.A. (1978). *Organizational learning. A theory of action perspective*. Reading, MA: Addison-Wesley.

Astley, W.G. (1985). Administrative sciences as socially constructed truth. *Administrative Science Quarterly*, *4*(30), 497-513.

Checkland, P. B. (1985). From optimizing to learning: A development of systems thinking in the 1990s. In R. L. Flood & M. C. Jackson. (1991). *Critical systems thinking: Directed readings*. John Wiley & Sons.

Chen, S.J., & Hwang, C. (1992). *Fuzzy multiple attribute decision making*. Berlin: Springer Verlag.

Greenberger, M., Crenson, M.A., & Crissey, B. (1976). *Models in the policy process: Public decision making in the computer era*. New York: Russell Sage Foundation.

Denzin, N.K., & Lincoln, Y.S. (2005). *Handbok of qualitative research* (3ʳᵈ ed.). Thousands Oaks, CA: Sage.

Eden, C., & Ackermann, F. (2001). Group decision and negotiation in strategy making. *Group Decision and Negotiation, 7*, 119-140.

Epstein, J.M., & Axtell, R. (1996). *Growing artificial societies: Social science from the bottom up.* Cambridge, MA: MIT Press.

Holland, J. (1995). *Hidden order: How adaption builds complexity.* Helix Books.

Huff, A.S. (Ed.). (1990). *Mapping strategic thought.* Chirchester: Wiley

Kelly, G. (1955). *The psychology of personal constructs.* New York: Norton.

Kirschner, P.A., Buckingham-Shum, S., & Carr, C.S. (2003). *Visualizing argumentation: Software tools for collaborative and educational sense-making.* Springer Verlag.

Klir, G.J., & Folger, T. (1985). *Fuzzy set, uncertainty and information.* Englewood Cliffs: Prentice Hall.

Kolodner, J. (1993). *Case-based reasoning.* San Mateo, CA: Morgan Kaufman.

Kosko, B. (1992). *Neural networks and fuzzy systems.* Englewood Cliffs, NJ: Prentice Hall.

March, J.G., & Simon, H.A. (1958). *Organizations.* New York: John Wiley & Sons.

Morgan, G. (1997). *Images of organizations* (2ⁿᵈ ed.). Thousands Oaks, CA: Sage.

Nonaka, I., & Takeuchi, H. (1995). *The knowledge creating company.* Oxford: Oxford University Press.

Newell, A., & Simon, H. (1972). *Human problem solving.* Englewood Cliffs, NJ: Prentice-Hall.

Rittel, H.W.J., & Webber, M.M. (1973). Dilemmas in a general theory of planning. *Policy Sciences, 4*, 155-169.

Rosenhead, J., & Mingers, J. (2001). *Rational analysis for a probelmatic world revisited: Problem structuring method for uncertainty and conflict.* Chichester: John Wiley & Sons.

Schreiber, G., Akkermans, H., Anjewierden, A., De Hoog, R., Shadbolt, N., Van de Velde, W., & Wielinga, B. (2000). *Knowledge engineering AND management. The commonKADS methodology.* Cambridge, MA: MIT Press.

Schein, E. (2002). The anxiety of learning. An interview with Edgar Schein by D. Coutu. Harvard Business Review.

Weaver, W. (1948). Science and complexity. *American Scientist, 36*, 536-544.

Zadeh, L. (1973). Outline of a new approach to the analysis of complex systems and decision processes. *IEEE Transactions on Systems, Man and Cybernetics, 3*(1).

Zadeh, L. (1996). Fuzzy logic = Computing with words. *IEEE Transactions on Fuzzy Systems, 4*(2), 103-111.

Zadeh, L. (2001, September 18-20). Perception-based decision analysis. *Proceedings of the VIII SIGEF Congress,*, Naples, Italy.

Endnotes

[1]   This is where the metaphor of organizations as systems for information processing comes from (March & Simon, 1958; Morgan, 1997), that can be interpreted as the natural evolution of the paradigm of Taylor's organization machine, with the difference being that the decisional and cognitive functions prevail over the executive and manual; but the structure remains the same.

[2]   This conclusion is justifiable with regard to the preceding studies and in particular to the experience conducted by Greenberger et al. (1976) with reference to the consultancy offered by the RAND corporation to the city of New York in terms of urban planning and management. When the consultants of RAND applied their methodologies of cause effect optimization modeling to organizational processes, the results were discordant in the various organizational realities in which these methods were applied. The traditional methods worked well in those organizations such as the fire brigade, characterized by well-defined tasks, almost military hierarchies and low levels of sophistication of duties, but failed in more destructured realities, such as the public health department.

[3]   Rosenhead and Mingers (2001) draw the following classifications from the literature:

a.   **Messes vs. problems (Ackoff, 1979):** The problems are analytical abstractions of complex questions in which a plurality of factors intervene (*messes*). The operation of analytical reduction transforms messes into resolvable problems whose solutions are, however, an abstraction that has not corresponding effective implementations in the real world.

b.   **Tame vs. wicked (Rittel & Weber, 1973):** A problem is *tame* if it admits a consensual representation on the part of groups who are interested to resolve it. A wicked problem admits instead different levels of explanation and the nature of the solution depends on the level selected.

c.   **Soft vs. hard systems (Checkland, 1985):** Others have underlined the problem of the analytical irreducibility of complexity. Simon affirms that the rationality of organizational actors is limited and that in general, the activity of solving problems by humans is limited by physiological, spatial, and temporal restrictions (1961, 1981). Zadeh (1973) states with his prinicple of incompatibility that there is a trade-off between precision and meaning in the representation of a complex problem. Klir and Folger (1985) demonstrate an ample case history of computationally intractible problems, that is, problems that are impossible to resolve in any case, even with the availability of very powerful computers and lots of time. Weaver (1948) classifies problems in three categories: (1) problems of organized simplicity (machines), those that can be analytically modelled, (2) problems of disorganized complexity (aggregates), statistically treatable problems such as in the kinetic theory of gases, (3) problems of organized complexity (systems), for which there are no standard modeling techniques.

4   Many authors prefer to connote the mapping phase with *problem setting* and that of information processing with *problem solving*. At any rate, to us it seems purely academic and excessively reductive as well as misleading to consider the representation of the problem or its construction as something separated from its resolution, since usually the two steps are strictly intertwined.

5   In Zadeh's definition of soft computing, agent-based modeling is not included. In a wider sense, however, the connotation of "soft" indicates the capacity of such techniques to tolerate uncertain information, both in the data, and in the description of the characteristics of the model. In this sense even systems based on agents can be included in this category in that they only weakly specify the behavior of the system that instead emerges even from the simplest interaction between agents.

6   Genetic algorithms were first proposed by Holland (1995) and his research group on complex systems at the Santa Fe Institute.

Appendix A

The Construction of Verbal Models:
Modelling Customer Satisfaction

Abstract

This appendix will present a concrete and detailed example of the construction of verbal models through the application of the methodology presented in Chapter X. In particular, we illustrate a case study from our own research carried out in a large Italian automotive company and related to the analysis of the voice of customer (VOC) in the development of new products. In current approaches to new product development, the VOC analysis is a fundamental step in the early design phases and the main critical aspects concern the translation of customers' wishes and requests into functional and technical specifications for concept development. Traditional models for VOC analysis usually neglect the importance of collecting qualitative information provided by customers and do not consider the way such information is processed by customers. Our hypothesis is that customers satisfaction has to be analyzed with a cognitive approach, according to the steps of the methodological approach presented in Chapter X: Eliciting/mapping individual customer's explanation linking the satisfaction level to product's characteristics and constructing verbal models in order to identify product's attributes that are more influential on customer's satisfaction.

Critical Issues in Voice of Customer Analysis[1]

Nowadays, a firm's approach to product design is based on the simultaneous involvement of teams composed of controllers, designers, marketing, and logistic experts from the first development phases of a new product or a service. This approach allows new products or services to be presented in time, costs to be minimized, and profit to be maximized throughout all the product's life cycle. In particular, in one of the early phases of new product design, the *performance requirements analysis*, marketing experts collect and analyze the voice of customers (VOC) in order to elicitate customers' needs and wishes and to define the relative importance of the product's characteristics. Then customers' preferences have to be analyzed in order to identify functional specifications for the design of the new product.

Usually customer's preferences are expressed through the natural language. In traditional approaches customers are asked to evaluate attributes and characteristics of the product on the basis of given evaluation criteria, and to express their judgements through numeric scales. Customers' preferences are then elaborated through statistical analysis and compared with the same values of competitors' products.

The current approach faces numerous problems due to oversimplification of customer reasoning and incapability to deal with qualitative verbal information. Four critical points are present in the first step of the process:

a.   **The item's meaning:** The traditional approach does not take into account that: (1) each customer attributes a subjective meaning to a given evaluation item; (2) the evaluation criteria do not have the same importance; (3) different customers use different parameters and criteria in the evaluation process.

b.   **The item's ratings:** Customers are not able to express precise evaluations because there is no threshold in the transition between verbal evaluations expressed on a given verbal scale; moreover, it has been proven that different individuals attribute different meaning to the same rating value.

c.   **The representation of the evaluation process:** Scarce attention is paid to the cognitive structure of customer evaluation processes. It's usually supposed that the customer's satisfaction has a rational and addictive structure in which interactions and trade-offs are neglected.

Thus, the outputs of the first step, obtained according the traditional methodologies often are very unreliable and not sufficient to describe the shades of meaning of customers evaluations. The lack of reliability of the importance of product's characteristics, which is the result of the first step, seriously affects the whole process of new product's development.

In order to overcome the critical issues of the current approach, we have applied the methodology presented in Chapter X to collect and analyze the VOC based on fuzzy verbal models.

The Representation of Customer Evaluation Process

The Representation of Customer Judgements

The first step (elicitation) consists of a structured interview, which allows the customer to formulate their judgements in a natural language. The interviewee is asked to specify his/her wishes and to *explain* the reasons of his/her choice by an explanatory discourse until a requested detail level is obtained. Through explanations, customers make explicit the link between the product attributes and components to their satisfaction degree. As showed in Chapter XI, there are several mapping techniques to represent explanation. In this appendix we show how an explanation can be adequately represented by an explanatory tree.

As shown in Figure 1, the final evaluation concerning an attribute C of the event X (i.e., Comfort(car)) is separated into a set of more detailed evaluations "C1(X) is V1" and "C2(X) is V2" aimed at explaining it. The explanatory discourse develops to a further detail level, in which the evaluation "C1(X) is V1" is explained by "C11(X) is V11" and "C12(X) is V12."

According to Zadeh's nomenclature for the "branching questionnaires" (Zadeh, 1976), by *fan* of the tree we mean a node of a tree with the branches connected to it. Each fan has a root (*the explanandum*) and one or more branches (*the explanans*), which constitute admissible explanations of the evaluative claim associated to the root. Both explanans and explanandum are called *facts*.

To each branch a quantity e_i^j called *explanation force* is associated. The symbol e_i^j indicates that the fact i-th is an admissible explanation for the root j-th. As we will show later, the term e_i^j can be derived from the analysis of the explanation. The explanation forces represent the importance that customers give to the attributes of the product.

For a given fan with $n \geq 1$ branches, the whole explanation force of the explanans will be equal to 1:

Figure 1. An example of an explanatory tree

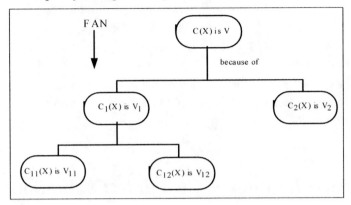

$$\sum_{i=1}^{n} e_i^j = 1 \qquad \text{with} \qquad 0 < e_i^j \le 1$$

The structure of a fan FAN_j is described by the following relation:

$$FAN_j = \sum_{i=1}^{n} e_i^j F_i,$$

where n is the number of explanans, $F_i := \text{"}C_i(X)$ is $V_i\text{"}$ is the fact associated to the i-th explanans and the summation indicates the combination of explanans. Each tree is formed by one or more fans. For example, the tree of Figure 2 is described as follows:

$$TREE_1 = FAN_1(FAN_3)$$

or, in a more explicit way, as:

$$TREE_1 = F_1\left(e_2^1 F_2 + e_3^1 F_3\left(e_4^3 F_4 + e_5^3 F_5\right)\right).$$

Given a *fact* in the form "X is V," the term X is a linguistic variable while V is an element of a term set $T(X)$; each term in $T(X)$ is a label of a fuzzy subset of a universe of discourse U. The term set is generated by the Cartesian product between a set of linguistic modifiers $MOD(X) = \{very, quite, \ldots\}$ and a couple of antonyms $ANT(X) = \{n, p\}$. For example if $ANT(X) = \{LOW, HIGH\}$ and $MOD(X) = \{very, quite, almost, u\text{-}\}$, where u- is the unit term, we get a term set $T(X)$ of eight terms:

Figure 2. The tree TREE1

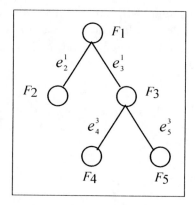

$T(X)=\{very\ low,\ quite\ low,\ almost\ low,\ low,\ quite\ high,\ almost\ high,\ high,\ very\ high\}$

Given a term set T of cardinality j, we represent each term V_i of T by means of fuzzy sets with triangular membership function μ_{V_i}:

$$\mu_{V_i}(u) = \begin{cases} (j+1)u - (i-1) & if \quad \dfrac{i-1}{j+1} \le u \le \dfrac{i}{j+1} \\ -(j+1)u + (i+1) & if \quad \dfrac{i}{j+1} \le u \le \dfrac{i+1}{j+1} \\ 0 & otherwise \end{cases} \qquad (1)$$

$i = 1,...j;$ \qquad\qquad with $u \in U = [0,1]$.

For example, given the term set $T_5 = \{very\ low,\ low,\ average,\ high,\ very\ high\}$ the term *average* (j = 5, i = 3) is represented by the following function:

$$\mu_{V_i}(u) = \begin{cases} 6u - 2 & if \quad \dfrac{2}{6} \le u \le \dfrac{3}{6} \\ -6u + 4 & if \quad \dfrac{3}{6} \le u \le \dfrac{4}{6} \\ 0 & otherwise \end{cases} \qquad (2)$$

To represent the meaning of a *fact* we use a couple of values, according to the dual truth model presented in Chapter XIII. According to the dual truth model, given the truth functions of a couple of antonyms *LOW* and *HIGH*, represented on *U* as and with $u\ U = [0,1]$, we obtain for a generic term $V(X)$ a couple of logical values through the following formulas:

$$(a,b) = (\sup\{\min(\mu_{LOW}(u),\mu_V(u))\}, \sup\{\min(\mu_{HIGH}(u),\mu_V(u))\})\ u \in U \quad (3)$$

$$(a,b) = \left(\frac{j+2-i}{j+2}, \frac{i+1}{j+2} \right) \quad (4)$$

where j is the cardinality of T and i is the position of the term V_i in T.

We can calculate the couples of truth values for terms belonging to term sets of different cardinality. Table 1 shows these couples for terms belonging to the term sets T_3, T_5 and T_7. It is possible to note that different truth couples are associated to the same linguistic term V and that the values of depend on which term set V belongs to. For example, the values of the term *very low* change from (0.86, 0.29) to (0.89, 0.22). It is easy to verify that, as the evaluator expresses their judgement *very low* by using a more precise term (i.e., belonging to a higher cardinality term set), the dissatisfaction degree increases while the satisfaction degree decreases[2].

The Interpretation of the Fan

This part of the model refers to the calculation of the explanation forces. In this section we are going to show how this result can be accomplished through an analysis of the explanation tree by means of the fuzzy implication connective.

Table 1. Couples of values related to verbal judgements of three different term sets

Term set cardinality			
	3	5	7
VL (very low)		(0.86, 0,29)	(0.89, 0.22)
L (low)	(0.8, 0.4)	(0.71, 0.43)	(0.78, 0.33)
MLL (more less low)			(0,67, 0.44)
A (average)	(0.6, 0.6)	(0.57, 0.57)	(0.56, 0.56)
MLH (more less high)			(0.44, 0.67)
H (high)	(0.4, 0.8)	(0.43, 0.71)	(0.33, 0.78)
VH (very high)		(0.29, 0.86)	(0.22, 0.89)

Usually the explanatory discourse develops according to propositions like this: "$C(X)$ is V *because of* $C1(X)$ is $V1$, …, $Cn(X)$ is Vn." The component of this proposition are the explanandum, a set of explanans and a relationship between explanans and explanandum. What is the logical relationship marked by the term "because" and how can we adequately represent it?

The sentence "$F1$ because $F2$," expressed by an evaluator E_i, given the hypothesis that $F2$ is a necessary and sufficient explanation of $F1$ for E_i, could be put in the form "$F2$ explains $F1$" which, in turn, could be transformed in the conditional statement "If $F2$, then $F1$."

It's well known that a conditional proposition can be represented by a fuzzy ply operator:

$$\Im(p,\ q): [0,1] \times [0,1] \text{->} [0,1]$$

such that, given two propositions *ant* and *cons*, whose truth values are, respectively, p and q, yields the truth value of the conditional proposition *If ant, then cons*. Thus, to calculate the truth of the proposition "If $F2$, then $F1$," we need a suitable ply operator.

Relevant studies (Baldwin & Pilsworth, 1980; Fukami et al., 1980; Mizumoto & Zimmermann, 1982) have shown that an ideal operator doesn't exist. Several authors have proposed axiomatic structures in order to determine one or more ply operators that should satisfy some intuitive criteria. On the basis of the axioms proposed we can reject those operators that fail in the satisfaction of such criteria, but the final choice will depend on the specific context of application. Thus, to choose a specific operator, we must specify what kind of behavior we expect from our model and, particularly, what exactly we mean by the concept of *explanation force*.

The choice of the ply operator can be done between those satisfying a set of axioms corresponding to some rational and intuitive criteria. A complete review of the several axiomatic approaches can be found in Klir and Yuan (1995)[3].

Between the ply operators presented by Klir and Yuan several ones satisfy the axioms. For our purpose, we choose the simplest of them, i.e., the Goguen operator $\Im(p,\ q)$:

$$\begin{cases} 1 & \text{if } p \leq q \\ \dfrac{q}{p} & \text{if } p > q \end{cases}$$

The Sensitivity Parameter

A default explanation develops according to sentences like, for example, "John's performance is <u>high</u> because his skills are <u>high</u>," which can be transformed in "If John's skills are <u>high</u>, then John's performance is <u>high</u>."

The default explanation represents a trivial explanation discourse like the following: B is V, because A_1 is V, ..., A_n is V. In a general sense, we could say that the default explanation is equivalent to the absence of an explanation since it represents an obvious interpretation of the reality.

Let's associate to each branch of a given fan a sensitivity parameter si, which represents customer's sensitivity towards the explanans i-th. In the default explanation we suppose that customer's sensitivity is the same for all the explanation factors, so s_i is the same for each i. In order to calculate the sensitivity parameter s, a comparison of the truth values of explanans and explanandum belonging to a given fan is performed through Goguen fuzzy ply operator.

For a given fan with n branches, the explanation forces are calculated by normalizing the values of the sensitivity parameters s_i associated to each branch according to the following relation:

$$e_i^j = \frac{s_i}{\sum_{j=1}^{n} s_j} \quad \forall i = 1, \ldots, n \tag{5}$$

Consequently, for the default fan we obtain:

$$e_i = 1/n \quad A i = 1, \ldots, n$$

i.e., the relative importance which the evaluator attributes to each explanans is the same.

Any relevant explanation expresses the necessity to move from the default explanation in order to give different weights to relevant facts experienced by the explainer. For example one could say: "*John's performance is average, because his professional skills are high and his ability in problem solving is average.*" In such a situation the speaker focuses his attention on John's ability in problem solving in order to obtain a greater increase of his global performance: John should improve his ability in problem solving rather than his professional capabilities.

In a real explanation, we assume that the sensitivity parameter s is expressed in the following way:

$$s_i = 1 + d_i \tag{6}$$

where, as we show in the following, '1' is the default value and d_i represents the *incremental sensitivity* induced by the real explanation. Consequently our aim is to calculate d_i.

Let's consider the fan:

$$FAN_j = F_j(e_i^j F_i + e_k^j F_k)$$

We suppose that the fan FAN_j should be decomposed in the two propositions:

If F_i, then F_j
If F_k, then F_j

whose truth values are:

$$\Im(t(F_i), t(F_j)) \text{ and } \Im(t(F_k), t(F_j)) \tag{7}$$

According to the dual truth model above illustrated, each fact is represented by a couple of truth values. Thus, we can interpret the (7) as follows:

$$\Im(t(F_i), t(F_j)) = \Im[(a_i, b_i), (a_j, b_j)] = [\Im(a_i, a_j), \Im(b_i, b_j)] = [LV_{ij}, RV_{ij}]$$

$$\Im(t(F_k), t(F_j)) = \Im[(a_k, b_k), (a_j, b_j)] = [\Im(a_k, a_j), \Im(b_k, b_j)] = [LV_{kj}, RV_{kj}]$$

and setting:

$$d_{ij} = RV_{ij} - LV_{ij} \text{ and } d_{kj} = RV_{kj} - LV_{kj}$$

we can obtain the following values by the (6):

$$s_{ij} = 1 + d_{ij} = 1 + RV_{ij} - LV_{ij}$$
$$s_{kj} = 1 + d_{kj} = 1 + RV_{kj} - LV_{kj}$$

Finally we obtain the *explanation forces* of facts F_i and F_k by the (5). It is easy to verify that if the evaluations contained in the explanans and in the explanandum are equal we obtain $s = 1$ because in this case $RV = LV$. The sensitivity parameter will be equal to zero if $t(explanans) = (0,1)$ and $t(explanandum) = (1,0)$ because, in this case, $LV = 1$ and $RV = 0$. In this situation, in which the evaluator is absolutely unsatisfied by the explanandum and absolutely satisfied by the explanans, the explanans does not contribute to the explanation.

An Example

Let us suppose that we need to interview a customer about a car cabin and that he expresses his evaluation in the following way: *"The cabin is average because the Robustness is high, the Spaciousness is high and the Comfort is low."*

The evaluations *low, average and high* belong to a five element term set. We can represent this composite evaluation through the explanation tree depicted in Figure 2, in which verbal evaluations are represented by means of the dual truth model.

Through the procedure shown in the previous section, by using the Goguen fuzzy ply operator we can obtain for each branch the results illustrated in Table 2. The comfort is the attribute which scores the highest importance because it is relatively unsatisfied compared to the remaining explanation factors.

It's possible to verify that by calculating the explanation forces (i.e., the importance of the explanans) according to the proposed model we associate the greatest importance to the explanation factor that the explainer feels relatively unsatisfied, i.e., whose evaluation is the most negative of the whole set of explanans belonging to the same fan.

Figure 3. An example of explanation

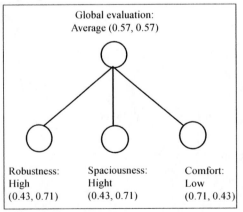

Table 2. Calculation of explanation forces e_i

EXPLANANS	EXPLANANDUM: Car's cabin is Average (0.57, 0.57)		
	Robustness [High: (0.43, 0.71)]	Spaciousness [High: (0.43, 0.71)]	Comfort [Low: (0.71, 0.43)]
(RV)	0,8	0,8	1
(LV)	1	1	0.8
Incremental sensitivity d	-0,2	-0,2	0,2
Sensitivity s	0,8	0,8	1,2
Importance	0,28	0,28	0,44

For example, let us consider an explanation like the following: "*X is average because $C_1(X)$ is low and $C_2(X)$ is high*," where *average, low* and *high* belong to a five elements term set T and $F_1=C_1(X)$ *is low* and $F_2=C_2(X)$ *is high* are the explanans of the global evaluation F=*X is average.*

The calculation of s_1 and of s_2 shows that a greater importance is associated to the explanans F_1 than to F_2. We can interpret this fact by saying that s_1 is greater then s_2 because the attribute C_1 is felt relatively unsatisfied in comparison with $C_2(X)$.

The Aggregation of the Individual Preferences

The last part of the model deals with the issue of determining the evaluation of the product by a group of customers. Though we did not discuss this aspect in depth in Chapter X, it is important to underline its importance in all cases in which an aggregate/collective evaluation is needed.

The aim is the definition of a group tree which we call the *customer tree.* In order to accomplish this result, we need to introduce some basic operations which will allow us to determine the structure of the group tree.

Operations on Explanation Trees

Two basic operations are defined for the explanation tree: composition and reduction.

a. **Composition:** Given n trees $TREE_1$, $TREE_2$, ..., $TREE_n$ with m levels of explanation the composition operation allows to create a composed tree TREE with $m+1$ levels defined in the following way:

$$TREE = e_1 TREE_1 + ... + e_n TREE_n$$

For example, consider the two trees:

$$TREE_A = F_1\left(e_2^1 F_2 + e_3^1 F_3\right) \text{ and } TREE_B = F_4\left(e_5^4 F_5 + e_6^4 F_6\right),$$

where $F_i = X_i$ is V_i, and X_i is an attribute of the evaluated object while V_i is a verbal judgement. Through the composition we obtain the tree:

$$TREE_C = F_7\left(e_1^7 TREE_A + e_4^7 TREE_B\right) =$$
$$= F_7\left(e_1^7 F_1\left(e_2^1 F_2 + e_3^1 F_3\right) + e_4^7 F_4\left(e_5^4 F_5 + e_6^4 F_6\right)\right)$$

b. **Reduction:** The reduction allows us to eliminate a level in a given tree. For example given the tree:

$$TREE = F_1\left(e_2^1 F_2\left(e_4^2 F_4' + e_5^2 F_5\right) + e_3^1 F_3\left(e_6^3 F_6 + e_7^3 F_7 + e_4^3 F_4''\right)\right)$$

we could eliminate the level of the explanation formed by the facts F_2 and F_3. Once F_2 and F_3 have been eliminated, the fact F_1 is explained directly by means of the facts F_4', F_4'', F_5 and F_6. In this example, the facts $F_4' = X_4$ is V_4' and $F_4'' = X_4$ is V_4'' are referred to a same explanation factor X_4 with eventually different evaluations V_4' and V_4''. By eliminating the facts F_2 and F_3 we obtain:

$$TREE = F_1\left(e_2^1 e_4^2 F_4' + e_2^1 e_5^2 F_5 + e_3^1 e_6^3 F_6 + e_3^1 e_7^3 F_7 + e_3^1 e_4^3 F_4''\right)$$

By assuming $e_i^k e_j^i = e_j^k$ we have:

$$TREE = F_1\left(e_4^1\left(F_4' + F_4''\right) + e_5^1 F_5 + e_6^1 F_6 + e_7^1 F_7\right)$$
$$= F_1\left(e_4^1 F_4 + e_5^1 F_5 + e_6^1 F_6 + e_7^1 F_7\right)$$

The fact $F_4 = F'_4 + F''_4 := (X_4 \text{ is } V'_4) + (X_4 \text{ is } V''_4) = X_4 \text{ is } V_4$ contains the aggregated evaluation:

$$V_4 = f(V'_4, V''_4).$$

where f is an aggregation operator. The symbol '+' indicates that the aggregated fact F_4 is obtained on the base of the individual facts F'_4 and F''_4. The values of the new explanation forces and are unknown in this phase. The calculation of the explanation forces can be performed according to the procedure shown in the following, once the evaluations V_1, V_4, V_5, V_6, and V_7 have been determined.

The Construction of the Customer Tree

The construction of the *customer tree* is carried out by merging more individual trees. This operation is made up by successive compositions and reductions: The composition allows us to create the group explanation levels while, through the reduction, the individual levels are eliminated. The reduction entails the aggregation of the individual evaluations by means of a suitable aggregation operator. The procedure, illustrated in the following example, starts from the top of the trees and is performed for each level.

Let us consider two trees formed by three levels of explanation and representing the explanation of two evaluators A and B:

$$TREE_A = F'_1\left(e^1_2 F'_2\left(e^2_5 F'_5 + e^2_6 F'_6\right) + e^1_3 F'_3\left(e^3_8 F'_8 + e^3_9 F'_9 + e^3_{10} F'_{10}\right)\right)$$
$$TREE_B = F''_1\left(e^1_2 F''_2\left(e^2_5 F''_5 + e^2_7 F''_7\right) + e^1_4 F''_4\left(e^4_8 F''_8 + e^4_9 F''_9\right)\right)$$

In the above relation the facts F'_i and F''_i contain the evaluations of a same item X_i expressed respectively by A and B. The aggregated tree can be obtained through the following steps:

*   **Step 1.** Build a new tree TREE by composing the two trees $TREE_A$ and $TREE_B$:

$$TREE = F_1\left(e^1_2 F_1\left(e^2_2 F'_2(...) + e^2_3 F'_3(...)\right) + e^1_3 F''_1\left(e^2_2 F''_2(...) + e^3_4 F''_4(...)\right)\right)$$

The composed tree TREE is formed by four levels since a further level representing the group global evaluation contained in F_1 is added to the three existing levels. The changes in the index of the explanation forces are due to the introduction of a new knot in the tree (F_1).

- **Step 2.** Reduce the composed tree TREE by eliminating the individual level formed by the facts F'_1 and F''_1:

$$TREE = F_1\left(e_2^1 e_2^2 F_2'(\ldots) + e_2^1 e_3^2 F_3'(\ldots) + e_3^1 e_2^3 F_2''(\ldots) + e_3^1 e_4^3 F_4''(\ldots)\right) =$$
$$= F_1\left(e_2^1 F_2'(\ldots) + e_2^1 F_2''(\ldots) + e_3^1 F_3'(\ldots) + e_4^1 F_4''(\ldots)\right)$$

After the reduction, the level of the individual global evaluation F'_1 and F''_1: Is eliminated and substituted by the level corresponding to the group global evaluation $F_1 = X_1$ is V_1 where $V_1 = f(V'_1, V''_1)$ and f is a suitable aggregation operator f.

- **Step 3.** The sub-tree F_2 representing the group evaluation X_2 is V_2 is formed through the composition of the sub-trees F'_2 and F''_2.

These steps are repeated for the sub-trees F'_3, F''_4 on the second level and then on F'_5, F''_5, F'_6, F''_7, F'_8, F''_8, F'_9, F''_9, F'_{10} on the third level.

The final result is the tree TREE:

$$TREE = F_1\left(e_2^1 F_2\left(e_5^2 F_5 + e_6^2 F_6 + e_7^2 F_7\right) + e_3^1 F_3\left(e_8^3 F_8 + e_9^3 F_9 + e_{10}^3 F_{10}\right) + e_4^1 F_4\left(e_8^4 F_4 + e_9^4 F_9\right)\right)$$

Calculation of the Group Explanation Forces

In order to complete the definition of the *customer tree*, the group explanation forces must be calculated.

The experimental results (see next section) showed that usually most of the explanation factors are shared. Even so, some explanans are expressed only by a sub-group of individuals. The number of persons who chose a given explanans is kept into account in the calculation of the group explanation force which will depend on the portion of customers who used the given explanans during the interview.

Once the *customer tree* has been determined both in structure and in group evaluations, it is possible to assign to each branch i a sensitivity parameter s_i, by means of the procedure above illustrated.

Now we define a *group sensitivity parameter s'$_i$* in the following way:

$$s'_i = s_i \eta_i$$

where represents the part of customers who used the explanans i-th. The explanation force associated to each branch of a given fan can be calculated by normalizing the s'_i associated to the branches of the fan through the following formula:

$$e_i = \frac{s'_i}{\sum\limits_{j=1}^{n} s'_j}$$

The Aggregation of Individual Evaluations

To carry out the merging of the individual trees in order to determine the *customer tree*, we need to calculate the group evaluations associated to every single explanation factor. The problem can be formulated in the following way: given n evaluations $V_1, \ldots, V_n$ of a same entity X, find an operator:

F: $V_1, \ldots, V_n$ -> V

such that V is the group evaluation of X. To achieve this result, we use the OWA operator already introduced at the end of Chapter XII and XIII (Yager, 1988, 1993)[4]. An OWA operator of dimension n is a mapping:

$$F : R^n \rightarrow R$$

that has an associated vector $W = [w_1, w_2, \ldots, w_n]^T$ such that:

1) $w_i \in [0,1]$, 2) $\sum_i w_i = 1$

and:

$$F(a_1, a_2, \ldots, a_n) = \sum_i w_i b_i$$

where $(a_1, a_2, \ldots, a_n) \in R^n$ and b_i is the i-th largest of the a_p, hence an ordering of the a_i is requested to perform the calculation of $F(a_1, \ldots, a_n)$. Yager (1991) shows that the OWA operators have the basic properties associated with an *averaging operator*. The pure average is the OWA operator whose weighting vector is $W = [1 / n, \ldots, 1 / n]$.

It is possible to demonstrate that for any OWA operator F we have:

$$\min(a) \leq F(a_1, a_2, \ldots, a_n) \leq Max(a_i)$$

i.e., the OWA operators provides a gradual transition from the *'and'* and the *'or'* fuzzy logical connectives. Given an operator F with a weighting vector W it is possible to define the following *orness* measure:

$$\text{orness}(W) = \frac{1}{n-1} \sum_i ((n - i) w_i)$$

F is called an *or-like* (*and-like*) operator if orness(W) > 0.5 (< 0.5).

In our case we suppose that the value $a \in [0,1]$ represents the truth value of the proposition "*The evaluator E_i is satisfied.*" In this hypothesis, the *or* aggregation (max) yields the greatest available individual satisfaction level (i.e., the group is satisfied if *at least* one evaluator is satisfied), while the *'and'* aggregation yields the lowest satisfaction level (i.e., the group is satisfied if *all* its members are satisfied). For this reason Yager defines the orness measure as an optimism indicator in the aggregation: Any other operator would provide a certain degree of optimism ranging from absolute pessimism (orness(W)=0) to absolute optimism (orness(W)=1).

Yager shows that the calculation of the weighting vector W can be performed by means of fuzzy quantifiers: Given a monotonically nondecreasing fuzzy quantifier Q(r) with r , the weights can be obtained through the following formula:

$$w_i = Q\left(\frac{i}{n}\right) - Q\left(\frac{i-1}{n}\right) \tag{9}$$

where n is the number of the evaluators.

Yager also demonstrates that the w_i can be interpreted as the group incremental satisfaction obtained if the evaluator i is satisfied, provided that i-1 evaluators are satisfied.

If the weights are calculated by means of a given fuzzy quantifier Q, it is possible to verify that the value can also be interpreted as the truth value of the proposition *Q evaluators are satisfied.*

It's worth to note that by choosing a quantifier Q we also establish an aggregation criterion. For example, let's consider the quantifier *most* depicted in Chapter XII, Figure 3: The aggregation criterion corresponding to this quantifier is "*most evaluators* should be satisfied." In the same way we could establish other criteria by using different quantifiers, such as *all, a lot of, at least half of evaluators* and so on.

By using the (9) with n=10 we have the following weight vectors for the quantifiers *most* and *at least 80%*:

$$W_{most} = [0 \ \ 0 \ \ 0 \ \ 0.2 \ \ 0.2 \ \ 0.2 \ \ 0.2 \ \ 0.2 \ \ 0 \ \ 0]^T$$
$$W_{at\ least\ 80\%} = [0 \ \ 0 \ \ 0 \ \ 0 \ \ 0 \ \ 0 \ \ 0 \ \ 1 \ \ 0 \ \ 0]^T$$

In contrast with a pure averaging operation, the use of the OWA operators allows us to prevent from undesired compensation between positive and negative evaluation which eventually could shifts the group evaluation toward the value "average." For example, if we consider the quantifier *most* we can observe that such a quantifier carries out an aggregation which does not keep into account the highest and the lowest available satisfaction level. The use of this quantifier entails an aggregation criteria according to which the group satisfaction we obtain is equal to zero if less than 30% of evaluators are satisfied and the group incremental satisfaction gained by satisfying more than 80% of evaluators is zero as well. Consequently, given a group of 100 evaluators, because of the ordering, the group evaluation will depend on the judgements belonging to the interval ranging from the 30th to the 80th best evaluation.

In our model a verbal evaluation V_i, expressed by an evaluator E_i is represented by a couple of truth values V_i =. According to this representation, the aggregation procedure develops for both values and yields the aggregated couple V:

$$F': [(V_1,\ldots,V_n)] \rightarrow (V)$$

where $V=(a,b)$' a and b are respectively the value of the group dissatisfaction and satisfaction degree and F' is an OWA operator.

Given two verbal evaluations $V=(a_1,a_1)$ and $V=(a_2,b_2)$, the ordering is defined in the following way:

$$V_1 > V_2 \Leftrightarrow \begin{cases} a_1 < a_2 \\ b_1 > b_2 \end{cases}$$

The calculation of the aggregated evaluation is performed as follows:

$$F(\underline{V}) = F(V_1,...,V_n) = \underline{V}' * W = \left[(a_1',b_1'),...,(a_n',b_n') \right] * W =$$
$$= [(a_1',...,a_n') * W, (b_1',...,b_n') * W] = (a,b) \tag{10}$$

where $\underline{V}$ is a vector of n verbal evaluations, $\underline{V}'$ is the ordered vector, W is the weigthing vector associated to F, $(a'_1,...,a'_n)$ and $(b'_1,...,b'_n)$ are the ordered left values and rigth values vectors and (a,b) is the aggregated truth couple. The final result will depend on the chosen fuzzy quantifier. For example we can aggregate so that *most, at least half, almost all* customers will be satisfied. In this way we have a high degree of flexibility in the aggregation (for example we could fix a given grade of *orness* or *optimism* in the aggregation).

The flexibility in the aggregation prevents that the group evaluation tends to shift toward the evaluation *average*, because of undesired compensations between positive and negative evaluations and allows us to aggregate the individual opinions according to several criteria.

For an example of calculation through OWA see the end of Chapter XII.

The Field Results

In this section we are going to show the results we obtained by interviewing a sample of customers of a large automotive company. Customers were asked to judge several characteristics of a given model of car.

The interviews were constructed according to the approach illustrated in Chapter X. People were asked to express a global judgement about the car's cabin and then to explain their evaluation through a set of explanans. To help the customers we provided them with a list of proposed explanans, taken from traditional questionnaires based on large marketing analysis. Nevertheless, the customers were free to accept the list, to exclude one or more items in the list and to insert new explanans according to their point of view.

At the first level customers had to explain their global satisfaction by means of a list of functions (such as *spaciousness, robustness, comfort* and so on). At the second level they were asked to explain their evaluations about the functions by referring to the several macrocomponents, such as the steering wheel, the seats, the door panel etc.

At both levels customers could express their evaluations through a verbal scale: They were left free to use one of the scales constituted by three, five or seven elements

Figure 4. Part of an explanation tree

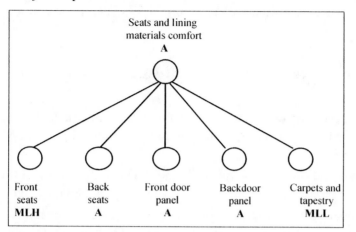

showed in Table 1, according to the grade of precision or vagueness they wanted to associate to their judgements.

Once data had been collected, the analysis of the VOC was performed as showed in the flow diagram in Chapter X Figure 1. From individual interviews we derived explanation trees characterized by three levels: The global satisfaction, the evaluations of product's functions and the evaluations of product's components which realize functions.

The Interview Analysis

A first examination of the interviews showed that customers shared substantially proposed explanans, both in functions and components. Only few customers excluded some items or added new ones. The majority of the customers preferred to express their judgements by means of the seven terms evaluation scale.

The experiment showed that customers seemed to appreciate this way to express their opinions and that they understood easily the mechanism of the explanation. We collected 50 interviews and every interview took about 20 minutes. The first result of this analysis was that most people used the same categories to explain their judgement. From a pragmatic approach this means that a classical marketing analysis is sufficient to detect the explanation categories.

Once the interview has been represented by means of an explanation tree, it's possible to understand what functions are really important for customers, what kind of relationships there are between functions and components, and the importance of a single component. A part of an explanation tree, drawn from a real interview, is depicted in Figure 4 where MLL = more or less low, A = average, MLH = more or less high.

Individual Tree and Evaluation Aggregation

Through the merging operation above defined, it is possible to determine the *customer tree*, whose structure is richer and more complex than individual trees, but it's quite similar.

OWA operators allows us to aggregate the individual preferences in several ways, depending on the particular fuzzy quantifier (i.e., aggregation criterion) we choose.

The first level of explanation is formed by the product's functions contained in Table 3 together with the group global evaluation. The aggregated evaluations of the functions contained in each column were obtained by using four different criteria: The pure *average* (uniform quantifier), a window quantifier (*Most*), a step quantifier (*At least 85%*) and the pure *and* aggregation (min operator, i.e., the classical quantifier *for all*).

These criteria are characterized by increasing degree of pessimism in the aggregation.

The different results are to be read in the following way: what is the group evaluation if one wants the *average (The majority, at least 85% of, all)* customers be satisfied? By using different aggregation criteria we can describe the VOC from different points of view, in a more complete and reliable way, in order to detect hidden, but precious, information. The advantages over traditional methods are the followings:

a.   **Flexibility:** The aggregation can be performed according different criteria.

Table 3. Group evaluations

	Aggregation criteria			
	Average	Most	At least 85%	And
Global evaluation	MLH	MLH	A	A
Accessibility	MLH	MLH	A	A
Spaciousness	MLH	MLH	A	A
Comfort	MLH	A	MLL	MLL
Design	MLH	A	A	VL
Easy use of controls	MLH	A	A	A
Robustness	MLH	A	MLL	VL

Table 4. Functions' importance ranking according different aggregation criteria

Aggregation criteria	Ranking of functions' importance					
Pure average	Accessib. 0.166	Spacious. 0.166	Comfort 0.166	Design 0.166	Easy use 0.166	Robust. 0.166
Most	Comfort 0.178	Design 0.178	Easy use 0.178	Robust. 0.178	Accessib 0.146	Spacious 0.146
At least 85%	Comfort 0.184	Robust. 0.184	Design 0.158	Easy use 0.158	Accessib 0.158	Spacious 0.158
All	Robust. 0.198	Design 0.198	Comfort 0.169	Easy use 0.145	Accessib 0.145	Spacious 0.145

b. **Reliability:** It is possible, by choosing a suitable quantifier, to prevent the regression of the group evaluation towards the evaluation *average*.

c. **Completeness:** We get more detailed and richer information.

The Customer Tree Analysis

Once the group evaluations has been determined, it is possible to calculate the importance of product's functions and components.

By using several aggregation criteria, different scenarios are obtained. In Table 4, some examples of calculation of functions' importance are showed: According to the pure average the functions are equally important, while more articulated situations are obtained by means of the quantifiers *most, at least 85%* and *all*. For example, according to the criterion *At least 85%*, the functions *comfort* and *robustness* of the cabin are the most important ones. This means that, in order to increase customer satisfaction, technicians should improve these aspects of the cabin.

Since different criteria give different importance rankings and, hence, different information to technicians for product's development, the decision maker should explicitly specify which criteria he uses and why; for example he could choose one of the possible ranking according to his grade of optimism or to firm's profitability objective (e.g., the firm needs that at least 80% of potential customers will be satisfied by the new product).

On the other hand, the simultaneous application of different criteria can also highlight some relevant facts. For example, Table 4 shows that the functions *accessibility and spaciousness* are in any case less important than others, while *comfort, robustness* and *design* score always the highest importance. As shown above, through the fuzzy implication operator we are able to define the importance of the explanans of a same fan. In this way, we can calculate the importance of the functions, and, for each function, the importance of the components which perform it. The importance indicators thus obtained depends on the relative satisfaction between explanans and explanandum and on the number of evaluators.

In Figure 5 we show the results regarding the robustness of the car's cabin. The *global importance* of a component is calculated by means of a correlation matrix which keeps into account that a macrocomponent may carry out several functions. The value of the *global importance* indicator depends on:

Figure 5. The components importance related to robustness according to the criterion at least 85%

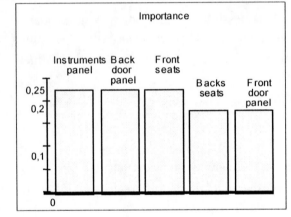

Figure 6. The components' importance related to the whole cabin according to the criterion at least 85%

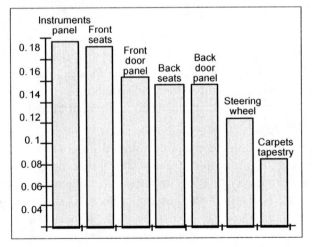

a.   The importance of a component for each function

b.   The importance of the functions which are performed by the component

c.   The number of functions realized by the component

In Figure 6 the global importance of the main components is plotted. These values could be used to calculate the cost of each subsystem. Thus the amount of the cost of components will depend on the level of importance given by customers to the several components of the product

The values of the component's global importance together with the values and the ranking of functions' importance allow technicians to understand which components should be modified and, for each component what are the component's characteristics which should be improved.

For example, if we consider the functions' importance obtained through the quantifier *at least 85%* contained in Table 5 and the component *front seat*, we can argue that, in order to enhance component's performance, technicians should make it more comfortable and robust rather than improving its design to increase spaciousness and accessibility to the cabin.

Conclusion

The proposed model allows us to obtain several advantages over the traditional methodologies in each phase of the entire procedure. The most important ones regard: (a) the representation of the individual evaluation process, (b) the aggregation of the individual preferences, (c) the determination of the importance.

Traditional questionnaires, because of their complex and rigid structures, are closed artifacts. They force customers to express their judgements according to top-down imposed criteria and by means of a numerical scale. The use of numerical scales is based on two erroneous assumptions: (1) that every person gives the same meaning to a given item of the scale, (2) that customers express precise and not ambiguous judgements. The information thus obtained is not reliable both from a qualitative and quantitative point of view. In our procedure, customers express their evaluations by verbal expressions through the natural language. The model of the dual truth allows us to manage easily the ambiguity and the complexity of human language. Thanks to an explanatory discourse, customers are compelled to explain their judgements, thus bringing to the light the criteria they use to evaluate a given product. Through the structured interview, we can discover the logical connections between the product's attributes and the customers' wishes and then define a mathematical representation of the evaluation process.

In the traditional context there is no attempt to understand how the customer evaluation process develops, because customer satisfaction is supposed to have an additive structure and can be analyzed on the basis of a questionnaires made up of independent items.

In our model, a rational aggregation procedure is available. We can determine the group satisfaction for the product as well as for every single attribute according to different criteria. In this way, by analyzing the customer evaluations from different point of view, we are able to get complete and reliable information.

The calculation of the explanation forces yields significant and complete indicator of the importance of functions and components of the product.

The classical questionnaires ask customers to state explicitly, usually on a numeric scale, how a component or a function is important. Usually this kind of information turns out to be quite useless if we do not also take into account the satisfaction level associated to a given attribute of the product.

With our model it's possible to link to each component more significant importance indicators which consider the customers level of satisfaction, the number of customers who chose that component as explanans, the number and the weights of the functions which the component performs.

The practical results we obtained during the experimental testing of the model induce us to deepen and strengthen some aspects of the model on theoretical grounds. Particularly, deeper studies regarding the concept of *default explanation* and the semantics differences between the concept of explanation and the concept of implication are needed.

Our further objective is to define a rule based system which allows us to describe effectively the link between customer satisfaction and product's characteristics.

References

Arrow, K.J. (1963). *Social choice and individual values.* New York: Wiley.

Baldwin, J.F., & Pilsworth, B.W. (1980). Axiomatic approach to implication for approximate reasoning with fuzzy logic. *Fuzzy Set and Systems, 3,* 193-219.

Cholewa, W. (1985). Aggregation of fuzzy opinions: An axiomatic approach. *Fuzzy Set and Systems, 17,* 249-259.

Dubois, D., & Koning, J.L. (1991). Social choice axioms for fuzzy set aggregation. *Fuzzy Sets and Systems, 45,* 257-274.

Dubois, D., & Prade, H. (1980). *Fuzzy sets and systems: Theory and applications.* New York: Academic Press.

Fukami, S., Mizumoto, M., & Tanaka, K. (1980). Some considerations on fuzzy conditional inference. *Fuzzy Set and Systems, 4*, 243-273.

Fung, L.W., & Fu, K.S. (1975). An axiomatic approach to rational decision making in a fuzzy environment. In L.A. Zadeh, F. King-Sum, K. Tanaka, & M. Shimura (Eds.), *Fuzzy sets and their applications to cognitive and decision processes.* New York: Academic Press.

Herrera, F., Herrera-Viedma, E., & Verdegay, J.L. (1996). Direct approach process in group decision making using linguistic OWA operators. *Fuzzy Set and Systems, 79*, 175-190.

Klir, G.J., & Yuan, B. (1995). *Fuzzy set and fuzzy logic: Theory and applications.* Englewood Cliffs, NJ: Prentice Hall.

Mizumoto, M., & Zimmermann, H.J. (1982). Comparison of fuzzy reasoning methods. *Fuzzy Set and Systems, 8*, 253-283.

Montero, F.J. (1985). A note on Fung-Fu's theorem. *Fuzzy Sets and Systems, 17*, 259-269.

Ovchinnikov, S. (1991). Social choice and Luckasiewicz logic. *Fuzzy Set and Systems, 45*, 275-293.

Yager, R.R. (1988). On ordered weigthed averaging aggregation operators in multicriteria decisionmaking. *IEEE Transactions on Systems, Man and Cybernetics, 18*(1), 183-191.

Yager, R.R. (1991). Connectives and quantifiers in fuzzy set. *Fuzzy Set and Systems, 40*, 39-76.

Yager, R.R. (1993). Families of OWA operators. *Fuzzy Sets and Systems, 59*, 125-148.

Zadeh, L. (1976). A fuzzy-algorithmic approach to the definition of complex or imprecise concepts. *Int. Journal of Man-Machine Studies, 8*, 249-291.

Zadeh, L. (1981). PRUF: A meaning representation language for natural languages. In E. H. Mamdani & G. R. Gaines (Eds.), *Fuzzy reasoning and its application.* London.

Endnotes

[1]   The research that this paper was the result of a fruitful co-operation between the Deptartment of Computer Science and Systems (DIS), University of Naples Federico II and the Fiat Research Center (CRF). G. Zollo directed the research

while A. Cannavacciuolo together with A. Iuliano of CRF coordinated the field activities. L. Iandoli and C. Ponsiglione developed most of the practical activities as ATA fellows at Dept. of Computer Science and Systems.

[2]   It is possible to demonstrate that, if the cardinality of the term set becomes very high (that is if precision increases), the left value will tend to be equal to the fuzzy complement of the right value. This means that, by using term sets with a very high value of cardinality, we do not need a truth couple but of a single value to represent an evaluation. In other words, if precision increases, then ambiguity decreases. In the real world, however, humans express their evaluations by using only small cardinality term sets. For this reason, any evaluation expressed in a natural language it's characterized by a certain degree of ambiguity which cannot be represented by means of a single truth value.

[3]   Given two propositions *ant* and *cons* whose truth values are p and q, a suitable operator   should satisfy the following axioms:

1. $p < q => I(p, x) > I(q, x)$.

The truth value of fuzzy implication increases as the truth values of the antecedent decreases.

2. $p < q => I(x, p) < I(x, q)$.

The truth value of fuzzy implication increases as the truth values of the consequent increases.

3. $I(0, p) = 1$.

The falsity implies everything

4. $I(1, q) = q$.

If the antecedent is absolutely true, the truth of the conditional proposition is equal to the truth of the consequent.

5. $I(p, p) = 1$.

Fuzzy implication is true whenever the truth values of the antecedent and consequent are equal.

6. (p, q) is a continuous function.

The axioms 1,2,3,4,5 are fuzzy counterparts of the properties of the traditional ply operator. Furthermore, if (p, q) satisfies the axiom 6 then little variations of p and q give little changes in the explanation forces.

[4]   The problem of calculating the evaluation of a same item expressed by a group of evaluators is the object of several studies (Cholewa, 1985; Fung & Fu, 1975; Montero, 1985). It is well known that Arrow (1963) showed that it is impossible to find a completely rational aggregation operator; fortunately, the negative implications of Arrow's theorem are not valid in a fuzzy representation of the individual preferences (Dubois & Koning, 1991; Ovchinnikov, 1991).

A suitable operator which, given n individual opinions, yields the group opinion can be determined by an axiomatic approach. A complete review of the axioms can be found in Dubois and Koning (1991). The authors classify the axioms in:

a. Imperative, whose violation leads to counterintuitive aggregation modes.

b. Technical, which facilitate the representation and the calculation of the aggregation operator.

c. Facultative, which is applied in special circumstances.

Herrera et al. (1996) demonstrated that the OWA operators satisfy all the necessary axioms and fail only on technical axioms.

Appendix B

Organizational Learning and Social Computation

Abstract

In Chapter XVIII we outlined the characteristics of a computational approach to support organizational analysis. Agent-based modeling, one of the several methodological tools presented in Chapter XVIII, is particularly suited for the modeling of learning processes in complex networks. In this appendix we want to provide the reader with an example of how it is possible to construct agent-based systems in order to simulate the collective behavior of social aggregates. We present a mathematical model aimed to represent and simulate adaptive organizational learning processes. With adaptive organizational learning processes we mean a learning process taking place in a social network in which individuals, by means of social interaction and subjective interpretative processes, contribute to the construction and the accumulation of shared experience. The proposed model implements a multiagent system aimed to represent a social network of interacting heterogeneous 'virtual people' operating in a virtual environment, here modeled as a network of resources. Learning for an agent means passing from an initial state to a target one through the identification of optimal paths within the environment by exploiting personal characteristics as well as interaction with other agents and the environment; such interaction allows agents to exchange information, to construct a collective memory on the basis of past individual experiences and to have access to resources.

Organizational Learning and Collective Cognition

Collective cognition has been the subject of many studies in research on organizational cognition. Some scholars have underlined the metaphorical nature of collective cognition by recognizing, however, the potential of such metaphors in providing explanations about how people think and act within organizations (Morgan, 1997). Lant and Shapira (2001) classify approaches to organizational cognition within a dichotomy between information processing approaches starting from March and Simon and Simon's work (1958), and the sense-making approaches, in which organizations are considered as interpretative systems (Daft & Weick, 1984). Moving along the continuum between information processing and interpretative approaches, other research efforts have been directed toward methodological issues concerning how to represent and model collective cognition and information flow in groups and organizations, such as mapping (Eden & Ackermann, 1992; Huff, 1990), social network analysis, and qualitative methodologies such as ethnography and discourse analysis (Heracleous & Barrett, 2001).

More recently, a multidisciplinary approach to collective cognition has emerged at the cross point between sociology, cognitive psychology and computer science, known as social computation (Conte, 1999; Tefstation, 2001). According to the social computation perspective, social behavior emerges from interactions among "cognitive" agents within social networks. Such an approach assumes heterogeneity, bounded rationality, localization and interdependence of cognitive agents, and absence of any centralized control mechanisms. Consequently, in the social simulation view, aggregate behavior and attributes are not merely metaphor or extension at the collective level of individual constructs, but properties observable at an aggregate level and arising from distributed ongoing interaction within a community of "thinking" agents.

A further advantage of social computation is that the development of simulation models based on interacting agents permits to construct virtual evolving social environments that can be used as virtual laboratories; through such computer models, called agent-based models, it is possible to explore the dynamics of social phenomena emerging from the bottom, starting form the microspecifications describing agents cognitive models and behavior (Epstein & Axtell, 1996). An agent-based simulation model can provide a computational demonstration that a set of hypotheses, related to individual agent behavior and cognition (microspecifications), is sufficient to generate certain macroscopic regularities appearing as recurring patterns.

In a social computation perspective, collective cognition can be characterized in at least one of the following ways: (1) as distributed individual cognition; (2) as sharing of cognitive assets (e.g., rules, values, schemata); (3) as emerging aggregate property (e.g., in terms of emerging dominant behavior, beliefs, social action).

In particular, agent-based models can provide explanations for the self-organizing behavior of complex systems, which is difficult to describe through other methodological approaches:

- *Qualitative methodologies* such as narratives and storytelling are mainly descriptive and can not be used for forecasting and what-if analysis.
- *Quantitative methodologies* such as structural equations become analytically intractable when system complexity exceeds certain thresholds.
- *Statistics* cannot be used to grasp the dynamic nature of social phenomena, e.g., their evolution through time, but only to describe significant correlation between static variables.

We focus on social networks and consider them as complex adaptive systems characterized by the following properties: Interaction between cognitive agents, lack of centralized control, agents adaptation and continuous evolution, presence of unpredictable changes, and the bounded rationality of agents.

The aim of this appendix is to present an agent-based model of a firms network in order to answer to the following research question:

a.   Which are the advantages and the limitations of using computer based models to investigate collective cognition?

b.   To what extent can the computational approach be used to model collective cognitive constructs such as collective memory and learning, and their influence on social action?

c.   How can research and practice on organizational cognition and learning benefit from a social computation view?

Modeling Organizational Learning Through a Computational Approach

A Generative Epistemological Perspective to Organizational and Social Studies

According to the generative epistemological approach, a possible way of explaining the emerging of macroscopic regularities in an organization is to answer to the following question (Epstein & Axtell, 1996): "*is it possible to generate observed macroregularities at the collective level from microspecifications governing local and de-centralized interactions of autonomous and heterogeneous agents?*"

Some possible examples of research questions related to collective learning and formulated according to the generative perspective could be the following:

a.   Is it possible to identify factors favoring the emergence of stable and shared learning patterns within an organization?

b.   If so, to which extent such patterns can be related to individual behaviors and subjective characteristics of organizational members?

c.   Is it possible to reconstruct the dynamics leading to a stable pattern? What types of interventions can influence such dynamics?

d.   What is the role played by factors such as imitation processes and group characteristics within learning collective processes?

The issue of providing explanations of social phenomena through the analysis of the behaviors of individuals belonging to a collectivity is one of the main objectives of organizational and social science research. A new way to look at the problem is to simulate the interaction of autonomous agents provided with bounded rationality and power to act within a framed environment bearing both resources and constraints to agents' actions. The first attempts to apply agent-based computer models to social science can be found in Shelling's work (1978). More recent research efforts in this direction include the work of Albin and Foley (1990), Axelrod (1995), Bull (1999), Conte (1999), Edmonds and Dautenhahn (1999), Epstein and Axtell (1996), Gilbert and Conte (1995), Holland and Miller (1991), Heyligen (1999), Gabriel and Bernstein (2000). According to this perspective, hypotheses can be tested through generative experiments. A generative experiment consists of (Epstein, 2000):

a.   Placing an initial population of heterogeneous and autonomous agents in a virtual environment.

b.   Letting them interact and evolve according to some predefined behavioral rules (*microspecifications*).

c.   Observing if such microspecifications are *sufficient to generate* expected or plausible macroscopic regularities.

In other words, an agent-based model provides a computational demonstration that a set of given microspecifications is sufficient to generate the observed regularities. Actually, according to the generative perspective, one is interested in discovering which dynamics create stable configurations starting from a system of interacting individuals. Those dynamics are generated by a set of local rules that agents apply repeatedly. The variety of the local rules allows us to model the plurality of subjective behaviors of organizational members within a same system.

The epistemological perspective followed by agent-based models applied to social science is the opposite of the one followed by traditional social research, usually based on a *top-down* approach deliberately aimed to suppress subjectivity and individual characteristics, as it happens, for example, in economics where one of the main assumptions is the existence of completely rational and identical economic agents.

If, on one hand, such approaches are able to build powerful analytical models, and on the other hand, they ignore a very often fundamental component of social dynamics, that is the variance and the multiplicity of individual behaviors. Furthermore, traditional approaches are usually focused on the study of static equilibrium, while they neglect the temporal dynamic leading to the achievement of equilibrium conditions.

Finally, a further advantage of the generative or *bottom-up* approach lies in the possibility of build up at a very low cost a *virtual laboratory for social experiment* in which it is possible to test theories related to the formation of social dynamics and structures. In their model of artificial society, *Sugarscape*, Epstein and Axtell (1996) have proven that the explicative power of generative models is very high if compared to the relatively low implementation and computational efforts; a further remarkable result is that the number of microspecifications able to generate a very large class of complex social phenomena such as demographic and economic processes is surprisingly low.

The use of an agent-based methodology is strongly coherent with the theory of organizational learning described in this book, for many reasons.

First, learning is considered as an emergent property of social entities in which individual and collective learning are strictly related.

Second, learning through emergence produces the institutionalization of new shared practices, behaviors, rules, and values. In other words, the construction of a collective memory.

Third, agent-based models permit us to observe the intrinsically unstable and chaotic properties of learning in social systems and to observe both the factors and the mechanisms that dynamically may trigger or suffocate learning.

Fourth, this kind of model allows researchers to model both individual initiative and diversity and the conditioning power of collective constructions and conformism.

Artifacts and values enter the picture as conditioning agents. An artifact or a value can be considered as a particular kind of agent, which is an agent that orders or suggests to human agents what should or can be done. For instance a traffic light is an agent telling drivers when to go or to stop.

Our ambition is to use the agent-based approach as quantitative methodological counterparts of theories such as the Berger and Luckmann social construction of the reality or the actor network theory of Callon and Latour, though we are pretty aware of still being very far from this result.

The Agent-Based Computational Models

According to the so-called generative approach, organizational complexity can be interpreted and analyzed through the concept of *social intelligence* (Edmons & Dautenhahn, 1999), that is intelligence possessed by a social network as a whole and produced by interactions among heterogeneous individuals and by de-centralized decisional processes.

Studying social intelligence means exploring the interface between an individual and its social network, that is to analyze individual capabilities from the point of view of the individual/individual and individual/society/environment interaction, by taking into account individuals' specificities. Thus, social intelligence can be generated by virtual collectivity formed by autonomous, intelligent and socially situated agents (Conte, 1999).

In the case of the analysis of organizational processes, autonomous agents are members of a social network and operate in a virtual environment by interacting with both resources, constraints, and other agents. Interconnections generated by these interactions create a double network structure:

1. A network of environmental resources and constraints, that we define organizational environment or simply environment.
2. A social network made up by relationships that individuals establish dynamically among them.

Autonomy allows agents to have *social responsiveness* (Conte, 1999), that is the capability to act on the basis of their own subjective deliberateness in order to filter inputs coming from external world, to benefit from available messages and resources, and, if necessary, to give feed-back to the social networks.

In order to represent an organizational process through a multiagent model we need to characterize three basic elements:

- **Agents:** They can be the "people" of the virtual social network, each having internal states and behavioral rules that may be modified through interactions with other agents or with the environment or artifacts defining constraints or providing suggestions to the virtual people.

- **Environment:** A network of renewable resources and environmental constraints.

- **Rules:** Of behavior governing agent/agent and agent/environment interactions. Rules can be shared, i.e., they belong to the collective memory, or individual.

Agents are usually characterized by the following properties:

- **Heterogeneity:** Populations of agents should be formed by individuals with different characteristics;

- **Autonomy:** There is no centralized control of agents' behavior. The individual behavior evolves according to rules governing interactions among individuals and among individuals and the environment; it is important to remark that agents are never entirely free since they are conditioned to a certain extent by existing collective rules and values belonging to the collective memory.

- **Bounded rationality:** Agents have bounded rationality, that is they have a local vision of the environment and a limited capability of searching and elaborating data and information.

In this book, we adopt the ant-system technique for modeling agent-based systems (Dorigo et al., 1996). The ant-system algorithms belong to a class of intelligent computation techniques derived from the observation of social insects such as ants, termites or bees. It has been applied in operation research for it represents a powerful heuristic algorithm in many search problems, like the traveling salesman problem.

There is a huge availability of modelization techniques and software tools. Among the most diffused, we remember two pen source platform: SWARM developed at the Santa Fe Institute (www.swarm.org) and NetLogo developed by the Northwestern University of Chicago (www.netlogo.org).

Figure 1. Ant systems as analogy with real ant behavior (Adapted from Dorigo et al., 1996)

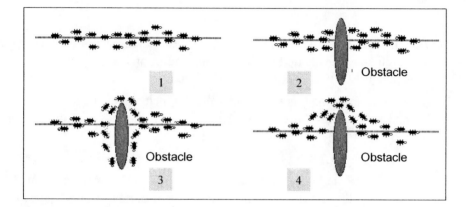

Both those platforms are inspired by the analogy between complex social systems and natural systems such as colonies of social insects like ants or bees.

The Ant Colony Systems

Ant systems try to imitate the mechanisms through which ants search for food in the environment. Ants are able to identify the shortest path between the nest and the food without using visual information. Ants are blind, thus during their search for food or water they leave on the ground an intense-smelling substance, called *pheromone*, which is able to attract other ants. In this way the amount of pheromone left on the soil is able to indicate to ants the preferential direction for food (see sequence 1-4 in Figure 1). For example, when an obstacle is found between the food and the nest (1, 2), ants will distribute themselves in a random way around the obstacle (3), but, after a while, the distribution of pheromone will be more intense on the shortest path and ants will converge rapidly on it (4).

It is interesting to note that ant behavior is due to an indirect form of communication called *stigmergy*. Grassé (1959), in his study on termites, defined stigmergy as "the stimulation of workers through the performance they have achieved." He observed that social insects are able to communicate by means of small signals able to trigger a chain reaction. In this way a coordination of individual activities is generated. What distinguishes stigmergy from other forms of communication is that information is released through a physical substance that can be manipulated by other individuals, and that it is local and it is available only to insects passing across specific sites. The resulting process is self-catalytic as, through positive feedback, it brings about a reinforcement of emerging trends and a rapid convergence.

Following this natural analogy, in the ant system algorithm, artificial ants cooperate to identify the optimal solution through information exchange. Information can be of two different type:

- **Local information:** It is a measure of the estimated cost of a move within the search space evaluated during the algorithm and usually measured as a distance between two sites within the environment;
- **Global information:** It is a measure of how much a path or a move are desirable and it is based on the accumulation of pheromone left by other ants on the path.

Each artificial ant is an agent that imitates real ant's behavior. Artificial ants have a memory in which they store past actions, live in a discrete time, and their moves are transitions between two discrete states (Dorigo et al., 1996). The environment in which ants move is modeled through a graph made up of a finite number of states having certain characteristics that make them more or less desirable to ants. In each step, each agent decides, on the basis of the available local and global information, which will be the most advantageous move. The agent's choice is determined by the calculation of a transition probability which is higher the more the move has been done by other agents and the less the distance[1].

The algorithm makes agents evolve through several iterations. In each iteration, all ants complete their paths from an initial site to a final one. At the end of each iteration, a certain amount of pheromone is deposited on all intermediate states forming the paths[2].

The algorithm stops when, after a certain number of iterations, ants converge to a unique path or alternatively when a maximum number Nc_{max} of iterations is achieved[3].

A Computational Model of Organizational Learning

In the proposed model, a collective learning process takes place through iterated exploration of a virtual environment by a group of heterogeneous individuals modeled as virtual agents. Each iteration is an attempt to identify a path within the environment leading from an initial starting point to a final state connected by an admissible sequence of intermediate states.

Social interaction processes able to influence learning are based (1) on the implementation of mechanisms of communications among individuals who exchange information about the most advantageous paths, (2) on the presence of a distribution of incentives able to attract individuals, (3) and on the availability of a shared memory built through shared rules and dynamically updated by the pheromone traces accumulated during past explorations.

In our model, pheromone plays the role of a communication mechanism as well as of a collective memory in which organizational members store perceptible traces associated to past successful individual actions and behaviors. As many kind of signals, also pheromone is characterized by a certain degree of volatility.

Model Description

In our model each individual (agent/ant) is described by a profile of c competencies each assuming a certain value $v \in \{1, 2, ..., v_{max}\}$. The learning process is represented as a sequence of moves through which each organizational member modifies his/her competencies profile. Individuals are supposed to have bounded rationality as they are not able to see all the opportunities offered by the environment, but only a limited part.

The representation of the environment in our model has a slightly different semantic structure from the one usually employed within current literature on multiagent models. Within traditional multiagent models, the environment is a "landscape, that is a topography of renewable resource that agents can 'eat' and metabolize. Such landscape is modeled as a lattice of resources bearing sites" (Epstein & Axtell, 1996).

In our model the environment is a network whose nodes are associated to admissible states, i.e., competencies profiles, and resources are represented by rewards that agents receive when they reach a given profile. The passage from a node to another means for an agent to modify his/her competencies profile and to gain a reward once a new profile has been reached.

We can say that the main difference with respect to the issue of modeling the environment between our approach and classic multiagent models is that, in the latter,

Figure 2. representation of the environment and of admissible moves

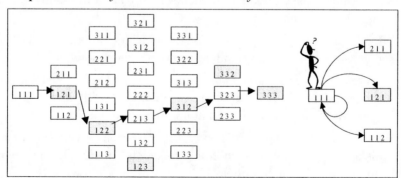

nodes are simply intended as 'virtual places' that individuals pass through, whereas in our model nodes are states of a process through which individuals modify their own characteristics. The number of admissible profiles, represented as vectors of length c, is $np=(v_{max})^c$. The search space formed by those vectors is depicted in Figure 2[4].

Each individual is allowed to increase the value of only one competency from v to $v + 1$ at a time; consequently individuals are allowed either to move from a level to the successive one or to remain in the same level (Figure 2). Moves towards other nodes within the same level are not allowed.

Once a new competencies profile has been reached by an individual, it becomes part of the individual experience together with all previous profiles, since the path describing the generation of the current profile is not discarded, but stored in a sub-jective memory. In our model the role of collective memory is emphasized through the pheromone deposited along individual paths.

Among all admissible profiles, there is a subset of *target profiles* to which rewards are associated (the dark knots in Figure 2) that we term *incentive*. Target profiles can be considered as special profiles characterized by higher importance than ordinary profiles; for example they could be profiles that in the past were related to better performances according to company's experience and/or they could be desired profile for new tasks and activities.

Target profiles can be considered as artifacts, i.e., think of desired job descriptions, that "demand" people to be reached.

The population of individuals is made up by heterogeneous individuals character-ized by aptitudes and personal characteristics influencing individual behaviors. In our model individuals are supposed to cooperate at least at a certain degree and no mechanism determining conflict or competition among agents is considered[5]. In particular, in the simulations presented in the next section, each individual is characterized by:

- An initial *competencies profile*, represented through a vector of c elements.

- A degree of *propensity to exploitation* through imitation $a \in [0,1]$: This value is a measure of the individual's tendency to move towards knots characterized by high levels of pheromone.

- A degree of *propensity to exploration* through innovation $b \in [0,1]$: This value is a measure of the agent's tendency to prefer unexplored nodes.

- A degree of *propensity to communication* $r \in [0,1]$: This value is a measure of the agent's will and/or ability to communicate with other agents through the deposit of larger than usual amount of pheromone.

- A value p, representing agent's *potential*; after each move, a portion of poten-tial is spent by the agent. Consequently agents with low level of p may stop during the algorithm iterations.

- A *level of inertia Lin*, representing the agent's aptitude and/or will to not modify its state.

The main elements of agent-ant model are summarized in Table 1.

An individual is supposed to produce added value V_i each time that she/he improves her/his competencies profile. The overall added value V for the organization is the sum of individual added values. The individual added value is formed by two components: The added value obtained after each step and an extra added value obtained when the individual reach a target profile.

We suppose that in order to modify competency profiles, both individuals and the organization, as a whole, must bear a cost K, whose value depends on the specific case. In particular, the organizational cost can be considered as the amount of money K_i needed to increase the value of a given competency C_i (for example it might represent a training cost). Furthermore, individuals pay their fees through a decrease of their potential; thus potential can be interpreted as a measure of individuals' capability to cover long paths and to achieve profiles characterized by high competencies values.

The overall training cost is obtained through the sum of all m individual costs determined by the modifications of the competencies profiles of the whole population. Our algorithm tries to maximize the following *group gain* function:

$$g = \frac{\sum_{i=1}^{m} V_i}{\sum_{i=1}^{m} K_i} = \frac{V}{K} \tag{7}$$

Table 1. The components of the model

Agent	Individual described by means of an initial competence profile and of some parameters related to potential, inertia, propensity to exploitation, exploration, and communication
Group of agents	Set of social interacting heterogeneous individuals
Search space or environment	Organizational environment represented as a set of possible paths linking an initial and an arrival point through multiple possible different paths of intermediate states
State	Competence profile
Resources	Incentives
Move	Incremental learning through modification of agent's current competence profile
Path	Learning pattern followed by an individual to achieve a certain competence profile
Pheromone	Collective memory
Iteration	New attempt of the agents community to improve their performance on the base of past results
Distance	Costs and efforts sustained by an agent to achieve a new competence profile

Each individual decides whether and how to modify his/her current competencies profile by calculating a transition probability. In our model this calculation is influenced by the following parameters:

- *Accessibility* (η) is proportional to the inverse of the cost that an individual must pay to increase the value of a given competency and to the inverse of the distance between the current and the next admissible profile;

- *Degree of membership to collective memory* (τ): This variable corresponds to pheromone, thus the more other agents have visited a node, the more the node belongs to the collective memory and agents are prone to imitate other agents' past choice.

- *Incentive (I)*: The transition probability towards a node increases if that node bears a target profile;

- The propensity to exploitation α and to exploration β.

Each individual calculates the transition probabilities of all admissible states and does not modify his/her profile in the following cases: (a) The transition probabilities are zero, (b) his/her potential is exhausted, (c) probabilities are less that agent's level of inertia.

During each iteration, all individuals construct possible solutions given by a set of paths through the environment. At the end of each iteration, the best solution, that is, the one with the highest gain, is identified and tagged with an amount of pheromone accumulation for the next exploration. If the ith profile does not belong to the best path, the pheromone evaporates. Furthermore, the more the propensity to communication of the best individual, the more the current best solution will be visible to other agents in the next iteration. This rule represent a mechanism of social feedback[6].

When a path allows individuals to reach one or more target profile, a further reinforcement of that path, called target path, is effected

In the next section some results obtained through a computer simulation in order to show how the model allows us to provide answers to some relevant questions in the analysis of collective learning processes:

1. Is it possible to identify convergent collective learning paths?
2. Is it possible to reconstruct paths corresponding to stable learning patterns?
3. To which extent long term results depend on initial conditions, such as individual characteristics and to which extent individual and group performances may be improved if some parameters are changed?

Figure 3. The simulation of the model

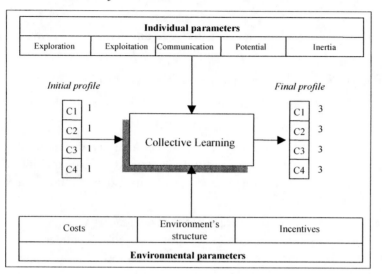

4.   How results are influenced by different incentives policies?
5.   Is it possible to identify effects attributable to group composition?

The Results of the Virtual Experiment

We considered profiles formed by four competencies C1, C2, C3 and C4 assuming value in $\{1,2,3\}$, with $v_{max} = 3$. Consequently the search space is made up of $np = (v_{max})^c = 3^4 = 81$ profiles.

The key elements considered for simulation are represented in fig. 3. Different simulations can be run by acting on one of the following four dimensions: individual parameters, environmental parameters, initial profiles, and final profiles.

In the following examples, we suppose that there are two technical (C1, C2) and two relational (C3, C4) competencies (e.g., C1 = knowledge of CAD tools, C2 = knowledge of computer simulation tools, C3 = leadership and C4 = team working); we further assume that the improvement of relational competencies is characterized by higher costs since we suppose that a more expensive training effort is needed to increase their value. An initial population of 20 agents with different characteristics is considered. Individual characteristics and incentives are randomly distributed. The same starting competence profile (1,1,1,1) is assumed for all individuals.

Convergent Patterns and Optimizing Behavior

The first objective of the simulation is to try to answer to the following questions:

a.   Is it possible to identify convergent collective learning paths?
b.   Is it possible to reconstruct paths corresponding to stable learning patterns?

In other words, our aim is to verify if the algorithm, given the conditions specified above, implies the convergence of individuals toward a dominant path. If this path exists, one may verify if the mechanism producing such solution is associated to any optimizing behaviors.

The answer is affirmative to both questions. The generative approach permits not only to identify possible convergent solutions, but also to understand how those solutions have been generated. Simulation results show that after 9 iterations almost all individuals converge towards the common path:

$\{(1,1,1,1); (1,2,1,1); (1,2,1,2); (2,2,1,2); (2,2,1,3); (3,2,1,3), (3,3,1,3), (3,3,2,3), (3,3,3,3)\}$

It is interesting to analyze the individual paths. For example, we can observe that individuals improve first the technical competencies and then spend the remaining potential to acquire also relational competencies, whose improvements require higher costs. Some individuals are not able to complete the path because their values of potential and inertia are, respectively, either too low or too high. It is possible to notice that some individuals reach the target before others and that the remaining ones tend to converge on the dominant path after a certain delay.

The objective function is the group gain g; the result depicted in Figure 4 clearly shows the presence of an optimizing group behavior.

During each iteration, the environment exploration process is repeated starting from some initial conditions that are always the same; but after each iteration the population's memory is updated by the experience deriving from the previous exploration. Thus individuals start a new exploration by exploiting experience previously determined through the accumulation of pheromone along preferential paths.

By observing Figure 5, it is possible to notice an optimizing group behavior since the gain oscillates before converging to a saturation value rather higher than its initial value. This is due to individuals' attempts to explore the environment and to look for new solutions; the gain diminishes when the new experienced solutions are actually worse than previous ones.

Figure 4. Group gain optimization after several iterations

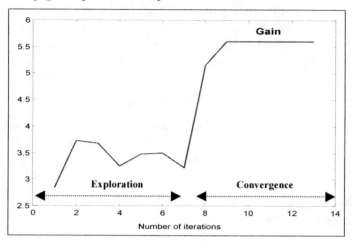

Figure 5. Individual gain optimization after several iterations for each agent

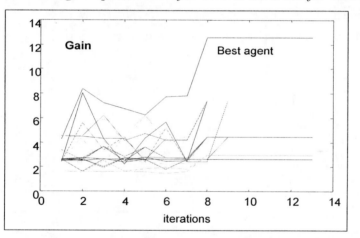

Factors Influencing Individual and Collective Learning

In this section the aim of the simulation is to answer to the following question:

- To what extent long do term results depend on initial conditions, such as individual characteristics?
- To what extent may individual and group performances be improved if some parameters are changed?

As stated above, different individuals show different performances. Figure 5 shows a comparison among individual gains. Individuals do not achieve the same gain because they have different characteristics such as values of potential, inertia, propensity to exploration and exploitation, but also the low potential individuals tend to conform to the best performer evolution.

At each iteration the best individual is able to influence the others to an extent depending on the best individual's communication propensity r.

Actually, if we diminish the propensity to communication of the best individual, we obtain a drastic diminution of the group gain function and a remarkable increase of the number of iterations needed to achieve the highest value of the gain, even if the individual performance of the best ant remains unaltered (Figure 6).

Further simulations aimed at verifying the influence of individual characteristics on the learning performance have showed that:

a. Performances increase if the degree of cooperation among group members, evaluated through the propensity to communication, increases.

b. A trade-off among exploration and exploitation obviously exists, but a certain prevalence of imitative behavior is desirable.

c. Heterogeneous group in terms of individual characteristics show better performances than homogeneous ones.

Figure 6. Group gain sensitivity to best agent's communication propensity

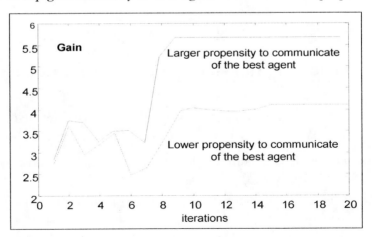

Incentives Distribution

The aim of this simulation is to observe if and how results are influenced by different incentives policies. Incentives associated to target profiles can be varied in order to simulate the effect on the community of particular organization's policies aimed to achieve specific results. In this way the effects of different policies can be compared and evaluated.

Results showed in Figures 4, 5, and 6. have been obtained in presence of a random distribution of incentives. Let us compare these results with the ones obtained by assuming a different distribution of incentives, for example by assigning larger incentives to profiles showing higher values of relational competencies.

Results obtained in this experiment are showed in Figure 7. It is possible to note a remarkable sensitivity of agents' behaviors to the distribution of incentives. For example, Figure 7 shows that, with an undifferentiated distribution of incentives within the search space, we obtain only one profile with excellent results as regards relational competencies, whereas a focused distribution of incentives brings about 18 excellent profiles.

Group Composition

In the previous simulations, we have always assumed that individuals were characterized by a same initial profile. Let us suppose that we have individuals with starting profiles such that it is possible to cluster individuals in two subgroups: A *first group* with high technical competencies and a *second group* with high relational competencies.

Figure 7. Comparison of the effects of different incentives distribution policies

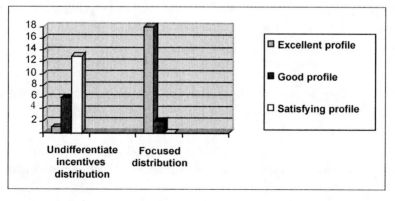

Results show a partition of the initial group into two distinct sub-group. For example, the best individual is able to influence prevalently the search of his/her own group; thus if we diminish of 20% the propensity to communication of the best individual of the first group, the total performance diminishes, but this diminution is due only to the first group since the gain of the second group remains unaltered.

This result is due to the structure of the virtual environment in which 'people' move. Each individual has bounded rationality and consequently can see only those profiles that are visible from his/her current position. Thus, the first group tends to prefer the upper part of the search space where technical profiles are mostly allocated, whereas the second group will move in the lower part of the search. The probability of interaction between individuals belonging to different groups is thus rather low and the partition of the initial group in two distinct noninteracting subgroups gives rise to a specialization process that induces a half of the initial population to prefer "technical" paths and the other part to choose "relational" paths.

Conclusion

In this appendix, a model aimed to simulate collective learning processes through agent-based modeling techniques has been presented. We have focused our attention on learning processes following some ideas presented in the literature on organizational learning that emphasize the role of adaptive learning and the impact on individual learning of communication and interactions among organizational members.

Our intention here is to present a new methodological approach to the study of orga-nizational phenomena based on a computational perspective. In order to accomplish this objective, we presented the results of some simulations aimed to illustrate:

a.   What the potentialities of the model are in reproducing collective learning processes.

b.   To what extent this methodological approach can be generalized and adopted as an analytical tool for organizational research.

c.   An insight into some possible applications.

As regards the former point, results showed in this book seem encouraging since the model is able to reproduce some well known or expected behaviors as illustrated in the previous section.

Perhaps the most interesting result regards the possibility of modeling the dualism between exploration and exploitation in organizational learning. As stated through the transition probability rule (1), the individual's choice is determined through a weighted combination of his/her propensity to exploration and to exploitation. From the algorithmic point of view, a right balance between exploration and exploitation ensures a satisfying search for interesting solutions in the environment: Exploitation focalizes the search towards optimal solutions, exploration diminishes the risk of a premature convergence to a local maximum.

But there is more than algorithmic issues in this aspect of the model. According to March (2001), the search for balance between exploration and exploitation is also at the base of the adaptation of organizations to the environment and to their "pursuit of intelligence." Exploration means "discovery, novelty, innovation;" exploitation means "refinement, routinization, production, and implementation" (March, 2001). Excessive exploitation can determine obsolescence, whereas excessive exploration can imply the *failure trap*, which is the inability to make new ideas productive because the organization has not the necessary experience to exploit their potentialities and individuate their most proper employment.

Possible applications of the model can be identified from these preliminary analysis: Career path definition, training plans, group composition, analysis, and simulation of management policies concerning incentives allocation. In all these fields the proposed model can be used as a decision support tools to perform a "what if" analysis.

As regards the possibility of concrete applications and a possible generalization of the model, further studies are needed to test its applicability and to enrich the model itself, for example to calibrate a model's parameters on an empirical basis or by adding other microspecifications aimed at representing individual conflict and concurrence mechanisms. Despite the current limitations of the model, as shown in the literature on *social intelligence*, agent-based models by their proper nature can be applied to a very large class of phenomena by simply adding further microspecifications. Actually their basic concepts are very general: A community of interacting agents, an environment in which agents operate and interact and some rules of behavior. In this simple framework it is easy to recognize the basic structure of many social phenomena, such as demographics, the transmission of culture, conflict, economics, and the emergence of a group.

In a much broader sense, agents belonging to a social network provided with bounded rationality and following some rules that govern local interaction and induce agents to pursue individual optimum can be also seen as computational nodes of a parallel computer whose interconnections evolve through time. In this sense, organizations, or more in general social networks carry out social computation able to solve problems that agents are not able to solve alone. This observation brings to a very stimulating research perspective in the study of social networks when considered as a set of computational interacting nodes; the computational perspective directs research on two axis: (1) The identification of microspecifications characterizing local interactions to be encoded as local node algorithms; (2) the comprehension of how complex phenomena can be generated and generatively explained on the basis of those simple mechanisms.

References

Albin, P., & Foley, D.K. (1990). Decentralized dispersed exchange without an auctioneer: A simulation study. *Journal of Economic Behavior and Organization, 18*(1), 27-51.

Argyris, C., & Schön, D.A. (1978). *Organizational learning. A theory of action perspective*. Reading, MA: Addison Wesley.

Axelrod, R. (1995). *The convergence and stability of cultures: Local convergence and global polarization*. Working Paper 95-03-028. Santa Fe, NM: Santa Fe Institute.

Bull, L. (1999). On evolving social systems: Communication, speciation and symbiogenesis. *Journal of Computational & Mathematical Organization Theory, 5*(3), 281-301.

Conte, R. (1999). Social intelligence among autonomous agents. *Journal of Computational & Mathematical Organization Theory, 5*(3), 203-228.

Daft, R.L., & Weick, K. (1984). Toward a model of organization as interpretation systems. *Academy of Management Review, 9*(2), 284-295.

Dorigo, M., Maniezzo, V., & Colorni, A. (1996). Ant system: Optimization by a colony of cooperating agents. *IEEE Transactions on systems, man, and cybernetics, 26*(1), 29-40.

Eden, C., & Ackermann, F. (1992). The analysis of causal map. *International Journal of Management Studies, 29*(3), 310-324.

Edmonds, B., & Dautenhahn, K. (1999). Social intelligence. *Journal of Computational & Mathematical Organization Theory, 5*(3), 199-201.

Epstein, J.M., & Axtell, R. (1996). *Growing artificial societies: Social science from the bottom up*. Cambridge, MA: MIT Press.

Epstein, J. M. (2000). Modelli computazionali fondati su agenti e scienza sociale generativa. *Sistemi Intelligenti, 2*.

Gabriel, S.A., & Bernstein, D. (2000). Nonadditive shortest paths: Subproblems in multiagent competitive networks models. *Journal of Computational & Mathematical Organization Theory, 6*, 29-45.

Gilbert, N., & Conte, R. (Eds.). (1995). *Artificial societies: The computer simulation of social life*. London: UCL Press.

Grassé, P. P. (1959). La reconstruction du nid et les coordinations interindividuelles chez BellicositermesNatalensis et Cubitermes. La théorie de la stigmergie: essai d'interprétation du comportament des termites constructeurs. *Insectes Sociaux, 6*, 41-81.

Holland, J., & Miller, J. (1991). Artificial adaptive agents in economic theory. *American Econoi Review, Papers and Proceedings, 81*(2), 365-370.

Heracleous, L., & Barrett, M. (2001). Organizational change as discourse: Communicative actions and deep structures in the context of information technology implementation. *Academy of Management Journal, 44*(4), 755-778.

Heyligen, F. (1999). Collective intelligence and its implementation the web: Algorithms to develop a collective mental map. *Journal of Computational & Mathematical Organization Theory, 5*(3), 253-280.

Huff, A.S. (Ed.). (1990). *Mapping strategic thought*. Chirchester: Wiley.

Lant, K.T., & Shapira, Z. (Eds.). (n.d.). *Organizational cognition: Computation and interpretation*. Mawah, NJ: Lawrence Erlbaum Associate.

Schelling, T.C. (1978). *Micromotives and macrobehavior*. Norton.

Tesfatsion, L. (2001, October). Special issue on the agent-based modeling of evolutionary economic systems. *IEEE Transactions on Evolutionary Computation, 5*(5).

Endnotes

[1]   The agent's choice is determined by the calculation of a transition probability:

$$p_{ij}^{k} = \begin{cases} \dfrac{\left[\tau_{ij}(t)\right]^{\alpha} * \left[\eta_{ij}\right]^{\beta}}{\sum\limits_{u \in J_{k}}\left[\tau_{iu}(t)\right]^{\alpha} * \left[\eta_{iu}\right]^{\beta}} & \text{if} \quad j \in J_{k} \\ \\ 0 & \text{otherwise} \end{cases} \tag{1}$$

where J_{k} is the set of all states accessible to the kth ant from the state i, τ_{ij} is the amount of pheromone on the arch (i,j), η_{ij} is the accessibility expressed as the inverse of the distance between i and j, α e β are, respectively, the importance associated to τ_{ij} and η_{ij}, that is the different weights attributed by an agent to local and global information when making a decision.

[2]   This information is updated through the following global updating rule:

$$\tau_{ij}(t+1) = \rho * \tau_{ij}(t) + \sum_{k=1}^{m} \Delta\tau_{ij}^{k} \tag{2}$$

where $\Delta\tau_{ij}^{k}$ is the incremental amount of pheromone left on the arch (i, j) by one or more of the m agents calculated as follows:

$$\Delta\tau_{ij}^{k} = \begin{cases} \dfrac{Q}{L_k} & \text{if } (i,j) \in \text{ to the path of ant k} \\ 0 & \text{otherwise} \end{cases} \tag{3}$$

where Q is a constant and L_k is the length of the path covered by the kth ant. The (3) ensures that shortest paths are reinforced through a positive feedback mechanism. The parameter $\rho \in [0,1]$, representing the persistence of pheromone between the instants t and $t + 1$, is introduced in order to avoid an unlimited accumulation of pheromone through time.

[3]   The ant system algorithm provides optimal solutions for problems of relatively small size. This limitation has induced researchers to improve the algorithm's performance. One of the improved versions of ant system is called Ant-Colony-System (ACO, Dorigo et al., 1997). The ACO differs from a basic ant system for three main reasons:

- There is a rule of global updating that keeps into account only the path realized by the best ant at the end of each iteration:

$$\tau(r,s) = (1 - \rho) * \tau(r,s) + \rho * \Delta\tau(r,s) \tag{4}$$

where $\rho \in [0,1]$ is the persistence of pheromone and

$$\Delta\tau(r,s) = \begin{cases} \dfrac{Q}{\left(L_{globalbest}\right)} & \text{if } (r,s) \in \text{ best ant's path} \\ 0 & \text{otherwise} \end{cases} \tag{5}$$

where $L_{globalbest}$ is the length of the best path; the best path is the shortest path leading from the nest to the food among all paths 'discovered' by ants until a certain iteration;

- The rule of state transition (1) is modified in order to establish a better balance among exploration of new nodes and exploitation of the local information through the introduction of random parameters;

- Ants modify automatically the amount of pheromone associated to an arch when they visit it:

$$\tau(r,s) = (1-\varphi) * \tau(r,s) + \varphi * \Delta\tau(r,s) \qquad (6)$$

where $\varphi \in [0,1]$ and $\Delta\tau(r,s)$ can be a constant τ_0. This rule implies that locally the pheromone diminishes when an ant chooses a given arch (r, s). Consequently other ants tend to visit mainly unexplored nodes, thus ensuring a better exploration of the search space.

The last two points are needed in order to prevent premature convergence. In the next section we illustrate the application of an Ant Colony System to the simulation of processes of organizational learning.

[4] It can be demonstrated that the search space formed by those vectors is characterized by the following properties (figure 2):

- Vectors are distributed on several levels; vectors belonging to a same level are such that the sum of their elements is a constant $v \in \{c, c+1, \ldots, c * v_{max}\}$;

- The number of levels is equal to $l = c * v_{max} - c + 1$;

- The search space is similar to an 'oval ball' since the number of strings increases moving from the first to the $(l-1)/2^{th}$ level, and diminishes from $(l-1)/2^{th}$ to the last level.

[5] Of course it is quite straightforward to introduce conflict mechanisms in such models, for example by modeling ants that cancel pheromone's traces left by enemies.

[6] Given a knot i, the global updating rule is the following:

$$IF(i,t+1) = \begin{cases} [1 - r(fglobalbest)] * IF(i,t) + r(fglobalbest) * \dfrac{1}{cglobalbest} & \text{if } i \in \text{best path} \\[2ex] [1 - r(fglobalbest)] * IF(i,t) & \text{otherwise} \end{cases} \qquad (8)$$

where $IF(i, t)$ is the amount of pheromone left on the ith node at the instant t, $cglobalbest$ is the cost associated to the best path, $fglobalbest$ is the individual who identified the best path.

About the Authors

Luca Iandoli received his master's degree in electronics engineering in 1998 from the University of Naples Federico II and a PhD in business and management from the University of Rome Tor Vergata in 2002. Currently, he is a professor in the Department of Business and Managerial Engineering, University of Naples Federico II. His current research interests include application of computational techniques to business and management, human resource management, organizational learning and cognition, information technology and organization. His papers have been published in the *Fuzzy Economic Review*, *Small Business Economics*, *Journal of Global Information Technology Management*, *Human Resources Management Journal*, and *Journal of Information Science and Technology*. He is a member of the editorial board of the *Fuzzy Economic Review*, *Journal of Information Technology: Cases and Applications*, and *Journal of Global Information Technology Management*.

Giuseppe Zollo is a full professor of business economics and organization in the Department of Business and Managerial, University of Naples Federico II. From 1985-1986, he was a visiting research associate in the Department of Economics of Northeastern University, Boston. He has published in several journals and has presented papers at international conferences on innovation management, organization, small innovative firms, and managerial application of fuzzy logic. In 1992, 1993, and 1995, he received the Entrepreneurship Award at the RENT-Research in Entrepreneurship Workshops organized by the European Institute for Advanced Studies in Management; in 1994, he received the Best Paper Award from FGF, Universitat Dortmund at the IntEnt '94 Conference. Moreover, he is a member of several editorial boards of international and Italian journals. He is vice president of the International Association for Fuzzy-Set Management and Economy (SIGEF) and director of the University of Naples Center for Organizational Innovation and Communication (COINOR).

Giancarlo Michellone has been president of Trieste's AREA Science Park since 2007. He began his career at FIAT in 1969, becoming director of the New Product Unit at the FIAT Research Centre. In 1984 he founded the Innovation Department of FIAT Auto and subsequently became executive vice president of FIAT Auto and Product Planning and Development. In 1989 he was appointed president and CEO of the FIAT Research Centre. He has been a member of the executive committee of the FIAT Group and its vice president. He is the author of 139 patents and holder of numerous positions among which: vice president of the Union of Industries in Turin, member of National Research Council (CNR) Scientific Committee (since 2006), and member of the Transport Advisory Group of the European Union for the 7th Framework Programme.

Index

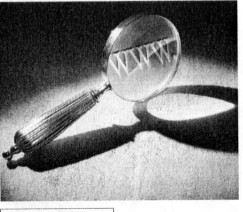